African Traditional Religion in Biblical Perspective

by

Richard J. Gehman

**Published by
Kesho Publications: Kijabe, Kenya**

This book may be purchased direct from

Richard J. Gehman
P.O.Box 21010
NAIROBI, Kenya

Also by the same author

Doing African Christian Theology: An Evangelical Perspective,
Evangel Publishing House, 1987.

Printed by
Kijabe Printing Press
P.O. Box 40, Kijabe, Kenya

First printing, 1989.

ISBN 9966-860-07-X

DEDICATION

To my wife, Flo,

whose love, encouragement and support

made this book possible.

CONTENTS

Page

Introduction: Rev. Dr. David Kitonga 6

Forward: Mr. Jon Arensen 8

Preface 10

PART ONE: FOUNDATIONAL ISSUES FOR
AFRICAN TRADITIONAL RELIGION

Chapter 1   Studies in African Traditional Religion 15

Chapter 2   Origins of Religion 32

Chapter 3   Focus of African Traditional Religion: Man 50

PART TWO: MYSTICAL POWERS IN
AFRICAN TRADITIONAL RELIGION

Chapter 4   Summary of Mystical Powers in Africa 67

Chapter 5   Case Study of the Akamba: Mystical Powers 80

Chapter 6   Mystical Powers Worldwide 98

Chapter 7   Mystical Powers in Biblical Perspective 106

PART THREE: THE SPIRIT WORLD IN
AFRICAN TRADITIONAL RELIGION

Chapter 8   Divinities in Africa 124

Chapter 9   Summary of Spirits in Africa 136

Chapter 10   Case Study of the Akamba: Ancestral Spirits 149

Chapter 11   The Spirit World: Worldwide 165

Chapter 12   The Spirit World in Biblical Perspective 171

**PART FOUR: THE SUPREME BEING IN
AFRICAN TRADITIONAL RELIGION**

Chapter 13 Summary of Belief in the Supreme Being in ATR 189

Chapter 14 Case Study of the Akamba: The Supreme Being 195

Chapter 15 The Supreme Being Worldwide 211

Chapter 16 Truth in ATR in Biblical Perspective 216

Chapter 17 Error in ATR in Biblical Perspective 226

PART FIVE: CONCLUDING OBSERVATIONS

Chapter 18 The Relationship of Biblical Christianity to ATR 245

Chapter 19 Syncretism 270

Chapter 20 Conclusion: A Christian Attitude 285

Appendix A – Survey of Literature Available on ATR 292

Appendix B – Testimonies of Former Medicine Men and Women 293

Appendix C – Further Examples of Mystical Powers Among the Akamba . 297

Permissions and Acknowledgements 301

Bibliography of References Cited 303

Index of Authors and Subjects 309

INTRODUCTION

This book is excellent, thorough and full of insights. Dr. Gehman has combined long experience in teaching with a wide range of understanding of African Traditional Religion. He has critically reflected on the key issues facing the African Christian believer related to the traditional African religion. The book is very objective and attempts to present the facts within the biblical perspective.

I am impressed with the accuracy of his use of Kikamba. This book is representative of the traditional Akamba beliefs and practice. The book touches on all the main themes of Akamba traditional religion.

The rapid growth of the church in Africa is widely known. The church growth rate is phenomenal. What is often not considered, however, is that this church growth is from among those Africans born in African traditional culture. What is desperately needed is increasing maturity. Problems develop when there is rapid church growth numerically without accompanying maturity. The African churches need much discipleship. Therefore, this book is most appropriate for it deals with the issue of syncretism. The number of African Independent Churches has increased and many of them are not founded on biblical principles but more on African traditions. For this reason we must understand African Traditional Religion in the light of biblical revelation. African Traditional Religion is not just the concern of African traditionalists. ATR also concerns Christians who seek to relate their Christian faith to their traditional religion. This book is therefore appropriate for our time.

Dr. Gehman comes across powerfully on the biblical perspective. He is committed to biblical Christianity. ATR is examined in the light of biblical revelation. The author is sincerely committed to the Christian Gospel.

Although many elements in ATR are not compatible with the Gospel, there are many traditional beliefs and practices in ATR which are useful and advantageous for bridging the Gospel. Dr. Gehman points to the many similarities between African traditional culture and Hebrew culture as found in the Old Testament.

Dr. Gehman has written this book with great sensitivity and respect for the integrity of his African brothers and sisters. Therefore, he has rendered the book useful not only for missionaries but for Africans as well. The author has written as a contemporary missionary who is aware of the pitfalls of former missionaries. The younger generation of Africans may know their traditional culture and religion in general terms, though often not with great detail. This book will make a significant contribution to the Africans' own understanding of their traditional culture. I do not hesitate to recommend this book to the African reader because of its factual accuracy and its sensitivity to the integrity of the African and his culture.

This book serves as an excellent textbook. It reflects a high degree of professionalism. It is particularly good for students of the Bible such as pastors and those with inquiring minds because it stimulates the thinking concerning ATR as it relates to the African Christian faith.

This is a book whose time has come. I do not hesitate to recommend this book both for the African and expatriate alike who seek to relate the Christian faith to African Traditional Religion.

David Kitonga Ph.D. (Michigan State University)

Dr. David Kitonga is the Regional Coordinator for Africa, Partners International (formerly known as Christian Nationals -CNEC). He has taught at Daystar University College and has been a pastor in Nairobi and Machakos.

FORWARD

Early books about missionary work in Africa are almost inevitably negative about the traditional religions which the Africans were practising. Missionaries of that time did not study the traditional religions and as a result they did not understand them. African Traditional Religions were usually considered to be evil, Satanic, and something that had to be totally rejected by its adherents if they were to become Christians.

However in more recent years a reaction as set in against this totally negative position. A number of Africans went overseas for further training and upon their return to Africa some of them began to study and defend African Traditional Religion. They focussed on the good to be found in these religions rather than on the negative. Many books have been written by these men proposing a number of different points of view. Some propose that African Traditional Religion is equal to Christianity and therefore that Christianity has little to offer the African people. Others propose that the good aspects of African Traditional Religion can be a base upon which Christianity can be built. Still others state that although there is good in African Traditional Religion, Christianity is quite different and stands apart.

However the people holding the above positions have one thing in common. They all call for an African theology. What is meant by an African theology is a Christianity which fits Africans. One which meets both their spiritual and cultural needs. The Pan-African Christian Leadership Assembly in 1976 made the following statement: "Imported Christianity will never, never quench the spiritual thirst of African peoples." There are a number of books written about the need for a solid application of Christianity in Africa but there is little consensus on how to go about this. What needs to be the basis for such an African theology?

This book is unique in that it is not vague about the basis for such an African theology. Dr. Gehman states uncategorically that the basis for any such study is the Holy Scriptures. Other authors study African cultures and desire to start there and build Christianity from that starting point. However Scriptural norms, not cultural norms, are the basis for this book.

When a person, who originally practised a traditional religion, becomes a Christian, there are a number of issues that he must deal with. It is not realistic to tell a new Christian to ignore the spirit world, to stop venerating the ancestors, and to stop going to a diviner unless specific reasons are given to do so and unless the church offers functional substitutes for these practices.

In this book Dr. Gehman shows that he has a good understanding of African Traditional Religion. He spent 17 years teaching and as the principal of a seminary in Kenya. This gave him access to a large body of material written by the students who did research papers on the subject of African Traditional Religion. During this time he lived in the Ukambani region of Kenya where Akamba religion was a focus of his studies and he shows an in depth knowledge of this subject.

The author also has a deep knowledge of the Scriptures and this book draws on his understanding of both subjects: African Traditional Religion and the Scriptures. In this book he deals with specific aspects of African Traditional Religion and then looks at the Scriptures to see if this activity is in line with Scriptural teaching. This is an approach that has been needed for a long time and one that I find particularly useful.

I recently saw a situation where newly converted Christians were wrestling with the issue of divining the future. They were asking the questions of whether or not as Christians they should still go to a diviner. The missionary in the area was both sensitive and insightful and would not give them the typical answer - "We westerners don't practice it so neither should you." Instead a Bible study was organized to see what the Scriptures had to say about the subject and then the African Christians decided for themselves what they should do based on those Scriptures.

In such a situation this book will be very helpful. Dr Gehman has not avoided sensitive issues but deals with them fairly and in the light of Scriptures, with plenty of Scriptural evidence for his conclusions. Of course African traditional religions vary a great deal within Africa and there are many aspects which are not covered in this book. In one religion a certain traditional practice may have positive ramifications which can be incorporated into Christianity, whereas in another area a similar practice may be inappropriate. Even though a reader may not agree with all the author's positions on certain issues this book will cause him to grapple with the issues in a new way.

I feel this book has been needed in church and missionary circles for a long time. African church leaders need to take an honest look at the church in Africa and see why they have gotten so far away from their cultural roots. Missionaries need to be made more aware that much of what they teach is not Christianity but western culture. Hopefully both can learn from the contents of this book and thereby promote the growth of God's church in Africa: a church that is both true to the Word of God and meets the deep spiritual and cultural needs of the African peoples.

Jon Arensen
    Anthropology Coordinator for SIL in Africa,
    Candidate for Ph.D., Oxford University.

PREFACE

This volume is intended to serve as a textbook for serious students interested in learning African Traditional Religion (ATR) from a biblical perspective. The major emphasis is on two elements: 1)ATR as traditionally practiced in Africa, and 2)ATR as interpreted by the Holy Bible. Thus the viewpoint contained herein is more than a generally Christian viewpoint, as noble as that may be. Rather, we intend to expound relevant biblical teaching and apply it to the issues in our study.

African Traditional Religion. ATR is composed of three basic components: belief in the Supreme Being, the spirit world (spirits subordinate to the Supreme Being) and mystical powers. Throughout Africa different peoples emphasize one of those elements. Some, for instance the Murle of the Sudan, emphasize the Supreme Being. Others, like the Zande, focus on magic and mystical powers. Many Bantu, such as the Akamba, focus on ancestral spirits. Some like the Yoruba have a fixation on the divinities. Thus each of the African peoples has its own religious flavour, emphasizing one or the other of the three main components of ATR. But throughout Africa there is a widespread belief, to one degree or another, in the Supreme Being, the spirit world and mystical powers.

Hence, various authors have divided their study of ATR in similar ways. E. Geoffrey Parrinder in his study, *West African Religions* (1961), divides the subject into four parts: 1)The Supreme Being; 2)The chief divinities, including non-human spirits; 3)The divinized ancestors; and 4)The charms and amulets. E. Bolaji Idowu basically follows the same pattern except that he treats divinities and spirits separately (Idowu 1973:139).

John Mbiti in his book, *African Religions and Philosophy* (1969), includes the categories mentioned above but adds a few more and distributes the emphasis as follows: 1)The Supreme Being (45 pages); 2)Spiritual Beings, Spirits and the Living-Dead (16 pages); 3)Mankind, including the cycle of life (74 pages); 4)Specialists (24 pages); 5)Mystical Power, Magic, Witchcraft and Sorcery (10 pages); 6)Evil, Ethics and Justice (11 pages).

In this book we shall divide our study into those three major parts mentioned above: the Supreme Being, the spirit world and mystical powers. Good reasons could be given to commence our study with the Supreme Being. Since all African peoples believe in the Supreme Being who is the Creator of all, and since He is the ultimate Power and ultimate explanation of everything, it may seem logical to commence our study with the traditional belief in God.

However, we shall be guided by the purposes of our study. As the reader will discover, a central thesis (emphasis) of this book is that the traditional belief in God is both the great strength of ATR as well as, paradoxically, its chief weakness. Therefore, in order to understand the traditional belief in and practices related to the Supreme Being, it is necessary to understand the other emphases of ATR. We cannot assess the traditional belief and practice related to the Supreme Being without relating that to all the other beliefs and practices of ATR.

Biblical Perspective. Our goal is to help in the development of mature Christian thinking about African Traditional Religion. As Christians we need to think "Christianly," and this means biblical thinking. Not only do we need a correct factual understanding of ATR both in the past and the present, we need a Christian discernment of the true origin and nature of ATR through the study of the Bible. We shall, therefore, seek to evaluate Traditional Religion in such a way that we can preserve that which is true and good in ATR. At the same time we shall need to reject any error found in ATR.

In the midst of Africa's quest for authenticity, the Church of Jesus Christ desperately needs a wholesome balance, stressing both the positive and the negative in biblical perspective. Scripture becomes the normative standard whereby we judge truth and error.

Scripture exhorts us not to believe every spirit, "but test the spirits to see whether they are from God; because many false prophets have gone out into the world." (I John 4:1) The word, "test," means "to examine and prove," even as gold is tested in fire. This gift of the Spirit, "distinguishing of the spirits" (I Cor. 12:10), is a crying need in the Church. Only after we "examine everything carefully" can we then "hold fast to that which is good." (I Thess. 5:21)

This then is our aim: to examine carefully some of the crucial issues in ATR in the spotlight of God's Word so that we may discern between truth and error.

The Church in the 20th century finds herself in a similar conflict as she did in the early centuries of the Christian era. Being confronted with the counter-claims of non-Christian religions, she is tempted to indulge in syncretism, compromising the Gospel, sacrificing the distinctiveness of the very message she proclaims. But this book seeks, by the grace of God, to be loyal to our Lord who said, "I am the way, the truth and the life; no man cometh unto the Father but by Me." (John 14:6)

Each of the major parts on Mystical Powers, Spirit World and the Supreme Being, will contain several complimentary chapters.

The purpose of the first chapter in each major part is to survey in brief the general beliefs and practices of ATR. This will be followed by a chapter giving a case study of the Akamba in eastern Kenya. If we would limit ourselves to generalizations, we would loose some of the concrete dynamics of traditional religion. And we would also misrepresent the enormous differences among the traditional beliefs and practices of Africa. On the other hand, if we would content ourselves with a specific example of ATR, omitting generalizations, we could become lost in details and loose the continent wide perspective. We have, therefore, chosen to combine the two emphases of generalizing and particularizing. By including the Case Study of the Akamba, this book has the added bonus of providing an in-depth contribution to our ethnological understanding of the religious traditions of an important African society.

This volume is in reality two books in one, an evangelical textbook for the study of ATR in biblical perspective, plus collateral reading on the Akamba. The Case Study of the Akamba serves as an illustration of ATR but is not essential for the flow and argument of the book.

Included in each part of our study will be reference to the traditional religions worldwide. These chapters are very brief. But their inclusion is very significant and purposeful. ATR is cut from the same cloth as all other religions of mankind. The fact that we are focusing on ATR does not mean that we are discriminating against ATR. For our study will reveal that the traditional African stands in solidarity with mankind as a whole outside of Christ. The truth and error in ATR is representative of all non-Christian religions throughout the world.

In biblical perspective we affirm that the fundamental elements of ATR are not unique to Africa. Belief in God, divinities, spirits, ancestors, magic, witchcraft and sorcery are universal. They have been believed and practiced by peoples around the world from antiquity past until the present. By demonstrating that these beliefs are universal, we shall avoid any temptation to single out ATR as uniquely in error or unusually rich in religious understanding. The African peoples are one with mankind who are all made in the image of God and have all rebelled against their Creator.

The final chapters of each major part deals with ATR in biblical perspective. This focus is the whole reason for writing this textbook. We seek to assess, evaluate and weigh various traditional beliefs and practices in the light of God's Word.

To prepare the reader for a study of ATR themes, we shall begin with Part One on Foundational Issues for ATR. After surveying the various studies on ATR, we shall give attention to two fundamental questions: the origin of ATR and the focus of ATR on man. The concluding part of the book will treat the relationship of Biblical Christianity to African Traditional Religion.

The author wishes to acknowledge with gratitude the contributions which many have made to the composition of this book. The author's pilgrimage in researching ATR began in 1973 when Mr. Desmond Hales, formerly Principal of Scott Theological College, gave the author a sabbatical in order to prepare a syllabus for the teaching of ATR in the College. From that study came a mimeographed version of *African Traditional Religion in Biblical Perspective* which ended up being used as a textbook on ATR in seven Bible Schools and Colleges in Kenya and Tanzania of the Africa Inland Church . We readily acknowledge that without the initiative of Mr. Desmond Hales this book in all probability would not have been produced.

Further acknowledgement must be given all the students who studied ATR in Scott Theological College from 1973 to 1984. They have enriched my appreciation and understanding of Africa and her peoples. Through their dialogue and contributions from their own observations and experience the author's perspective has deepened. Some of their valuable contributions have been included in this book which I gratefully acknowledge. Without that invaluable experience, this book would not be published.

In 1980 the author began the studies which led to a Doctor of Missiology from the School of World Mission in 1985. The resulting dissertation was entitled, *Ancestor Relations Among Three African Societies in Biblical Perspective*. This present book is derived in part from that dissertation. A special word of thanks belongs to my mentor, Dr. Dean Gilliland, for his generous support and encouragement in my research. The author is deeply indebted to his dear wife, Mrs. Florence Gehman, for her support, encouragement and loving patience during those arduous years when study was combined with ministry responsibilities at Scott. To her this book is dedicated.

In fact this book is indebted to many people. A special word of thanks must be given to those who have read the manuscript and contributed helpful suggestions, including Dr. Paul Bowers, Rev. Daidanso ma Djongwe, Dr. David Kitonga and Mr. Jon Arensen. Clerical help, pastoral encouragement, the approval and co-operation of the A.I.M. International for my studies, support from church leaders and a host of others have all contributed. To them I gratefully give my thanks. The footnotes acknowledge the sources of my information and quotations from many books. If there are any omissions or errors in misrepresenting the facts, my sincerest apologies.

PART ONE

FOUNDATIONAL ISSUES FOR
AFRICAN TRADITIONAL RELIGION

PART ONE

FOUNDATIONAL ISSUES FOR
AFRICAN TRADITIONAL RELIGION

Chapter 1

STUDIES IN
AFRICAN TRADITIONAL RELIGION

REASONS FOR STUDYING ATR

Some Christians in Africa may ask, "Why study African Traditional Religion (ATR)? We have forsaken our old religion and have embraced the Christian faith. Jesus Christ is now our Lord and Saviour. What further need do we have to research ATR?"

Some church workers may also ask, "What is the use of researching ATR? We need to be current and up to date. ATR is a passing phenomenon. If you are interested in studying history, you may study ATR to help you understand the past. But ATR is irrelevant for understanding the present, younger generations."

Is the study of ATR relevant to our contemporary life at the close of the 20th century? Or is the chief benefit of ATR a knowledge of history, knowing how our ancestors once lived? A knowledge of ATR is imperative if we are to understand and minister in post independent Africa. Perhaps we can best illustrate the contemporary relevance of our subject by briefly recounting an extended legal wrangle in Kenya. For five months the nation was captivated with the unprecedented struggle between a widow and a clan.

A prominent Nairobi advocate, the leading African criminal lawyer in Kenya, Mr. S.M. Otieno, died suddenly of a heart attack. When his wife had announced plans over the radio to bury her late husband at his farm near Nairobi, his clan objected. His clan claimed that Mr. Otieno should not be buried by his wife near Nairobi but by his clan according to customary law at his ancestral home.

The protracted legal struggle lasted five months while the body of the deceased lay unburied in the city mortuary. The story became top news in Kenya with thousands crowding the law courts daily and the newspapers giving the story extensive front page coverage. The story became the chief topic of conversation for thousands. The daily narrative brought suspense and surprises, such as when Mrs. Otieno announced that she had been born again. And in the end the Nairobi All Saints' Cathedral refused to hold the S.M. Otieno funeral service at the cathedral as the clan had desired. For five months there were suspense and surprises. At first Mrs. Otieno was granted permission by the Judge to bury her late husband but the burial was stopped by a counter injunction from the deceased man's brother. A full trial ensued with the Judge awarding burial rights to the clan. Thereafter, Mrs. Otieno took the matter to the Court of Appeals which handed down its decision five months later, giving the body to the clan for customary burial.

This fascinating case could be viewed from different angles. In one sense, it was a tribal problem. Though the late Mr. Otieno was a Luo by tribe, he had married a Gikuyu woman. Emotions ran deep. The thousands of excited, cheering Kenyans crowding the court were largely Luo. They jumped and danced, flinging their hands in the air, frenzied and excited, unable to contain their happiness when the judges awarded the body to the Umira Kager clan. The clan accused Mrs. Otieno of being a rebel. In the end she refused to participate in the burial of her late husband in Luo land. Accusations were made. When the final verdict was announced, Mrs. Otieno was warned that the clan could not guarantee her bodily safety if she attended the funeral because of her alleged bitter arrogance. Nevertheless, they also declared that if she did not attend the funeral, she would be treated as non-existent with a veiled threat of confiscating her property.

Another way of assessing this legal wrangle is to contrast the traditional with the contemporary, the customary law with the common law. The late Mr. Otieno was a metropolitan and a cosmopolitan. Though he undoubtedly honoured the traditions of his ancestors, he had moved away from his deep attachment to the Luo customs of his rural community. He never built a house in Luo land, never owned land there and seldom visited his roots. Nor did his children learn to speak Jaluo. He had married a Gikuyu. He also had attended a mission sponsored school and was a baptized member of a Christian church. Indicating his own wish, he told his wife and many others that he desired to be buried at his farm near Nairobi.

However, his clan would hear nothing of Mr. Otieno's wish. They contended that Otieno was born a Luo and died a Luo. Though he had married a Gikuyu wife, though he was a baptized Christian and though he lived in Nairobi as a metropolitan, never owning land back home and seldom returning to his roots, his clan said he should be buried in the traditional Luo manner at his ancestral home. "In Luo customs, a man cannot marry a woman from a different tribe and become a member of that tribe. He remains a Luo." "Born a Luo, always a Luo." According to Luo traditions, women and children had no say over funeral and burial matters and, therefore, the duty fell to his brother to bury Mr. Otieno.

In the end, the Court of Appeals ruled that when there is conflict between common law and customary law, the later is given precedent. They declared that the courts of Kenya are guided by African customary law provided that such laws are "not repugnant to justice and morality." And the judges concluded that the advocate for Mrs. Otieno had failed to demonstrate that traditional Luo burial customs were opposed to justice or morality. On the surface one might say, therefore, that the struggle was simply between Luo customary law and the English common laws used in modern Kenya.

However, we believe that beneath the surface there was an even more fundamental reason why the clan felt obligated to bury the deceased. And that reason was religious.

Throughout the five months of extended hearings both sides readily acknowledged that changes are taking place in Luo customs. For instance the Luo men no longer remove their front six teeth as traditionally practiced. But we ask, why are some customs changing and not others? Why do the Luo insist on traditional burial ceremonies? Why do Luo customs of burial persist into the 21st century?

The cultures of Africa today are no more what they used to be. In so many areas the traditional customs are changing— technologically, educationally, politically, culturally and to some extent religiously. Yet we find that during times of crises, especially death, even professing "Christians" revert to traditional beliefs and practices. The fact is that superficial customs change easily with the passage of time. But the deep core world view beliefs of a people are very persistent.

Beneath the explicit struggle over traditional values versus contemporary values, is the traditional world view of the Luo which is religious at heart. The fact is that African Traditional Religion provides the basic pre-suppositions for much of traditional African culture. And this was only alluded to briefly in the public press.

Said Mr. Otieno's brother, "If my late brother's body is not buried at home, Wambui [the late Mr. Otieno's widow] and her family will have bad luck." Ghosts and spirits would haunt the family members, so they contended. Indeed, the clan said that if the courts did not grant them authority to bury the body at the ancestral home, they would follow traditional burial rites practiced when someone drowns and his body is lost for burial. They would take a local fruit tree, *yago*, and use it to represent the late lawyer's body. Traditional prayers and rites would be said before the branch of the tree is buried. And all of this is intended to prevent bad luck. Nothing much more was said in the public press. But a knowledge of the Luo traditional religion helps one to understand the thinking of the Luo clan.

For the Luo believe that when a man dies, his soul (*chuny*) continues to live, being transformed into an ancestral spirit known as *jachien*. Although the body dies, the Luo person remains very much alive and active among the members of the clan. While the body corrupts in the ground, his spirit continues to interact with the living, for good or ill.

These ancestral spirits, the "living-dead" in the words of John Mbiti, can bring benefits to the living. But more frequently they produce the problem of "ghostly vengeance." When unhappy, these ancestral spirits return and haunt the living. Ancestral spirits are notable for their troublesome relations with their descendants. When an ancestor is offended by the living, his aggrieved spirit becomes a menace to the living, haunting the living by causing sickness and death.

In order to avoid the problem of being haunted, the Luo must keep the traditions laid down by the community. To break traditions of society will surely bring revenge from the ancestral spirits. Such traditions include the proper mode and place of burial.

Because the spirits of the dead are dreaded and feared, the Luo have the custom of driving away the ancestral spirit at the funerals. At the funerals attended by Hauge in recent years, "a war dance in full regalia [dress], complete with spears and shields" was performed, "accompanied by frenzied [wild, emotional excitement] drum beats and other loud noises from various instruments." (Hauge 1974:113) The intention is to drive away the spirit of the deceased together with other ancestral spirits who may attend the funeral to harm those present. In 1910 Stam reported the same phenomenon. "At the burial, frantic dancing takes place, and the surrounding atmosphere is furiously beaten with clubs, to drive the spirit of the defunct out of the neighbourhood, because it is supposed to bring on sickness and even death." (Stam 1910:361)

This custom is widely practiced even today. People come to the funeral with all their cattle from distant places. While drums are beat and emotions are high, they drive the cattle and the spirits of the deceased a long distance to some river or lake to escort the spirits of the dead so that they will not haunt the living. The people then return with their cattle. Years ago on such occasions the Luo in a frenzied state would fight with spears and take revenge on their enemies. It was a frightening occasion. The purpose was preventive, to drive the ancestors away to prevent them from harming the living.

This fear of death and the dead is reflected in the comment made by Millikin in 1906. "As soon as the person has expired the relatives in the same *boma* commence howling and crying, and in some cases this is done before the sick person has expired but close to death." (1906:54) The Luo believe the howling and crying are capable of driving away the ancestors (Hauge 1974:114).

Thus we find here in Luo traditional religion the reason for the Luo insistence on customary burial at the ancestral home in modern Kenya. Customary burial is more than tradition. Any failure to follow the ancestral traditions will bring revenge upon the living. Thus we can see that ATR is not dead. Nor is it irrelevant. In order to interpret and understand the actions and words of people today, one must understand the traditional religious world view which provides the assumptions for customary laws.

Most of those Luo who participated in the legal proceedings were professing Christians who saw nothing wrong with those Luo traditional burial rites. Christian clergymen testified, defending those Luo burial practices. Quotations were made from the Bible to support some of their customs. They contended that "Christianity had taken a strong hold" among the Luo. They readily conceded that if Luo customs were contrary to Christianity they should be abandoned. But they did not believe there was anything in Luo tradition of burial that was irreconcilable with morality and the Christian faith.

Luo customs continue to change. Some Luo Christians affirm that Luo customs, offensive to the Christian conscience, are not forced upon born again believers when they die. Indeed, this often is true. But the judicial ruling indicates that the traditional clan custom has precedence over the stated preferences of individuals. And those burial traditions are religious at the core.

We can see from this current event in contemporary Africa, therefore, that a knowledge of ATR is most vital for a contemporary understanding of life and culture. ATR is not a religion in the western sense of the word which is separated from the rest of life. African Traditional Religion permeates the social life of the traditional African; it is the total traditional world view with all the values and beliefs.

This revival of the religion of Africa is not confined to this one incident in Kenya. Reports from all over Africa confirm the same thing. African traditional culture is being revived everywhere and with it, ATR.

As evangelical Christians we need to think through our traditional religious heritage. We must evaluate these ATR beliefs in the light of the Bible so as to know what is moral and just, what is good and upright before the Lord.

Why then should we study African Traditional Religion?

1. ATR should be studied for its own sake.

Men climb mountains to explore the unknown, risking their own lives many times, just because the mountain is there waiting to be explored. Astronomers examine the heavenly bodies just because the astronomical expanse is there.

Even so we ought to study the traditional religion of Africa because it is one of the world's religions of a great people with a great past. ATR was formerly embraced by a whole continent. And even today, over 100 years since the introduction of the Christian faith, ATR persists and shapes the attitudes and actions of large numbers of people. God has endowed man with curiosity so that we may explore, research, learn and grow in our understanding of God's universe in the light of God's special revelation. ATR is one of those legitimate areas of learning.

2. ATR is the religious background of African peoples whom Christians seek to evangelize today.

The Christian Church is seeking to evangelize and disciple large multitudes of peoples in Africa today. And their religious background is ATR. In order to build bridges of communication with them, we must understand the beliefs and practices of the traditional African.

All learning proceeds from the known to the unknown. What the person believes and knows forms the basis for further knowledge. Therefore, a communicator must know intimately those with whom he would communicate in order to relate his thoughts to the problems and needs of that person.

This is true in every area of communication. In teaching, this is the principle of the dynamic of teacher-student relationship. Unless students are well known to the teacher, the lesson will seem irrelevant and theoretical, for the instruction will be without meaningful application.

In public speaking, the first and most fundamental step in preparing a speech is to analyze the occasion and audience. Unless the speaker knows the audience's fixed attitudes and beliefs and knows their thinking on the subject he wishes to expound, he cannot speak effectively and persuasively.

Therefore, we study ATR in order to be better prepared to evangelize and disciple the peoples for Christ.

3. Many professing Christians rely on ATR in times of crisis.

Witchcraft and sorcery are great temptations. Reliance upon the ancestors is a felt need during times of emergency, even for many Christians. The traditional help derived from the medicine man is often felt strongly during times of great need.

Mbiti speaks of a "religious concubinage" in which people embrace "the good" in both Christianity and ATR.

The following pertinent observation is made by Idowu:

> While, as we have said, every African may wish to be regarded as connected with one or the other of the two 'fashionable' religions, most are at heart still attached to their own indigenous beliefs. It is now becoming clear to the most optimistic of Christian evangelists that the main problem of the church in Africa today is the divided loyalties of most of her members between Christianity with its western categories and practices on the one hand, and the traditional religion on the other. It is well known that in strictly personal matters relating to the passages of life and the crises of life, African Traditional Religion is regarded as the final succour by most Africans (Idowu 1973:205, 206).

The degree to which this is true undoubtedly varies with the particular church and individual. There are well-taught, mature believers in Africa as well as weak, biblically illiterate ones. There are genuine Christians transformed by the power of God as well as nominal followers of the church. Nevertheless, even in the best taught churches where the power of God is working mightily through the Word, the tendency for relapse into the old ways is very real.

Daidanso ma Djongwe, a Chadian who is also a leader of the Association of Evangelicals of Africa and Madagascar, affirms that ATR is a major problem in the African Christian Church whenever suffering comes. Suffering and sickness lead the people back to ATR. In fact, Daidanso contends that few African Christians respond well to problems of sickness. Many feel that their ancestors are not pleased with them. Only a few African Christians have a mature biblical attitude during times of sickness and death (Daidanso ma Djongwe:1988).

The Luo of Kenya are a case in point. Traditionally, they bury the body with the head facing the gate of the homestead. The male is buried on his left side and the wife on her right side. If trouble develops in the family even twenty years after a person dies, they may fear that the improper burial, failure to follow the Luo traditions, has resulted in the family trouble. The only resolution is to rectify the error in burial.

One Luo Christian left instructions how his body should be buried in a non-traditional manner. But his own brother would not follow his wishes, preferring instead to follow the Luo traditional culture. Whether one is buried on his left side or his right side is in itself inconsequential. But if the reason is fear of the ancestral spirits, then there is lack of faith.

Another Luo Christian woman buried her deceased Christian husband in a Christian manner and contrary to some of the Luo traditional practices. She persisted in doing this despite the objections of her extended family. But years later when trouble haunted the home, when one family member died and another went mad, she was literally compelled by the other family members to un-do the mistakes of the past and re-bury her husband according to Luo traditional ways.

In view of this common problem of Christians yielding to traditional pressures and resorting to traditional religious practices, the Christian Church should seek to understand the appeal of the traditional religion and evaluate this in biblical perspective. Why do Christians resort to the traditional resources in times of need? Is this merely a sinful relapse brought on by the Devil, or can we learn some felt-needs which the Church has not yet met with its present approach to ministry and teaching? Wherein does the Scripture speak to the problems facing African Christians? In order to answer these questions we must have a thorough grasp of ATR.

4. The Christian Church in Africa needs to contextualize her faith so that it becomes truly rooted in the life of the peoples.

The Gospel in its *content* is unchanging and supra-cultural. It is relevant to all men in every culture because it is God's message addressed to mankind which is one in origin, nature and spiritual need. Throughout Africa, the unadulterated gospel of Jesus Christ has met the needs of the human heart. David Barrett has demonstrated this through his statistical study of the remarkable church growth in Africa. He further affirms, "Christianity has been accepted by Africans from the earliest days as a genuinely African religion, with roots firmly in African soil." (Barrett 1973:168)

But the manner of *expression* and *communication* of this Gospel varies from people to people. The manner of *worship*, the expression of praise and gratitude, the ways of *communicating* the Gospel will differ. The *music* of the church should be rooted in the traditional culture. The *gifts* of helps and governing within the church should take on a local flavour. "The formalized ecclesiastical expressions of faith" should have the indelible marks of a particular people. To be sure, there are biblical guidelines, but no biblical formula that is inflexible and uniform for every culture. The Holy Spirit stamps everyone with the mark of divine life, but this life then reflects the cultural diversity of the peoples.

Today there is a cry throughout Africa for a genuine, authentic African Christianity, one which is truly rooted in the lives of the indigenous peoples. The Gospel must be communicated in culturally relevant ways which people can grasp. The Gospel must come alive to the people by clothing the biblical message in African culture and life-ways.

The needs and problems of people are essentially the same. Mankind is one in his nature. But, though peoples are basically the same, their cultures are in many ways unique and distinctive. The teaching of Scripture should be applied and related to the particular cultural context in which the African church finds herself. In this sense, the theologians of the West wrestled with different kinds of problems than those found on the African continent. Africa must take the unchanging truth of Scripture and apply it to her particular needs, and in this sense, develop an "African Christian Theology." (refer to Gehman 1987)

For all this to happen we need to know the context of African Christianity. This surely includes African Traditional Religion. We need to evaluate it and understand it in the light of God's Word. Where truth is found, we must preserve it. Where errors exists, we must expose it by the standard of Scripture.

5. The revival of ATR brings a sense of urgency to this study.

Most African nations have been liberated from colonial rule within the past generation. They are now seeking African identity. Rejecting many of the customs and ways of Europeans, they are seeking to re-assert their own traditional ways, including their religion.

As an example of this we remember Kwame Nkrumah of Ghana who was the forerunner of the advocates of the "African personality." In order to restore the African "soul," he abolished the formal Christian prayers offered at the beginning of Parliament, a custom instituted by the "Christian" colonialists, and he reinstated the pouring of libation to the ancestors.

University students today, taught that they have been deprived of a rich cultural tradition by the colonialists, are re-asserting their desire to return to many of the religious traditions of the past. Selectively and tentatively they are experimenting with traditional religion. Through the universities there has sprung up a renewed commitment to ATR once again.

Okot P'Bitek closes his book, *African Religions in Western Scholarship*, with this opinion.

> But the basic conflict is between fundamental assumptions of Western civilization and the fundamental assumptions of African civilization. The assumptions of Western man have their roots in Judaism, the Greek and Roman experiences, the Christian faith and industrialization. True Uhuru means the abolition of Western political and economic dominance from Africa, and the reconstruction of our societies on the basis of African thought systems. The study of African religions is one important way of understanding African ways of thought (P'Bitek 1971:119).

When Traditional Religion is so closely associated with nationalism, the Christian Church is posed with a serious problem. An non-thinking negative attitude is not the answer. Surely, the Christian need not reject all the pleas for "authenticity," "self-identity," "African personality" and "African culture." But a passive, blind acceptance is not possible either for a Christian who desires to remain loyal to his Lord. A passive attitude leading to compromise spells disaster for the Christian Church.

What is desperately needed today is a biblical understanding of ATR as evangelicals search the Scriptures under the guidance of the Holy Spirit. The traditional religion of Africa must be evaluated in the light of God's eternal and unchanging Word. Only then can we sort out the culturally relative elements and the supra-cultural absolutes. And only then can we maintain a biblical Christianity with a genuine, authentic stamp of Africa upon her.

SURVEY OF LITERATURE ON ATR

Where can we find literature on the study of African Traditional Religion? Who wrote it and how reliable is it? The elementary formal study of ATR began during the colonial period when Europeans entered the continent towards the end of the 19th century and the early part of the 20th century. The fragmentary and provisional nature of that study is self evident today and the quality of the studies gradually developed through the years.

Articles in Anthropological Journals. Brief articles of a few pages were written in various anthropological journals based on some field observation. Much of what is written has little to do with the religious beliefs and practices of the peoples. One must search through the indexes. Their value varies, depending on the nature and extent of the research and the quality of the researcher. In many ways the earlier magazine articles have their primary value in giving us an historical understanding of what was understood and said about ATR in the earlier days of research.

Ethnographic Studies of African Peoples. Some rather substantial and creditable studies have been made by anthropologists from the earliest days. Religion is usually treated in one chapter or so along with all the other cultural features. See Appendix A for a selected list of some of the more prominent ethnographies. It is significant that included among these early ethnographical studies is that of an African, the late Mzee Jomo Kenyatta. In 1938 he wrote the pioneering book, entitled, *Facing Mount Kenya*, an anthropological study of his own people, the Gikuyu of Kenya.

African Traditional Religion of Particular African Peoples. While the books listed above contain, at the most, a chapter or two on the religion of the peoples, as time passed, specialized studies were made of the religion of a particular ethnic group. A selected bibliography can be found in Appendix A. As one may expect, the African contributions to this aspect of study began to increase during the latter years, beginning in the 1960's.

Occasional Papers, University Research, and Ethnographic Surveys. Various universities throughout the continent and in Europe have provided means for researching, preserving and publishing research materials on African cultural and religious themes. For instance, the Department of Religious Studies and Philosophy of Makerere University has mimeographed many volumes in the series entitled, *Occasional Research Papers*. The Royal Anthropological Institute of Great Britain and Ireland has published *Occasional Papers*. And the International African Institute has published various Ethnographic Surveys of Africa which include brief treatment on religion.

General Surveys of African Traditional Religion. In addition to the various studies made of particular peoples mentioned above, there has developed a number of standard books useful in their general survey of traditional religion throughout Africa.

1954 Parrinder, E.G. *African Traditional Religion*
1959 Temples, P. *Bantu Philosophy*
1961 Parrinder, G. *West African Religion*
1963 Taylor, J. *The Primal Vision*
1969 Mbiti, J. *African Religions and Philosophy*
1969 Parrinder, G. *Africa's Three Religions*
1970 Mbiti, J. *Concepts of God in Africa*
1973 Idowu, B. *African Traditional Religion: A Definition*
1983 Adggbola, E.A. Ade. *Traditional Religion in West Africa*

There are many other books on ATR in addition to the ones mentioned above. They vary in quality and perspective. With the rapid change of African culture and religion, the older substantial studies by ethnographically trained scholars fill a void difficult to fill today. Yet their viewpoint is etic, that is, foreign, that of westerners who sought to understand the traditional beliefs of the Africans. Today many African scholars are rising up and seeking to provide an insider's perspective, frequently called an emic perspective. They are now supplementing the void from the past.

LIMITATIONS OF PAST STUDIES

The question may legitimately be asked, why prepare another book on African Traditional Religion? Have we not demonstrated that there are indeed many books written on ATR? And are not these books already written by authoritative authors? To this we must reply that many excellent books by competent authors have indeed been written. They have in fact been utilized in the preparation of this book. But their main limitation is that they do not seek to assess and evaluate ATR in the light of God's Word; they do not approach the study with rigorous commitment to biblical pre-suppositions which would enable the authors to make an evangelical evaluation of African Traditional Religion.

By pre-suppositions, we mean that which is assumed before one approaches the study of traditional religion; that which is taken for granted and underlies all interpretation and explanation of ATR.

We are not denying the need for objectivity in the sense of studying things as they are without distortion and misrepresentation. There is always a danger of "reading into" traditional religion what is not there, or "reading out" what is not indigenous. No one is exempt from these twin dangers. For the sake of honesty and personal integrity, we must be faithful to the facts.

However, the notion of objectivity is highly abused. The dictionary defines objectivity as "without bias or prejudice; detached; impersonal." The first two terms are loaded. The popular meaning of "bias" is to warp or slant the truth. The dictionary defines "prejudice" as pre- judgment, "a judgment or opinion formed before the facts are known; preconceived idea...a judgment or opinion held in disregard of facts that contradict it." If objectivity is the opposite of bias and prejudice, then every scholar, especially a Christian scholar, must be objective. The suggestion of twisting or distorting the truth, or being closed to the facts should be repulsive to everyone, and especially to a Christian who serves God, the Source of all Truth.

But if objectivity merges with the other synonyms, "detached, impersonal," how can a Christian, let alone a human being, become detached in the strict sense of the word? It is true that an objective, detached approach to study is essential for any creditable research. But this cannot be done in any mechanical sense. To be human involves personal attachment and involvement. A coldly detached, impersonal character may describe a machine but not a man. The very nature of a Christian is one who is *committed* to Jesus Christ.

This basic truth escapes many peoples. While we thoroughly agree with Idowu on the need for "openness and sympathy" when studying ATR, we strongly disagree with him when he assumes you can approach the study of ATR without any preconceived notions. Idowu advocates the W.C.C. slogan, "The world provides the agenda." "This is a wise approach," Idowu writes, "in that, if properly followed, it ensures that one does not enter the field with any preconceived notions."

(Idowu 1973:17) This is humanly impossible.

The fact is that every person approaches the study of anything, including African Traditional Religion, with presuppositions of one sort or another. And the limitations with most studies of ATR is that they do not bring with them a rigorous commitment to biblical presuppositions as understood by evangelicals. As invaluable as many books are on ATR, there are few which seek to develop a "Christian perspective" and none which relates ATR directly to the study of Scripture. None actually examines the teaching of Scripture to assess and evaluate ATR.

The late Okot P'Bitek (1970) is a vivid illustration of this truth that all research is done with commitment to prior presuppositions. His basic criticism of all past and present studies of African Traditional Religion is that they are not objective. He claims that they are all coloured by cultural and religious bias. Expatriates study and write on the subject with their biases. So do the African nationalists today, such as Jomo Kenyatta, Leopold Senghor, J.B. Danquah, K.A. Busia and John Mbiti. Okot P'Bitek laments, "...instead of carrying out systematic studies of beliefs of their peoples, and presenting them as the African peoples actually know them, African scholars, smarting [reacting] under the insults from the West, claimed that African peoples knew the Christian God long before the missionaries told them about it." (1970:46) What he pleads for is "objectivity." "We must reject all forms of subjectivity, whether the subjectivity arose from anti-Christian or from pro-Christian prejudices." "...Religions must be studied and presented as accurately as possible, so as to discover the African world view." (1970:113)

Yet P'Bitek does not recognize that he himself is committed to a certain perspective. He brings to his study of ATR a certain pre-understanding which helps him shape his perspective of traditional religion. Ali Mazuri, writing the epilogue of the book, comments on the passionate commitment of Okot P'Bitek. "Here also is African scholarship in a mood of unabashed [courageous] commitment." (1970:9) Following are some of the basic assumptions underlying the writings of P'Bitek.

a. He is biased against the Christian faith.

You can almost see the sneer on his face when he writes of "the followers of Joshua the Messiah (alias Jesus Christ)." (1970:25) With apparent approval, he narrates extensively the attack of Celsus against Christianity around A.D. 177-180. He says, "The poor Jesus hired himself out as a workman in Egypt, and there learned the art of magic, and, full of conceit because of those powers, and on account of them gave him the title, 'God'." (1970:27)

b. He embraces the liberal higher critical view of the Bible.

His educational exposure to Christianity was obviously of a radical liberal nature. Speaking of the development of the Christian God, he asserts "JHVR or Yahweh was at first only one of many deities of the ancient Jews." (1970:81) It was Jeremiah and Ezekiel who "invented the idea that all other deities except JHVR were false and that he punishes divinities." While the Jewish religion was very simple, Paul Hellenized Christianity, introducing the metaphysical. "It would be inexact," P'Bitek contends, "...to suppose that the Christian *Theos* [God] is the same as Yahweh of the Old Testament." (1970:86)

c. He rejects belief in an infinite, eternal and personal God.

He laments that the African deities have been robed with "awkward Hellenic garments" by such men as Kenyatta and Idowu. Instead, he contends that as most of the Africans "did not hold beliefs in any deity similar in conception to the Christian God, we may refer to traditional Africans as *atheistic* in their outlook." (emphasis mine; 1970:100)

P'Bitek then asks, "But will the African deities survive the revolutions in science and philosophy which have killed the Christian God?" Without any apparent regret, he responds, "I doubt it...The Christian God has become intellectually superfluous [unnecessary] and, moreover, the metaphysical statements about him [pertaining to the essential nature of reality] do not make sense to modern men." (1970:112)

d. He is an African nationalist, passionately committed to an "African thought system" and opposed to all that is "foreign," including Christianity. He writes,

> ...if the leaders sincerely believe that the social reconstruction in Africa should be based on the African world view, their religions must be studied and presented as accurately as possible, so as to discover the African world view. Christian sex ethics, its other worldliness, and its preoccupations with sin are three important areas which African intellectuals and leaders can explore, because, here, Christianity contrasts vividly with African religions." (1970:113)

We can only conclude that in fact Okot P'Bitek is no more objective than the intellectuals whom he rejects. In fact, he calls for "counter- selection" and "purposive-discrimination." Since former scholars persistently distorted ATR in the past, he claims, it is now necessary to engage in "a process of counter-selection" in order to correct the human error of the past (1970:123).

Okot P'Bitek may have desired to approach the subject with a "scientific attitude." But as Kraemer points out, "The scientific attitude in such cases is just a fancy name for personal taste." (Kraemer 1963:52) The intention of a scientific attitude is excellent in trying to be objective. But the scientific method has a serious weakness. It does not include any standard or measurement which can be used in deciding truth and error. Since science cannot produce truth, truth must be imported. And the standard by which P'Bitek desires to measure ATR is a non-Christian commitment to the African world view which he no doubt selectively assesses according to his own personal taste. His own standard of measurement is himself with his own preferences and dislikes.

Thus we conclude that we all approach the study of ATR with our particular perspective. What is lacking in all the previous studies of ATR is a rigorous biblical assessment, relating ATR to the teachings of the Bible. Herein lies the need for another look at traditional religion through the perspective of the Scriptures.

LIMITATIONS OF THIS PRESENT STUDY

All research has its limitations determined by the inescapable reality of our human nature. Being limited as finite human beings, we can only produce limited contributions to any subject. Thus we are attempting a new approach to the study of African Traditional Religion in order to rectify some of the limitations of previous studies. But we must also acknowledge the limitations of this present study and the perspective of the author.

Limitations of an Evangelical Perspective. This book, no less than the writings of P'Bitek, is written from a particular perspective. With the same unabashed commitment found in the writings of Okot P'Bitek, the author of this book is fervently committed to a set of presuppositions which are evangelical in nature. And our desire is to set before the reader some of these assumptions.

As we study the phenomenon of ATR we must remember that no data is impregnated with meaning. Whatever data we handle must be given meaning and interpretation, consistent both with the facts and our world view. It is our pre-understanding, our assumptions, our presuppositions which help fashion the interpretation of the facts.

We have sought diligently to be fair and objective, without twisting or distorting the facts to suit our theories. If in fact evidence can be deduced to demonstrate factual error, we welcome any notification of such errors. But many times the root of disagreement does not lie in the raw data but in the presuppositions which help us to interpret that raw data. Anyone who disagrees with the interpretation of the data herein presented should also consider the presuppositions of this study, for therein may be one cause for the different perspective.

However, the evangelical presuppositions of this book do set it apart from most other books on African Traditional Religion in its attempt to assess and evaluate ATR from a biblical perspective. **The basic presuppositions of this book are:**

1. The belief in the absolute and final authority of the Bible for all faith and conduct is the one fundamental presupposition which is the foundation for this book (Ps.119:89; Isa.40:8; Mt. 5:17,18; Lk.24:27, 44; Jn. 10:35; 17:17; I Cor. 2:12, 13; II Tim. 3:15-17; I Pet. 1:10-11; II Pet. 1:21; Rev. 22:18, 19).

Thus we affirm the divine authorship and consequent unity of the Scriptures. We also reject the liberal higher critical approach to the Scriptures represented by Idowu who writes,

> If we take, for example, the spiritual journey of the Hebrew minds, we shall see the stages which were covered from a henotheism [belief in many gods with one supreme god among them] which was deeply tinged [coloured] with ethnocentricity [national self-centredness] to the ethical monotheism of Deutero-Isaiah." (Idowu 1973: 142)

For Idowu, the theological journey of the Hebrews began at the Exodus with a belief in many gods but with one supreme god among them, and proceeded to a belief in one Creator God in the post-exilic period. Such a view believes in the evolutionary development of man's comprehension rather than the progressive revelation of God.

We affirm, instead, that the Bible is the Word of God in that the words of Scripture teach only that which God desired to teach, each part of Scripture bearing proper relationship with all other parts. Scripture is marked by unity and the absence of all contradictions because the Holy Spirit is the divine Author.

Arising out of this faith in the inspired, infallible and inerrant Word of God, grow these further assumptions which form the basis for our study.

2. We acknowledge the general revelation of God, given to all men in nature and conscience which is not sufficient for salvation but which leaves men without excuse (Rom. 1:18-20; 2:14-16). We therefore, accept all truth wherever it is found as being derived from common grace.

3. We affirm that all men, by virtue of their Adamic nature, are sinners in rebellion against the Triune God and living under God's wrath (Rom.3:9-18; 5:12-21).

4. We further believe that salvation from eternal condemnation is a free gift of grace, received alone through faith in Jesus Christ (Rom. 3:21-20; Eph. 2:1-10).

5. We acknowledge the existence of a personal Devil and spirit beings who, in their fallen state, can molest and harm unbelievers (Eph. 2:2; 6:12). But we also affirm our faith in the omnipotent God whose power is infinitely greater than any creature and who pledges to preserve His children from all evil (Rom. 8:31-39).

6. We are bound by Scripture to believe in both heaven and hell; hell where all unrepentant sinners shall be banished from God's presence and judged by His wrath in conscious torment forever; and heaven where God's people, sinners redeemed by the blood of the Lamb by grace through personal faith in Christ, shall live forever in conscious fellowship with God (Mt.8:12; 25:41, 46; Rev. 21:27).

Limitations of Personal Understanding. At the same time we readily admit that the perspective found in this book is *an* evangelical perspective, not *the* evangelical perspective. Other evangelicals may disagree with various view points. Our stated presuppositions do not take into consideration the particular historical, cultural and experiential background of the author. Such cultural differences contribute to different perspectives on the subject.

Furthermore, the author's experience and research has been confined largely to East Africa in general and to Kenya in particular. We have tried to consider ATR throughout the continent of Africa but for obvious reasons we have not been able to research other areas to the same depth. This will be reflected, for instance, in our limited treatment of Divinities which is largely a West African phenomenon (though also found among the former kingdoms in Uganda).

In one sense, this book represents a perspective of someone who has not grown up within any of the traditional religions of Africa. Those who learn ATR from second hand experience have a very different view of things from those who have grown up with ATR. That may be one reason, for instance, why the late Byang Kato takes such a divergent view of ATR from Mbiti (cf. Kato 1975, pages 27-46; Mbiti 1986: Dedication). The late Byang Kato was reared in a traditional African home where ATR was a daily experience, while John Mbiti grew up in a Christian home.

However, what is found in this book is not the result of mere contact with books, nor from a few months of interaction with people. Through the teaching of ATR over a period of eleven years in a theological college classroom, the author has had ample opportunity of grappling with these issues, inside the classroom and out in the field. Through dialogue, discussion, interaction and inquiry the author has grown in his comprehension of the subject. Through this learning experience the author has gleaned from personal contacts a deeper appreciation and understanding of ATR. While the perspective contained in this book in all of its details is not embraced by everyone, this book does reflect the perspective of many Africans who have themselves grown up in ATR.

Limitations of Balance. The reader may discover that certain topics in ATR are treated more briefly, with less detail, than other topics. The Case Study of the Akamba, for instance, may at times seem to be unbalanced for a purported pan-African survey of ATR. Our discussion of ancestral spirits and mystical powers may appear to be excessive when compared to some other books on the subject. On the other hand, our discussion of man in his concrete experience of the supernatural may seem rather limited.

Each author must determine his priorities and objectives. For some reason Mbiti has chosen to discuss spiritual beings, spirits and the living-dead in only 16 pages and mystical powers he discusses in only 10 pages, all from a book totaling 277 pages (Mbiti 1969). Our own purposes have led us to examine carefully in the light of biblical teaching the main themes of ATR, namely, mystical powers, the spirit world, and the Supreme Being. Therefore, the accent in this book has the apologetic purpose of interpreting these basic elements in ATR in the light of Scripture.

Limitations of Generalizations and Specificity. Many books on ATR have the admirable advantage of restricting their research to one particular African ethnic group. They have the freedom to explore, investigate and interpret on the basis of specific phenomena which they observe. However, human nature yearns to generalize, seeing the relationship of the particular to the universal.

Therefore, more recently, other textbooks on ATR have been written which generalize for all of Africa. While these books have the advantage of enabling one to grasp ATR for the whole continent, they tend to minimize the great differences between one ethnic group and another, with over 1,000 such peoples in Africa. One serious criticism of such books is that they gloss over the great differences and paint something which is far more homogenious than is actually true.

This introduces us to the question of whether we are capable of discussing African Traditional Religion (in the singular) or whether we must reckon with

1,000 differing African Traditional Religions (in the plural). This seems to be a needless bone of contention. Idowu writes on *African Traditional Religion* (1973) while Mbiti writes on *African Religions and Philosophy* (1969). And yet even Mbiti composed a later book entitled, *An Introduction to African Religion*.

It is our contention that either singular or plural is acceptable if one understands the issue. Just as there is not one ethnic group in Africa, but 1,000, so there is not one formulation of religious beliefs and practices, but many. The deeper you go into the study of religious beliefs in ATR, the more conscious you are of diversity.

Yet, in all the diversity, there is also unity. All African peoples are united on certain issues: a belief in the Supreme Being who is Creator of all things, the existence of spirits, life after death, a living relationship with the ancestral spirits, and the practice of magic, witchcraft and sorcery. The individual expressions may be different, but a general similarity prevails throughout the continent, so that we may speak of African Traditional Religion in the singular.

The generalizations of ATR found in this book are generally representative of ATR as attested by the large body of literature available on the subject. However, these generalizations should be accepted for what they are. Generalizations do have exceptions. And generalizations do tend to gloss over significant differences in traditional beliefs among the African peoples.

Our case study on the Akamba is meant to avoid the pitfalls of generalization by an examination of what one particular ethnic group believes and practices. This case study of the Akamba will help us make ATR concrete and specific, instead of general and abstract. The Akamba Traditional Religion will vividly illustrate ATR and serve as a counter balance to the broad sweeping generalizations one is prone to make about ATR. While we do not want to exaggerate the extent to which these beliefs are representative of the hundreds of other ethnic groups in Africa, it would appear that they are indeed representative of many African peoples, though certainly not all. We may do injustice to the facts if we either exaggerate the similarity of the Akamba with other Africans, or if we minimize the relationship of the Akamba Traditional Religion with other Bantu and African peoples.

In seeking to present to the reader what traditional Africans believed and practiced we do fall into the danger of minimizing the differences. Of this limitation we should be aware in our present study.

With these introductory remarks concluded, we proceed to consider two important foundational issues in our study of ATR, namely, the origins of ATR and the focus of ATR.

REVIEW QUESTIONS FOR CHAPTER 1

1. Enumerate all the reasons why a growing, witnessing Christian would benefit by studying ATR?
2. Why is it harmful for a Christian worker to be ignorant of the African traditional beliefs, even though he may know the Bible well?
3. Discuss what is meant by "presuppositions."
4. How does Okot p'Bitek illustrate the truth that everyone has his own as-

sumptions and pre-understanding when studying ATR?

5. Evaluate some of the presuppositions upon which this study of ATR is based.

Suggested Reading and Thought Questions for Advanced Study:

Anderson, J.N.D. *Christianity and Comparative Religion*, 1970, pp.7-30.

Idowu, E. Bolaji. *African Traditional Religion: A Definition*, 1973, pp 76-136.

Mbiti, John. *African Religions and Philosophy*, 1969, pp. 1-28.

Parrinder, E.G. *African Traditional Religion*, 1962, pp. 9-28.

P'Bitek, Okot. *African Religions in Western Scholarship*, 1970.

Shorter, Aylward. *African Christian Theology*, 1977, pp. 38-60.

Smith, Edwin ed. *African Ideas of God*, 1966, pp. 1-35.

1. What do you think should be the title of our study, "African Traditional *Religion*" or "African Traditional *Religions*"? Why? Is one necessarily wrong to give the alternative answer? Why?

2. As you approach the study of ATR, are you completely free from all presuppositions and pre-understandings? If not, discuss some of your own presuppositions which you bring with you to your study of ATR. How are your presuppositions similar to or different from the presuppositions of this book?

3. How can an evangelical Christian be objective in his study of ATR if he has prior commitment to a higher authority? Will this not distort his perspective of ATR? Why? What steps should you take to ensure a fair, objective study without distorting the facts?

4. Think through and enumerate all the difficulties you will face in your desire to understand ATR as it really is (and was).

Chapter 2

ORIGINS OF TRADITIONAL RELIGION

The existence of religion, any religion, demands an explanation. Even the most irreligious man is compelled to offer his theory for the origin of religion. Man has been defined as "the incurably religious animal." For everywhere and in every age he has professed some belief in supernatural powers which aid him in life. There is an ultimate Ground of Being. Until the emergence of humanism and its offspring, Marxism, we know of no human group without religion. And even humanism and Marxism have the characteristics of a religion without belief in the supernatural.

NATURALISTIC THEORIES

Those who do not believe in the Supreme Being, divinities or in the supernatural realm have been diligent to offer a naturalistic explanation for all religion. Christianity and ATR are thus treated along with all other religions. Anthropologists in the past have generally considered all religions as an *illusion*. Evans-Pritchard observes that "with one or two exceptions, whatever the backgound may have been, the persons whose writings have been most influential have been at the time they wrote agnostics or atheists." (Evans-Pritchard 1965:14,15) Anthropologists in general have been "bleakly hostile" toward religion. For them, all religious faith is an *illusion*. Since they do not accept the supernatural, they cannot accept any God who would reveal Himself and His will to mankind. Thus they laid hold of the theory of evolution to explain a natural development of religion. An excellent book on this subject is by E.E. Evans-Pritchard, entitled, *Theories of Primitive Religion*. Here then is a brief summary of some of man's theories for the origin of religion.

Psychological Theories

These theories find their explanation of religion in man's intellect. As "primitive" man pondered and reflected and thought upon various experiences, he gradually evolved a religious belief.

Fetishism. Charles de Brosses in 1760 contended that religion originated in fetishism, the worship of inanimate things and of animals.

He observed that many people believe that every external object in nature possesses life and magical powers. The Portuguese word, *feitico*, means "charm" and was applied to relics, rosaries and images of the 15th century which were thought by the Roman Catholic Church to have magical powers. *Feitico* itself is derived from the Latin word, *factitius*, meaning "magically artful." When Portuguese explorers ventured into West Africa, they found Africans reverencing and venerating trees, plants, pebbles and claws of animals. These revered objects were called, *feitico*, which became anglicized to be *fetish*. These fetishes (objects containing supernatural powers) thus formed the most basic and elementary form of religious belief, Charles de Brosses thought.

Auguste Comte, a 19th century philosopher, used the term, *fetishism*, to refer to a general theory of religion. In 1850 he wrote that the religious period of humanity began with *fetishism* when Man believed that all physical objects were animated by life similar to the life in man (Hays 1958:68).

Comte then theorized that religion evolved from fetishism to polytheism and finally monotheism. This was the prevalent naturalistic theory from the middle of the 18th century until the middle of the 19th century.

Dream Theory. Edward Tylor coined the word, "animism." By this he meant that peoples believe that non-living objects have life, personality and even souls. He published his views in the book, *Primitive Culture*. This book is still used in African universities today.

In Tylor's opinion, the belief in spirits and gods arose from man's experience of dreams, visions, disease and death. When man slept at night he dreamed that he was on safari hunting or visiting in some distant place. Yet his family could testify that his body remained in the house during sleep. This led to the conclusion, Tylor conjectured, that man is made of two parts: a material body and a non-material soul which could leave the body and travel at night. At death the physical body remained lifeless. But people believed that after death the soul left the body and became an ancestral spirit. Finally, early man decided that even material, non-living objects had souls. From this idea of souls arose the idea of non-human spirits and eventually, a belief in gods.

Tylor, who was convinced of the theory of evolution, thought that animism was man's first religion. Evidence for this was his belief that "primitive" people were animists. He further claimed, "no savage tribe of monotheists has ever been known." This uninformed opinion was later proved incorrect. Tylor thought that religion began with animism, and evolved into polytheism. In polytheism there is belief in many gods such as the sun gods, moon goddesses, thunder gods and earthquake gods. Finally, polytheism evolved into monotheism.

A minimum definition for religion suggested by Tylor and still popular today is the "belief in spiritual beings." Therefore, he concluded that religion was universal since all peoples believed in spiritual beings of one kind or another.

Monotheistic Theory. Andrew Lang, a student of Edward Tylor, was a confirmed animist for he thought that belief in souls and spirits may have arisen from psychical phenomena such as dreams. He also believed that religion evolved.

However, in 1898 he wrote a book, *The Making of Religion*, in which he attacked the views of his teacher, Edward Tylor. Andrew Lang felt that Tylor was guilty of blindness in refusing to admit that "primitive" people were monotheists.

Lang tried to demonstrate that pre-literate peoples had a concept of a High God. But Tylor simply dismissed such evidence as ideas which came from the missionaries.

Lang suggested that belief in a creative, moral, omnipotent and omniscient God probably arose among "primtive people" from observing the design of the universe. He contended that the idea of a soul-ghost and the idea of a god have totally different sources. In fact, he claimed that monotheism may even have preceded animism since belief in a Creator God is found among most "primitive" peoples all over the world.

Magico-Religious Theory. This theory says that magic must have preceded religion because religion (belief in spiritual beings) is too advanced for "primitive" peoples evolving from primate creatures. The first step in the evolutionary development of religion must have been magic.

Sir James Frazer, born in 1854, was a brilliant anthropologist who wrote *The Golden Bough*. Frazer suggested three stages of development: magic, religion and science. Sir James thought that early man first turned to magic as a means of gaining his desires. By means of magic, man tried to enlarge his family, increase his harvest, bring good fortune on his hunting trips and curse his enemy. But when intelligent people saw that magic did not always work, they turned to religion and began to believe in spiritual beings who might aid them. Religion developed from belief in spirits and gradually evolved into belief in many gods and finally one God. The last stage in man's development is the age of science when men advance beyond the need of either magic or religion. Science is all man needs today, without any dependence on magical or religious practices.

In 1909 R.R. Marett published his book, *The Threshold of Religion*. He criticized previous scholars, including Tylor and Frazer, who conceived early man "exactly as if he were an Oxford professor who sat down and mused on the nature of things and then got up and fitted his actions to his conclusions." (Hays 1958:140) Marett concluded that the beginnings of religion were less intellectual and reflective and more emotional. Awe, wonder, fear, and admiration were at the root of religion.

Psychoanalytic Theory. Sigmund Freud, famous for his theories of psychology, wrote a book entitled, *The Future of an Illusion,* in which he speculates on the origin of religion.

Freud spins a theory like a spider spins a flimsy web. He dreams up the theory that the development of a person through several stages is a repetition, a recapitulation of the development of the human race. By tracing the growth patterns of a human being, we can understand the evolution of the human race and thereby know the development of religion.

In the first stage, an infant is unable to satisfy his desires through physical activity. He cannot walk or move by himself. He is completely dependent upon his parents. Therefore, he substitutes thought for action. He uses imagination and wishful thinking to bring about his desires. Freud called this, "omnipotence of thought."

In the same way, magical societies are the first step in the development of religion. In this, Freud followed Sir James Frazer and the school of Magico-

Religious thought. When man is frustrated with unfulfilled desires, he turns to magic by which he tries to gain his desires. Magic is simply wish-fulfillment similar to the practice of children. Man uses certain medicines and recites certain words in order to attain his desires. Magic is the use of spells or verbal charms, spoken or sung, as part of the ritual to bring about desired results. By wishful thinking he believes he can influence the course of his life.

The second stage through which a human being passes involves dependence on his parents whom he both loves and hates. This is similar to the development of religion in societies.

Freud constructed a myth to explain the origin of religion. It is based on the Oedipus complex, the notion that a prime motivating force in life is the desire of the son and daughter to commit incest with the parents. Here, then, is Freud's myth.

In the early days of mankind when men were ape-like, the dominant father-male kept all the females for himself in a large harem. The male offspring, however, resented their father's action and rose up against this monopoly. They killed the father and ate him as cannibals so that they could rape the females. However, the sons became grieved over their own actions subsequently, feeling guilty. They instituted taboos on eating their father who became their totem. A totem is an animal or plant species thought to have blood relationship with the clan. Ceremonially, they ate the totem to commemorate their guilt. And instead of claiming the females for themselves, they established a rule against incest because of their guilt feelings.

In this allegorical tale, Freud theorizes the origin of religion. All gods are merely the father-male, devoured by the sons, and projected by them. "God" is an unreal idea produced by a diseased mind. Religion is a neurotic illusion. According to the theory of the Oedipus Complex, children both love and hate their parents. The son unconsciously wants to kill the father and rape his mother, while the daughters unconsciously want to kill the mother and be possessed by the father. On the surface, however, the children show respect and affection for the father who is idealized in the father-image of god. Religion is, therefore, the result of psychological tensions, frustrations and illusions.

For Freud, this explains the presence of taboos, totemism and exogamy (social regulations forbidding marriage outside the same kinship group) found in "primitive" religion. Taboos against incest are the result of compelling, compulsive neuroses, desiring to commit incest yet feeling guilty about it. Taboos take on religious meaning as they are associated with totemism. Each clan identifies itself with an ancestor symbolized by a totem animal or plant. Totemism usually involves the ceremonial eating of the totem animal which otherwise is protected by taboos.

The third and last stage of individual development is maturity in which the person accepts reality and adapts to it. He no longer depends upon wish-fulfillment of magic to satisfy his desires. He no longer submits to taboos and guilt feelings of religion. He faces life as it really is and adjusts to it.

This corresponds to the age of science in which all religious ideas are cast aside as false impressions and men face the hard, cold facts of life, without resorting to wishful thinking of the supernatural. A mature person no longer suppresses his natural urges but expresses his hostility and biological drives. Gods and ghosts are mere escapes from reality. We have now learned to live without the supernatural.

Sociological Theories

According to the psychological theories, religion originated through the exercise of the mind as man reflected upon life. In actual fact, however, religion is a vain illusion, a false impression, these men say. Nevertheless, religion had value because it provided security and assurance in the midst of problems. Thus religion can serve a useful purpose, even though it is an illusion. These theories, stressing the intellect, assumed that religious world views were systems of belief and concepts which were independent of outside influence. Religion simply evolved in the minds of people as they thought and reflected on life.

After some time, however, many scholars began to reject the various psychological theories which stressed the intellect and reasoning as the origin of religion. How could a vain fantasy, a mere mistake, an illusion have produced universal and enduring laws and religion? According to the sociological theories, religion originated as a product of the social structures of society. Men create their own gods in the image of their society. Thus religion is a functional part of every culture and not something independently coherent as an abstract religion. Religion as an institution is intimately linked with the rest of culture and is in fact a reflection of the social structures.

Various men have expounded their theories that religion began as a reflection of society. Max Mueller suggested that henotheism (a belief in one dominant god among many gods) arose among peoples before the development of nations. Robertson Smith theorized that religion among the Hebrews and their Semitic societies arose out of a sacred relationship with certain totemic animals. Robertson Smith contended that religion began for sociological reasons. The clan became idealized as god, as the clan idealized and divinized itself. Periodically, the clan members expressed their unity by sacrificing to their totemic animal and eating their feast together.

Instead of believing that beliefs and dogma shape culture, the functionalists, who promoted the sociological explanation for the origin of religion, asserted that action controls beliefs. Ritual action is logically prior to ritual belief, they say. Religious belief is thus born out of social behaviour.

In 1912 Emile Durkheim spelled out his views in the book, *Elementary Forms of Religious Life*. Like Robertson Smith, Emile Durkheim contended that religion began as a clan cult which was totemic in nature, that the clan god was the clan itself divinized and that totemism is the most elementary form of religion. He taught that religion is always a social phenomena. Society appears to have absolute powers, gives a feeling of perpetual dependence and is an object of venerable respect. Thus society is projected into the image of god.

Levy-Bruhl (1856-1939) believed that the mentality of people is derived from their social structures. And all societies can be divided into "primitive" and "civilized." "Civilized mentality" is trained to analyze and think logically, always seeking the causes of natural phenomena. He thinks in terms of cause and effect. When something cannot be accounted for scientifically, the "civilized mentality" assumes the reason is lack of knowledge.

In contrast, "primitive mentality" is supernaturally oriented. "Primitive" people do not inquire into objective causal connections for they are "prelogical" and mystical. By "prelogical" he simply means "unscientific" and "uncritical." Those who are prelogical interpret everything by the unseen, supernatural causes. "Primitive" people do think coherently but they begin with different presuppositions. While "primitive" ideas may seem strange and illogical to the "civilized," "primitive thinking" is indeed logically coherent. They simply begin with a different set of presuppositions.

Marxism

Marxist interpretation of religion is similar to and compatible with the sociological theories. For the disciples of Karl Marx believe that religious belief is a reflection of the underlying sociological factors

Communism Rejects All Religion. For world communism, religion is only an illusion because matter is all that exists. There are no spirits, no souls, no gods, no angels, no demons, no after-life, nor any future judgment. Matter is the sole element in the universe. Certain laws within the material universe propel humanity forward irresistibly until communism will inevitably prevail throughout the whole world.

How then did religion originate? By *economic determinism*.

Communists theorize that man's chief instinct is self-preservation. Everything man does is *determined* by man's effort to survive. Self-preservation involves the means of producing the necessities of life. Therefore, Marx concluded, that the means of production, his tools and technical processes, constitute the fundamental force in history.

And the means of production inevitably produce and generate the social system, laws, state, ideals, politics, morals and religion. Man is therefore, not free to choose anything. For the ruling class, governed by the instinct of survival, automatically defends the current mode of production even to death.

Marx, therefore, rejected every effort to impose moral dogma as an eternal and ultimate law. Marx contended that all moral theories are the result of the economic stage which society has reached. Religion is used by capitalist societies to defend the landowners from the poor peasants under their control. The ten commandments are a clever tactic to prevent the workers from revolt. Capitalism has invented the state with its laws, religion with its moral obligations, to subject the masses of poor workers so that the capitalists can continue enjoying the benefit of slave labour.

Karl Marx summed up the communist view of religion by calling it "the opium of the people." Religion lulls people to sleep with its faith in God and future hope of heaven. Only when people reject religion and overthrow the ruling class can the working class gain justice.

Nicolai Lenin said religion is "a kind of spiritual gin in which slaves of capital drown their human shape and their claims to any decent human life. We must combat religion...this is the ABC of materialism and consequently of Marxism."

For Lenin, the evils of religion lay in the intoxicating effects which remove men from the real world. Religion, like alcohol, intoxicates a person so that a drunkard is not in touch with reality. Instead of rising up in revolt against the oppressors, the working class only dreams of future heaven with mansions and streets of gold. Thus the poor, oppressed workers are deprived of a decent life in this world because they dream and hope for a better life in heaven.

Communism is a Religion. Despite Marxist's repudiation of religion, communism is in itself a form of religion without any belief in the spiritual realm. Notice the similarities between Christianity and Communism.

   a. Both revere and obey their Leader — God and Marx.
   b. Both rely on an authoritative book — the Bible and the writings of Marx and Lenin.
   c. Both extol lofty ideals of justice, equity and brotherhood.
   d. Both condemn the evils in society.
   e. Both provide an answer to the problems of society.
   f. Both give an answer and meaning to life.
   g. Both require absolute obedience and commitment.
   h. Both require self-sacrifice.
   i. Both are zealous in winning converts.
   j. Both require faith and confidence.

Thus Marxism, though it rejects all forms of religion as an illusion, proves to be a pseudo-religion of the anti-christ himself.

Conclusion

These naturalistic theories, developed by men who were frequently brilliant, illustrate the vanity of men apart from the gracious revelation of God. These theories are mere guesses, the result of conjecturing and theorizing. There was no proof whatsoever to support their opinions. They took the field data and fashioned their own interpretations.

The hostility that these anthropologists had toward Christianity and the work of missionaries is a reflection of their own antipathy to their rejected past. Having rejected the Christian faith, they used their anthropological discipline as a weapon to dismiss the Word of God as unreal. Cultural relativism was a rejection of absolute truth and the assertion that all values are historically conditioned.

Many of their theories are not only out-dated today but are offensive. They are racist and reflect a condescending attitude toward many peoples in the two-thirds world. But we must point out that although they reflected the prejudices of the 19th century toward "primitive" people, they similarly reflect their bias against Christianity. For their assumption is that all religion is essentially an illusion, an empty dream. Christianity may well be an advanced religion above ATR, but it also is an illusion. When men come of age, they remove all remnants of religion, including Christianity. The age of science with its "civilized mentality" is devoid of all religion, including Christianity of the biblical variety.

The fact is that these theories are all based on an outright denial of the Supreme Being who has revealed Himself to mankind. More than that, they do not hold water. If religion were a mere deception, an illusion, how can we explain its universality and persistence in countries that are religiously atheistic? If religion is developed to give security and comfort, why do religions develop beliefs in evil spirits which torment, in devils and demons which molest and frighten? If religion is outgrown with the age of science, why do we find hunger for spiritual things among a generation of Russians reared under atheism and materialism?

We can only conclude with a hymn of gratitude to God, that by grace He has made known to His children the truth through our Lord Jesus Christ in the Scriptures. We can pray with our Lord when He said, "I praise Thee, O Father, Lord of heaven and earth, that Thou didst hide these things from the wise and intelligent and didst reveal them to babes." (Mt. 11:25) For those who have found faith in Jesus Christ, can turn to the written Word of God to learn the origin of the world religions and of the Christian faith. To the Bible we shall now turn for divine insight.

BIBLICAL THEOLOGY

Briefly, we shall survey the familiar account of Scripture concerning the origin of traditional religion of all peoples. Much of this will be a mere basic review of biblical knowledge which students may already possess. But this seems necessary if we are to provide a biblical perspective of ATR. How do we assess ATR along with all other world religions? What value do we see in ATR? These are fundamental questions being asked today.

There are two elements which need to be maintained in balance, and as it were, in tension. Unless we give adequate stress to both the negative and positive elements revealed in the Word of God, we shall be unbalanced. Probably it would not be erroneous to say that all Christian scholars of world religions recognize both the negative and positive in traditional religions. But we maintain that in order to hold a biblical view of traditional religion, we must hold to both the positive and the negative elements as presented by Scripture. This of course is our own understanding of what the Bible teaches.

Positive Elements

1. The one true and living God, sovereign and eternal.

Naturalistic theories must begin with man who ever stretches onward and upward. But the revealed Word of God begins with the Creator. "In the beginning GOD..." (Gen. 1:1)

Throughout Scripture, God is pre-eminent and sovereign, the explanation of all things. Listen to the eloquent words of the Lord Himself spoken by the prophet Isaiah.

> Thus says the Lord, the King of Israel
> And His Redeemer, the Lord of hosts:
> I am the first and I am the last,

And there is no God besides Me.
And who is like Me? Let him proclaim and declare it;
Yes, let him recount it to Me in order,
From the time that I established the ancient nation.
And let them declare to them the things that are coming
And the events that are going to take place...
Is there any God besides Me,
Or is there any other Rock?
I know of none (Isa. 44:6-8).

In His love, wisdom and power, He created the heavens and the earth, and all that in them is (Gen. 1,2). He also created angelic spirit beings to praise Him and serve Him (Col. 1:13-17; Isa. 6:1-4; Heb. 1:7).

2. The creation of man in the image of God.

The crown of God's creation is man, made in the image of God (Gen. 1:26,27; 5:1). To search the depth of meaning is beyond the scope of this survey. Let it be sufficient to say that the image of God included both personality and moral rectitude.

Man as a person is made in God's image. He has a *mind* to think and reason (Gen. 2:15,20), a *will* enabling man to obey from the heart and not by mere instinct (Gen. 2:16,17), and *emotions* whereby man can express joy and sorrow, gratitude and thanksgiving, awe and worship.

Man as a moral being, created morally pure and clean, is made in God's image (Col. 3:10). Man was created with a disposition predisposed to love and serve the Creator. His moral capacity distinguished him from all other earthly creatures for he was given the capacity to discern between right and wrong.

Because of the divine image implanted within man, Adam and Eve were enabled to:

a. Fellowship with God (Gen. 2:8; 5:24)
b. Obey God (Gen. 1:16, 17)
c. Fulfill God's purpose in ruling the earth (Gen. 1:26,28)
d. Worship and praise God.

Thus man in his originally constituted nature was intended to be personally related to God in love, fellowship, service and worship. In one sense there is an infinite divide between God and all of creation even as there is a divide between the infinite and the finite. In another sense there is a great divide between God and man created in His image on the one hand, and all other creatures on the other, because of the divine image stamped in the very nature of man. Mankind is unique and distinct from all other creatures.

3. The revelation of God to man.

Important in the understanding of traditional religion is the knowledge that God has revealed Himself to man in several ways. In the Bible God takes the initiative to reveal Himself to man. A knowledge of God is not the result of perceptive men discovering the Creator but of the Creator disclosing Himself to man.

Idowu, however, declares,

> It is certain that, at the beginning, man worshipped he knew not what. A person of special perceptive ability had an experience which gripped him and changed the course of life for him, and he could not help making this known. [italics mine] (Idowu 1973:15)

Thus, according to Idowu, did Moses pass through "stages of his theological development until it came to flowering at Mt. Sinai." And Muhammed did the same.

Not so in the Bible. Throughout Scripture God is the pre-eminent and sovereign Lord who supernaturally discloses Himself to people, line upon line and precept upon precept.

Man's knowledge of God can never be to man's credit, as Idowu implies, but is only by God's grace. Therefore, we reject Idowu's theology expressed in these words,

> What we regard loosely as the concept of God with reference to any particular people or race is thus only a result attained by the few privileged ones through their spiritual discernment and mental or intellectual efforts... [italics mine] (Idowu 1973:143).

By way of contrast, the Bible teaches that if any man knows any truth about God, the credit belongs to God's gracious revelation and not to man's "mental or intellectual efforts." God has been pleased to reveal Himself to mankind and not just to the "few privileged ones."

God has revealed Himself to mankind through two different ways: General Revelation and Special Revelation.

a. *General Revelation*

In nature. The truth that God created all visible things is proclaimed to all men everywhere (Ps.19:1-6). The two invisible attributes of God, "His eternal power and divine nature, have been clearly seen, being understood through what has been made." (Rom. 1:20) The provision of rain and fruitful seasons is universal testimony of the goodness of God (Acts 14:15-17).

In conscience. Not only has God revealed Himself in nature external to man, but God has also revealed Himself to man through man's conscience.

The Law of God, a sense of what is right and wrong, has been written upon the very heart of man (Rom. 2:14,15). Consequently, we find all men everywhere conscious of right and wrong.

The existence of God has been inscribed in every man's heart so that man cannot escape Him (Acts 17:21-31). God has "set eternity in their heart" (Eccles. 3:11), so that man is ever conscious of that which is beyond this life.

General Revelation, however, has limitations in its purpose. It was intended to point men to God but it was inadequate for purposes of redemption. As Adeyemo points out,

> Like the Mosaic Law, general revelation could be termed a 'schoolmaster' commis-

sioned with the task of pointing men and women to the existence of a holy and righteous God...[but] It was never meant to be redemptive, and it is not...Thus it is evident that general revelation does not possess any soteriological merit by its very essence, and is limited as a vehicle of knowing God by the radical nature of man's fall, the effect of the fall upon man and the deception of man by Satan. This, in effect, calls for special revelation to meet man's need (Adeyemo 1979:24,26).

b. *Special Revelation*

Because of the limitations of General Revelation and because of man's sin, God has, from the beginning, given to men special revelation concerning Himself and His will for mankind.

Primeval Revelation. God spoke to man concerning His judgment which fell upon man in his sin. To Adam and Eve (Gen. 3:14-24), to Lamech (5:28,29), and to Noah (Gen. 6:1-12), God explained the nature of the judgment which God pronounced upon man. Because of man's sin against God, there was revealed to them the consequences of their disobedience.

Also revealed by God was His provision for the satisfaction of His wrath. Adam and Eve were provided skins for clothing, thus typifying the shedding of blood necessary for man's acceptance with God (Gen. 3:21). The first promise of redemption was here given (Gen. 3:15). Sacrifices were instituted by God with the first people (Gen. 4:4,7) and continued, thereafter, as exemplified by Noah (Gen. 8:20ff).

God's moral law was not only written in man's heart, but specifically given in early revelation. The sanctity of the Sabbath Day (Gen. 2:1-3), the sanctity of life (Gen. 4:9-15,23,24; 9:5,6), and the sanctity of blood which represents the life of man (Gen. 9:4), were some of the moral commandments which God gave to the first men.

The cultural mandate, "Be fruitful and multiply, and fill the earth, and subdue it; and rule over the fish of the sea and over the birds of the sky, and over every living thing that moves on the earth" (Gen. 1:28), clearly outlines man's responsibilities as master under God of the earth.

Biblical Revelation. In His providence, God chose Abraham and his seed to become the people of God through whom the nations of the world might receive the light of the Gospel (Gen. 12:1-3). Through the prophets of Israel, God gave to mankind the Word of God in written form, the Bible. The centrality of the Jewish people in God's self-disclosure is evident in Scripture. To the Jews "belongs the adoption as sons and the glory and the covenants and the giving of the Law and the temple service and the promises, whose are the fathers, and from whom is the Christ according to the flesh." (Rom. 9:4,5)

Jesus Christ, the Word of God made flesh (Jn. 1:1-18) is the final and ultimate revelation of God (Heb. 1:1-3). He is known by faith alone through the pages of Scripture as the Holy Spirit illumines our minds (I Cor. 2:10-14).

4. Traditions of Revelation passed down by generation.

It is appropriate here to stress that these traditions are not of equal value to God's revelation in Scripture. Far from it. All truth and error must be judged by the written Word of God. But we need to recognize this element of tradition if we are to understand traditional religion as it is found in Africa today. This is a mere summary of what could be said concerning this important issue.

In the early records of Scripture, we discover that not all men outside the covenant people of God were without the true knowledge of God, or at least without some knowledge of God's special revelation.

Canaanites: Although most Canaanites were degenerate and without a true knowledge of God, Melchizedek was "a priest of God Most High" (Gen. 14:18-24). Unless we understand Melchizedek to be the preincarnate Son of God, we are bound to accept the conclusion that here was one, outside the circle of the Abrahamic covenant, who still clung to the revelation of God given in the earliest times. Here was a representative of the Canaanites who actually served as a priest (and king) of the Most High God and to whom Abraham was obligated to give his tithe.

Philistines: Generally, there is no evidence that these people knew and served God. Yet, we find an integrity and honesty that shamed Abraham (see Gen. 20:1-18; especially vss. 4-6,11). Though Abraham thought there "was no fear of God in this place," Abimeleck behaved "in the integrity of his heart and the innocence of his hands."

Mesopotamians: The pure faith once delivered to the fathers, was fast becoming adulterated. Yet, Abraham and his father, Terah, were true followers of God and called out of their native land to serve Him. But the family descended from Terah was plagued with idolatry and for that reason Abraham was called upon to separate himself from them, being sent to Canaan. But among the Mesopotamians were some who still clung to God in true faith.

Balaam, who finally yielded to his base desire for gain, is another example of a Gentile who knew about the Lord and occasionally obeyed Him (Numb. 22-24; especially 22:8,18; 23:12,26; 24:2,13).

We believe, further, that there is evidence both in Scripture and in history to indicate that the earliest knowledge of God and His will was carried to Africa by the sons of Ham (Gen. 10:6-20). The sons of Ham included:

Cush, the father of the Ethiopians, not only those who settled in Africa but those scattered in southern Asia and Arabia.

Mizraim, the father of those who settled in Egypt. In fact, Mizraim is the ancient name for Egypt, both upper and lower.

Put, the father of the Libyans in the wider sense of those who spread over northern Africa as far as Mauritania.

A study of these African ancestors and the path of their migration would be fascinating. No doubt the Nilotics and others migrated southward by way of the Nile to Africa south of the Sahara. With them came the traditions rooted in primeval revelation. From thence, we may trace the widespread tradition of sacrifices and strong belief in the Creator God.

Biblical revelation was transmitted to Africa through the Jews in dispersion. Many Jews were scattered in Egypt in dispersion. From them we may trace the Jewish beliefs and practices which are found in Africa. Jewish settlers lived in Egypt (I Kings 14:25ff; II Chron. 12:2ff) and along the Nile in Migdol, Tahpanhes and Noph (Memphis) as well as in the country of Pathros in upper Egypt (Jer. 43,44; see Josephus Ant.X,ix,7).

These are but the barest of outlined suggestions which should be developed further. In brief, we find here sufficient evidence in Scripture to supply the answer to the question, "How did traditional Africans receive such true knowledge of God and know so much truth and virtue before the missionaries came with the Gospel?" Because God has not left them alone but pursued them with His love and grace.

Negative Elements

But what has been said thus far is only a partial answer. We must place equal stress on all the biblical teaching concerning the negative elements which have contributed to ATR.

1. All mankind is in rebellion against God.

Man is not merely falling short of God's glory, lacking sufficient knowledge and grace to enable him to do better. He is in rebellion against God and His will. Sin has affected every aspect of his being, even the divine image within man. Consequently, he no longer has a reliable conscience nor a will inclined to do God's will.

Adam and Eve, though they were created holy, were granted a free will to obey God or to disobey Him. Temptation came from without, through the beguiling serpent. But sin required the consent of the will (James. 1:14; 3:6).

The nature of that first temptation is significant. Satan questioned God's Word (Gen. 3:2-4a), cast doubt on the character and integrity of God (Gen. 3:4b,5), and exalted human ambition, sensuality and selfishness above faith and obedience to God and His Word (Gen.3:5,6).

The results of yielding to temptation were disastrous. Death, both physical and spiritual, came to Adam and Eve and all their descendants as God had warned (Gen. 3:24; 5:5; Eph. 2:1). All their descendants inherited a corrupt nature, subject to death and judgment (see Rom. 5:12-21; Ps. 51:5; Eph. 2; Rom. 1-3). The mind became debased (Rom. 1:21, 28; Eph. 4:17, 18). Their conscience became unreliable (I Tim. 4:2; Tit. 1:15; Jer. 6:15; Prov. 16:25). The will was no longer inclined to do the right (Rom. 7:14-25). And the whole natural universe was affected by sin (Gen. 2:17-19; Rom. 8:20-21).

Straightaway, the human race reflected the fallen state. Cain became degenerate in his character and envious of his brother's favour with God. Hatred filled his heart, resulting in murder (Gen. 4). Lamech, the first polygamist, likewise became a murderer (Gen. 4:23, 24). "The wickedness of man was great on the earth, and...every intent of the thoughts of his heart was only evil continually," so that God brought universal judgment upon the earth by a flood (Gen. 6:1-8). After the flood man was moved to make a name for himself instead of magnifying the Name of the Creator (Gen. 11:4). Man refused to spread abroad to populate the earth as God had commanded. Instead, men built the tower of Babel on the plain of Shinar. The idolary found at Babel has been repeated countless times as people seek to glorify themselves instead of their Creator.

The Word of God concerning all men everywhere is full of far reaching implications.

> There is none righteous, no not one;
> There is none who understands,
> There is none who seeks for God;
> There is none who does good.
> There is not even one (Rom. 3:10-12).

2. Man attempts to deify the creature.

All of man's religion and culture is an attempt to dethrone God and exalt the creature. All men, because of their sinful nature, deify the creature and make idols of the finite.

The whole temptation and sin of Eve was directed against the will of God. The temptation was given in these words: "For God knows that in the day you eat from it your eyes will be opened, and *you will be like God*, knowing good and evil." (Gen. 3:5)

Ever since that time, men are trying to elevate themselves. That is, they are trying to remove God from His throne. They are rebelling against the lordship of the Creator.

The building of the tower of Babel is a rank example. Not only did they disobey God but they were ambitious for their own name, rather than the name and will of God Himself (Gen. 11:4).

This tendency towards idolatrous pride can be illustrated many times in Scripture:

Nebuchadnezzar, King of Babylon, was elevated in pride, ignoring the very One who placed him on the throne (Dan. 4:17, 25, 28-32, 34, 35).

The King of Tyre said in arrogance, "I am a god, I sit in the seat of the gods." (Ezek. 28:1-9)

Herod the King accepted the acclamation of the people who said, "The voice of a god and not a man." (Acts 12:20-23)

The anti-christ, who will be the very personification of sin, will demand exclusive worship by the peoples of the earth (Rev. 13:5,6,8,15).

Most people surely do not think they are guilty of such idolatry. Do they not acknowledge one living God? But in many subtle ways they suppress the knowledge and will of God and treasure creaturely objects and desires in the place of God.

Lamenting the people who forget God, David cries out, "Put them in fear, O Lord; Let the nations know that **they are but men**." (Ps. 9:20)

3. Man suppresses the truth revealed to him by God.

The extensive discussion of the Gentiles in Romans 1 is applicable to all peoples without the Gospel. This is demonstrated by the same condemnation brought against the Jews in Romans 2 and with a universal conclusion for all peoples in Romans 3:9-20. The conduct of fallen men toward the Creator is most damning.

Man suppresses the knowledge that God has given him (Rom. 1:18). Although he possesses a knowledge of what is right, he wickedly represses it, hinders it, opposes it and does all he can to resist it.

Man is not thankful for the knowledge granted him (Rom. 1:21). Unthankfulness is a characteristic of sinful man which will become more prominent in the end of the age (II Tim. 3:2). Man simply refuses to acknowledge the gifts of God with gratitude.

Man is dissatisfied with the truth of God, so he prefers to trade it away and exchange it for a lie (Rom. 1:23,25). This word, "exchange," is a term used in the market place for bartering. Not content with the treasure of God's truth, man bartered it away for a "lie."

Man refused to retain the knowledge of God in his mind and "did not see fit to acknowledge God any longer." (Rom. 1:28) Men do not think it is worth the trouble to retain the knowledge of God and so they suppressed the thought.

Consequently, God gave men up to:
    perverted religions. vss. 24,25
    perverted passions. vss. 26,27
    perverted minds. vss. 28-32

4. Man is uniformly described as without God, without goodness and without hope.

Writing to the Gentile converts in Ephesus, Paul says, "Remember that you were at that time separate from Christ, excluded from the commonwealth of Israel, and strangers to the covenants of promise, having no hope and without God in the world." (Eph. 2:12)

He exhorts them not to walk as the Gentiles walk, "in the futility of their mind, being darkened in their understanding, excluded from the life of God, because of the ignorance that is in them, because of the hardness of their heart." (Eph. 4:17, 18)

Before they turned to Christ, they were "dead in...trespasses and sins." (Eph. 2:1)

They were "children of wrath, *even as the rest*." (Eph. 2:3)

This does not mean that the Ephesians did not know a lot of true things about God, nor that they were without religion. Quite the contrary! See Acts 19:21-41. The Ephesians were very religious. But there is a world of difference between knowing *about* God and actually knowing Him personally. Though religious, the Ephesians were without hope, without God, without the life of God; they were dead spiritually, ignorant intellectually and hardened in their hearts.

Writing to the Galatians, who were likewise Gentile converts to the Christian faith, Paul says, "at that time, when you did not know God, you were slaves to those which by nature are no gods. But now...you have come to know God, or rather be known by God..." (Gal. 4:8)

Paul contrasts the non-Christians with the Christians in Thessalonica. The former "have no hope" while the believers alone have hope (I Thess. 4:13).

5. Man is subject to demonic influences.

Some of the angelic beings created by God were led by Satan in rebellion against God. Satan is called "Beelzebub, prince of the demons" (Mt. 12:24) and "the prince of the power of the air" (Eph. 2:2). The evil spirits active in the world today are none other than the great multitude of angelic beings that followed the lead of Satan in rebelling against God (see Mt. 25:41; Rev. 12:4,7).

Spirits are actively deceiving men. Christians are called upon "to test the spirits to see whether they are from God." (I Jn. 4:1)

These demonic spirits provide the dynamic in heathen worship. The gods which the Gentiles worship are but demons (I Cor. 10:20).

The Apostle forewarns us that Satan will be actively working in the end of the age. His work in the anti-christ will be "with all power and signs and false wonders, and with all the deception of wickedness for those who perish, because they did not receive the love of the truth so as to be saved." (II Thess. 2:9,10)

Christians are exhorted to equip themselves for a spiritual battle, "For our struggle is not against flesh and blood, but against rulers, against the powers, against the world-forces of this darkness, against the spiritual forces of wickedness in the heavenly places." (Eph. 6:12)

We conclude, then, that mankind lives in darkness, not only because of darkened hearts, but because of the evil forces of darkness at work within the Kingdom of Darkness.

Conclusion

This brief survey of biblical teaching demonstrates that man is a divided creature. Because he is in rebellion against God, many of his deeds, including his religious worship, are subtle acts which remove God from His rightful place of sovereignty. Yet, man, made in the image of God, cannot escape God. So he recognizes Him, and displays a form of godliness.

Man is ever suppressing the truth, hindering the knowledge of God and refusing to have God in his mind. Yet, man cannot escape. God confronts him daily in his conscience and through nature.

Therefore, man can, at the same time, reflect beauty and ugliness, loveliness and hatred, purity and uncleanness.

In biblical perspective, however, this still is inadequate. It is not as though the positive and negative elements are held in equal tension. It is not as though man is a little good and a little bad. James asks the question, "Does a fountain send out from the same opening both fresh and bitter water? Can a fig tree, my brethren, produce olives, or a vine produce figs? Neither can salt water produce fresh." (James 3:11,12)

When we examine more closely that which appears lovely and beautiful from a distance, we frequently find it overshadowed by evil. Corrupt motives can render a noble act worthless before God. Self-centred attitudes toward God and man can nullify worthy deeds. Sinful behaviour can mar beautiful prayers and thoughts.

Apart from the grace of God found in Jesus Christ there is no hope. "For as many as are of the works of the Law are under a curse; for it is written, 'Cursed is every one who does not abide in *all the things* written in the book of the Law, to perform them.'" (Gal. 3:10)

Deeds which appear good before men are all negated by the sin in every man. But thank God, "Christ redeemed us from the curse of the Law, having become a curse for us..." (Gal. 3:13)

REVIEW QUESTIONS FOR CHAPTER 2

1. What is meant by naturalistic theories of the origin of traditional religion?

2. Why have non-Christians spent so much effort in seeking an answer to the origin of religion?

3. Summarize three of the naturalistic theories for the origin of all religion (including Christianity). Why do you believe they are inadequate and in error?

4. Traditional Religion contains error with a mixture of truth, according to most scholars. According to Scripture, what is the explanation for traditional belief in God and morality?

5. According to Scripture, what is the explanation for the evil in traditional religion?

6. Can a Christian look upon any culture as free from the corrupting influences of sinful human nature? Why?

Suggested Reading and Thought Questions for Advanced Study:

> Conn, Harvie. *Eternal Word and Changing Worlds*, 1984, pp. 11- 124.
> Evans-Pritchard, E.E. *Theories of Primitive Religion*, 1965.
> Hays, H.R. *From Ape to Angel*, 1958.
> Keeley, Robin ed. *The Lion Handbook of Christian Belief*, 1982, pp. 206- 307.
> Lessa, William A. and Evon Vogt eds. *Reader in Comparative Religion*, 1965, pp. 7-105.
> Sharpe, Eric. *Comparative Religion: A History*, 1975.
> Tisdall, W. St. Clair. "Comparative Religion." *The International Standard Bible Encyclopaedia*, James Orr, ed., 1939, pp. 691-694 Vol. II.

1. How could intelligent, well educated men develop such naturalistic theories which look so foolish to us today? What was their pre-understanding and motivation? How do the pre-suppositions of men explain why even today many brilliant, highly educated men hold similar naturalistic theories concerning the origin of all religion?

2. As a believer in Jesus Christ, what do you believe is the true explanation for the origin of ATR? for the origin of all other religions? for the origin of the Christian faith? (study the biblical teaching of natural revelation)

3. Virtually every scholar of ATR will acknowledge both positive and negative elements in traditional religion. Why is it essential to maintain a biblical balance in viewing the positive and negative elements of ATR? What dangers

can you fall into if you don't maintain a biblical balance?

4. The debate rages, whether ATR is primarily the product of each African ethnic group or whether ATR is the result of borrowing. What light does Scripture shed on the origin of ATR, whether it originated from the African peoples themselves or through diffusion and/or borrowing? Discuss.

Chapter 3

THE FOCUS OF AFRICAN TRADITIONAL RELIGION: MAN

In traditional African culture there was no separate compartment known as African Traditional Religion. For traditional religion permeated the whole of life. One could not point to anything and classify it as secular, for all of life was sacred with spiritual dimensions. Strictly speaking, ATR is not a religion as understood in the West, a set of dogmas, but is life, experiential.

Therefore, we could study man and his life-way as part of ATR. In fact, this has been done by many and with good justification. For man's origin and nature, his life-style and future destination, are all religious in nature. The focus of ATR is indeed on man himself.

African Traditional Religion centres on man. The whole emphasis is upon man gaining the power needed to live a good life. Life revolves around man and his interests and needs.

John Mbiti goes so far as calling ATR, "anthropocentric," (man centred).

> African philosophy is basically anthropocentric: man is at the very centre of existence, and African peoples see everything else in its relation to this central position of man. God is the explanation of man's origin and sustenance; it is as if God exists for the sake of man. The spirits are ontologically in the mode between God and man; they describe or explain the destiny of man after physical life...Animals, plants, land, rain and other natural objects and phenomena, describe man's environment, and African peoples incorporate this environment into this deeply religious perception of the universe (1969:92).

But while man is the focus of ATR and he himself is part of a study of ATR, we shall include the study of man in the Foundational Issues of ATR. For not only is the study of man part of ATR, man forms the context in which ATR functioned. ATR was practiced by the traditional man and woman in concrete situations of life. ATR is not primarily ideology but the practice of people based on a traditional world view. As Idowu says, "There can be nothing like religion in the abstract or religion considered apart from persons who worship and practice the tenets of their faith." (Idowu 1973:12) ATR is best understood in the concrete, as lived out and practiced by the people themselves.

Therefore, we shall look upon the study of man, his nature and life cycle, as the context in which the traditional African experienced and practiced his religion. We need to understand the African traditional life of man in order to understand how his religious beliefs and practices were operative.

GENERAL SUMMARY

Man in Africa is a Family

Man as an individual is only a modern western development rooted in industrialization and urbanization. But in traditional societies throughout most of history, man was not primarily an individual but a member of a community. Indeed, the culture reflected in the Hebrew Old Testament is more like ATR in this respect than western society. As industry moves into Africa and cities grow in size, we are experiencing the break down of the traditionally extended family and an increase of individualism. The need for orphanages we see today, totally unknown and unthinkable in traditional culture, is a growing phenomena. Even homes for the aging are being built. Modern education is revolutionary, undermining traditional values and relationships. Yet the past tradition continues to influence the present.

"The deep sense of kinship, with all it implies, has been one of the strongest forces in traditional life," says John Mbiti. "I am, because we are; and since we are, therefore I am. In traditional life, the individual does not and cannot exist alone except corporately...He is simply part of the whole." (Mbiti 1969:104,108)

Man Gains and Loses as a Member of the Family

A person must surrender any individualism. As part of the community, he must be ready to share without condition. Certain individual traits are surely permitted. People are not identical. But whatever variation is allowed, the community determines the limits. Any loner, any individual off by himself, will be feared and rejected as a possible witch.

In return for what he loses, however, he gains even more. He has a deep sense of security. He belongs to the whole community. Not just one mother or one father cares for him. There are many fathers and mothers. Whenever trouble arises, he can rely on the whole extended family and even the clan to support and strengthen him.

Members of the Family

In western society, the primary family (or nuclear family) is predominant. This includes only one mother and one father and their own children. Though close relationships may prevail between other relatives, this need not be. In fact, one can and usually does live quite independently of brothers and sisters, uncles and aunts.

But in Africa the family is extended. Included are the brothers and sisters of parents with their families as well as grandparents. Relationships between uncle and nephews can be just as close and even closer than between the actual parent and child. Children are often closer to their grandparents than they are to their own parents, because the elderly grandmothers care for the children throughout the day while the parents are away working. Thus a person has many fathers and many mothers and a multitude of brothers and sisters.

In addition to the extended family, there is also the larger community of the clan and tribe. This is not limited to those living, but extends backward to the ancestral spirits who are considered a vital part of the community. Nor is the community limited to them. The African community also includes the unborn.

When the late Jomo Kenyatta dedicated his book, *Facing Mt. Kenya*, (n.d.) to Moigoi and Wamboi, he expressed his purpose thus: "for perpetuation of communion with ancestral spirits through the fight for African Freedom, and in the firm faith that the dead, the living and the unborn will unite to rebuild the destroyed shrines."

Thus the sharing community is broad in this tripartite formula: the dead, the living and the unborn.

"Existence-in-relationship sums up the pattern of the African way of life," as Swailem Sidhom phrases it. (Dickson 1969:102)

Growth and Development of Man

A child grows into adulthood not only physically, but socially and religiously. Therefore, rites and ceremonies are performed to mark the passage of a child from one stage of growth to another.

These rites of passage (ceremonies marking the stages of growth) vary from people to people, but generally they occur during the following occasions: birth, puberty, marriage, child birth and death. John Mbiti has a lengthy discussion of these stages of growth and development in his book (1969:110-165). For our purposes, we shall focus on the religious nature of the rites of passage.

Birth. Birth is always an important moment in the life of the family. Religious attitudes and activities surround the whole process of birth and childhood. Children receive their importance from the traditional meaning of immortality. Since personal immortality is only possible when children remember them, the birth and survival of great numbers of children are religiously important. Thus, there are many customs and prayers in order to ensure the safety of the new-born child. Prayers are said to God and to the ancestors. Offerings are made to the ancestors. Purification ceremonies are observed for the mother. Amulets are used to protect the child from harm and danger.

After the birth of a Gikuyu child, for instance, the mother shaves her head and the husband sacrifices a sheep to God and the living-dead as a sign of thanksgiving. The ancestors are brought into the picture because the new baby is in fact "their" child as much as the living.

Furthermore, the Gikuyu place a small wristlet of goat skin on the child to symbolize the bond between the child and the entire tribe. Thus there is a sacred link between the life of the new born child and the past generations which cannot be broken.

Puberty. Puberty marks the transition from childhood to adulthood. For many African peoples this is marked by the rite of circumcision, though for others as the Luo, there are different rites associated with this point of transition. For many peoples an uninitiated person is not a full member of the tribe. Therefore, he will be despised and regarded as a mere boy or girl unless they are properly initiated. The Nandi girl who avoids female circumcision (clitoridectomy) is regarded as a "nobody," incomplete, a mere child. Hence there is tremendous pressure placed upon the youth to conform.

Superficial observation of the circumcision rites may suggest that the religious significance is minimal. But further investigation often dispels this idea. When Myrtle Langley studied the life crisis rituals among the Nandi she made the following discovery.

> It was only after the repeated insistence of Christian informants that they could not take part in the traditional rites, or at least certain parts of them, because of their religious significance that I eventually forsook my previously held view that such insistence was missionary-inspired, and proceeded to piece together what information I could glean from literature, oral tradition and current practice (Langley 1979:115).

And she discovered that religious symbols and appeals to God occur frequently throughout the Nandi rituals.

Marriage. Marriage and the birth of children are central to all life in Africa. Unmarried men or women are unthinkable in traditional African society. There is no traditional category for single ladies or single men. He who refuses to marry is "a curse to the community, he is a rebel and a law-breaker, he is not only abnormal but 'underhuman.' Failure to get married under normal circumstances means that the person concerned has rejected society and society rejects him in return." (Mbiti 1969:133)

Marriage was entered through the mutual agreement of the families concerned. Marriage was not an individualistic consideration of the man and woman but it was a family decision. To seal the agreement a bride price was required to ensure that the marriage bond was permanent.

Once again, traditional religious beliefs are common in these ceremonies. A traditionalist will often say, "If you don't get married and have children, who will pour out libation to you when you die?" Marriage is the focal point of all existence. Both the living and departed together with those yet unborn meet together at this key point. For the very future of the community depends upon a succession of descendants.

Since children are the major concern of people, marriage that does not produce children is considered a failure. For this reason many brides are pregnant before marriage because of the overriding concern of bearing children. If a wife does not bear children, this becomes the motive for the husband to marry a second wife.

In every traditional Nandi marriage, libation is poured to the ancestors, requesting cattle, children, a good harvest and other kinds of blessings. Feasting with food and beer occur through out the night. Early in the morning libation is again poured out to the ancestors, a special fire is made from the wood of a sacred tree and prayers are offered to God.

If there is an unusual delay in the bearing of children after marriage, the wife must first consult with a woman dealing with herbs. If she is unsuccessful, she will consult with a diviner to determine the cause of infertility. The cause may either be the displeasure of the ancestors or witchcraft. The diviner will then provide the solution.

Polygamy was the form of marriage with the most prestige and honour. Polygamy is the state of having a plurality of husbands or wives, being the opposite of monogamy. In Africa the polygamous marriages are usually polygynous, one man with more than one wife. Popularly, the plurality of wives is called polygamy, though technically, this should be called polygyny.

Polygamy of necessity was always a minority form of marriage but it had the greatest prestige and honour. Economically, the more children one had, the more workers were available to labour in the *shamba* (garden). Socially, the greater the man's wealth, made possible by many wives and children, the greater will be his status in the community. Religiously, the more children one had, the more likely that his name and memory could be carried on, thus extending a man's personal immortality. The living-dead depended upon the living descendants to remember them with food and offerings in order to extend their immortality.

If a man died, levirate marriages were sometimes practiced. That is, the brother of the deceased inherited the wife so as to continue raising children for the deceased. Thus traditionally there were no bachelors, unmarried women or widows. Marriage was the standard relationship of all mature men and women. Children were the necessary desire for survival, physically and spiritually.

Death. Death does not terminate the existence of a human being. He continues to live on as an ancestral spirit. And he continues to maintain living relationships with the living, bringing both benefits and trouble. Death is, therefore, the necessary door through which the living pass in order to take up the inevitable role as the living-dead. Death is the transition to the final destiny of all men and women.

However inevitable and certain death may be, it usually is thought to be caused by external forces. Therefore, death is followed by thorough investigation as to the cause of death, whether by witchcraft or an evil spirit or a disgruntled ancestral spirit. Witchcraft may need to be counteracted and the villain punished. The ancestral spirit may need to be appeased and the wrongs righted. In all these matters the traditional medicine man has a central function.

Because the departed dead now enter into a new relationship with the living, elaborate ritual is followed in order to ensure peace and harmony with the spirit world. Death disrupts the peaceful balance prevailing in the world. Ritual and ceremony are necessary in order to restore that peaceful balance.

Conclusion

Thus the traditional person in Africa is communally oriented, intimately related to his family, clan, tribe and to his ancestors. He grows and develops from birth through puberty and marriage. Death is the passage into the final stage of his relationship with the community as he becomes a "living-dead."

Within this concrete community of relationships the traditional African utilized all the supernatural, metaphysical powers at his disposal. The unseen world interpenetrated the seen, the world of spirits intermingled with the world of mankind. The world of spirits and mystical powers were just as real and practical as their houses, gardens, sun and rain. The mystical powers of magic, witchcraft and sorcery were at man's disposal for him to achieve his goals in life. For most Africans the ancestral spirits were a constant frame of reference for all activities. They sought their favour and blessing that they might become more powerful in the community with wealth, prestige, status and authority. They feared their anger and displeasure and thus always tried to follow the traditions of the ancestors. However, for some Africans the ancestral spirits were not at all prominent, for such people as the Murle of Sudan and the Masai of Kenya. The Supreme Being, the Creator of all, was also a metaphysical reality on whom they called when all other help failed. When death and sickness struck, when drought and pestilence came, and when all other help failed, the people were able to call upon God for assistance.

Thus the concrete traditional African man in his earthly life is the context in which ATR was practiced and followed. Traditional religion was not practiced in a segregated, compartment of life, but was lived out throughout life, integrating and permeating all of life. ATR drenched the African as rain drenches the parched ground. ATR was relevant in all situations and conditions of life. For the African depended always and completely on the supernatural powers of the world about him to aid him in his quest for posterity, prosperity and position.

CASE STUDY OF THE AKAMBA

The Akamba are the fourth largest ethnic group in Kenya numbering 1,725,800 in the 1979 census. The people (plural) are called Akamba, one person, Mukamba, their language is Kikamba and the place of their abode is Ukamba (or Ukambani). The Akamba, a Bantu people, migrated from the plains around Mt. Kilimanjaro. They were originally migratory pastoralists with many cattle and no oral tradition of crop production during the early years. When the Akamba moved northward into present day eastern Kenya the fierce Masai led them to seek protection in the mountainous areas. Gradually, the Akamba developed a sedentary life, supporting themselves with agriculture. Trading between the coast and the hinterland became an important feature of Akamba culture. The mountainous areas are fertile but much of Ukambani has poor soil and limited rainfall with eastern Ukambani (Kitui) having large tracts of uninhabitable waterless land bordering the Nyika (treeless wilderness). Today the Christian church is firmly planted in most of Ukambani. Primary and Secondary Schools dot the countryside. Cultural change has been revolutionary within the past ninety years. Yet the deep seated values of the traditional world view persist even within the Christian church today.

Creation of Man

Man (*mundu*) is the creation of the Supreme Being. Man is neither eternal nor self-existent. Nor is he the product of evolution. *Mundu* is a created human being through the sovereign act of the Creator God.

The Akamba have a creation myth, although there are no "elaborate myths of creation among the Akamba people." (Ndeti 1972:28) In brief, the Akamba believe that "God (*Mulungu*) made the first pair (or two pairs, in another version) of husband and wife, and brought them out of a hole in the ground (or from the sky, according to another tradition)" (Mbiti 1966:14). While the location of the hole is uncertain, many believe it was on Nzaui hill.

Lindblom recorded the narrative of the more common version of man's creation (Lindblom 1920:252). Kivuto Ndeti, some sixty years after Lindblom, has recorded another version of man's creation (Ndeti 1972:30). The significant difference in this later version is the creation of the ancestral spirits (*aimu*) before the creation of man himself (Ndeti 1972:30).

Whether Lindblom's version is the original one, or whether both versions have roots in antiquity, we are unable to say. However, one fact is certain. God created man, male and female.

Nature of Man

Essentially, man is dichotomous in nature, composed of *body and spirit*. Man dwells in his body (*mwii*). Within man's body is his spirit (*veva*). The noun, "spirit", comes from the verb meaning "to breathe". "The spirit is the 'life-principle' and its existence is manifested through breathing." (Mbiti 1971:130) One may describe death by saying, "His breath is gone." When one dies the body was cast off into the bush to be devoured by the hyena or other carnivorous animals. But the spirit continues on in the spirit world where the spirit then becomes known as *iimu* (*aimu*, plural). But a human being is more than a body with a spirit. *Mundu* is a community. This community among the Akamba, like other African peoples, extends beyond the living members of the clan and tribe. It incorporates those who have died and those who are yet unborn. Man "is a physical representation of the dead, living and the unborn. Thus *mondo* [*mundu*] is a community incorporating three principles — life, spirit and immortality." (Ndeti 1972:114) Those who depart from their bodies do not depart from the community. The dead are not really dead for they have merely made a transition to the spirit world which is near the physical world. Mbiti calls them, "the living-dead" because they still live among the members of the living community, even though they are dead.

This concept of man has many implications in the social life of the people. Since this is an attempt to paint the world view of the Akamba we shall not delve deeply into the social implications. But several things should be sketched briefly, relating the abstract concept of man to the concrete implications.

Mundu as community is born, reared, married, matured and deceased within an extended family. This community extends from the smaller units to the Akamba "nation" as a whole.

The smallest social unit among the Akamba is the *musyi* (family or home). Central to family is the man with his wife or wives and their children, together with the extended family with strong ties over three generations — grandparents, parents and children.

Children are an essential part of each marriage. This is due in part to the necessity of rearing children who will offer sacrifices and maintain personal immortality for the parents by remembering them after death. The more children one has, the greater will be his labour force to care for his gardens and cattle. Increased labour force will increase one's wealth, and consequently, the more children one has, the greater will be his social prestige. One's stature in the community is related to leadership positions. The greater one's authority and influence in this life, the greater will his be after death. In light of these cultural values, polygyny was a prestigious form of marriage.

Because of the frequent tribal wars and intra-tribal conflicts before colonialism, the male population decreased, creating a disproportionate number of women for every male. Therefore, polygamy was quite prevalent, though monogamy has "a wide distribution contrary to the opinions of many writers on the Akamba." (Ndeti 1972:66) In fact, polygamy can never be the normal form of marriage since that would require twice as many women as men, which is not the case, since the birth rate of male and female is about equal.

The family (*musyi*) formed a closely knit community in which every member contributed to the welfare of the whole community. This basic social unit also was "the means by which the Akamba religious principles are carried out. It is a 'holy alliance' and all the members of the *mosie* [*musyi*] are bound by the rituals to lead a clean life in the totality of *mosie* [*musyi*]." (Ndeti 1972:68) Within the Akamba context this meant that the veneration of the ancestors (*aimu*) was the responsibility of the head of the family. But *musyi* is an elastic word which can even refer to a village or larger unit.

The second largest social unit is the clan (*mbai*). The clans are not territorial units but members who are descended from some real or mythical ancestor. The number of clans is continually increasing. Anyone with a very large family prides himself by calling his family after his own name, as *Mbaa Mbuu*, the descendants of *Mbuu*. For this is the potential beginning of a new clan (*mbai*).

Each clan has a totem, that is, some animal, plant or inanimate object which is said to stand in a special relationship to them. A totem is thought to have some blood relationship with a specific family group. Totems are usually some plant or animal. These totem relationships among the Akamba, Ndeti contends however, are not of a religious nature but "a means of regulating and utilizing the environmental resources." (Ndeti 1972:72) Each clan refrains from killing and eating their totem, therefore, helping to preserve that species. But each clan is noted for certain characteristics and codes of behavior which are said to originate from the founder of the clan. The Lion Clan does not eat liver because the lion is thought to refrain from eating the liver. But the Lion Clan is noted for its courage and intelligence. The Hyena Clan is known for its greed and the Hawk Clan for its tendency to steal.

More important than the relationships between the clan members and their totem, is the relationship among the clan members themselves. The social impact is extensive. Exogamy is practiced, with no one being allowed to marry within their own clan. They have an absolute duty to help each other in need. One individual can bring trouble to the whole family through the offended ancestors if he transgresses some tradition. So the clan members are responsible to be faithful to the ancestral traditions of the clan. Punishment is meted out to those who violate the codes of the founder. Thus the clan "provides codes and means of social control among its members, and also it is one of the greatest benefactors of its members." (Ndeti 1972:73)

However, clan traditions are collapsing today. They are not nearly as strong in many parts of Ukambani as they were prior to Independence. Marrying within the clan, a traditionally abhorrent practice, is not unknown today. Instead of seeking justice from the clan, the tendency is to resort to the Law Courts. Nevertheless, clan justice is carried out in many places. And clans do frequently join together to assist some members to obtain further education.

The largest unit to which a member belongs is the whole tribe. But even as the clan can be sub-divided into sub-clans or minor groups within the clan, so the Akamba are generally divided into larger groupings, the Machakos (or Masaku) Akamba and the Kitui Akamba. Each grouping implies a togetherness with the potential for opposition to others. Thus the Akamba stand together in their family units (*musyi*) and in their clans and larger groupings of Masaku or Kitui. They also divide, compete and fight with non-members. This traditional animosity even extends within the churches today. It was within these social structures, the family and the clan, that the people governed themselves. The Akamba are known for their relative individualism and independency. The family (*musyi*) was the centre for learning all the traditions of the Akamba. "The Akamba government, therefore, was a collective responsibility based on the assumption that man is ultimately responsible for the protection of himself and whatever proceeds from him." (Ndeti 1972:97)

The Akamba were ruled by the elders in various councils called *nzama* (council).

> In the traditional Akamba social order, man was never defined as merely an economic being. A poor man in his old age merited as much respect as a rich man. Old age in the mind of the Akamba represented a unique veneration. The community thought of an old person as having trans-human capacities— near to the deity by age and wisdom (Ndeti 1972:104).

The elders, deciding by consensus in the council, made the judicial decisions for the community, but the people executed the decisions. Crimes which threatened the whole community would be dealt with severely through collective retaliation.

As man was born into the Akamba community, he underwent a process of humanization and maturation, passing through various stages of development. Each of these stages reflect his relationship with the broad Akamba community, both the living and the living-dead.

Life Cycle

Birth. Conception is believed to be the result of both the husband and the ancestral spirits (*aimu*) playing their roles. While the biological mechanism of conception is understood by traditional Akamba, they believe that the ancestors play an important part in child birth. They "are supposed to create and shape the child in the woman; they also decide whether it should be a boy or a girl." (Lindblom 1920:29-30; Hobley 1910:89)

Whereas, the expecting mothers in the past would live primarily on milk and porridge made from the flour of sorghum and millet, this practice has now ceased, no doubt due to the fact that the Akamba have relatively few cows as in the past. Today they eat honey which was taboo in the past. But they do abstain from eating any meat from an animal killed by a poisoned arrow.

Pregnant women are not isolated. They continue their normal work responsibilities until time of delivery. When the time for birth has come, they deliver while standing upright in their house, or visit the hospital or dispensary nearby. If the mother has a history of deaths in childbirth, they will offer sacrifices to the ancestral spirits to protect the newborn child.

Even today a very tiny child will be wrapped up and placed in a large clay vessel to keep it warm. This child is called *Muinde*, a word derived from the verb meaning "to put somewhere under to help it get ready and ripe." (Lindblom 1920:31,32)

After birth a ceremony follows. Two small children, a boy and a girl, with their heads smeared with fat, go to the river for a small quantity of water to wash the baby and prepare the porridge. One of the children has a piece of skin, in which the baby is carried, bound to his back so that he can carry the new born infant to the entrance of the village and back. "This rite ushers in the important phase of a child's life during which it is carried on its mother's back." (Lindblom 1920:33) Prayers and libations are also offered to the ancestral spirits. A piece of hard ugali is ceremonially thrown over the roof and a prayer offered to the ancestors, informing them of the birth and requesting their help for growing safely.

A new born child is called, *kiimu*, meaning literally, "a little spirit." The child is not thought of as part of humanity until the fourth day. He is still part of the spirit world from whence he came. Precaution is necessary to protect the child from the ancestors, lest they snatch the infant away. The *kiimu* may be hid and a special door constructed in the house for the mother to use in order to confuse the spirits desiring to take the child.

A charm is given the child to protect him from danger. In the past a necklace made of fine iron chain was hung around the neck. Today the charm more likely is made of goat's skin or a cloth with magical medicines (*muthea*) placed inside. It is hung around the neck or placed on the right wrist for a boy or the left wrist for a girl. By placing this charm on the child, the parents thereby declare that he has now become a human being and ceased being a "little spirit."

Circumcision. Circumcision among the Akamba is the initiation into adulthood, marking the transition from childhood to manhood. An uncircumcized male child is known as *kivisi*. For anyone to call an adult, *kivisi* (an uncircumcized male), is to use abusive language. Circumcision is the gateway to manhood. Circumcision is a pre-requisite for marriage and the privilege of establishing a home. Both men and women submit to circumcision "if they wish to be regarded as members of the tribe." (Lindblom 1920:42)

There were three initiation rites performed in Ukambani. The first circumcision, literally "the minor circumcision", sometimes known as the small or real circumcision, is primarily the physical cutting of the foreskin of the penis for men and the cutting of the clitoris for women. There was no set age for the first circumcision. Children were frequently circumcised around 15 years or more, though boys could be circumcised as young as 10. Donald Jacobs reports that the age could range from four to the time of marriage (1961:44).

Dancing and drinking of beer accompanied the ceremony. Special porridge (*ugali*) made from millet flour and cow fat was prepared. Goat meat was also devoured. "Sacrifices are made to the ancestral spirits, but presumably only in order that the wounds may heal quickly. Circumcision is not to be regarded as a genuinely religious act among the Akamba." (Lindblom 1920:44) This first circumcision was essential but the least esteemed.

The Great Circumcision was essential for all males and it was the more important of the two. This was the occasion when the youth were taught and advised, and thus prepared for adult responsibilities. The Great Circumcision was a "secret school" conducted in the bush and away from the villages of the people. Girls and boys were taught separately. They learned how to sing, dance and do the work of an adult. The boys stayed in the bush for a week, learning how to fight and how to raid cattle. Their teacher, known as their "protector," instructed the young men how to approach the young ladies, how to attract them and how to treat them as their future wives.

The young ladies were similarly taught female responsibilities as future wives, how to fetch firewood and water and how to tie things traditionally. During this week of the Great Circumcision the boys and girls remained in separate groups.

Social relationships are important among the Akamba. This emphasis on living with people was stressed. How to communicate and relate well with others was taught. The initiates were charged with their responsibility to honour their parents and older people.

Throughout the seven day ceremony there was dancing, singing and ritual coition between the conductor and his wife. While the Akamba are quite modest in daily life, the singing and talking is quite obscene during the ceremony. This is intended to show that "no feelings of shame exist under these circumstances." (Lindblom 1920:50)

Various tests of endurance were given. Frightening experiences were encountered with a "rhino" charging the group. The young men were taught how to use the bow and arrow to fight the "rhino." If one failed, he was mocked the rest of his life. A very bitter juice of a yiumba tree was poured on the private parts in order to prove whether they could endure suffering.

For the Akamba, both the first and second circumcision were essential. One was traditionally regarded as an inferior person, improperly educated and not a true member of the tribe to forego either the First Circumcision or the Great Circumcision. A period of time elapsed after the First Circumcision before one experienced the Great Circumcision. There was no physical circumcision during the Great Circumcision, but several marks were made along the private parts to show that the individuals had undergone the second circumcision.

After completing the Great Circumcision a ring was given to each one. The girls were to be given a goat and the boys a cow by their parents. If they were not given, the youth were instructed not to speak to their parents until the animals were given.

Only two rites of circumcision were known in Machakos. But a third ceremony, known as the Circumcision of Men, was practiced in Eastern Ukambani among the Kitui people. This was very secretive. Only those initiates who underwent the Circumcision for Men knew anything about it and they were sworn to secrecy. This one is more related to religious practice and the intention is "that the Kamba youth may reach the culmination of the education and knowledge that the tribe can bestow on the individual." (Lindblom 1920:61) To become a real man, and recognized as an elder with dignity among the Eastern Akamba, this rite must be experienced.

Traditional circumcision, however, is dying out in Ukambani. Only in isolated areas, particularly the more rural parts of Kitui and Machakos, are traditional circumcision practices observed. Instead, boys go to the hospital for the physical operation. They are known to take the initiative at a young age to acquire finance for this minor operation. The traditional teaching and practices, however, which surrounded the second and third circumcision, are no more found in many parts of Machakos District and Central Kitui.

Part of the vital experience of youth before and after circumcision was the joining of traditional dance groups. There were many different kinds of dances with qualifications for the participation defined by the society. Some dances were for the entertainment of the youth at night after work. Other dances were for groups of young people, both male and female.

What were the traditional relationships between the youth as they danced together throughout the night? What was expected of them and what were the limitations? Lindblom observed, "Boys and girls who are duly circumcised and who have attained puberty amuse themselves at their favorite dance, the *mbalya*. This dance is engaged in almost daily and is quite erotic in character. In this dance the girls choose their male partners and it is during these dances that the basis of marriage is formed." (Lindblom 1920:407-412) Premarital intercourse is expected, but it is regarded as shameful for an unmarried girl to become pregnant (Middleton 1953:90) Abortion is sometimes practiced (Jacobs 1961:60).

Today, traditional dancing is fast fading away. Instead, young people use guitars, records and pop music to dance in the garden and at the disco. Only old women dance traditionally. When they die, the traditional beating of the drums will fade away, apart from public official ceremonies and those centres which seek to preserve the traditional culture of the peoples, such as the Bomas of Kenya.

Marriage. Marriage was primarily for the perpetuation of the family, with children being central in the whole relationship.

Menstruation of females, unmarried and married, was therefore, of great significance. When a girl discovers that she is menstruating for the first time, she must go home immediately. Anyone touching the blood would cause sterility, either in the one who touches the blood or in the one with whom that person has intercourse. Following the first menstruation, the parents of the girl must have intercourse, "to purify the daughter."

> Menstruation plays a very large part in the ordering of the life of the Akamba village for it is thought that the menses is in some way connected with the world of spirits. In fact, it is believed that only during the menstruation can conception take place, for that is the time when the ancestral spirits are present. Consequently, on the night of the first menstrual day the husband has intercourse with his wife (Jacobs 1961:59).

Marriage traditionally was not at a set age, the girl could be 18 and the boy

24, or they could marry much younger. Sometimes a man could be forced to marry somebody who is ten years older or younger than himself.

Only the parents of the boy were responsible for finding their son a good wife to marry. They had to search for a good girl, well behaved and from a lovely home. Many a time they had to pay the dowry completely before the son could be given the daughter for marriage. Many of the arrangements were done by both the parents. Whether the girl agreed or not, they had to marry.

Sometimes a small girl was engaged when very young and when the boy was also young. But as they grew up together, they eventually became married.

In other places and on other occasions the boy and girl could make a secret agreement to marry, after which they sought the permission from the boy's father, who in turn would seek the approval from the girl's father. But in traditional marriage the boy and girl had no right to make the final decision. The son had no right to choose a girl for himself. Only the parents had the right to do so.

Engagement took place when the parents of both the boy and the girl agreed. This was followed by an elaborate series of gifts leading to the decision of the bride-wealth. Two goats were immediately sent to the prospective father-in-law as the initial bride-price. Payment of the bride-price covered many years and normally continued after marriage.

The bride-wealth (the expression for bride-price in Kikamba means literally "to buy a girl"), was a form of commitment by both families to the marriage relationship. As many as 75 goats and several cows were required, together with gifts of beer, and produce from the fields. The exact amount of the bride wealth varied from place to place. Other reports gave the number of goats to be 46, with two cows and two bulls. "But beer is an integral part of the bride-wealth and dare not be omitted." (Jacobs 1961:61) Concluding this agreement between the families, the boy's parents slaughtered a bull for the covenant between the two families.

When the final covenant and agreement was made, the boy's parents were free to come for the bride to take her back for their son. This usually was done at night or when the girl was fetching water away from the house.

The girl's parents gave her proper marriage advice and concluded with a blessing. Milk and water were used. The parents of both sides spread it over their bodies and they would say, 'May you multiply till you fill the earth.'

There is virtually no wedding ceremony as in the West. There is no word in Kikamba for "wedding" as such. "The only ceremony marking the entry of the girl into the new home is observed at the door of the hut. The suitor's mother rubs fat on the girl's neck after which she is invited into the house." (Jacobs 1961:62) The important "ceremonies" are the mutual arrangements between the two families, the exchange of gifts and the feasts with the two families. Marriage is not primarily between two individuals but a covenant between two families.

Death and Burial. Only in old age is death considered normal among the Akamba. Death is called, *kikw'u*, taken from the verb meaning, "to be called" (*kwitwa*). Death is, therefore, viewed not as a mere happening but a snatching of life. Something comes to take away a person maliciously. Thus death is an enemy.

Therefore, the Akamba always seek the medicine man to inquire into the metaphysical (supernatural) causes of death. Even though death may be caused by an apparent accident, the question is raised, "Why did that accident occur? Who caused it?" For the ultimate explanation of death is not natural but metaphysical (supernatural). The medicine man, through his communication with the ancestral spirits, determines what the true cause is.

Certain omens indicated pending death when someone was sick, such as the screech of the owl. Owls were thus feared. Old cooking pots were placed on the roofs to keep the owls away. When death was considered imminent, the dying man would try to talk with his close relatives, giving words of blessing, instruction, handing down (bequeathing) to family members the future family leadership and possibly uttering some curses on family members. These final words were most important and every family member tried to understand them.

Most ceremonies after death centred around the death of a married man, especially the older ones. An unmarried person is not fully human and fails to attain personal immortality. The more powerful the person is in this life, the more elaborate the ceremonies will be for him after death, for the more potentially dangerous he will become as an ancestral spirit.

Customs of burial in Ukambani varied considerably from place to place and from time to time. Mourning began immediately after death and intensified during the time of burial. The mourning was shorter for the death of women and children and longer for fathers and grandfathers.

Burial customs were very important. When ill fortune followed the burial of someone, they assumed that the ancestral spirit was displeased. This led to changes in burial practices. The body was covered by skins or blankets and could not be seen by unauthorized persons. Only approved individuals who were old men, sexually inactive, could handle the body. A young man could never touch a dead person for fear that he might pass death on to the family through sexual activities.

In preparing the body of a barren woman for disposal, a stick of appropriate size was placed in the vagina to remain there permanently in order to prevent barrenness from flowing out through the vagina into the vagina of another woman. If a married woman died, the first thing asked of the women in the family was whether the deceased had died during her monthly period. If she had, the husband was then required to have sexual intercourse with her dead body before burial so that the family might be purified. To bury a woman having her menstrual period would make the family unclean, resulting in continuous deaths.

Traditionally, the corpses were disposed by tossing the body into the bush far from the home so that the hyenas would devour it. Gradually, this custom changed and regulations developed as to where and how a corpse would be buried. After the burial a sacrifice was made to the ancestral spirits.

After disposing the body, purification was necessary in order to remove death. This was a ritual sexual intercourse to render death harmless. The bereaved person had to have ceremonial coition (sexual intercourse) before any other member of the family was permitted to engage in sex. The widow would perform this with the man inheriting her, the widower with another wife or with another woman. Menstruation brought ceremonial uncleanness. Therefore, any woman in the family with her monthly period had to be cleansed also through ritual coition. Anyone who had touched the corpse had to be cleansed by a specialist.

Conclusion

Today, there are widespread changes throughout Ukambani. The active presence of the Christian church has wrought a cultural revolution. The presence of schools, the introduction of a money economy, industrialization and westernization have all contributed to the transformation of traditional culture. Many traditional rituals are no longer practiced as they used to be generally speaking. Some traditions have changed. Dowry has frequently become a commercial exchange whereby money, houses or cars are demanded as fees before the daughter is given in marriage.

But if the rituals and ceremonies are greatly changing, the deep levels of traditional world view linger on. The meaning of death lingers on for many. Since death cannot happen accidentally, according to traditional Akamba custom, even weaker Christians may seek answers from the medicine man. The practice of visiting a medicine man after someone dies to learn the cause of death and obtain further protection is widespread among the traditionalists. Even Christians may leave the Christian funeral led by the pastor and resort to the medicine man for traditional help. Death is thus greatly feared and the deep levels of the Akamba traditional world view still linger on, even though the external forms are changing.

REVIEW QUESTIONS FOR CHAPTER 3

1. Mbiti says that ATR is "anthropocentric" (man centred). Do you believe he is justified in saying this? Why?
2. Describe the benefits and problems that arise from the ATR view of man as an integral part of the community.
3. How did religious beliefs enter into every major happening of a person throughout his development?

Suggested Reading and Thought Questions for Advanced Study:

Adggbola, E.A. Ade. *Traditional Religion in West Africa*, 1983, pp. 73-127; 259-337.
Field, M.J. *Religion and Medicine of the Ga People*, 1961, pp.161-206.
Mbiti, John. *African Religions and Philosophy*, 1969, pp.92-165.
Melland, Frank H. *In Witchbound Africa*, 1967, pp.48-117.
Parrinder, E.G. *African Traditional Religion*, 1962, pp.134-141, 90-100.
Parrinder, Geoffrey. *West African Religion*, 1961, pp.95-114.
Kenyatta, Jomo. *Facing Mt. Kenya*, n.d., pp.3-221.
Setiloane, Gabriel. *The Image of God Among the Sotho-Tswana*, 1976, pp.1-43.
Talbot, P. Amaury. *Tribes of the Niger Delta*, 1967, pages 144-257.

1. Many African languages have no indigenous word for religion but have had to borrow one (eg. *dini* from Kiswahili). Does this mean that Africans have not

traditionally believed in any religion? What does this tell you of the nature of ATR as it affects the totality of life?

2. In describing man in African society, Mbiti states, "I am, because we are; and since we are, therefore I am." What essentially does this mean? How does this traditional African concept of man match with the Old Testament view? What contemporary forces are at work to destroy this African tradition? Should the Christian church seek to preserve this African traditional perspective? Why? How?

3. Write down the traditional duties of the following persons among your peoples:

a. grandparents, b. fathers in the nuclear and extended family, c. mothers in the nuclear and extended family, d. brothers in the nuclear and extended family, e. sisters in the nuclear and extended family, f. the clan, g. the tribe.

To what extent are these traditional duties changing in contempoary society? To what extent have these traditional duties both hindered and helped in the proclamation of the Gospel?

4. Describe some of the admirable traditional customs among your peoples surrounding the pregnancy, birth and naming of children which glorify God and accord with the Scripture. What efforts have been made (or should be made) to incorporate them in the African expression of the Christian faith?

5. Describe the traditional initiation ceremonies which traditionally took place among your peoples at the time of puberty. To what extent are these traditions continuing, changing or disappearing? To what extent do they present a problem to the Christian church? What practical steps should the church take to meet the felt need of the adolescent initiates and how can we fulfill the function of the traditional initiation rites today?

6. Polygamy is one of the biggest obstacles to the growth of the Christian church in Africa. How serious is this problem among your churches? Discuss the motives for polygamy among African men. How can the Christian church best deal with this problem from a biblical perspective?

7. Describe the traditional burial customs among your people. Include all the activities and ceremonies from the moment of death to the events subsequent to the burial. What traditional elements have been eliminated in Christian funerals to ensure that they glorify God? What traditional elements have remained in Christian funerals to reflect the African Christian nature of the funeral? To what extent does the traditional African world view of death persist among Christians and create a problem in maintaining a strong biblical church? What should the Christian church do to help believers develop a truly biblical perspective of death? Itemize detailed, practical steps to be taken.

PART TWO

MYSTICAL POWERS IN
AFRICAN TRADITIONAL RELIGION

Chapter 4

SUMMARY OF MYSTICAL POWERS IN AFRICA

PROMINENCE

The belief in mystical power filling the universe is common throughout Africa. It is experienced daily in every village and city. Endless stories of the effects of this unseen force are told by young and old.

In the words of John Mbiti, "The whole psychic atmosphere of African village life is filled with belief in this mystical power. African peoples know that the universe has a power, or force or whatever else one may call it, in addition..." to the living-dead, spirits and the Supreme Being (Mbiti 1969:197). Mystical powers such as magic, sorcery and witchcraft affect everyone for better or for worse.

Referring to sorcery and witchcraft, John Middletown writes,

> It is no exaggeration to say that one cannot gain any fundamental grasp of the attitudes which people have towards one another nor can one understand many aspects of their behaviour in a wide range of social situations without a fairly extensive knowledge of their ideas regarding good, evil and causation, and their associated beliefs in witches and sorcerers. (Middletown 1963:1)

MAGIC AND RELIGION

According to Noss, one specialist in world religions, magic refers to "an endeavor through utterance of set words, or the performance of set acts, or both, to control or bend the powers of the world to man's will...It is discernibly present when emphasis is placed on forcing things to happen rather than asking that they do." (Noss 1963:20)

As we have seen, a distinction between magic and religion was made by Edward Tylor and popularized by Sir James G. Frazer. This difference is implied in the definition given above. Frazer believed there was a difference in the time of their development and basic nature.

Magic is the manipulation and use of impersonal powers through ritual and ceremony. Whereas religion is the belief in unseen spirits, deities and gods and the attempt to pray to them for aid. Religion prays to the gods while magic commands the impersonal forces of nature. Religion says, "Thy will be done." Magic says, "My will be done." Religion shows an attitude of submission to the supernatural beings, whereas magic seeks to control and use the powers of nature for man's own purposes.

Idowu reflects this well established distinction made by anthropologists and scholars of religion. In E. Bolaji Idowu's helpful discussion on this subject (Idowu 1973:189-202), he defines magic as "an attempt on the part of man to tap and control the supernatural resources of the universe for his own benefit...Magic serves man's egocentricity [self centredness] and is for him a shortcut to spiritual bliss." In contrast, Idowu argues that "religion is essentially a matter of reciprocal relationship in which man depends upon Deity for the fulfillment of personal, basic needs which are more than material (although those are included) with the belief that the transcendental Being on whom he depends is capable of fulfilling these needs. Religion implies trust, dependence and submission." (Idowu 1973:190)

However, this traditional distinction between magic and religion has been called into question. Frazer, committed to evolutionary presuppositions, wrote that religion was "the despair of magic and merely succeeds it in time." That is, when magic failed, man turned to religion. Today such naive views are rejected.

Jevon and Idowu teach the very opposite, that religion was prior to magic, with magic being a lapse in the evolution of religion (Idowu 1973:192). The fact is that no empirical evidence can demonstrate which came first, magic or religion. For this question we are wholly dependent upon special revelation. We are thrown upon the Word of God to give us light. Our earlier discussion on the origin of ATR points the way to the biblical answer for the question which came first, magic or religion.

Not only has the priority of magic been questioned, but many students of ATR affirm that religion and magic cannot be separated. Jomo Kenyatta states that "magical practices and religious rites go hand in hand, and sometimes it is not easy to separate the two, especially in dealing with beneficial magical practices." (Kenyatta n.d.: 270) He shows that prayer to the ancestral spirits is combined with use of magical ritual. The Yoruba call upon a divinity in connection with magic. This is true throughout much of West Africa. Guner Wagner has also demonstrated that magic and religion are combined among the Abaluyia (Forde 1954:27ff).

It appears that the emphasis on difference brings more confusion than clarity. From a biblical perspective there is more similarity between magic and religion than difference. Trust and dependence are characteristic of both religion and magic. It is obvious that a person has confidence in the magical rites. The idea that religion has "no immediate practical result in mind," as Malinowski suggests, is nonsense (Noss 1963:16). Religion has importance both in the present and the future. Others suggest that religion is primarily concerned with morality, for it believes in a good God, whereas magic is amoral without any relation to God. There is truth in this. But even this is an oversimplification. For certain kinds of behaviour are demanded before magic will work. And the moral behaviour required of man in traditional religion is not always so closely linked with belief in God.

Numbers of scholars today define religion in such a way that magic may be included. Commenting on the function of magic, William Howells writes,

Human nature, as I said, really wants magic, and gets true good out of it. It is not comforting for man...to realize how helpless he can be, and magic enables him to avoid realizing it; it gives him a soothing conviction that he can take care of himself, because nature can be bossed around by pulling imaginary wires. It is another form of religion which acts to quiet the nerves of individuals and of society and to allay the urges of panic and disunion [italics mine] (Howells 1948:63).

Howells thus explicitly includes magic with religion. Edward Sapir says, "Religion is man's never-ceasing attempt to discover a road to spiritual serenity across the perplexities and dangers of daily life." (Davis 1968:55) By this definition, we may incorporate magic as part of religion.

In conclusion, we note that the distinction between magic and religion arose out of an evolutionary view of religion. It has been taught repeatedly by anthropologists. But an increasing number of scholars today accept the fundamental similarity between magic and religion. Magic can no longer be separated from religion as some have done. Magic is part of all idolatry in opposition to personal faith in God.

KINDS OF MAGIC

There are various kinds of magic which have widespread application.

a. "White Magic" and "Black Magic"

Good magic ("white magic") must be distinguished from bad magic ("black magic"). These expressions, black magic and white magic, are found both among African peoples and Europeans, describing their own belief in magic (Parrinder 1974:116).

"Good magic" is primarily used for protection against the evil forces that are found everywhere. The use of charms, amulets, herbs, seeds, powder, skins, feathers, chanting of magical formula, cuts on the body and many other magical practices are used to protect individuals, cattle, houses and possessions from evil powers. They are given by the medicine man, the most respected man in most of the African communities.

In addition to protection, good magic may also be used to bring rain by the rainmaker and predict the future by the diviner. With the help of the medicine man, magic can also be used to win a lover, produce abundant crops, gain more children or cattle, and in general, increase one's personal fortunes in life.

Good magic is openly favoured by society and used for man's benefit. But bad magic is secretly practiced without the approval of society and for evil purposes.

In contrast to the positive benefits received from good magic, black magic is intended primarily to harm people and property. Therefore, black magic is feared by people. Society opposes it. It is practiced at night and without approval. Mbiti points out that "a great deal of belief here is based on, or derives from, fear, suspicion, jealousies, ignorance or false accusations, which go on in African villages." (Mbiti 1969:199)

Black magic is therefore associated with sorcery. Both sorcery and witchcraft are the most feared parts of African Traditional Religion.

b. Imitative Magic and Contagious Magic.

Sir James G. Frazer wrote much about certain types of magic. He made popular the term, "sympathetic magic." By this he meant that magic depends on an apparent association or agreement between things.

One kind of sympathetic magic is known as "imitative magic" (sometimes called, "homeopathic magic"). By this he meant, "like produces like" or "the effect resembles the cause." That is, things that look alike have an effect upon one another. The most widespread practice throughout the world of hurting someone with imitative magic is by hurting an effigy (image) of that person. The magician prepares an effigy of mud, wood or other material. He then tries to hurt the effigy with needles, knives, thorns or other weapons. Whatever damage is done to the effigy, results in harm done to the enemy.

Other examples of imitative magic are also found in Africa. Rainmakers spit water into the air in order to imitate the falling of rain. Medicine men plaster spots on the body of a person suffering from a rash and then wash away the spots. This imitates the removal of the rash. Hunters make an effigy of animals which they desire to kill.

The second type of sympathetic magic is called "contagious magic." This means that "things which have once been in contact with each other continue to act on each other at a distance, even after the physical contact has been removed." For this reason, people are often afraid to leave around their hair, finger nails and toe nails, clothes, feces, or other items which once were in personal contact with them. People fear that these things may be used to harm them with black magic.

Even a footprint may be used with medicines in order to bring harm to the man who once had contact with that piece of soil. Women have refused going to the hospital for child birth because of fear that the after-birth may be used against them. Some hospitals, therefore, return the placenta and umbilical cord of the baby so that the mother can bury the afterbirth. Some nurses even make a profitable business by selling the afterbirth to the mothers. In West Africa servants follow their chiefs around in order to catch the chief's spit in a container. This is not for sanitary purposes, but in order to keep the spit away from the black magician.

We should point out that good magic and bad magic can be either imitative magic or contagious magic. Both can be used for good or bad.

We may also note that scholars have discerned other principles underlying the logic of magic in addition to the principles of similarity and contiguity observed by Frazer. Magical power is enhanced by repetition. The more words are repeated, the more effective they will become. Likewise, the more unusual the ritual may be, the more potent will be the effects.

c. Personal Magic and Public Magic.

A further difference may be made between personal magic and public magic. Much of the magic used is to serve personal needs. Individuals may purchase various charms for protection against evil forces. Leather packets containing dried leaves or a text of the Koran for Muslims may be hung around the neck. Knots are worn which tie a spell from affecting the wearer. Iron bracelets or chains are used against sorcery. Horns of wild animals may be stuffed with leaves and powders, after spells are pronounced over them. These are worn to give protection, like that powerful protection exhibited by the animals whose horns they were. In like manner, teeth of lions, crocodiles and snakes are wrapped in leather and worn on the body.

In addition to personal magic, there is also public magic. This is intended for the household or village. Many houses are protected by the use of charms hung over the doorway or placed in the roof. Fields are frequently protected from witchcraft by means of charms. These may be a few pieces of straw placed on a bamboo pole, or a packet of bones, feathers, sticks, skins or leaves buried in the field. In West Africa, villages are often protected by an arch or small door way leading into the village. These arches are made of palms. Attached to them are bones, leaves or a dead bird.

CHARMS AND MEDICINES

Charms are produced by medicine men out of materials such as herbs, roots, barks, insects, skins and bones, leaves and animal horns. They are empowered magically through the repetition of set words. Charms may be used for a variety of purposes: attracting a lover, gaining employment, protecting from witchcraft, productivity of gardens, accumulation of wealth, protection from sickness and most anything else that is needed. Today we hear of charms being used to protect warriors from the deadly bullets in modern warfare.

Charms and medicines partake of the same nature. Charms may be a kind of medicine and medicines have the effect of a charm. But generally speaking, charms are used as protective magic and medicines are used for healing magic. The effectiveness of medicines depends on two ingredients: the materials and the use of words. Magic always depends on the use of special ingredients and the spoken words of some powerful person.

WITCHCRAFT AND SORCERY

Terminology

Anthropologists have studied mystical powers under such topics as witchcraft, wizardry, sorcery, evil magic, fetishism and the like. Lack of agreement in the use of words has led to some confusion. It must be admitted that Africans do not make such theoretical differences. We cannot make a general statement and apply it to everyone because beliefs vary from people to people. English words are usually not an exact translation of the vernacular languages.

Nevertheless, we note the distinctions that have been made by leading anthropologists in order to read books and discuss with understanding.

Evans Pritchard broke new ground in 1937 by observing magic and witchcraft among the Azande (Evans-Pritchard 1937). Another book particularly helpful for study of witchcraft in East Africa is edited by John Middleton and E.H. Winter in 1963, *Witchcraft and Sorcery in East Africa*.

Evans-Pritchard, "one of the greatest authorities on the subject," said this.

The chief difference between a sorcerer and a witch is that the former [sorcerer] uses the technique of magic and derives power from medicines, while the latter [witch] acts without rites and spells and uses hereditary psycho- psychical powers to attain his ends. Both alike are enemies of men. Witchcraft and sorcery are opposed by good magic. (Evans-Pritchard 1937:21)

Other anthropologists like Geoffrey Parrinder and John Middleton make the same general distinctions between witchcraft and sorcery as outlined by Evans-Pritchard.

Sorcery is defined as the use of black magic and medicines against others. Sorcery may be practiced by any individual who buys specially prepared charms and then places them near someone's house.

In contrast, the witch possesses mystical and innate power within herself as an individual. She does not use rites or spells and operates without medicines or material apparatus. Witches are thought to be able to do extraordinary things beyond human abilities. By merely looking at someone, or wishing evil on someone, the witch will bring harm. The act of witchcraft is a psychic act.

A sorcerer is not a threat to society as a whole, since he is moved against an individual. His sorcery is, therefore, directed toward an individual alone and perhaps only once. But a witch performs her evil work because of her very nature. Her unsatisfied desire for human flesh makes her a threat to everyone. No one is safe from her hunger for human flesh. In contrast, one can remain untouched by sorcery by staying on good terms with everyone.

It is true that many Africans make this difference. Evans-Pritchard found that the Azande distinguish between a witch and a sorcerer in this manner. Dr. Field, who has made most valuable studies of West African witchcraft, makes the same distinction. Speaking of witchcraft she writes, "Its distinctive feature is that there is no palpable apparatus connected with it, no rites, ceremonies, incantations or invocations that the witch has to perform." (Parrender 1961:166)

Similarly, the Amba of Uganda make this distinction between witchcraft and sorcery (Middleton 1963:277-299). Anyone can practice sorcery, say the Amba. A sorcerer does not act in any unusual way but simply uses certain methods which enable him to accomplish his evil purpose. In contrast, one must be born a witch or introduced into the secret community of witches in order to practice witchcraft. He possesses mysterious and superhuman powers like the ability to remove a man's intestines without making a visible cut.

According to E.H. Winter who lived among the Amba,

"Sorcery is set in motion by ordinary motives of envy, jealousy, and hatred. It is activated by the elements of daily life, by social situations which give rise to feels of envy, jealousy, and hatred. It is activated by the elements of daily life, by social situations which give rise to feelings of ill will...by contrast, the activities of witches are ultimately inexplicable. Witches although they may harm people in all sorts of ways, for instance by causing a man to trip over a fallen branch, are concerned basically with the satisfaction of their abnormal desire for human flesh...," a thought utterly rejected by the normal Amba (Middleton 1963:280).

According to Okot P'Bitek, the Central Luo also make this distinction (P'Bitek 1971:121-144). Witchcraft is an involuntary act, either inherited from or blown into him by his father. A witch is forced to do his evil deed. He acts blindly without any motive. When the *Jok* power comes over him, he is overcome. He is described as a "victim, a prisoner, an instrument of the power in him."

P'Bitek mentions two kinds of witchcraft. The evil eye (*layir*) is a rare power possessed by people with bloodshot eyes. By merely looking at a person he can unwillingly bring harm. *La tal* is one who can cause death, by causing a person to dry up and waste away. Contrary to the strict definition of a witch, however, the *La tal* would use material substances and spells. These materials were placed in the roof or garden of the intended victim. At times the *La tal* would enjoy a feast of human flesh by digging up the corpse of a dead person. Several witches lay on a grave, urinate and defecate, dig up the body and eat together. Legs and arms would be used for stirring dishes and a skull used as a water cup. Though witches were pitied because of their uncontrollable urge, they were severely punished when caught.

In contrast, the sorcerer (for which the Central Luo had no specific term), was a responsible person in full possession of himself. He used medicines and poisons to harm his victim.

For our purpose of studying the various beliefs in mystical powers, this traditional distinction is useful. But it must be repeated that many, many Africans do not make such a distinction. The Akamba and Gikuyu of Kenya are examples. The English term, witchcraft, is used in popular speech to refer to all harmful employment of mystical powers which, according to Evans-Pritchard, is strictly speaking, sorcery. No verbal distinctions are made in Kikamba.

For these reasons perhaps, John Mbiti, himself a Mukamba, comments, "I am inclined to use the term 'witch' or 'witchcraft' in this broader sense; and here theologians may wish to part company with anthropologists." (Mbiti 1969:202) Mbiti, however, has given no theological basis for such a statement.

Characteristics of a Witch

In general, witches are marked by the following characteristics:

1) Most witches are female, but not all of them.

2) Witches are evil within themselves, and perform wicked deeds because of their wicked nature. Some believe witches are what they are because of a witchcraft substance within their intestines which can be seen and felt. Because of this physical feature, they are abnormal and prove to be a threat to everyone, not only their enemies.

3) Witches, like sorcerers, are against society and greatly feared by the people. But witches are always dangerous to everyone, whereas sorcerers are only dangerous when excited by ill will.

4) A witch, strictly speaking, does not use medicines or material apparatus. Nor does she perform rites or utter spells. Her whole art of witchcraft is innate, an act of the mind.

5) While the bodies remain at home, their spirits fly away at night and congregate with other witches. They enjoy dancing completely naked, eating human flesh and sucking their blood. Unsatisfied hunger for human flesh is characteristic of witches.

6) Every kind of misfortune and evil may be blamed on witches and witchcraft. The wasting away of a person's body and the swelling of his internal organs is evidence that a witch is eating his soul and drinking his blood. The effect is proof of the cause.

Sorcery and Black Magic

As we have stated before, sorcery, the use of mystical powers of black magic, is opposed to the welfare of the people. Sorcery uses medicines, charms and black magic. Hence, black magic is closely associated with sorcery. In fact, a sorcerer may be called a black magician. Parrinder speaks of "offensive magic" to describe the attacking quality of "black magic", in contrast to "white magic" which is usually "defensive" and protective from the attacks of witchcraft and sorcery.

Speaking of the Azande concept, Evans-Pritchard says good magic is moral and right because it is used to protect people from unknown enemies. But bad magic is evil because it is directed against definite persons. If a good person knows a criminal, he will take him to court. But the sorcerer has no legal case against his enemy, and therefore, uses black magic to destroy him.

A wizard is by definition a "male witch, a magician and sorcerer." Parrinder suggests it is best to limit the wizard to a dealer in black magic. A wizard is, therefore, a black magician or a sorcerer.

Sorcery is specifically associated with poison. Among the Gusii of Kenya, the use of poison is a sign that sorcery has been used. Some people have claimed to be sorcerers even though they admit that the only way they can kill people is by poison. The logic here is that the kind of person who would seek to murder his own family must be a sorcerer.

The very name for "witchcraft" among the Gikuyu is *orogi*, meaning "poison." The one who uses this poison is a witch, *morogi*. It should be pointed out that the Gikuyu do not distinguish between a witch and a sorcerer. Even though Kenyatta uses the terms, "witch" and "witchcraft," what he describes is really sorcery according to the anthropological distinctions.

Kenyatta claims that the "*orogi* is pure and simple poison" made from various poisonous herbs (Kenyatta n.d.:294). But this substance truly becomes *orogi* only when it is properly mixed with other magical substances and energized over by ritual formula. The ingredients added to the poison are parts of human, animal and reptile flesh. The chief human parts needed are male and female genital organs, breasts, tongues, ears, hands and feet, blood, eyes and noses. These parts are extracted from the dead bodies of those killed by the witch.

All kinds of other harmful and magical medicines are used by the sorcerer. These may be placed in the victim's food, water or beer. It is secretly placed in his house or sprinkled around the house.

In addition to these medicines, other methods are used by the sorcerer. He may use animals such as snakes or leopards to destroy an enemy. Some people believe he can beat the grave of a dead man and cause the corpse to rise. By piercing the head with a long needle, the corpse becomes foolish and subject to the desires of the witch. He then sends the body on errands to injure his enemies.

MEDICINE MEN AND OTHER SPECIALISTS

Many tasks in African traditional culture may be performed by one specialist, or they may be divided among many different kinds of persons, each a specialist in his field. Mbiti rightly observes that a sharp distinction is "chiefly an academic" one. Thus a medicine man may also be a diviner or a rainmaker or even a priest. Or these specializations may be divided among different persons.

Briefly, let us mention several specialists, understanding that this is an abbreviated generalization of ATR. We shall give primary attention to the medicine man who is in many African cultures a dominant figure.

Medicine Men. There are found in all African societies those specialists who assist the people in fighting off attacks from witches. Traditionally, these specialists have been called "witch-doctors" in English. This word simply meant a traditional doctor who helped the troubled, sick and dying who had been bewitched. Witch-doctors were traditional doctors dealing with the problem of witches.

However, the term, "witch-doctor," has developed negative connotations over the years. This title, therefore, is not highly favoured today. Other terms have been used instead, such as "witch finder" or "doctor." Perhaps the term most favoured is "medicine man." The medicine man is the traditional doctor who seeks to help the sick and needy who are troubled by witchcraft. In this context a medicine man is not a pure herbalist. He is the "doctor" of traditional African culture, endowed by his ancestral spirits with the power of counteracting witchcraft. In our presentation we shall refer to this specialist, traditionally called "witch doctor," as the medicine man. These medicine men are not the pure herbalists but the mediums who use their powers with the spirit world to help those troubled by witchcraft.

What are the characteristics of a medicine man?

1)*Medicine men are highly respected people.*

They are not merely accepted, but highly respected and feared. Mbiti speaks of them as "the friend of the community." Some may reject Mbiti's strong affirmation of the medicine man. But we do agree that in contrast to the anti-social behaviour of the sorcerer, the medicine man is regarded as socially accepted and approved.

This may be illustrated by the medicine man among the Akamba. Because of his unique relationship to the ancestral spirits, he is given special honour. When walking on the path, the Mukamba medicine man leads the way before everyone else. When he needs a new house, the whole community joins in to build the house for him. The old women and young people dance on the new site, a practice not performed for any other. At the funeral of a medicine man, the old men dance, the only time this is ever done. An old man once told Lindblom, "We Akamba have no chiefs and are not used to them. But if any of us may be compared with them, it would be the *mundu mue* [medicine man]." (Lindblom 1920:258)

The Nandi medicine man is called a *njorik*. An essential part of his training is the learning of self confidence. He learns to believe in himself and feel that he has special status among the people. He has powers not available to others.

Therefore, he is taught to have pride and a sense of satisfaction in his new position. And the Nandi all recognize and accept the greatness of his powers.

The Azande of Sudan express much doubt about their medicine men. They know many are pretenders. Yet the medicine men hold a most important place in Zande society. Witchcraft is a daily happening with all its dangers. Only the medicine man has that special power to fight this evil. He alone can see the magic flying toward its victim. He alone fights with the evil powers and overcomes witchcraft before their very eyes. As a result, only the political leaders have greater influence than medicine men.

2)*Medicine men are public servants fighting witchcraft.*

This is the real difference between witches and medicine men. While the witches are anti-social and hated by the people, the medicine men are highly respected in their community for their ability to fight witchcraft. They can find the witch, heal the sick, provide protective magic, and control the nature spirits and the ancestral spirits. The duty of the medicine man is to serve as a doctor for those attacked by witchcraft. For this, he may use herbal plants, ancestral spirits or psychical methods.

This can be illustrated by the Azande. The Azande medicine man is both a diviner and a magician. When he is called by someone troubled with witchcraft, his first job is to find the witch. (Thus some specialists have suggested his title should be, "witch finder," though this is only part of his broad duties.) The medicine man arouses himself through the use of medicines, dancing and drumming. Once the witch is known, the medicine man may be called upon to provide charms and magic to prevent further attacks of the witch.

In a general sort of way this main point can be shown to be true, that medicine men are public servants fighting witchcraft. As Parrinder observes, the medicine man "is no more a witch than an Inspector of the C.I.D. is a burglar." (Parrinder 1958:181) However, this general truth can be overstated. We shall see that their activities are not always positive and for the good of the community. It is because of their enormous powers that they are greatly feared.

3)*Medicine men use the same powers as witches.*

This point is very important, though we shall only introduce it at this stage. Generally, medicine men are said to be good people, while witches are rejected by the community as bad people. But in preparation for our later discussion, we need to understand that medicine men have this in common with witches and sorcerers: they use the same powers.

Africans believe in the existence of some "vital force," some spiritual power that fills the universe. This powerful energy is found in people, things, trees and animals. It is that which gives power to magical practices, provides power for medicine men and witches, and offers hope to all those in special need. The ability to use this power is a great benefit for one's honour and prestige.

This force is neutral and can be used for good or evil. A witch always uses this power for evil. But he can use the same power to benefit himself with improved crops. And he can use that power to reverse the evil spells he has made. Thus anyone with unusual success is suspected of using witchcraft.

On the other hand, a medicine man generally uses this power for finding a witch, protecting against witchcraft or healing one attacked by witchcraft. But at the same time he can use this same power for destructive purposes to attack innocent people.

A Diviner is "a specialist who seeks to diagnose disease, or discover the solution to problems, by means of inspiration or manipulation of objects through various techniques." (Parrinder 1962:103) Diviners work closely with the medicine men, and in fact may be medicine men themselves.

They use various equipment to divine, such as divining stones, seeds, nuts and gourds. Diviners may also serve as mediums to gain help from the ancestral spirits. When the diviner and the medium are different persons, the diviner is often a male and the medium a female.

A diviner may be a medium through whom the spirits speak to the diviner. Dreams and visions are different ways in which the diviners receive communication from the spirit world. Medicines, drugs and herbs are also some of the methods used by diviners. Various techniques are learned whereby the special knowledge is gained.

Rainmakers are essential in Africa wherever rainfall is marginal or unpredictable. The rainmakers not only study the sky and signs of weather but they also intercede before God, the spirits and the ancestral dead. Rainmakers are in fact a specialized form of the medicine man. Furthermore, they use magical chants and materials.

Prophets are specialists who predict future events. They served a vital service for the community by advising the warriors when and how to win their battles. Prophets frequently became famous for their knowledge of the future. Many times a prophet was a medicine man devoted to the specialization of prophecy. Usually, he was a medium who served as a mediator between the unseen realm of spirits and living mankind.

Priests in ATR were common place, especially in West Africa where they served at the shrines of the various divinities. In East Africa the priest is often a specialist among the medicine men. These priests were often called to their vocation and were always trained, learning their many prayers, ritual and sacrifices from their tutors. After being called by the ancestral spirits or inheriting the vocation from someone else, they must observe various taboos, such as abstaining from certain foods or mixing with people, or from sexual intercourse. The priest not only offers sacrifices but often serves as a medium.

Herbalists in traditional culture were familiar with the medicinal value of various herbs. The pure herbalist was distinct from the diviner who combined herbal remedies with divination and the mystical powers of the spirit world. Daidanso urges that we strike a balance on this question of traditional herbal medicines. To say that there were no pure herbalists is not true. Sometimes people were told to collect certain herbs, use them and be healed. But if that same herbalist/diviner required that person to return the next day with a hen or an egg, that showed a religious element was involved. In fact, religion permeated the whole life of the African. This frequently included prescription of healing for the sick. But not always.

Daidanso affirms that there are three kinds of activities in ATR: 1)Activities which are not committed to religious beliefs. Though this may be hard to find in traditional African culture, they can be found. 2)Activities which are religiously committed. 3)Activities which are mixed. Some herbal specialists freely give herbal medicines without any religious connotations. While others give the same herb for the same illness but with religious overtones. If it is known that a specialist mixes the herbal remedies with the religious, the Christian should refrain from visiting the specialist. Because other Christians will follow their example and become engaged in traditional religion (Daidanso ma Djongwe: 1988).

CONCLUSION

If we are to gauge the importance of a religious concept or practice by its prominence in traditional culture, then surely the ATR belief in mystical powers is of paramount importance. From the sheer preoccupation that Africans have given to witchcraft, sorcery and magic, we may affirm that belief in these mystical powers was a focal concern for ATR.

Mystical powers, an impersonal power (*mana*) which permeates the universe, can be used for good or ill. Within ATR there is a delicate balance maintained. Specialists with extra ordinary powers, either inherited, endowed by the ancestral spirits or purchased from local medicine men, are the mediums through whom the numinous powers may be tapped, either for good or ill. Access to these mystical powers by the ordinary African was through these specialists who served either the interests of the community or the malicious designs of individuals.

REVIEW QUESTIONS FOR CHAPTER 4

1. Define what is meant by magic?
2. Discuss the difference between witchcraft and sorcery according to the anthropologists.
3. Describe the general characteristics of a witch.
4. In what way is black magic and medicine associated with sorcery?
5. Discuss the various characteristics of a medicine man.

Suggested Reading and Thought Questions for Advanced Study:

Adggbola, E.A.Ade. *Traditional Religion in West Africa*, 1983, pp.55-70, 317-336.

Idowu, Bolaji. *African Traditional Religion: A Definition*, 1973, pp.189-202.

Mbiti, John. *African Religions and Philosophy*, 1969, pp.166-203.

Middleton, John and E.H. Winter eds. *Witchcraft and Sorcery in East Africa*, 1963.

Parrinder, E. G. *African Traditional Religion*, 1962, pp.113-134; 100-109.

Parrinder, Geoffrey. *West African Religion*, 1961, pp.137-186.

1. In what ways are magic and religion similar? In what ways are they different? Do your peoples traditionally use magic without any reference to belief in ancestors, spirits or God? Or are they inter-related? Is it legitimate today for an evangelical Christian to distinguish between magic and religion? Why?

2. Explain and illustrate from your own traditional beliefs the different kinds of magic:

  "white magic" and "black magic"

  "imitative magic" and "contagious magic"

  "personal magic" and "public magic"

3. Describe some of the traditional beliefs and practices of witchcraft and sorcery among your peoples. Do you believe the anthropological distinction between witchcraft and sorcery is helpful in understanding mystical powers? Explain why it is or is not helpful.

4. Mbiti declares that the medicine man is highly admired and respected, "the friend of the community." To what extent do you agree or disagree? Support your answer with thoughtful reasons and evidence.

Chapter 5

CASE STUDY OF THE AKAMBA: MYSTICAL POWERS

A dominant feature of the Akamba world view is belief in mystical powers. Though the Akamba cannot explain its nature or source, they can reiterate experience after experience of the reality of this power. This inexplicable power is resident in plant and animal life, manifest through spoken words, and mediated through specialists. This power can be for good or evil. The effectiveness of this power is recognized by the present government administration and used in settling land disputes. It is accepted by well educated, highly salaried persons living in Nairobi who travel long distances in their expensive cars over difficult paths into remote corners of Kitui in order to secure this power from known specialists.

WITCHCRAFT: " UOI"

Prominence

Virtually every unusual event or tragic experience can be explained by witchcraft. Anything from a poor harvest, sickness, death, accident or headache, to a quarreling relationship or unusual phenomena find their explanation in witchcraft. Nothing happens by chance to a traditional Mukamba. There is no "natural" death. Everything, from a fly falling into a cup of tea to a strange noise made by a bird in a tree has some metaphysical explanation. Since life is filled with such experiences, the belief in witchcraft permeates the world view of the Akamba. As Mbiti maintains, "Magic, witchcraft and sorcery play a prominent role in Akamba life. The people are saturated with beliefs, fears and superstitions connected with these practices." (Mbiti 1971:9)

The Akamba can tell innumerable stories of unusual experiences which can only be explained by mystical powers. To illustrate this we recount the story personally narrated by Ndeto. When he was a young boy of two years old, he was walking along a path together with his sister, near his home. They passed a woman carrying some maize. When Ndeto saw the maize, he began crying for some because he loved maize so much. In response the woman gave him two ears of corn Immediately, thereafter, he became seriously ill to the point of death. Upon reaching home they explained the full story to the mother who immediately concluded that the boy had been bewitched. In deep anger the mother visited the Chief to report the matter. The Chief accompanied the mother to the home of the suspected witch. With bitter feelings the mother accused the woman of b witching the child and threatened to kill her with a panga unless she reversed the witchcraft. Thereupon, the suspected witch accompanied Ndeto into a closed room where she was ordered to reverse the spell. While in the room the people could hear her talking and doing certain things. Thereafter, she brought Ndeto from the room and presented him to his mother, the child now recovering. To this day the woman lives in the village and is a suspected witch.

The Akamba are famous for their powerful witchcraft. The Akamba living in Machakos District recognize the witchcraft in Kitui to be far more powerful than theirs. Akamba from Machakos and even non-Akamba living in Nairobi travel to Kitui in order to enlist the help of specialists. But the Akamba in Kitui believe that the witchcraft at the coast is even more powerful than theirs. And the coastal peoples believe that those living in Tanzania have even greater mystical powers.

Definitions

The Kikamba term for inexplicable evil powers is *uoi*. No one can explain what this power is. People are more concerned with what *uoi* does than what it is. No traditional Mukamba has tried to analyze the nature and source of this power. But everyone recognizes the reality of *uoi*. The evil power finds its way into a human being from birth or from another person possessing it.

The evil person who taps the power of witchcraft (*uoi*) is called a witch (*muoi*). Most witches are women, and the most powerful witches are women.

Between 1954 and 1955 the British Colonial Government in Kenya tried to suppress witchcraft among the Akamba. Some 1,800 women and 150 men of all ages handed in their witchcraft objects (Nottingham 1959:5). This demonstrates the recognized fact that the vast majority of Akamba witches are women.

The witch does her work in secret, usually active at night. She walks at night, usually very fast. Animals may accompany. The witch moves bodily and not merely in her spirit. This evil person is anti-social and secretive, unwilling to divulge her knowledge or activities. With evil intentions she seeks to injure both her enemies and her prosperous friends.

The Akamba describe the witch as an evil person. She is driven by an inner urge to harm and kill. Failure to obey this urge might lead to a weakening of herself, or even death. Thirst for blood is found in her. Witchcraft is a power in the witch used consciously or unconsciously to bring evil upon another person.

At most, one can say that witchcraft is a power in nature which finds its way into a human being from birth or from one who possesses it. Even Christians know it exists and need not ask what it is or what it does. Witchcraft is a power which enables the witch to perform evil deeds, causing every evil experience encountered in life. Witchcraft is also a power which can be used to counteract those attacked by witchcraft.

Bewitching

1. Witch: *Muoi.* "To bewitch" in Kikamba is *kuoa*. For this purpose the witch (technically, a sorcerer) uses all manner of items which had association with the person who is to be bewitched. In this sense the Mukamba witch is pre-eminently a black magician.

The witch utilizes all manner of items which had once been in contact with the person. When the traditional Mukamba cuts his finger nails, toe nails or hair, he throws them into the bush or places them in an ant hill. If placed into an ant hill, the termites will eat them quickly and the witch would, therefore, be unable to secure them. If the nails or hair are buried, great care must be taken lest someone sees you. But the Akamba never burn the hair or nails lest this would bring harm to the owner. The person from whom the hair or nails had come would feel pain if those objects were burned.

The vital parts of a human being are also used in witchcraft. The parts of the human body with concentrated power are the extremities of the person and those organs where great power (potency) resides. These parts include hair, fingers, toes, the penis and the clitoris. These are mixed with other ingredients to form potent witchcraft. The penis and clitoris are used to produce the most potent form of witchcraft in killing people.

For this reason efforts were made to protect the corpse lest a witch would come at night and take part of the body for use in black magic. When the corpse was thrown into the bush years ago, a relative with a bow and arrow set up guard to watch the body at night. If anyone was found cutting parts from the body, he was killed on the spot. Burial of the dead may have arisen in part to protect the corpse from the witch. But even today the digging up of a corpse by a witch is not unknown. Sometimes a witch will take the feces of a child. At home he will utter some magical words. Thereafter, the child begins to die. At night the witch may come naked and count the cows. Taking up the cow dung he throws it while mooing like a cow. The cows then begin to die.

Contagious magic (see "Kinds of Magic" chapter 4) included the use of footprints. A witch will spit on a footprint of a person or take some of the sand in the footprint to mix with a dead hyena and the dung of an ox. This becomes deadly witchcraft to kill men and cattle or spoil the crops. The witch will take the sand home so that no one will see him treating the footprint. Or he will at night take a small bow and tiny arrows to shoot the footprint intending to harm the one who made the foot mark. The person so affected will then suffer pain in the soles of his feet. The practice of shooting the footprint is called *ndatho* (or *ndato* in Machakos). The practice of taking the footprint of a person to treat secretly for harmful purposes is known literally as "taking the footprint of a person" (compare Hobley 1910:93). The witch may also take cattle dung and use this to harm the whole herd of cattle from whence it came.

Even the personal name can be used against a Mukamba as part of black magic. Because the name bears an essential part of the person, harm can be brought to the owner through wrong use. For this reason it had been common for a Mukamba to withhold his name from a stranger. Or a pseudonym (false name) might be given, lest his real name be used by an ill-disposed person in witchcraft. The use of poisons by a witch is common. "*Muthea* is the Kikamba word for the black powder obtained by grinding between two stones the dried essence resulting from cooking certain insects together with the roots, bark or leaves of various trees and grasses." (Nottingham 1959:5) *Muthea* powder is composed of the liver of some animals like crocodiles, and roots or leaves of certain plants and trees. *Muthea* may contain nails, hair, bones and teeth of human beings. It may also include claws, fur, horns and skulls of certain animals.

In the 1950's a study was made of various items which have poisonous effects in Ukambani. The total number then counted was 75 trees, 30 grasses and 26 insects or reptiles. Many have "a venerable tradition for being poisonous among the Akamba." (Nottingham 1959:5) Some poisons are "so virulent (powerful) that the extract of a single leaf will cause death." (1959:6)

Thus a few grains of these poisons can be secretly placed in the bowl of a guest, or in the snuff box containing tobacco. Good manners among the Akamba required the host to eat first the food dished out for the guests. Just a few grains of *muthea* carefully concealed under a long finger nail when dipped into the communal calabash at the beer party would be sufficient to do its deadly work. The Akamba often love to grow long finger nails which can conveniently be used for that purpose.

Direct killing through witchcraft can allegedly be done through the use of a special mirror. The witch takes this mirror, draws seven lines vertically on the mirror, using blue and red. He then calls the person by name while looking into the mirror. If the person comes sideways, he has been treated and cannot be harmed. If he comes straight forward, the witch takes a knife, dips it in blood and draws a line across the mirror. The person will then die immediately.

It is alleged that some people are able to change themselves into an animal in order to devour someone's cattle. One man allegedly changed himself into a half-man and half-hyena. He then devoured goats and sheep. He was able to do this magical trick by jumping over a certain stick obtained from a witchdoctor. The story is told of one man in Kangundo who performed this trick, but unluckily, his stick was misplaced. As a result, the man disappeared forever. He could be found nowhere.

2. Charms: *Kithangona*. The witch is not restricted to the use of poisons. Nor is he limited to direct killings. He can reportedly use indirect means of killing or weakening a person. He is able to use other materials which produce evil effects. Through jealousy a person may wish to destroy the good crops which his neighbour has been enjoying. For this purpose the witch will plant a *kithangona* in the garden to destroy it. A Christian Mukamba tells of finding a horn from a bull with a few eggs buried in the soil. "As we were ploughing and sowing seeds the plough unearthed these. The man who was ploughing my garden was afraid to continue ploughing a bewitched garden. I encouraged him to continue ploughing because it was nonsense to me. When time for harvesting came, my garden had the best harvest of all those neighbouring mine."

Many such stories can be told of finding *kithangona* planted in someone's property in order to destroy. Musyima tells of weeding the maize in his garden when he unearthed a bottle of yellow liquid and four calf hooves placed under the best maize seedlings. For the Christian family no harm was brought.

For non-Christians, however, fear devastates the mental outlook of those finding *kithangona*. The witch may place it under the path over which his enemy will pass. Usually, it is placed near the door post entering his house or homestead or on a nearby path. When the enemy walks across the *kithangona*, he will allegedly become sick and begin wasting away.

Becoming a Witch

The most effective way of becoming a witch is through inheritance. A male witch passes on his powers to his son, while a female witch passes her powers on to her daughter. If the daughter refuses, she will be in danger of misfortune, such as failure to marry, failure to bear children or becoming mad or epileptic.

The details of transferring the powers of witchcraft from mother to daughter are not well known, since disclosure of such details would mean misfortune. However, certain aspects of the rite have been learned by talking with Christian women who were formerly witches.

Both the mother and daughter are naked during the rite. The daughter is shown some powders and the horns in which witchcraft is placed, together with nails, hair and bones of human beings. Horns of every size and shape are used in which to store the witchcraft, from wart hogs to gazelles. The mother instructs the daughter how to use witchcraft and where to keep it. A mixture of gruel and blood previously prepared in the shrine are drunk by both. They sing and dance, bumping their naked buttocks together various times. The mother sits down with her legs wide apart, facing her daughter who does the same thing. The mother places a horn between her legs. After saying some words, the daughter stretches forward to take the horn.

Incisions (cuts) are made by the mother in the daughter at five places: pubic area, tongue, fingers and buttocks. Blood is transferred to each other. Certain powders are rubbed into the wounds made by the incisions (cuts). Those areas become the source of emitting witchcraft. Any time a witch scratches her incisions, she can bewitch people. Thereafter, the spoken word or the pointing finger sends forth destructive power.

In order to seal this transaction certain acts of incest (sexual relations with close relatives) must take place. A male witch must commit incest with his daughter or a female witch must commit incest with her son. Alternatively, intercourse may take place with an animal.

The witchcraft medicines may not be kept at home. They are hidden in caves or near a big tree. For that reason they call witchcraft medicines, "that which is kept in the caves."

To buy witchcraft in Kitui or at the Coast, one inquiries secretly from his friends how he can meet the most feared witch in the area. When arriving at the house of the witch (he may cause you to wait for several days in order to know whether the person wants to purchase witchcraft from him or to bewitch him instead), the cost of purchase is stated. Mutunga said, "I was put into a bee hive, then thrown in a big fire which was made outside a small house. As the fire flamed upwards I heard someone call my name. I looked but did not see anyone. I was given something that looked like red seeds to swallow. I was told to recite some words after the voice. This I did." Incisions (cuts) were made, medicines inserted, as previously described, when the powers of witchcraft are transmitted from mother to daughter. Certain taboos were told him, including the taboo of never washing or drinking water for seven days after he reached home.

Others who purchase witchcraft at the coast are given some spirits which reside in a gourd. These spirits are called *majini* in Kiswahili. These *majini* become the servants of the witch. Whenever the witch wants to bewitch someone, he sends the *majini* to do certain things. The *majini* are not kept at home. Sacrifices are given to the *majini* such as a cow or goat, killed once per year. Blood is then offered to the *majini* to drink.

Witchraft when purchased must be confirmed and strengthened through the performance of some horrible deed, such as bewitching the husband, the firstborn or the mother-in-law, if the witch is a woman. The performance of these horrible acts is needed to strengthen the powers of witchcraft.

Law Enforcement: *King'ole*

The *king'ole* was the Akamba Supreme Court, composed of elders who were valiant men, excelling in their fields, such as hunting or fighting. The *king'ole* was the Council which controlled the evil practices of witchcraft.

The traditional punishment of a witch was death in Akamba culture. When someone was suspected of being a witch, a group of elders, called the *king'ole*, assembled and visited the suspect's home. If they found witchcraft paraphernalia, they took the suspect outside the village and shot him to death with arrows.

On other occasions they sent villagers to different medicine men to distant places, to inquire. Since each village had many jealousies and bitter enemies, and since the medicine man may in fact be a witch, they frequently visited distant medicine men to learn the truth. At least three medicine men were consulted to verify the reports. Such specialists would describe what they saw in their vision. For example, the medicine man would describe the witch as a short man with brown skin, living north of your house and being a practicingmedicine man. When the various villagers returned, they consulted one another to learn the various reports. If all medicine men were in agreement, the villagers would arrest the person and send word to the elders of that family and clan. A council was held in which the husband of the witch was present to hear the reports. After reaching a guilty verdict the husband was required by the *king'ole* to shoot the first arrow at his wife, but without a metal tip. Thereafter, the elders showered all their arrows on her body until she died.

This work of killing the witch was the responsibility of the *king'ole*. These elders were the military guard against witchcraft. The *king'ole* was the meeting of the adult population, dominated by the elders, for the purpose of condemning and executing the guilty offender.

With the coming of colonialism, such traditional controls of witchcraft were outlawed with the result that witchcraft tended to increase among the Akamba.

DIVINATION: " UWE"

The second kind of mystical power among the Akamba is beneficial, known as *uwe*.

Medicine Man: *Mundu Mue*

1. His Role. Basic to the Akamba world view is the cosmological balance between good and evil. The witch who employs the powers of witchcraft represents the evil within the created universe. Counter balancing this evil is the medicine man who employs the greater powers of divination (*uwe*) to counteract the evil.

The *mundu mue* (*andu awe*, plural) means literally, "the wise man." The medicine man is wise in that he knows and understands the use of local herbs for healing the sick. He is able to foretell the future, seek out the witchcraft which troubles people and in general help people in their needs.

According to Lindblom, the chief duties of the medicine man are "divination and the curing of illness." (Lindblom 1920:258) However, Ndeti believes that Lindblom's explanation of his chief duties is "limited, narrow and misleading." (Ndeti 1972:177) Traditionally, the medicine man is much more, Ndeti contends. He is the "wise man" who is consulted by the living on behalf of the living-dead (1972:117).

The medicine man is essentially the medium between the living and the ancestral spirits. All Akamba pass through the medicine man whenever they desire to communicate with their ancestors. The medicine man does not convey his own opinions to his client, but he communicates the messages of the ancestors to the living. Only the medicine man has the right and authority to know the requests of the ancestors.

The role of the medicine man is most essential in the traditional life of the Akamba. Should you remove the medicine man from Akamba life, one would need to replace him with another person who would fulfill a similar role. Whenever something goes wrong in the life of an individual or family, the Akamba resort to the medicine man for advice. His traditional role is comprehensive in traditional culture, being the one who is "consulted in all the more or less perplexing occasions of life." (Lindblom 1920:258) He serves as counselor, doctor and advisor. He is the defender of the community against the evils of witchcraft. Ndeti prefers to call the medicine man the "doctor." He has experimented with various herbs to determine which ones are effective for various diseases. The medicine man is "dedicated to the care of the sick through the use of local herbs...*mondo moe [Mundu Mue]* has learned over the years that sometimes he is unable to cure an ailment, even when he can diagnose it and knows what herbs would be suitable. In such cases, he directs his treatment to the psyche or the soul (Ndeti 1972:116).

In many ways the medicine man is similar to the shaman found in other parts of the world.

> The shaman, like the physician, tries to cure the patient by correcting the causes of his illness. In line with his culture's concept of disease, this cure may involve not only the administration of the therapeutic [healing] agents, but provision of the means for confession, atonement, restoration into the good graces of family and tribe, and intercession with the world of the spirit. The shaman's role may thus involve aspects of the roles of physician, magician, priest, moral arbiter, representative of the group's world view and agent of social control (Ndeti 1972:116).

Ndeti continues, "There seems to be no better definition of the role of *mondo moe [mundu mue]* in Akamba society than the one given in the above quotation." (1972:116)

And yet it would seem that the medicine man is more. He is the intermediary between the living and the ancestral spirits. His powers are obtained through the ancestors. His role is to communicate with the living-dead and to be their mouth piece. All this becomes abundantly evident in our discussion.

2. Becoming a Medicine Man. There are three basic ways of becoming a medicine man: through birth, through inheritance from the parent, or through purchase from another medicine man. But all of them achieve their status through demonstration of their abilities.

Through Birth. The most powerful medicine man is one who is born destined to be a medicine man. Such a new born child will be found with some abnormal appendages on his body. Or he may be born with divination pebbles (*mbuu*) in his hand or in the after birth. The mother will hide these divination pebbles and give them to him later as the credentials of a medicine man. The child will begin to appear abnormal and stand out from other children. He will have dreams and revelations from the spirit world and thereby confirm his calling. One aspect of his "abnormality" is his "desire for solitude." As he matures he will develop the character traits of a medicine man.

When the young man, predestined to be a medicine man, comes of age, between the age of 20 and 25, his father will kill a sacrificial goat and hold a feast for him. They will pray to the ancestral spirits to empower him with these confirmatory objects. From henceforth the burden of proving himself is upon the young medicine man. He must heal and divine successfully in order to demonstrate his ability. Not everyone succeeds in establishing a name for himself. The office of the medicine man is through special appointment by the ancestors. Nevertheless, each medicine man must demonstrate his effectiveness to the satisfaction of his clients. (See Appendix B for a vivid account).

Through Inheritance. A second way by which a person becomes a medicine man is through inheritance from the parent. The father or mother who is a medicine man is directed by the ancestors to appoint the son or daughter to be associated with him or her in the office. The male Wise Man chooses a son and the female Diviner selects a daughter. When the son or daughter matures, about the age of 20 or 25, the active partnership commences. If the son or daughter rejects this request, the ancestors become angry and may give the parent some poisonous medicine and order the parent to kill the child for refusing. As the child grows up in the parent's home, he or she begins learning the habits and practices of his father or mother.

The child may begin dreaming of securing certain herbs to heal people. He will grow in his interest in different types of trees and roots useful for medicines. But the day comes when that prospective medicine man must be initiated into the profession of being a Diviner, empowered with the powers of the spirit world.

Lindblom suggests that the hereditary nature of the Akamba witchcraft "may, to some extent, be due to the fact that the stimulation of the nervous system to which a medicine man is continually exposed, is inherited by one of his children and so makes him disposed to the profession." (Lindblom 1920:256) Ndeti rejects this explanation of Lindblom. Rather, Ndeti claims, that it is "the practical knowledge to which the child is exposed. He sees his father heal patients by giving them local herbs, and acquires the same knowledge because it brings honour, wealth, personal satisfaction and social prestige." (Ndeti 1972:117) (See Appendix B for a personal account of a former *mundu mue*.)

Through Purchasing. The third way by which a person can become a medicine man is by purchasing those mystical powers from a powerful Diviner. A Diviner who has purchased his powers is said to have the weakest power of all medicine men. They are often said to have fewer clients because they are known to be in the business mainly for money and not merely to help people. Their power is known to be less effective. Often the people who consult them are living at a distance and do not know them well. But their powers are also dependent upon the ancestral spirits who become their helpers.

If a Mukamba desires to purchase the powers of a medicine man he may go to Kitui or even Mombasa. With the payment of money or material things the Diviner will teach the client how to use his tools and how to communicate with the ancestral spirits (*aimu*) or the *majini* in Mombasa. A particular *jini* or two *majini* are given to the client to be his servants. An agreement is made between the medicine man, the client and the spirits. A bull or two is killed. The blood is given to the ancestral spirits together with the liver, heart and the pancreas. (See Appendix B for a personal testimony of one who purchased mystical powers to become a medicine woman.)

3. Specializations of a Mundu Mue. The Akamba medicine men specialize in different activities. One could divide the Akamba wise men and wise women into three categories. 1)Prophets (*athani*), 2)Diviners (*awe ma kuausya*), and 3)Herbalists who cleanse (*awe ma ng'ondu*).

Prophet. A prophet is one who predicts the future. He warns of impending danger such as drought, heavy rains, locust plagues and ensuing epidemics. The prophets are always associated with the ancestral spirits. They communicate with the ancestors who inform them what shall take place and what remedies may be taken to prevent disaster or to protect against approaching danger. Several times a week the prophet receives revelations from the spirit world. The prophets were the mouthpieces of the ancestral spirits.

If a revelation is given during the day, the prophet falls into a deep sleep during which time he dreams. When he awakes, he announces to the people all that he saw and heard. If the message is of impending danger, the prophet will also reveal the solution. The Akamba are reportedly saved when they follow the solution recommended by the ancestral spirits. Otherwise, they suffer the consequences.

The primary means by which a prophet receives his revelations is by a dream. But he might also be possessed by the ancestors.

Sometimes the *aimu* would appear in the visible but non-physical form. For instance, *Kathambi* appears various times to the prophets when they are sleeping or sitting down. *Kathambi* was always elaborately decorated. Whenever

Kathambi appeared, the prophet had to offer a sacrifice for her. Otherwise, no message was given and a curse was possible. *Kathambi* was known to be generous for she would disclose all that was needed by the people in order for the people to avoid disaster.On another occasion, a prophet admonished and advised the people concerning a great mistake they had made. During a *kilumi* dance a participant left the group to relieve himself. Though it was dark he saw someone standing in the cattle pen in the midst of the animals. Thinking that person was a thief the man threw a fire stick. But the person suddenly vanished. Instantly, his arm began to pain him. When he returned to the dance (*kilumi*), he told the prophet present what had happened. The prophet replied that he had made a great mistake for he had attacked the guardian of the cattle. Because of this, the *iimu* had become angry and struck his arm with pain. The prophet then informed the people not to repeat the same mistake and he offered a black she goat as a sacrifice. Immediately, the pain in his arm went away.

Probably, the most prominent Akamba prophets were Syokaiku, Syondonga, Syenze and Syokimau. The most famous prophet of all in Ukambani was Syokimau who foretold the coming of the white men a long time before they arrived in East Africa. Syokimau prophesied about the building of the Kenya Uganda Railway which was constructed at the turn of the century from Mombasa to Lake Victoria. In her vision she saw a long snake from waters to another water which carried people on it, understood afterwards as the Uganda railroad, extending from Mombasa to Lake Victoria. Syokimau also predicted that the white men would carry fire in their pockets which has been interpreted to be match boxes.

The prophet could help the Akamba spies during the days of their cattle raiding with the neighboring Masai and Gikuyu. Before the Akamba spies left their territory they consulted with the prophet to receive counsel and advice. Certain signs of fortune were given. If the spies would see a certain woodpecker during the day or if they spied a certain insect during the night, they would return home immediately. This insect cannot fly at night because of the cold. Such signs would foretell bad luck.

If the prophet predicted some pending disaster, he could also prescribe the means by which they would protect themselves. For instance, he might order the slaughter of a goat. The blood was mixed with a purifying medicine (*ng'ondu*) and sprinkled on all the people. Or he would prescribe a goat to be led away into the bush in order to carry the epidemic or disease away from the people. A most common method was to slaughter the kid of a goat and bury it on the path where the people would pass. If the epidemic would come, it would be vanquished when passing over that spot. Not only was the goat buried, but the blood was put into a container and mixed with cooked porridge and eaten by the people. The rest of the blood was sprinkled on the shrine (*ithembo*) and on the people.

Diviners. The more common wise man was the diviner, the *mundu mue wa kititi,* whom we have been calling the medicine man. This diviner used the divination balls (*mbuu*) of his profession, placed in the the small divining gourd. He would talk to the gourd as if he were talking to a spirit inside it. As he talked, he shook the divining balls in the gourd and poured them out at intervals. Different interpretations are based on different patterns.If a Mukamba became ill he would normally seek traditional herbal treatment. If the illness persisted or seemed unusually serious he would then consult the medicine man to know whether he was being troubled by an ancestor or whether he had been bewitched.

Whenever something goes wrong for an individual or a family, or whenever something unusual happens, he would traditionally feel a need for the divining skills of the medicine man to determine WHO had caused this problem and WHY. Steps would need to be taken in order to prevent continuing havoc and possible disaster. For this need the medicine man is indispensable.

If the medicine man divines that an enemy has bewitched him, he is able to treat the client with magical instruments and to attack the powers of the wizard. The medicine man places pegs in a circle in the ground and requests the patient to lie in the circle. The Diviner then goes around the person, speaking magical words and expressing the authority he has been given by his ancestral spirits to overcome the powers of the witch. He then smears the patient with magical powder. Some herbs are eaten. The patient then soon becomes well. Magical powder can also be given to harm the witch, if he so desires.

It is customary to take some payment for the wise man, though the exact payment differed from person to person, and from place to place. In some cases two goats were brought, one to be sacrificed to the ancestors by the medicine man and the other as payment to the wise man for his services. Sometimes part of the goat's skin is offered to the ancestors and tied on the thigh or arm. Payment might be in food stuffs, grain or currency. At the turn of the century the cost to consult the medicine man was two arrows or six cents (Lindblom 1920:261).

The act of seeking help from the medicine man is called kwausya in Kikamba. The client who comes for help is called a muausya. (For a detailed account see Lindblom 1920:258-268; Ndeti 1972:120,121; Beresford- Stooke 1928c:189) Lindblom contends that "the main part of each medicine man's practice consists of 'kuausya-ing,' i.e. with the help of the aimu [ancestral spirits] to predict things, to state also whether a project will succeed or not, find out the cause of a thing, etc." (Lindblom 1920:258).

The chief instrument which the medicine man uses to divine is a little bow, a traditional instrument constructed like a hunter's bow, but smaller. A taut string is affixed to the bow with a calabash between the string and bow, the calabash serving as a sounding board. (Today some medicine men have been known to use a concertina as a divining instrument.) The diviner plays the string and bow by hitting or plucking the string with a wooden stick, up and down, while singing. He asks the ancestral spirits to help solve the problem. His ear is placed near the gourd so that he can hear the sound of the vibrations which form the answers from the ancestors (Nottingham 1959:10).

Sometime thereafter, he takes his divining gourd containing the divination seeds (mbuu) and shakes it. He then pours out some of the divining seeds onto the skin, frequently a leopard skin in the old days, or a goat skin today. Lindblom theorized that the leopard represents strength and therefore enhances the powers of the wise man. Parts of the leopard, such as the claws, are ground into powder and eaten to gain the strength and courage of the leopard. The significance of goats, Lindblom suggests, is due to their close association with the ancestral spirits, being the chief animal sacrificed for the ancestors (Lindblom 1920:261).

The details of the divining vary from one diviner to another. The medicine man may count the divination seeds which come out of the gourd. Or the client may be asked to lay the seeds in piles of five each. During the time the divination seeds are being counted, the diviner is playing his divination bow. From the few remaining divination seeds, those less than five, the diviner makes his interpretation. At other times the total number of seeds might be counted. An even number of seeds means good luck while an odd number would mean bad luck. Sometimes the client is asked to spit on the divination gourd and ask his question. The divination seeds which then tumble from the gourd forms the basis for divination.

By interpreting the divination seeds which fall from the divination gourd, the diviner determines the message from the ancestors. Some representative answers might include the following. "The *aimu* now want the goat which you had promised your dead father." "You have misused something which belongs to the *aimu*." Such faults in neglecting or dishonoring the ancestral spirits necessitated restitution to be made for the ancestors in order for blessing to return upon the family. If the client requested the ancestors to increase his wealth, the *aimu* might respond that a goat or bull would be born every October. In order to protect the flock a small boy or girl had to walk around the flock to protect the animals from disease.

Sometimes the medicine man would advise the sick client that he should go to certain women, be placed in their midst, and have a traditional dance (*kilumi*) played. At the conclusion of the dance, some woman would be possessed by the ancestral spirits who would inform the sick person what was wanted, perhaps a goat, bull, or piece of cloth. Immediately, or soon thereafter, having fulfilled their request, the sick person would be healed.

Some medicine men, especially those from Mombasa or Zanzibar, use mirrors instead of the divining bow. These can tell the full identity when they first appear to the medicine man, a complete stranger. He can identify the client's problem before being told. Some allow the client to see his own house in the mirror and the witch actually planting a charm in his homestead.

Let us describe the divining of a particular medicine man. Mutiso described his visit to the medicine man when he went, seeking a job.

Inside the workshop the medicine man laid down a long skin and over it he placed a white cloth sheet. Then I was ordered to remove my clothes except my underwear. He took off his clothes and started his job. He took a gourd full of divination seeds and jumped over me while I was lying on the white sheet. Two balls came out. Then Mutua put on his special clothes, a red cloth with black stripes. Then he took his bow and inserted the half gourd (used for dipping) and then played the bow while dancing and jumping over me. He ran around me. He threw an arrow which dropped on my throat. Then he stopped his exercise. The medicine man took a razor blade and cut several lines on my chest. He then poured magical powders (muthea) on the cuts. He then crushed the two divination balls which had come out into powder and smeared it on the lines he had cut on my chest. Taking another horn he used the contents to smear more black powder on the lines. He then ran and hid behind the red curtain. When he reappeared, Mutua then gave me a little bag full of medicine (muthea) and ordered me to wear it on my body all the time. He then asked me for a she goat which I brought back to him. He instructed me not to return home but to go straight to Thika and look for a job. Soon after I arrived, I was employed and have remained employed ever since.

These diviners, though powerful and feared, are not always believed as illustrated in this story. One medicine man reported that his ancestral spirit said that the reason for the destructive birds destroying the millet was because of a failure to offer a sacrifice. If two black goats would be offered, the destructive birds would cease. When they offered the sacrifices, the medicine man informed the people that their millet was now being guarded by the ancestors and there was no need to send people to the gardens to watch over the crops. But Mwangangi did not trust the medicine man so he went early in the morning to watch over his millet field. There he saw an enormous creature with manlike features, large flaming eyes staring at him and about to attack him. Thereupon Mwangangi fled, being assured that the millet was indeed being protected by the ancestral spirits.

A Cleansing Herbalist. The third type of wise man (*mundu mue*) is a cleansing herbalist known as a *mundu mue wa ng'ondu*.

Lindblom defines *Muthea* as a "medicine of a more or less magic character." (Lindblom 1920:270) While the average Mukamba may know about the plant, they do not know how to use it effectively because only the medicine man has "the key" to its effective power, through the use of incantations.

Such magical medicines may be used to cure a woman of barrenness. The process of curing a barren woman is through the use of purification medicines (*ng'ondu*). The medicine man prepares the medicine from a particular tree. This herb is ground into powder and mixed with herbs and water. A part of the tree is tied together with a rag, then dipped in the *ng'ondu* herbs. The string is made from the bark of a particular tree which is then used to tie the rag onto the twig. The woman is then not allowed to remove this object, the rag tied onto the twig, until she gives birth to a child. The charm has magical powers of causing conception of the woman.

If the woman has a miscarriage or gives birth to an abnormal or dead child, this indicates that she had committed incest with a relative. A child born with yellow skin or a soft head or some other deformity indicates a problem of incest. Even if the girl does not become pregnant during incest, her future children in marriage will die. This requires different treatment to appease the ancestral spirits.

For this problem the purifying medicine (*ng'ondu*) is mixed with other herbs. While the woman stands, the *ng'ondu* is passed across her and eventually placed between her legs. A substance is given her in order to make her vomit the sin which she had committed. When she does give birth to a child, she dare not look at the infant until both she and her husband are treated with purifying medicine. It is applied to the eyes, the breasts of the woman, and on the sheets wrapped around the child. They must say then, "I had my eyes opened with *ng'ondu* to see my child."

This purifying medicine (*ng'ondu*) is also used to treat cattle for certain epidemics and to remove a curse placed upon a person. This specialist is called to remove the magical horns through the use of his purifying medicines.

This specialist, sometimes called a herbalist, should not be confused, however, with a true herbalist (*mukimi wa miti*). The true herbalist uses herbal medicine obtained from trees, bushes and herbs. This kind of herbal remedy is known to others beside the medicine man (*mundu mue wa ng'ondu*) and can be used by anyone who searches for the herb and prepares it for himself. But the herbalist is a specialist in his field.

Under the guidance of the ancestral spirits the herbalist (*mukimi wa miti*) identifies various roots and leaves which may be ground into powder and used for medication. Many of these medicines have been recognized by western medical practitioners, such as the World Health Organization (W.H.O.) of the United Nations. Many have been tested in laboratories and found to be curative.

In Kenya there has been established the Traditional Medicines and Drugs Research Centre at the Kenya Medical Research Institute (KEMRI) in Nairobi. Through scientific research they have established cures through traditional herbal medicines for 11 diseases including asthma, diabetes, epilepsy, hypertension and various cancers. They encourage collaboration between the traditional herbal medicine practioners and the conventional doctors. Use of traditional herbal medicines first entails the identification of medicinal plants followed by the collection, hygienic drying, grinding, mixing, packaging and storing of those medicines. The University of Nairobi has established a herbal medicine garden for scientific research into the medicinal value of various plants and herbs.

Whereas, the medicine man herbalist heals people through magical medicines, the true herbalist uses only natural methods. When the patient describes his illness, the true herbalist can identify the illness and prescribe the herbs for treatment.

Several examples are these. For the symptoms of chest pains, the inner bark of the *musemei* is chewed. To eliminate worms they chew the bark of the *mwooa* herb or the *mutonga tongu*. Malaria is treated by *muvau* or *mutuiie*.

Most of these herbs are very bitter. Patients are advised to mix the herb with water or soup to reduce the bitterness. Because the cure is through natural means only, Christians in Machakos regularly seek treatment from them without any sense of guilt.

One practicing herbalist, now 70 years old, described how she became a herbalist. It should be noted, however, that she is both a herbalist and a diviner (*mundu mue*).

> I became sick which was a sign that my spirit wanted me to start dealings with herbs. I was taken back to my parents' home. My husband took a goat and beer with him. My father also offered beer and a goat. My father and my husband respectively ground some herbs and put them into different gourds. These were put into two baskets. A bow was made for me with a string made from tendons of the two goats. I then used the bow for divination (singing to motivate the spirits to communicate with me), and the herb powder for treating. After some people had given me some money, I was able to treat them.

From that day onwards she became both a diviner and a herbalist.

A person can therefore be both a diviner and a herbalist, while others are a true herbalist only. Both Christians and non-Christians believe that these herbs have been created by God for the purpose of benefiting people by healing them. Anyone can gather these herbs from the bush to treat a particular sickness. These herbs often need no additional powers from the ancestors.

It is of interest, however, that many true herbalists also say magical words. Magical words are spoken by the true herbalist either to empower the herbs or to remove the harmful, poisonous effect. These words are spoken while standing on the eastern side of the bush and throwing ashes from the fireplace three or seven times, speaking the words as he throws. While some herbs don't need this empowering, most true herbalists say these magical words to enhance their effectiveness.

The exact nature of this power is not clear. Saying the magical words (*kuthyuua*) is a tradition handed down from the forefathers. It is, therefore, a kind of delegated power, assumed by some to come originally from God. The words themselves have power derived from the ancestors who handed the tradition over to the new generation of specialists.

It is of interest that even the true herbalist is sometimes instructed by his spirit. Wambua was told at night by his ancestral spirit which herbs to take from the field. He was then told to get a goat and traditional beer, to grind the herbs and mix it with the beer and part of the goat and then take it. Then his ancestral spirit brought a sick person to him. His spirit instructed him to give this herb to the sick person who was then healed.

There are those individuals who affirm that a traditional herbalist did not use witchcraft, sorcery or magic in his practice. We have found such evidence in parts of Machakos. However in Kitui it appears that mystical powers more frequently played a role in the use of herbal treatment.

From our limited research in this area, it would appear that the people knew of leaves and roots and were able to obtain these by themselves in order to treat physical illnesses. But such personal use of herbs was different from consulting a specialist. All those who were professed herbalists had the tendency of diagnosing and curing diseases through the use of herbal medicines in association with the spirits and magic. Such specialists are not prepared to teach others their skills, saying their knowledge was imparted by dreams.

While some may claim that the *mukimi wa miti* is a pure herbalist, the evidence given above suggests that even his knowledge and application of the herb is closely associated with spirits and magic. One Christian Mukamba from Kitui made this observation.

> The claim that Akamba herbalists are pure herbalists is a recent innovation and an academic approach. The typical tradition of all Akamba herbalists was associated with spirits and the use of prayers. In my home area in Kitui no Christian goes to a herbalist for medicines, because of their association with spirits and the medicine man.

Magic

Whereas, the witch specializes in black magic to the detriment of people, the medicine man engages in white magic which protects people from the witch and empowers him to achieve his desires.

A visit to the medicine man can provide the client with love magic by which the love of a woman or man can be won. The medicine man provides a kind of love potion. This can be used to win the love of another. If a man desired very much to sleep with a girl, he would purchase this love medicine and place it in a feather. "You, so and so, I have called you into my house," he would say. Then he would place the feather in the thatched roof of the girl's house. In a few days, the girl would show up. Another kind of love potion was placed secretly in the girl's food. But this kind of love will last only as long as the love potion endures. A stronger kind of love potion is used by a wife in a polygamous marriage. If she wants her husband to love her more than the other wives, she will go to a traditional doctor for the love potion. This type will last longer and is more effective.

Another kind of magic potion is used in seeking wealth and employment. Many people use this type of magic to acquire a job.

Early in the morning you rub the magic potion on your hands and swallow some medicines while saying these words, "I take this medicine to enable me to gain favor before the employers I will meet this day." When you approach the place of employment, you rub the medicine on your face, on the back of your head and on your toes and heels, saying these words. "If the back of the head ever became the face, let it be so today. If the sun ever rose from the west, let it be so today. I make all other job seekers the heel, the back of the head, while I myself the face and the toe. I now open my eyes to see myself being employed."

You then rub powder on your hands, saying, "I mix my words with the words of the employer like this powder in my hands." With these words you ask that the employer will listen and agree to the request. The job seeker then bites a piece of the stick which makes him attractive to the ears of the prospective employer. This advice was given by a diviner and herbalist who claims to have helped many find a job. He has also given magic potions to those wanting a girl friend or wanting to pass their examination. This magical medicine can also be used by businessmen in the market places in order to attract more customers for himself, causing the prospective customers to desert the other salesmen and resort to him.

Another kind of magical powder (*nzevu*) can be placed in the palm of the hand and blown into the air, while uttering words with a specific intention. The words then become potent and effective in fulfilling one's wish. *Nzevu* can also be used in land cases. This magic powder can be poured at the place where the case will be discussed. When the proper ritual and ceremonial words are spoken, the magical powder will stupefy the minds of the elders and favour the user of the magic. It blinds the eyes of the judge so that the verdict is decided in the way the user of the magic desires.

Protective amulets are available for almost every problem associated with witchcraft. Such amulets traditionally consisted of little horns from small antelopes and filled with a magical potion. Sometimes the fangs of a lion or a leopard were worn. They would be worn around the neck, the waist or on the upper arm. These days they may be placed secretly on the body but under the clothes so that they are not seen. (See Hobley 1967:24,25 for a fascinating description of the various charms available for protection.) Magic can be used to protect a home from witches. A medicine man comes, encircles the house, and buries a charm, a small horn with magical contents. If anyone tries to harm you, he will either die or be found outside your house, mentally confused.

Imitative magic, though present among the Akamba, is not so prominent. When Kenya demonstrated against Idi Amin's territorial ambitions against Kenya, the Akamba leaders of Machakos made a big doll representing Idi Amin. They shot it and burned it to harm Amin. This type of imitative magic, however, is more common at the coast than in Ukambani.

There is another type of magic which may sometimes be used for entertainment. *Syama* (magic) may be performed with the skill of hand by which a person is turned into an animal or snake. This is a form of clever use of the hand which cheats the mind and deceives the eyes.

But we cannot restrict *syama* to mere entertainment. It can also be used for a serious purpose of chasing away elephants from the gardens. Thus *syama* may be for entertainment or for a serious purpose, the latter assuming some supernatural powers. But *syama* always has a positive end result, either deliverance from danger or for entertainment. (See Appendix C for a discussion of further kinds of mystical powers among the Akamba.)

CONCLUSION

Mystical powers are a highly developed concept among the Akamba, as among most other African peoples. Through traditional means ATR provided protection and guidance in a world filled with malice and greed. Despite the availability of professional help from the medicine man, however, fear and suspicion were prevalent. It was this factor, providentially, that prepared many Africans for the preaching of the Gospel which offered security and hope through Jesus Christ to those living in fear.

REVIEW QUESTIONS FOR CHAPTER 5

1. Discuss the mystical power evidenced in such traditional practices as the curse, the oath, the evil tongue and the evil eye among the Akamba (see also Appendix C). Do you find anything comparable among your own peoples? Discuss the similarities and differences.

2. Discuss the person and work of the witch among the Akamba and all the evil powers associated with witchcraft. How does this compare or contrast with witchcraft among your own peoples?

3. Contrast and compare the witch (*muoi*) and the medicine man (*mundu mue*) among the Akamba.

4. What evidence do we find of spirit activity in and through the medicine man among the Akamba?

5. Among the Akamba the medicine man may specialize as a prophet, a diviner or a cleansing herbalist. Discuss the work of these different specialists. Compare these with the specialists among your own people.

Suggested Reading and Thought Questions for Advanced Study:

Crawford, J.R. *Witchcraft and Sorcery in Rhodesia*, 1967, (Shona of Zimbabwe).

Evans-Pritchard, E.E. *Witchcraft, Oracles and Magic Among the Azande*, 1937, (Azande of the Nile-Congo).

Field, M.J. *Religion and Medicine of the Ga People*, 1961, pp.110-160,

(Ghana).

Harwood, Alan. *Witchcraft, Sorcery and Social Categories Among the Safwa*, 1970.

Kenyatta, Jomo. *Facing Mt. Kenya*, n.d., pp.280-308, (Gikuyu of Kenya).

Maclean, Una. *Magical Medicine - A Nigerian Case Study*, 1974.

Marwick, B.A. *The Swazi*, 1966, pp.234-253, (Swazi of Swaziland).

Melland, Frank. *In Witchbound Africa*, 1967, pp.183-248, (Kaonde of Zimbabwe).

P'Bitek, Okot. *Religion of the Central Luo*, 1971, pp.121-153, (Luo of Uganda).

Setiloane, Gabriel. *The Image of God Among the Sotho-Tswana*, 1976, pp.45-63.

Talbot, P. Amaury. *Tribes of the Niger Delta*, 1967, pp.108-147.

1. Do research on witchcraft and sorcery among two other African peoples (from two of the books recommended above or among your own peoples). Compare the similarities and differences of these beliefs with those mentioned here for the Akamba. What does this tell you of the unity and plurality of African religions?

2. Research the calling, empowering and work of the medicine man (or a prophet, diviner or rainmaker) among your own people or from a written account. To what extent are the spirits involved in the life of each of these specialists, compared to the specialists described among the Akamba.

3. How is the pure herbalist different from the medicine man? Are there herbalists among your people who are pure herbalists or do they also have guidance and empowering from the spirit world?

4. Describe the traditional charms used among your people intended to protect from evil and misfortune. To what extent do Christians in your church continue to depend on traditional charms? Why do they continue this traditional practice?

Chapter 6

MYSTICAL POWERS WORLDWIDE

Africa is not alone in the experience of mystical powers of unseen forces. Pagan religious belief has been hard to eliminate in lands where the Gospel has been preached for centuries. Today, despite scientific knowledge, there is a revival of witchcraft, spiritism and the occult in the West and a persistence of belief in mystical powers worldwide. In fact belief and practice in the occult is the fastest growing religion of the United States and Western Europe (see Lindsey 1973).

From time to time even some western leaders depend on mystical powers for guidance and protection. Donald Regan, former White House Chief of Staff for President Ronald Reagan of the United States, disclosed in his book, *For the Record*, how astrology greatly influenced the schedules and plans of the former President and First Lady of the most powerful nation on earth. When plans were made for the Reagan-Gorbachev Washington summit in 1987, an astrologer cast the charts of both men and determined that 2:00 P.M. on December 8, 1987 was the most propitious moment for them to sign the intermediate-range nuclear forces treaty. The entire summit was built around that hour. Furthermore, President and Mrs. Reagan are known for their superstitions, observing rituals as knocking on wood and walking around and not under ladders. The President also puts a lucky gold charm in his pocket every morning. Although the President seems to have a deep Christian faith, he seems untroubled by the contradictions of depending on the mystical powers of astrology even while professing faith in Christ and the Gospel.

MAGIC

Many different kinds of magic have been used since ancient times and continue to be practiced throughout many parts of the world today. Magic is said to heal or bring disease, lead people to love or hate one another, produce children in the family or destroy them, increase the numbers of cattle and livestock or bring about devastating epidemics, cause a bountiful harvest or a destructive drought, protect from evil and death or bring about sickness and death.

Examples from every part of the earth can be collected in great numbers. Our purpose here is merely to illustrate briefly what could be demonstrated exhaustively.

Magical practices, complete with formulas and ritual, were prevalent in Europe. "Abracadabra" is a word of magical connotations. The first reference to "Abracadabra" is found in the second century after Christ when Quintus

Serenus Sammonicus, the personal physician of the Roman Emperor, used the word in order to relieve the Emperor of his fever. It was believed that if "abracadabra" was written on an amulet and worn around the neck for nine days, then thrown over the shoulder into water flowing eastward, the fever would be relieved (Newall 1974:12).

White magicians in Europe were known as "cunning folk." "Cunning" had different connotations in those days from today. "Cunning folk" were possessed with a special knowledge or cunning, believed to be from supernatural powers. These "cunning folk" were consulted for many problems, for instance to locate a thief, find stolen goods, identify a witch or cure a disease. These cunning white magicians were very popular in England (Newall 1974:61,62).

The Bishop of Troyes is an example of image magic. In A.D. 1308, this Roman Catholic Bishop was tried for the murder of Queen Jeanne, wife of Philip IV of France. He apparently sought the help of a witch who used the powers of a demon. A wax image was made and baptized with the name "Jeanne," representing the queen. Needles were then placed in the head and other parts of the body. As a result, the queen became ill and could not be cured. More pins were stuck into the image "until it looked like a pin cushion. Jeanne still refused to die. The Bishop, in a fury, cried out, 'How, devil, will this woman live forever?' He knocked the limbs off the image and tore it into bits; he trampled on the pieces and threw them in the fire. The queen died." (Howells 1948:51,52)

A report is given of a Christian pastor in Germany in recent years who was used to cure a woman possessed by a spirit and protected by a charm. When this lady fell into a spell, her whole character changed and she spoke with a deep male voice. One day the pastor noticed a leather packet on her neck. When he snatched it from her, a male voice like that of a well-known gypsy cried out, "Don't give up that sack." As soon as the pastor removed the charm, the spell was broken and the woman completely cured. Inside the charm was a little paper with these words, "I am he that holds the seven agues in hand and can send out the seven powers and if you hide this and live in my name, you will succeed in all things, and I will protect you." (Unger 1972:91)

Healing has always been a popular reason for magic. Dr. Kurt Koch reports on Harry Edwards in England, "one of the most dangerous healers in the Western world." An average of 10,000 letters were written to him weekly. He was president of the National Federation of Spiritual Healers with 2,000 members. This organization had been granted permission to give treatment in 1,700 British hospitals when their service was requested. Harry Edwards had developed the ability of healing the sick from a distance. Remarkable examples are recorded of people suffering from different illnesses being cured through him. He had also developed the ability "to travel out of his physical body to the place where his patient is, the so-called art of spirit traveling or excursion of the soul." When asked about his powers, he states that they stem "from his spirit guides on the other side." "In my view," Edwards writes, "this is the same divine power which streamed through the healer of Nazareth in Bible days and produced results that the orthodox regard as miracles." (Koch 1970:44-48)

Contagious magic is widespread. The Apaches in North America believe that anything closely associated with any person can be used to harm that person. Therefore, the afterbirth is never buried for fear of an animal digging it up and eating it. Instead, it is wrapped in an old cloth on which the mother has knelt. The bundle is blessed by the midwife and placed in a fruit-bearing tree. The thought is this. Even as the tree comes to life every year, so the child will be renewed every year. A prayer is said to the tree with these words, "May the child live and grow up to see you bear fruit many times."

DIVINATION

From ancient times until the present, man has been curious about his future and fortune. There have been many different ways used in telling the future (see "Divination" in Hastings ed. 1909:775-829).

Divination by Examining Dead Animals

Many peoples examine the liver in order to divine the future. This form of divination was found among the Babylonians in 2,000 B.C. Today it is still practiced in Asia, Africa and sections in the West. Ancient clay models of the liver have been discovered in which each part was inscribed with its meaning. Generally, a specialist is required to interpret the meaning of the liver or internal organs. Often the animal is first sacrificed and is then examined by a priest. There is complex symbolism as they interpret the internal organs.

Widespread is the practice of divination from the cracks which develop in scorched shoulder blades. It may have come from China where it was known 1,000 B.C. From there it spread to Japan, Siberia, Central Asia and westward to the Byzantine Empire, north Africa and parts of Arabia, Afghanistan and India. This was popular in Europe in the 15th and 16th centuries and can still be found among certain rural populations.

The shoulder blades of seals and reindeer are used among the Siberians. Domesticated animals, especially sheep, are used elsewhere. Scorching is omitted among the north Africans and Europeans. Instead, the shape, thickness and veining of the bone is studied.

Divination by Examining Living Animals

Nearly all peoples have considered the movement of birds or beasts to have special meaning. This form of divination is called "augury." The Etruscans of Italy divined the future by interpreting the flight or action of birds. With the spread of the Christian faith in Europe, this practice declined. But the belief spread eastward. Even today, the priests of Borneo and the Philippines foretell the future through the observation of the flight of birds and the examination of the gall bladder, an organ closely associated with the liver.

Living animals may serve in other ways to help people divine the future. Among the Melanesians there is a particular bird which makes a peculiar noise. This is taken to be a "no." Any other noise means "yes." The Melanesians thus ask the bird various questions. They can divine, "yes" or "no," through the bird's crowing and chatter.

Divination by Examining the Stars

The pseudo-science of telling the future by the study of the stars, known as astrology, can be traced back to 3,000 B.C. It was found in Sumeria, Chaldea and Babylon, then later spread to Greece, Rome and Europe.

It was based on the belief that the sun, moon and planets were living beings, gods, each possessing a preferred "house" among the stars. The path (zodiac) of the sun, moon and planets was divided into twelve parts, each represented by an emblem: ram, bull, twins, crab, lion, virgin, scales, scorpion, archer, goat, water carrier and fish.

Prediction of one's fortune including his life, death, wealth, marriage, children, friendship and fate in general was determined by a clever study of the relationship of the stars and their positions at the time of birth. For they assumed that the position of these deities influenced the affairs of the earth. The sun, moon and Venus were thought to control the zodiacal signs and thus influence the increase or decay, the light and darkness, cold and heat, life and death on the earth.

Despite scientific advance, today we find a revival of this pagan practice throughout the western world. There are more than 10,000 full-time astrologers in the United States and 175,000 part-time ones. Half of all the published newspapers in the United States, more than 1,200 daily newspapers, carry horoscopes which explain your fortune by the zodiac. "Christian" presidents are known to consult astrologers for guidance in making public decisions. A computer has been programmed by Time Pattern Research Institute to turn out a 10,000 word horoscope reading in two minutes. Their goal is to publish 10,000 such horoscopes monthly. Through western influence, astrology has been introduced to Africa in the form of horoscopes found in the newspapers. Thus the pagan influence from the West is infiltrating Africa through publicly sanctioned newspapers.

Divination by Mechanical Means

The Romans developed a system of little tablets with written symbols so that the future could be foretold. By A.D. 800 they had begun using cards. The system is quite simple. Meanings are attached to certain cards. After they are mixed up, the various combinations of cards are full of meaning as they are laid out on the table.

Ruth Montgomery, who uses these cards in our times in the West, does not even look at them. She claims they were blessed by a "sweet old gypsy." "Because she blessed them, they carry good vibrations. I don't know a single thing about telling fortunes with cards," she writes. "I simply have a person hold them so that I can pick up his vibrations." (Unger 1972:62)

Other mechanical means include throwing of dice or pebbles to observe whether an odd number or an even number appears. In the South Pacific a mangrove- embryo is used to determine the sex of an unborn child. The expecting mother throws it between her legs. If it flies straight, it signifies a boy, but if it flies crooked, the baby will be a girl.

Divination or fortune telling can also be done through the interpretation of the lines in a persons hands. This art was invented by the Babylonians over 4,000 years ago.

Divination by Possession

Peoples in Asia, Europe, the Americas and Africa, have all divined the future through specialists who became possessed, either by some ancestral spirit or by another spirit. Among the peoples of Siberia, a shaman is possessed by the ancestral spirits.

> The individual marked out by the might of the ancestors for shamanhood feels a sudden faintness and exhaustion...a heavy weight presses on his breast and suddenly wrings from him violent, inarticulate screams. (After wild paroxysms he sinks to the ground.) His limbs are wholly insensitive; he snatches whatever he can lay his hands on, and swallows aimlessly everything he gets hold of — hot iron, knives, needles...afterwards casting up dry and uninjured what he has swallowed (Rose 1909:777).

The Shaman then seizes a shaman's drum and exercises his gifts of divination. Sometimes the spirits speak through the mouth of the shaman or divination is made known through the drumming. He is able to foretell the future through the agency of the ancestral spirit.

Divination Through Dreams and Visions

Jeanne Dixon in the United States became "the most famous seeress of the century." Her first vision occurred in 1952 when a huge serpent slowly twisted itself around her body. Looking into her eyes the serpent breathed out love, goodness and strength. This vision she considers the key to other visions.

Her self proclaimed most important vision was in 1962 when she saw a baby born in the East with eyes full of wisdom. As he grew a cross formed above him and grew in size until people of every race knelt before this man. Her interpretation is that on February 5, 1962, a child was born somewhere in the Middle East who would revolutionize the world. By the end of the century all people will join together in a new Christianity with every denomination and religion united through this man (cf. Unger 1972:69).

Only time will verify or disprove the authenticity of this vision. It could prove to be empty self-delusion. Later she changed her opinion and said that the baby was to be the future anti-christ. Whatever the final assessment of Jeanne Dixon may be, we can at least affirm that modern man still seeks security and assurance through knowledge of future events through dreams and visions.

WITCHCRAFT

Witchcraft and sorcery are found in every corner of the globe. Of special interest is the witchcraft that became popular in Europe during the Middle Ages and the Renaissance, for witchcraft in Europe and Africa are "easily comparable." Parrinder has concluded his research by saying that there is "an astonishing resemblance between these modern African beliefs and those of

Europe centuries ago." (Parrinder 1958:138)
Following are some of the characteristics of European witches 200 years ago (see Parrinder 1958:9-116).

Night-Flying

It was thought that witches could ride at night time on certain animals in order to attend an assembly or coven with other witches in some lonely spot. This night activity was explained by the phenomena of dreams. While the body remains asleep, the spirit escapes and wanders about at night, so they thought. Certain ointments were allegedly used to make this night-flying possible. Sometimes it was said that this ointment was made from the flesh of unbaptized children. Thus witchcraft was primarily a night time activity and anti-social.

Animal Familiars

Witches were usually associated with some animal familiar, like a bird, hare, rat, toad, duck, lizard, goat or dog. The most common familiar was the black cat. Hence, for many Europeans, a black cat walking in front of them means bad luck. It was also believed that a witch could change herself into an animal. Hence, there was fear of vampires and werewolves which sucked the blood of a victim.

Eating Human Flesh

Witches were accused of killing and eating unbaptized children. Magical potions were sprinkled around the house of a victim in order to cause the parents to fall into a deep sleep. While they slept at night, the witch could enter the house, touch the infant with poisonous hands and cause the death of the child in a few days. Or the souls were eaten while the body still remained in the cradle, so they believed.

Other Activities

Some witches were accused of celebrating devilish sacraments in baptism and communion. Thus the Lord's Supper was celebrated in communion with the Devil and called the Black Mass. Like African witches, they were blamed for barrenness, impotence, dryness in nursing mothers, paralysis, leprosy, epilepsy, dropsy and other diseases. Horses going mad, plagues and pestilence, unusual weather and storms were all blamed on the witches.

Reginold Scot, who lived during the great fears of witchcraft, writes this observation of Europe in a manner similar to what we have found in Africa.

> For if any adversity, grief, sickness, loss of children, corn, cattle, or liberty happen unto them; by and by they exclaim upon witches. As if there were no God in Israel that ordereth all things according to his will...but that certain old women here on earth, called witches, must needs be the contrivers [causes] of all men's calamities...Insomuch as a clap of thunder, or a gale of wind is no sooner heard, but either they run to bells or cry out to burn the witches (Parrinder 1958:58).

Witch Hunts

During certain periods, both Europeans and American authorities engaged in witch hunts with the blessing and encouragement of the churches. When magic and sorcery were thought to be on the increase in the 15th century, England under Queen Elizabeth and James I brought many people accused of witchcraft to trial and execution. New England during the 17th century likewise saw a mania in witch hunts.

Scholars estimate that some 300,000 witches were killed in Europe and America. The worst persecution was in Germany with an alleged 100,000 witches burned. Estimates for England vary from 30,000 to 70,000. Clearly these are mere guesses with a real tendency toward exaggeration. Nevertheless, we are compelled to accept the historical fact that many thousands and tens of thousands of people were killed, largely on their own confessions of witchcraft activities.

Witchcraft Today in the West

Witchcraft is not only a topic of antiquity in the West. Witchcraft in the west is a modern phenomena. Referring to the explosion of the occult in the West, Parrinder says one could speak of this as a revival of the belief in witchcraft (Parrinder 1976:182). And Summers describes western spiritism as "modern witchcraft" (Summers 1973:xii).

The fact is that many of the modern rites and practices of witches have been used for centuries. Modern witches in the West can allegedly cause someone pain, sickness and death through psychic powers from a distance. They claim to be able to transform themselves into animals (Boa 1981).

CONCLUSION

From time immemorial peoples of all races and continents have believed in the mystical powers of magic, witchcraft and sorcery. Not only have they exercised belief in such numinous powers, they have found the explanation for life's fortunes and failures in them and sought refuge in their power. Africans are not alone in their traditional fear of mystical powers. Underlying all the diversity and dissimilarity of mankind, there is remarkable similarity. Beneath the differences of colour and culture there is the similarity of man's nature which has found a fascination for mystical powers.

REVIEW QUESTIONS FOR CHAPTER 6

1. Discuss belief in magic, divination and witchcraft found in other places throughout the world.

2. How widespread has this belief in mystical powers been throughout Europe and America?

3. What does this teach us concerning the universal nature of man?

Suggested Reading and Thought Questions for Advanced Study:

Hastings, James ed. *Encyclopaedia of Religion and Ethics*, Vol. VII, "Magic": pp.245-321.

Howells, William. *The Heathens: Primitive Man and His Religions*, 1948, pp.25-144.

Lessa, William and Evon Vogt eds. *Reader in Comparative Religion*, 1965, pp.413-465; 381-412.

Parrinder, Geoffrey. *Witchcraft: European and African*, 1963.

Thomas, Keith. *Religion and the Decline of Magic*, 1971.

Zwemer, Samuel. *The Influence of Animism on Islam*, 1920.

1. Why do you believe peoples all over the world have resorted to magic, divination and witchcraft from time immemorial up to the present day?

2. How can you explain the many similarities in mystical powers worldwide with the mystical powers in ATR?

3. Why is it wrong to single out ATR and find in traditional African belief some extraordinary superstition or error in mystical powers different from the other peoples of the world?

Chapter 7

MYSTICAL POWERS IN BIBLICAL PERSPECTIVE

NATURE OF ASSESSMENT

What are the different possible ways by which we could evaluate and assess traditional belief in mystical powers?

We could simply embrace uncritically the emic perspective. Whatever the traditional African has believed, we also believe. Without any sense of discernment, we could accept what they taught and believed. Because they believed it, we also believe it.

However, there are some weighty reasons militating against uncritical acceptance of traditional beliefs. Apart from the traditionalists themselves, just about everyone else evaluates ATR somewhat differently from the traditionalists. If in fact you would embrace en toto what ATR has taught and practiced, you would then become an adherent of ATR. But even those ardent nationalists who call for a return to traditional African culture make their own discrimination between what they are willing to accept and follow and what they reject. Thus there must be some other criteria by which we make a critical judgment of ATR.

Today many scholars of ATR assess traditional mystical powers in Africa by the measuring standard of natural science. Modern man, schooled with his anti-supernatural bias, is unwilling to accept the possibility of the supernatural.

For example, Evans-Pritchard writes, "Witchcraft is an imaginary offense because it is impossible. A witch cannot do what he is supposed to do and has in fact no real existence." (Parrinder 1958:166) You will recall the anthropological distinction between witchcraft and sorcery. Evans-Pritchard does believe in sorcery with its use of black magic and poisons. But he denies the reality of witchcraft which is psychic and uses no paraphernalia or poisons. By this he certainly does not mean that there are no people who *think* they are witches. In fact, he and others have compiled a vast array of confessions made by self-proclaimed witches, both in Europe and Africa. But he contends that, apart from personal confessions made by witches, there is no empirical evidence supporting the reality of witchcraft.

Many Europeans contend that witches in fact do not exist because witchcraft is an impossibility. Witchcraft is merely a means of interpreting the jealousies and hatred in society. They help to interpret life with its mysteries and help to channel feelings of aggression. Witchcraft is a means of releasing the tensions and frustrations in society in a communally accepted manner. Witchcraft is symbolic, but not a reality, for witchcraft is impossible.

It is rare among Europeans to find those anthropologists or students of religion who accept the objective reality of mystical powers in the African beliefs. Dr. Kurt Koch, a German evangelical who has counseled 20,000 people over the past forty years all over the world, especially those in occult bondage, has said, "If one talks to scientists today on the matter of occult subjection (i.e. depression that stems from demon possession), it is often almost like talking to a brick wall. Any psychiatrist who is not a truly born again Christian would simply deny the existence of occult subjection and oppression." (Koch 1970:30) In his book, he gives many examples of scientists, psychologists and even clergy who simply reject out of hand any possible supernatural evil power that could possess or manipulate man.

Unfortunately, this rationalism rooted in the West has begun to seep into Africa. For the African traditionalist there can be no question. Of course he believes in supernatural powers. There is more to life than what the scientist can explain. The unseen world of spirits, ancestors and mystical powers interpenetrates with our own world. But for those African scholars schooled in western universities or by professors taught overseas, there is frequently a serious erosion of faith in the reality of the supernatural.

As evangelicals we can neither accept the ATR interpretation uncritically nor can we accept the rationalistic assumptions derived from western unbelief. We are bound to the world view as taught in the Bible. And the world view of Scriptures is sufficiently close to ATR that we can understand and accept the realities as expressed by followers of ATR. Yet Scripture provides a necessary corrective so that we evaluate ATR from the divine perspective as found in the Bible.

AN EVANGELICAL INTERPRETATION OF MYSTICAL POWERS

1. Spirit Activity Behind Mystical Powers

A brief survey of biblical teaching on demonic spirits is appropriate here. But first we must hasten to counter any false assumption on the part of the reader. By no means are we suggesting that every alleged occultic activity in ATR is the result of the extra ordinary work of evil spirits. People, blinded by Satan, may be self-deceived in thinking that something is caused by witchcraft when in fact it has a very natural explanation. Or there may be specialists among the people who are frauds and who deceive their clients.

But the evangelical simply believes in the world of fallen spirits who seek to molest mankind and draw people away from divine worship and into satanic slavery. We cannot and will not make any judgment on particular cases. How much of traditional mystical powers may be the result of self-induced self-deception, or how much is the result of fraudulent specialists who cheat their clients, or how much is the result of actual spirit activity we cannot say. But we firmly believe that mystical powers among the Africans is not a mere illusion by a people lacking the benefits of modern education and science. African traditionalists experienced a reality which the Bible recognizes but which the naturalist in today's modern world cannot accept.

Satan, whose name means "Adversary," is depicted in the Bible as an adversary of both God and His people. As the Tempter, Satan approached Christ (Mt. 4:1-17). He approaches Christians today (I Cor. 7:5) in order to seduce them away from the will of God. He is able to deceive people, disguising himself as an angel of light (II Cor. 11:14). His deceitfulness is manifest in his supernatural power to perform signs and wonders (II Thess. 2:2). Being a spirit he is able to enter a human being and motivate that person to oppose Jesus Christ and his divine will (Jn. 12:27). Satan, the Adversary of God, hinders the work of God (I Thess. 2:18) and takes advantage of any opportunity to thwart the will of God (II Cor. 2:11).

Satan is also called the Devil. The meaning of "Devil" is one "prone to slander." The portrait of the Devil is that of a cunning, clever, powerful, deceitful schemer who at every turn challenges the reign and rule of God. The Devil is "the father of lies" (Jn. 8:44), an allusion to Genesis 3:1-16 and the temptation of Eve by the Serpent. The Devil not only tempted the first woman, but tempted the second Adam, even Christ.

Temptation by the Devil is attractive. For Eve, the attraction was to "be like God, knowing good and evil" (Gen. 3:5). For Christ, the attraction was to obtain the kingdoms of the world by circumventing the cross. But in both cases the real target was the truthfulness of God's Word (Gen. 3:1). And the Devil is not beyond the deceitfulness of quoting God's very words with distortion (Mt. 4:6).

But in every case the Devil is the opponent of the Kingdom of God. Satan is also allied to men and women who owe their allegiance to him and who derive their life style from him. As such they are called "children of the Devil" (I Jn 3:10), and "sons of the devil" (Acts 13:10). These human allies of the Devil, his very own children, sons and daughters, resemble the Devil and are said to be "from the Devil" (I Jn. 3:8). As such, the Devil is their "father" (Jn. 8:44) and they are his "children" (I Jn. 3:10).

The Bible divides history into "this age" and the "age to come." The two ages are contrasted. While "the age to come" is the Messianic age, "this age" refers to the one in which we now live, characterized by sin and misery (Mt. 13:22). It is significant that Satan is spoken of as "the god of this age." Satan has set himself against God and His people and seeks to direct all his own children to transgress God's law and rebel against Him. He is called "the ruler of the world" (Jn. 12:31; 16:11). He is "the prince of the power of the air" (Eph. 2:2). All peoples and their cultures are corrupted by sin and ruled by Satan, "the god of this age."

But Satan is not alone in the spirit world in his opposition to God. There are a host of fallen angels who, like Satan himself, rebelled against God and form the host which opposes their Creator. In the New Testament there are a number of significant passages that speak of powers and principalities who are allied against God (Eph. 1:21; 3:10; 6:12; Col. 1:16; 2:10; I Pet. 3:22; Rom. 8:38, 39). Without seeking to exegete these passages, we may observe that Satan has a kingdom of darkness comprised of unregenerate men and women together with his fallen angels. There is some kind of hierarchy within Satan's kingdom in which a vast array of spirit beings are opposing the Kingdom of God. "For our struggle is not against flesh and blood, but against the rulers, against the powers, against the world-forces of this darkness, against the spiritual forces of wickedness in the heavenly places." (Eph. 6:12)

Thus we find in Scripture clear teaching that allied against God and His Kingdom is Satan and his hosts of unclean spirits. They tempt people to transgress God's law, they oppose God and His will, they slander God and His people, they deceive people through various tactics, they perform wonders and signs which are counterfeit to the signs and wonders performed by God, they possess human beings, controlling them as slaves, and they are proponents of the Kingdom of Darkness.

The nations of the world, the peoples, their cultures and their life style are all under the control of Satan, "the spirit that is now at work in the sons of disobedience." (Eph. 2:2) We all once followed the standard of Satan himself, following the pattern of this age, before being redeemed through Christ. The purpose of Christ's coming was to destroy him who has the power of death, even the Devil (Heb. 2:14). We as God's children are called upon to engage in open conflict with satanic powers. And with the spiritual weapons of our warfare we shall overcome (Eph. 6:12).

The Bible teaches us concerning the reality of Satan and his kingdom of darkness. What of witchcraft in Africa and the world today? Is there evidence that this is Satanic? We have noted the conclusion of many scholars who accept a rationalistic explanation of witchcraft. While rejecting anything supernatural about witchcraft they explain any results as the result of poison, psychic powers and the use of drugs. This is true of Margaret Murray who wrote "one of the most outstanding modern books on witchcraft" (Parrinder 1958:12. See Murray 1962:158, 231-35, 280).

Montague Summers wrote a classic on *The History of Witchcraft and Demonology* in 1926 (Summers 1969) on European witchcraft. While he admits "gross superstition" and "unbridled imaginations," he maintains that when every allowance is made and every possible explanation exhausted, "a mass of solid proven facts" cannot be adequately accounted for by medical or psychological knowledge, "save by acknowledging the reality of witchcraft and diabolic contracts." (Summers 1973:64) In contrast to Murray who also studied European witchcraft, Summers concluded that Satanic and demonic influence and activity occurred in medieval European witchcraft.

Kurt Koch, who has counseled thousands of people throughout the world who have been emotionally disturbed, comments, "My counselling work continually supplies evidence to the effect that magic in any form is the work of the devil, whether it sails under a black, white or neutral flag." (Koch 1981:77) Although some people claim to use only "white magic" together with Bible verses and prayer, Koch believes it "remains black magic under a different guise." (Koch 1981:77)

John Montgomery readily acknowledges the reality of the para-normal, but he maintains that it is only a short step from the para-normal to the demonic and easily taken. Furthermore, he writes,

> this subject poses the fewest complexities of interpretation. The reason is simply that here one reaches the 'black' end of the occult spectrum; grayness disappears and all becomes clear — hideously clear. The problem in determining whether demon possession occurs and whether witchcraft works is absurdly simple. The documentation is overwhelming. Even if 99% of all witchcraft cases are thrown out — and that would be difficult to do — the remainder would easily establish the reality of the phenomenon

The biblical testimony is clear. And for those whose world view is open to the reality of demonic spirits, the evidence is inescapable. The inspiration and the dynamic of witchcraft is demonic.

Demonic Activity in Magic and Divination. From a biblical perspective, the definition of magic by Noss, given in chapter 4, is inadequate. Though modern science rejects all supernatural reality in mystical powers, the Scripture clearly and repeatedly teaches that demon activity lies behind the occult. Magic is not only "an endeavor...to control." It involves living, intelligent demonic beings. The definition of magic given by the English dictionary is also inadequate. Magic is defined in the dictionary thus: "1. The *pretended* art of producing effects or controlling events by charms, spells, and rituals *supposed* to govern certain natural or supernatural forces; sorcery; witchcraft. 2. Any mysterious, *seemingly inexplicable* or extraordinary power or influence. 3. The art of producing baffling effects or *illusions by sleight of hand,* concealed apparatus." [italics mine]

Magic, of course, can be a play thing, using a quick hand unnoticed by people. This form of magic is for entertainment and has a very natural explanation. Magic may also be an intentional deception by a specialist in order to defraud people and obtain their money. But "if magic is genuine and not mere deception or hocus-pocus, it must be personal. Living, intelligent spirit beings become the real agents." Therefore, Unger would define magic along with divination as "The divinely forbidden art of bringing about results beyond human power by recourse to superhuman spirit agencies." (Unger 1972: 76)

Divination is closely related to magic, and therefore, may be discussed together. If magic is "the forbidden art of bringing about results beyond human power by recourse to superhuman spirit agencies," then divination is just one kind of magic. For divination is the art of foretelling future events and determining the cause of some misfortune. It is the art of gaining knowledge which is otherwise withheld from human beings.

Divination is related to magic even as prophecy is related to miracle. Miracles imply divine power at work, while magic implies demonic power in operation. Prophecy is divine knowledge of the future imparted by God, whereas divination is superhuman knowledge acquired through demonic influence. Divination is the devil's counterfeit of true prophecy while magic is Satan's substitute for miracle.

Both magic and divination originated in man's rebellion against God. God had commanded Adam and Eve, "Be fruitful and multiply, and fill the earth and subdue it." (Gen. 1:28) This of course was to be done in dependence upon the Creator and according to His will. But Satan, the father of all lies, offered knowledge and power apart from God. In tempting man to disobey God, the Liar said, "you will *be* like God, *knowing* good and evil." (Gen. 3:5) Man rebelled against God's will in his quest for *knowledge* and *power* like unto God's. Thus magic is as old as the fall. Magic is at its very heart, rebellion against God, whether it be white magic or black magic. Magic is "the very antithesis of the commandment of God as it reveals a hunger for knowledge and a desire for power in opposition to the will of God." (Koch 1981:61,62)

Therefore, magic and divination are two aspects of rebellion against God. In magic and divination man depends upon human effort and demonic powers for the purpose of controlling and subduing the earth and acquiring knowledge of the unknown. Man has two choices: either submit to God in obedience, depending upon Him for power, or rebel against God in subduing the earth by means contrary to the will of God.

The Christian faith, as the only true "religion," is total submission to God in faith, and obedience to His divine will and purpose through Jesus Christ our Lord. But magic is a departure from true religion. To this extent the traditional distinction between magic and biblical religion is true. Magic says, "My will be done" whereas the Word of God says, "Thy will be done."

Magic is sometimes thought of as a crude science based on erroneous assumptions, manipulating the impersonal forces of the world through incantations, medicines and magical rites. Other times magic becomes personal in which living, intelligent, personal agents are invoked. Whenever magical powers are real, either in impersonal magic or personal magic, we may assume the active influence of demons and fallen spirits.

The Bible recognizes the reality of magical powers. The Egyptian magicians were able to perform miracles similar to those miracles produced by Moses by the power of God up to a certain point (Ex. 7:11,22; 8:7,18,19; II Tim. 3:8). God did not dismiss Egyptian magic as superstition. Rather, the greater power of the Lord was demonstrated defeating the Egyptian magicians. Though the power of the Babylonian magicians was demonstrated to be inferior to that of God's power, yet the reality of their power is assumed (Dan. 1:20; 2:2, 27; 4:7, 9; 5:11). We are warned that the end of the present age will be marked by a renewal of demonic power and influence (Rev. 9:1-20). The authority of the anti-christ will be confirmed by miracles and signs (II Thess. 2:9-12; Rev. 13:13-18). Scripture always assumes the reality of demonic forces, even though it teaches the deceptive nature of many of Satan's tactics.

Demonic Activity in Witchcraft and Sorcery. Witchcraft mentioned in Scripture is different from that which has been defined by Evans-Pritchard. The witch of the Bible is really a sorceress, for she used magical words, incantations and occult medicines. The Hebrew word, *mekassepa* (Ex. 22:18), and the Greek word, *pharmakeia* (Gal. 5:20), refer to the use of drugs, charms and magical incantations. The so-called "witch of Endor" was not really a witch or a sorceress, but a woman who communed with the spirits, a woman who communicated with the dead (I Sam. 28:3,9ff).

All forms of witchcraft and sorcery are forbidden in Scripture because of their association with demonic activities. Sorcery is associated with practices of spiritism (II Kings 23:24), spiritual harlotry (Nah. 3:4) and idolatry (Mic. 5:12). The evil of witchcraft is in its dependence upon the creature in defiance to the will of God. That men seek the wizard rather than God is evidence of demonic idolatry, removing God from His rightful place in pre-eminence (Isa. 8:19).

2. Specialists Deceive People

We have dwelt long on the issue of demonic activity in traditional mystical powers. We have seen that for these reasons mystical powers are treated with utmost severity by the living God.

Nevertheless, we readily admit and must fully affirm that a large portion of what is claimed to be mystical power is none other than deception by the specialists themselves. The medicine men themselves as well as the diviners and rain makers, the witches and sorcerers, are often guilty of deception for purposes of personal gain.

To say this is to simply to recognize the obvious. Africans themselves are conscious of deceit by many diviners, medicine men and sorcerers. Many Azande affirm that "the great majority of witch-doctors are liars whose sole concern is to acquire wealth." A Kisii sorcerer explicitly acknowledged his effort to appear terrifying in order to strike fear in the hearts of others. He shaved one side of his head, assumed a fearsome name, and assumed a haughty appearance in order to impress people with his powers. So conscious are the Akamba of the deceitfulness of their medicine men that they traditionally sent emissaries to three different medicine men from distant villages to inquire into the question whether a particular person was in fact a witch. They wanted to avoid any collusion or duplicity.

James Rand, a professional magician in the United States, has used his expertise to expose many psychics, astrologers, spiritualists, faith healers and mystics. While western nations have increasingly rejected the Christian faith, westerners have turned to the occult and eastern religions in growing numbers. Para-normal phenomenon, such as mind reading, bending spoons, making objects move mysteriously and speaking to the dead, have become popular in the West. However, James Rand has exposed many to be charlatans, nothing but fakes. Through various tricks, such as deception, sleight of hand, use of ear phones and radio transmitters, and other standard tricks of the trade, these self-proclaimed miracle workers and psychics have been proved to be frauds.

Kurt Koch firmly believes in supernatural demonic activity. Yet he acknowledges that there are many frauds, swindlers and charlatans among fortunetellers in the West. He estimates that "probably more than 90% of all fortune-telling is really fake."

The Bible likewise recognizes the deceitful nature of many magicians. Paul encountered "a certain magician, a Jewish false prophet whose name was Bar-Jesus." (Acts 13:6) When this magician opposed the preaching of Paul, the Apostle filled with the Holy Spirit said, "You are full of all deceit and fraud, you son of the devil, you enemy of all righteousness, will you not cease to make crooked the straight ways of the Lord?" (Acts 13:10) But though Bar-Jesus was a deceiver, Paul also recognized the activity of Satan in his false trade. He was an enemy of all righteousness and a son of the devil (see Acts 13:6-9).

3. People are Self-Deluded

Not only do we affirm that Satan and his hosts of unclean spirits are the dynamic behind mystical powers and that specialists frequently cheat people through clever deceit. We also affirm that the peoples are blinded by sin, slaves of the Evil One and living under the delusion of darkness.

A study of Scripture indicates that Satan can delude people and cause them to live in fear. Not all the claims of witches and sorcerers should be accepted at face value. Self delusion is an activity of Satan and just as real as any other mystical power.

We should note that the Christian church herself has recognized this fact. Geoffrey Parrinder quotes at length the Council of Ancyra in the ninth century.

> Some wicked women, reverting to Satan, and seduced by the illusions and phantasms of demons, believe and profess that they ride at night with Diana on certain beasts, with an innumerable company of women, passing over immense distances, obeying her commands, as their mistress, and evoked by her on certain nights...Therefore, priests everywhere should preach that they know this to be false, and that such phantasms are sent by the Evil Spirit, who deludes them in dreams. Who is there who is not led out of himself in dreams, seeing much in sleeping that he never saw waking? And who is such a fool that he believes that to happen in the body which is done only in the spirit? (Parrinder 1958:19)

This decree, known as Cap.Episcopi, branded "night-flying," "illusory." It became part of the canon law of the Roman Catholic Church.

Many confessions by witches in Europe reveal that "witches did sometimes confuse their dreams with reality."

> This is admitted by all writers...Hence, one writer, Sinistrari, declared, "There is no question that sometimes young women, deceived by the Demon, imagine they are actually taking part, in their flesh and blood, in the sabbats [Sabbaths] of Witches, and all this is merest fantasy...But this is not always the case; on the contrary, it more often happens that witches are bodily present at sabbats and have an actual carnal and corporeal connexion with the Demon" (Parrinder 1958:41).

Yet it must be admitted that later churchmen had a change of heart, saying that night-flying was possible "through the liberty that God allows to demons." This conclusion was based on the confessions of the many witches to their night-flying.

4. Use of Mystical Powers Forbidden by God.

The aim of demonic influence is to overthrow the Kingdom of God. This can be traced through the Bible, beginning with Genesis 3 and concluding in Revelation, the last book of the Bible. Indeed, the Book of Revelation may be viewed as the final struggle of Satan for victory and his final overthrow.

We have seen that the origin of magical powers was in the rebellion of man. Magic is evil because it replaces a personal faith in God. The ultimate aim of magic is the overthrow of the Kingdom of God. In view of this we can understand why Scripture from cover to cover warns against the use of mystical powers.

Old Testament Teaching. The first warning against mystical powers is found in Exodus 22:18, "you shall not allow a sorceress to live."

God further admonishes Israel, "You shall not practice augury or witchcraft." (Lev. 19:26) "If a person turns to mediums and wizards, playing the harlot after them, I will set my face against that person, and will cut him off from among his people. Consecrate yourselves therefore, and be holy; for I am the Lord your God." (Lev. 20:6) "A man or a woman who is a medium or a wizard shall be put to death; they shall be stoned with stones, their blood shall be upon them." (Lev. 20:27)

The primary concern in these chapters is holiness. The series of commandments in chapters 19 and 20, which appear loosely connected, are all related to the motif, "You shall be holy, for I the Lord your God am holy." (Lev. 19:2) This thought is repeated throughout the chapter. Israel shall obey these commandments because God says, "I am the Lord your God." Holiness of life is essential for this unique covenant relationship between God and Israel.

A medium is one who communicates with and is in personal contact with the evil spirits. These verses are not only relevant to those who practice black magic and behave in an anti-social manner. These verses apply to those specialists who are socially approved, yet who serve as mediums. For any Christian to consult a medicine man as described above is to commit spiritual harlotry. For the believer is "married" to God Himself in a covenant relationship. God jealously cares for His people as a husband cares for his wife. And any attempt to rely on specialists, who communicate with the spirits and who are empowered by the spirits, are in fact committing spiritual harlotry. We have betrayed our Maker and Redeemer. We have broken our marriage vow to cling only to our God. Instead, we are seeking help from the Kingdom of Darkness.

The most comprehensive passage in the Bible concerning the prohibition of pagan practices is found in Deuteronomy 18:9-14.

"When you enter the land which the Lord your God gives you, you shall not learn to imitate the detestable things of those nations." (vs.9) Israel was called unto the Lord in separation from the nations around them. The cultural distinctiveness of Israel is grounded in religious and ethical separation. Israel was chosen from among the nations and with Israel alone did God enter into a covenant relationship. Israel was to be separate unto the Lord.

This special relationship between God and Israel must be understood in the background of Genesis 1-11 and God's declared purpose to Abraham in Gen. 12:1-3. The nations had failed to obey God, resulting in their mass destruction during the Flood, and further judgment on the tower of Babel. God chose Israel that through them they might be a blessing to the nations. But God's people were called unto separation FROM the nations UNTO the living God. Lest Israel follow after the gods of those nations (Deut. 30:17), Israel was commanded to separate from them.

The Book of Joshua outlines the limited extent to which Israel obeyed God's command to destroy the Canaanites. The Book of Judges details the tragic results because they failed to obey God completely. The whole issue was faithfulness to God and the avoidance of idolatry. Not only did those nations deserve to die because of their sin (despite God's gracious forbearance of four generations, Gen. 15:16), but their presence in the holy land would prove to be a stumbling block to the people of God.

The preface to the series of prohibitions in Deut. 18:10, 11, underscores the importance of rejecting all that is detestable to God. In verse 12 God reminds us that because these nations practiced these "detestable things," God was driving them out of the land. Israel's failure to drive out the nations resulted in temptation. Because Israel succumbed to this temptation and followed the "detestable things" of those nations, Israel herself was carried away into captivity. Therefore, we should examine carefully all that is listed in this passage.

a. "There shall not be found among you anyone who makes his son or his daughter pass through the fire." (vs.10) Though the precise pagan practice is not known, the general meaning is clear. In some fiery way the Canaanites offered their children in consecration to Molech or some other deity. This was possibly done by placing a child in the arms of an idol of Molech, a hollow metal idol with fire burning inside. The child would, therefore, become a sacrifice, though the child may not have been burned to death. Though the RSV interprets this as a child sacrifice, the precise nature of this practice is not certain.

b. "One who uses divination." (vs.10) Among the Semitic nations there were three kinds of divination as illustrated in Ezekiel 21:21, where the king of Babylon is confronted with the question, which city to attack. "He shakes the arrows, he consults the household idols, he looks at the liver."

Examination of the liver is as old as the ancient Babylonians, Greeks and Romans. Yet it is as modern as the people in Burma, Borneo and Africa who practice the same form of divination today. The Hebrew word means literally, "to cut" or "to divide." As the animal is cut and the liver divided, the shape of the liver is examined. The belief is that the gods have shaped the organ, the seat of life, in such a way that one is able to learn the divine will by examining the liver.

Divination by arrows is called belomancy. The arrows were marked with the names of the cities to be attacked and then placed in a quiver. They were shaken together and thrown out in order to determine the will of the spirits. Whichever came out first, revealed the place of attack. Or if they were thrown up into the air, the direction they faced on the ground showed the direction of attack.

The third Semitic method of divination was "consulting the household idols" or the teraphim (see I Sam. 15:23; Zech. 10:2). This method is not known today. Some suggest that these idols were ancestral images raised to the place of household gods. Even as a spirit of a medium today makes contact with the dead by means of a picture of the dead, so the idols may been so used. But the precise practice is unknown today.

Astrology was also common in the ancient world. A careful study of the following biblical passages reveals that divination was closely linked with the worship of the golden calf, Molech and the stars (II Kings. 17:16; 23:5, 10; Ps. 81:12; Isa. 47:13; Amos 5:25,26; Acts 7:41-43) (Unger 1952:131-141).

From a biblical perspective, divination of any kind is forbidden. God has set Himself against these mystical powers. "Thus says the Lord, your Redeemer, and the One who formed you from the womb; I, the Lord, am the maker of all things...Causing the omens of boasters to fail, making fools out of diviners, causing wise men to draw back, and turning their knowledge into foolishness..." (Isa. 44:24, 25)

c. "One who practices witchcraft"

d. "One who interprets omens"
There are in this verse three separate words used for various forms of divination, translated by the NASV, "one who uses divination, one who practices witchcraft, or one who interprets omens." While the general meaning is clear, we are not able to distinguish precisely between these different terms. What is clear from the Scripture, however, is that any and every form of divination is forbidden by God. Even if divination is for a "good" purpose and is socially accepted in the community, divination is sin and contrary to the will of God. Judgment is pronounced upon all diviners and those who consult them.

> Stand fast now in your spells
> And in your many sorceries
> With which you have labored from your youth;
> Perhaps you may cause trembling.
> You are weaned with your many counsels.
> Let now the astrologers,
> Those who prophecy by the stars,
> Those who predict by the new moons,
> Stand up and save you from what will come upon you.
> Behold, they have become like stubble,
> Fire burns them;
> They cannot deliver themselves from the power of the flame.
> (Isa. 47:12-14)

e. "a sorcerer." It is significant that the Authorized Version uses "witch" and "witchcraft" nine times in the Bible, whereas, the NASV generally avoids the use of those words, substituting instead, "sorcerer" and "sorcery." The first prohibition against the use of mystical powers in the Mosaic law occurs in Exodus 22:18 as we have seen. The NASV reads, "You shall not allow a sorceress to live." The Authorized Version substitutes "witch" for "sorcerer." The same applies to Deuteronomy 18:10 where the same word is used.

The reason for this change is evident. Both the Greek and Hebrew words which are translated "witch" and "witchcraft" in the Authorized Version refer to that practice which involves the use of herbs and material objects. In anthropological terminology today, a "witch" is someone who acts without rites or spells and uses no herbs or medicines. Hence the NASV lists "sorcery" as one of the "deeds of the flesh" (Gal. 5:20), whereas the Authorized Version says "witchcraft."

Beyond this technicality, the biblical command is clear. Those who by use of drugs, herbs or by other means sought to bring about supernatural effects for the harm of others or the protection of the client are totally forbidden. "The condemnation of sorcery is absolute. Religion cannot flower in an atmosphere of such aberrations [deviations from divine commandments] and *those who practice them are an abomination to the Lord* [italics mine], and worthy of death." (Wright 1953a:446)

Not only was Israel forbidden to peer into the future through the means of diviners, they were forbidden at a deeper level to make any attempts to control the future. Any such activity reflected lack of faith in the living God and a defiant dependence on the occult (Cole 1974:174). Whereas, the Eastern religions distinguished between those magical practices which were permitted (white magic) and those which were forbidden (black magic), "in Israel no distinction was made between permitted and prohibited magic. Every magical art, even for a purpose that is not evil, is forbidden, since it constitutes an attempt to prevail over the will of God, who alone has dominion over the world. Thus it is not without reason that in Israel the concepts of magic and idolatry were identical." (Cassuto 1967:290)

The sentence of death upon these individuals, indicates the absolute, unqualified and unrestricted manner by which God has forbidden such magical practices.

f. "one who casts a spell." The Hebrew word means "to tie a magic knot or spell, charm." It refers to a magician who uses words or things, such as the tying of knots, to cast a spell.

While sorcery is generally a negative practice, designed to harm another person or his property, magic may have positive connotations, providing benefits for the client who desires a new job, a rich harvest or a wife to marry. But from the biblical perspective, all such mystical powers, even "innocent" ones as the ability to acquire employment, are evil and to be shunned by the Christian.

Since all genuine magic is the display of supernatural power, it is personal. That is, genuine magic is the result of living, intelligent spirit beings. Therefore, all such magic is evil. For these reasons the practices recorded in Deuteronomy 18 are described as "detestable things." They are forbidden, not because of some arbitrary will of God. They are forbidden because they are associated with the adversaries of the Kingdom of God. To participate in them not only reflects unbelief and disobedience, but involves the participant in the works of the Devil himself.

New Testament Teaching. The New Testament teaching is firmly built upon divine revelation in the Old Testament. Sorcery is listed among the works of the flesh (Gal. 5:20) and is closely linked with idolatry. Simon the sorcerer was sternly rebuked by the Apostle Peter and commanded to repent (Acts 8:9-24). Elymas the magician was rebuked as "the son of the devil" and "enemy of all righteousness" (Acts 13:6-12). When the Gospel was received in Ephesus, the magical charms and medicines of the converts were burned. The total value was 50,000 pieces of silver, representing a total worth of 50,000 working days (Acts 19:18, 19). Sorcerers are among those who are specifically excluded from the holy city, the new Jerusalem (Rev. 21:8; 22:15).

We conclude then that the whole of Scriptures, from the Pentateuch through the Old Testament prophets and to the New Testament, has forbidden the use of all mystical powers, whether they be socially acceptable or unacceptable, whether they are for the purported good of the people or for their harm, whether they are for personal gain or the benefit of the community. All mystical powers of magic and divination, sorcery and witchcraft are forbidden by God. All specialists who engage in communication with the spirit world, whether for good or ill, are under God's judgment. And any Christian who resorts to them for help is transgressing the will of God. Punishment for such practices in the Old Testament was death. Capital punishment was executed upon them because this constituted idolatry. For these sins, God punished the Canaanite nations. Because Israel followed after these idolatrous acts, the wrath of God was poured out upon them also, resulting in their captivity. And God who is the same yesterday, today and forever, has maintained the same standard throughout the New Testament and the present church age.

As Wolford observes, no activity whatsoever which seeks to gain access to the spiritual powers of the universe is acceptable for God's people. "He expects his people to look to Him and to Him alone for life and guidance. It is a life and death matter: death surrounds any hint of sorcery practices and life is found in God alone who is over all powers." (Wolford 1981:208)

CONCLUSION

What we have said in brief is this. The Bible teaches that behind genuinely extra ordinary, supernatural powers of traditional religion is the work of demonic spirits. Therefore, God forbids any involvement whatsoever with mystical powers of any sort, whether they are socially acceptable or anti- social. However, the Bible also acknowledges deceit and deception promoted by the specialists. And the people themselves, blinded by sin and living in fear, are often self-deluded in believing that a particular event is the direct result of some mystical power.

Everyone who comes to this subject is wearing a set of glasses which helps him determine what he accepts or rejects. These glasses are molded and shaped by his own past experiences, history and culture. Through long experience, I have discovered that the African is usually prone to assume the reality of the supernatural in some purported event. Whereas a westerner is more inclined to be suspicious and unbelieving. The African, because he has grown up with all these stories of mystical powers is more likely to believe in their reality. While the westerner, reared in a culture dominated by western scientism, is skeptical and doubtful. The stories of traditional mystical powers seem far fetched and unbelievable.

The four assertions made above are biblical and evangelicals everywhere believe them: Evil spirits are present and working in mystical powers, specialists deceive the people, and the people themselves mislead themselves. And the whole of Scriptures from cover to cover forbids any use of mystical powers, whether good magic or bad, protective or destructive, socially approved or anti-social.

But the application of these principles to particular events is something else. Who can say that this or that is without question the work of the devil, or the result of deceit or self-delusion? On this matter we need to be cautious. When people walking through the forests, hear the movement of the "spirits" as they hear the breaking of twigs and the rustling of leaves — is this self-delusion? Could that not have a natural explanation? How many westerners can remember experiences in their childhood when they thought they saw and heard ghosts while walking at night near a cemetery? We hear of spirits beating people with thorn branches and sticks. We hear of spirits speaking from horns, from inside the tent where a sick person is resting or from a gourd. Is this trickery by the specialist? Who can say? We only maintain that if it is not self-delusion or deceit by the specialist, then it is the working of the fallen angels who seek to build up the kingdom of darkness.

So we need to allow room for different perspectives on this subject and be willing to learn from one another. I suspect that the westerner must listen more carefully to the reality behind many of these stories of mystical powers. And that the African must be more open to the possibility of fraud and self- delusion.

One thing we can be sure of is that mystical powers as discussed above are contrary to the will of God and that the dynamic in all magic and divination, witchcraft and sorcery, white magic and black magic, medicine men and witches is from the kingdom of darkness.

What is the future of mystical powers? Most observers seem to agree that the answer to sorcery and witchcraft is modern advancement and enlightenment. Eliminate child mortality, provide better medical care, offer scientific education to the children and eliminate many of the past sources of tension, and you will find sorcery disappearing.

This opinion is based on the theory that witchcraft and sorcery have risen as a psychological response to stress. People by nature want to know **WHY?** Why did our house burn down? Why did my son become ill? Why did I fail in my hunting safari? Why is my wife barren? Why have our crops failed? **Why,** *why,* *WHY?* Witchcraft provides an answer.

Belief in sorcery and witchcraft is said to provide a means of release from social strains. The poor are envious of the rich. Wives are jealous of one another. Brothers come into conflict over personal interests. In all these points of interpersonal strain, the accusations of sorcery abound. If we can eliminate the tensions, the cause of witchcraft would be removed, we are told.

As Parrinder observes,

> Education will slowly dispel some superstitions. Medical and child care will remove many unexplained diseases. But nobler beliefs and a new religion would lift the load of false belief and prejudices. It took centuries for the superstition to disappear from Europe, and it will fade out in Africa in due course if the forces of enlightenment are maintained and increased (Parrinder 1961:171).

While much of what Parrinder says is true, he seems to ignore the biblical perspective. Scripture teaches that stress is not removed by improving health, education and welfare. The basic stress is caused by sin and man's separation from God. Anxiety over these things is due to unbelief in God. I do not refer here to mere infidelity. The Gospel teaches that "the just shall *live* by faith." His whole life rests in the sufficiency and goodness of God. In Him and Him alone will man find release from the tensions that make sorcery necessary.

The fact is that witchcraft has not subsided in modern Africa. "The truth of the matter is that the belief in witchcraft has not been reduced by missionary influence or contact with the West. On the contrary, it is possible to argue that belief in witchcraft has never been greater and that it is in fact growing rapidly in present-day Africa." (McVeigh 1974:168)

Mr. Felix Houphouet, President of the Ivory Coast, has been quoted as saying this. "For the Westerners belief in witchcraft may seem childish, but it is a great tragedy which takes place in Africa. From the African archbishop down to the most insignificant Catholic, from the great marabout down to the most insignificant Muslim, from the pastor down to the smallest Protestant, we all have in us an animistic past and perhaps two or three generations of Catholics, Muslims and Protestants." (cf. Hukema 1988) He believes that 75 years is not enough to change the traditional world view and destroy the belief in witchcraft.

The tragedy is that in our Bible Schools and Colleges as well as our churches the subject of witchcraft is not taught or preached. A major reason is because the older pastors remain faithful to the teaching of the earlier missionaries. Because the pioneer missionaries considered witchcraft superstition, they dismissed it as unreal. Consequently, the pastors have never been trained in our Bible Schools and Colleges to deal with mystical powers.

Another problem is that many second and third generation "Christians" have never been born again and do not know the reality and power of Christ in their lives. Consequently, they turn to witchcraft because they have never tasted the new life in Christ. So the growing phenomena of nominal Christianity goes hand in hand with a return to magic.

The fact is that the Gospel is the primary means by which sorcery and witchcraft will be removed. In Christ, man finds release from guilt and fear. By the Holy Spirit man experiences love and joy, and the sanctifying grace which removes selfishness, jealousy and hatred. Through the Word of God, man finds guidance through a life of trouble. Along with the Gospel are the accompanying fruits of the Christian faith which include hospitals of hope and mercy, schools of education and instruction.

Man by his sinful nature is envious and jealous. By nature he is anxious and fearful. Witchcraft and sorcery are only one means in certain cultures of expressing this and dealing with this problem. Modern civilization in the West has demonstrated to all willing to learn, that education and welfare do not remove superstition. Nor do they eliminate tensions of society. In the West today there is a dramatic increase in the occult. Westerners with all their history of education and religion are experimenting in the mystical arts of astrology, witchcraft, spiritism, necromancy and divination. Only the pure Gospel of Jesus Christ with the full teaching of the Word of God by the power of the Holy Spirit can remove this evil of mystical powers so that we may trust and obey God fully from our hearts.

REVIEW QUESTIONS FOR CHAPTER 7

1. How do naturalistic presuppositions affect a scholar's approach to mystical powers?

2. Discuss the three main explanations for mystical powers suggested by the author. Wherein do you agree or disagree? Support your answer with reasons.

3. Discuss the biblical teaching on the origin, nature and activity of evil spirits. How does this teaching of the Bible help us to understand the nature of the spirits active within mystical powers?

4. To what extent may a Christian engage in the use of mystical powers? May

a Christian seek help from the medicine man for good reasons? Why?

Suggested Reading and Thought Questions for Advanced Study:

Koch, Kurt. *Between Christ and Satan.*
Koch, Kurt. *Occult A.B.C.*
Koch, Kurt. *Occult Bondage and Deliverance.*
Michelet, Jules. *Satanism and Witchcraft.*
Montgomery, J.W. *Principalities and Powers: The World of the Occult.*
Summers, Montague. *The History of Witchcraft and Demonology.*

Check the following topics in various standard evangelical reference books on theology, in Bible dictionaries and encyclopedias: astrology, divination, enchantment, magic, occult, sorcery, witchcraft, wizard,

Baker's Dictionary of Theology, Everett Harrison ed.
Evangelical Dictionary of Theology, Walter A. Elwell ed.
The International Standard Bible Encyclopaedia, Geoffrey Bromiley ed.
The International Standard Bible Encyclopaedia, James Orr ed.
New Bible Dictionary, J.D. Douglas ed.
Unger's Bible Dictionary, Merrill F. Unger ed.
Wycliffe Bible Encyclopedia, Charles Pfeiffer ed.,
The Zondervan Pictorial Encyclopedia of the Bible, Merrill C. Tenney
  ed.

Make an inductive exegetical study of such biblical passages as: Ex 22:18; Lev. 19:26; 20:6,27; Deut. 18:9-14; Ezek. 21:21.

1. From what source or sources does the power and dynamic of mystical powers in ATR come from? Is it mere superstition, psychological, telepathy, paranormal phenomena, an illusion, deception or demonic? Support your answer with reasons.
2. From your own observation, how much of traditional mystical powers is due to spirit activity, how much is due to deception by the specialists and how much is due to self-delusion?
3. To what extent has the pastoral approach of your mission and church to mystical powers been biblical and helpful to the people? Describe. To what extent has the pastoral approach been inadequate, unhelpful or in error? Explain.
4. "Magic that protects from harm or enables one to find a job is good magic and acceptable for Christians to use." Discuss in the light of biblical teaching.
5. What specific actions should the church take to help Christians who are tempted to resort to magic and divination through the medicine man?
6. "The pastor is the Christian substitute for the traditional medicine man." Evaluate this assertion, its truth or error or its danger. If you believe there is any truth to that statement, discuss the implication for the minister of the Gospel. If you believe there are dangerous implications in comparing a medicine man with a pastor, please explain.
7. What specific biblical teaching should the pastors and evangelists provide

the Christians today,
    a. who seek protection from harm through charms?
    b. who seek guidance for the future from the medicine man?
    c. who are afraid of witchcraft and sorcery?

8. In what ways can the traditional belief in mystical powers become a point of contact for preaching the Gospel? In what way can the Christian church make positive use of traditional belief in mystical powers to teach the things of God? Discuss.

9. If these traditional specialists are no longer acceptable among Christians, what efforts should be made by the Christian churches to replace them with Christian substitutes, so that the traditionally felt needs of Africa will be fully satisfied in the Gospel of Jesus Christ?

PART THREE

THE SPIRIT WORLD IN
AFRICAN TRADITIONAL RELIGION

Chapter 8

DIVINITIES IN AFRICA

Even as man is both body and spirit according to ATR, so man's life-long experience is both earthly and spiritual, each affecting and interpenetrating the other. Mystical powers, those inanimate [non-personal], impersonal forces which pervade the universe, are an ever present reality to the traditional African. But we have seen that even those allegedly impersonal mystical powers are often animated and activated by spiritual beings.

The spirit world is alive with a variety of spirit beings. In this chapter we shall deal with a category of spiritual beings below the Supreme Being but above the ancestral spirits and nature spirits. These spiritual beings are said to be ministers of God, some of whom are said to have created the world. To distinguish them from the Supreme Being and the lesser spirits, we shall call them "divinities."

Parrinder states that the word "divinity" is a translation of various vernacular words in West Africa, such as *abosom* among the Twi and *orisha* in Yoruba. While Olodumare is never included among the *orisha*, there are a host of other divinities or gods which exercise great authority in the governing and operation of the world (Parrinder 1961:26).

Although we include divinities in our discussion of the spirit world, we should observe with Idowu, "Divinities and ancestors form separate homogeneous categories of their own. Divinities and ancestors could be described as 'domesticated' spirits — the ancestors have always been a part of the human family, and the divinities are intimately a tutelary part of the personal or community establishments." (Idowu 1973:173) Though they form "separate homogeneous categories," they are both spiritual beings anthropomorphically conceived (that is, thought of in the form of human beings). Moreover, by common consent, the divinities are part of the created universe, although some divinities themselves, as ministers of God, are said to have created the earth.

If there is anything which makes the traditional religions significantly different in various parts of Africa, it is this belief in divinities. If there is any reason we should speak of African religions (plural), rather than African religion (singular), it is this belief in divinities.

Africa may be roughly divided into two groups: those living in West Africa with large pantheons of gods (eg. *obosom* in Twi, *vudu* in Ewe-Fon, and *orisha* in Yoruba), and those people living in Central, Eastern and Southern Africa with no belief in divinities. Certain kingdoms in Uganda, like their counterparts in West Africa, likewise affirmed belief in divinities.

Parrinder observes that writers may not have paid sufficient attention to the pantheons of divinities in Africa. Instead, they have concentrated on the "ancestral cult." He comments that religion in West Africa "may be best understood by the student, and not inaccurately described, if it is roundly called 'polytheism.'" (Parrinder 1961:11) There "we find fully developed polytheism. Here are pantheons of nature gods, with their temples and priest, like the polytheisms of Egypt, Greece and India." (Parrinder 1961:44) Edwin Smith concurs with this judgment (Parrinder 1962:xiii). However, we shall note hereafter that some scholars, like Idowu, strongly object to this interpretation.

EXAMPLES OF DIVINITIES IN AFRICA

An excellent survey on West African religion with its myriad of divinities is a book by Geoffrey Parrinder, entitled, *West African Religions* (1961). In this book, the author has treated four groups of people in West Africa, namely, the Yoruba, Ewe, Akan and Ibo. We shall mention briefly some of the religious beliefs and practices relating to three of these West African peoples in addition to the ancient Egyptians.

The Yoruba

This large ethnic group is found primarily in Nigeria with some living in Dahomey. E.B. Idowu has made a major contribution by his interpretation of the Yoruba religious belief in his book, *Olodumare: God in Yoruba Belief* (1962).

The title for the Supreme Being among the Yoruba is Olorun, meaning "owner of the sky." Idowu has presented evidence that the older name for God is Olodumare. He is the almighty and eternal Creator, "the immovable rock that never dies" (Idowu 1962:33-37).

But in addition to Olodumare, however, and surpassing in cultic prominence, are the reported 1,700 divinities, "the largest collection of divinities in a single African people." In actual fact no one knows exactly how many divinities there are among the Yoruba. The name for divinities in Yoruba, *orisa*, means "legion." They are innumerable divinities, legion in number.

The supreme divinity is Orisa-Nla who acts as God's emissary. "Yoruba theology also calls him the off-spring of Olodumare in the sense that he derived immediately from him and that the attributes of Olodumare are revealed through him." (Idowu 1962:71) In fact Orisa-Nla is known by many of the attributes of Olodumare. God sent Orisa-Nla to create both the earth and man's body. Afterwards, Olodumare breathed into man the breath of life. Orisa-Nla is known as "the maker," "He who spreads over the whole extent of the earth," "the Proposer who wields the sceptre." As the creator, Orisa-Nla is the one responsible for the creation of hunchbacks, cripples and albinos.

White is the favourite colour for Orisa-Nla whose temples are white washed and contain white beads as symbols. Orisa-Nla represents the purity and high morality demanded of men. Snails are offered to him instead of blood.

Oduduwa is another powerful and prominent divinity. Conflicting Yoruba mythology says that after Orisa-Nla received his orders from Olodumare to create man, Orisa-Nla became thirsty and drank palm-wine excessively, falling into a drunken stupor. Consequently, Oduduwa quietly gathered the materials and created man's material body, thus supplanting Orisa-Nla in honour as the

Creator. Some regard Oduduwa as the ancestor of the Yorubas. His name means, "chief who created us."

Idowu concludes after his research that the divinity Oduduwa was once a powerful leader among the Yoruba. This individual had a dominant personality and was a capable leader. He lived and ruled in Ile-Ife, the capital city. When he died, an ancestral cult centred on him. Through the course of history, legends developed which eventually resulted in the present day beliefs of Oduduwa, the creator divinity (Idowu 1962:22-24).

Qrunmila is another divinity whose wisdom surpasses even that of Orisa-Nla. Having been with Olodumare during the creation, he knows all about man and divinities. Qrunmila has extraordinary insight and understanding. His wisdom and foreknowledge is second only to Olodumare himself.

The story is told that on one occasion, Olodumare was perplexed concerning the administration of the world. It was Qrunmila who had insight and provided the solution for Olodumare. Hence Qrunmila was made God's minister with whom all other divinities consulted. Consequently, Qrunmila is worshipped throughout Yoruba-land and known as the "universal king." His oracles are implicitly trusted as reliable and dependable.

Included among the divinities are various nature gods of the sky and the earth. In West Africa where thunder storms are fierce, the thunder gods are greatly feared. The Yoruba storm god is Shango who is sometimes thought to be the fourth king of Oyo. There are various conflicting stories of this tyrannical and powerful king who could send out clouds of fire and smoke from his mouth. One version says he hung himself after he used a charm to send lightning which accidentally killed his family. Other stories say he ascended into heaven. Whatever happened, he is now in heaven and controls the thunder and lightning. Shango is said to have been the principal national god. When lightning flashes, the people greet him with the words, "Welcome to your majesty" and "Long live the king." Shrines in his honour are placed outside the homes (Parrinder 1961:32-33).

The companion of Shango is Oya, the river Niger. She is so fierce and terrible that no one can look upon her. Oya is often identified with the wind that blows when no rain follows.

Orisha Oko is an important farm goddess among the Yoruba. Temples erected for her are the most common of all divinities. Women are her principal worshippers. The chief festival is at the time of the yam harvest. "It is said that in olden days there was considerable license at this festival, which showed the fertility of human beings likened with that of the soil." (Parrinder 1961:40)

Shopona is one of the four principal deities among the Yoruba. He is greatly feared and greeted as "Lord of the Earth." He is known exclusively as "King who is Lord of the earth." The reason he is so greatly feared is that he not only preserves the seed for the farmer but sends the scourge of smallpox. As king, he must ever be respected and thanked, even when he takes someone's life with smallpox. He is seen as dressed in red and roaming about in the dry season to cast his curse upon those who offend him. His shrines usually are outside the village. Since this cult was forbidden in 1917, it can be found in only scattered places these days.

These vast numbers of divinities among the Yoruba are worshipped daily in temples erected for their devotees. Priests offer sacrifices, sing hymns of adoration and offer prayers devotedly.

The Ewe

These peoples are are located in the southern parts of Ghana, Togo and Dahomey. Melville Herskovits has provided us with the standard work on the Ewe, entitled, *Dahomey, An Ancient West African Kingdom* (1938). They are reported to have so many divinities that no detailed account has ever been made of them.

The complexity and multiplication of the divinities and their cults are so great that no comprehensive account has yet been provided (Mercier 1954:211). Thus our knowledge is inadequate. But one thing cannot be denied, the predominance of divinities in the religious life among the Ewe cluster of peoples.

The supreme gods of the Ewe are Mawu-Lisa. They are twins. Mawu, the female, is represented by the moon, while Lisa, the male, is represented by the sun. As husband and wife, Mawu-Lisa had seven pairs of twins which became the major gods of the Ewe. Of special interest is the red wooden statue with large breasts and a crescent in one hand. This image of Mawu is the only known idol of the Supreme Being in Africa (Parrinder 1961:18).

Yet there appear to be a series of creators. For the Ewe believe that "some being must have existed before Mawu, a being who had the power of creating Mawu." When pressed they reply, "there may have been many Mawus." (Herskovits 1938:290; see Mercier 1954:217-219) Mawu is said to have been created by another god, Se. Yet we go back further and find that Nana Buluku or another Mawu were prior creators. And behind them is Da, a kind of force without which Mawu could not have created the world.

In addition to these supreme gods and divinities is the thunder god by the name, So. He is represented as a ram painted red with lightning coming from his mouth and two axes by his side curved like lightning. Thunder storms are frequent and awesome in West Africa so the thunder gods are powerful and feared. So strikes down the wicked and destroys the objects used by witches. Since those struck by lightning are thus judged by So, the dead corpses are not given a normal burial. During a thunder storm the priests walk through the village, beating a gong which represents his voice. But So is not only an angry god who casts down axes upon people and trees. He also owns the heavens and sends the people heat, rain, and gives fertility to men and crops (Parrinder 1961:31).

The Ewe also revere the earth divinity, known as Ayi and Li. A shrine is erected in his honour in every market. Chief in the pantheon of earth gods is Sapata. He is called, "king of the earth." He is also the god of smallpox who sends this disease among the people. When someone becomes ill with smallpox, they use mild inoffensive expressions (euphemistic phrases) to describe those sick, such as, "He has the king," or "It is the king who makes him suffer." One day a week is devoted to Sapata. No earth may be tilled on that day.

The Akan

The Akan are composed principally of the Ashanti, Fante and Twi groups, the most prominent being the Ashanti. They live in the southern half of Ghana and the eastern part of the Ivory Coast.

The best known studies of the Ashanti are by the anthropologist, R.S. Rattray (1923). A frequently mentioned work is by J.B. Danquah, entitled, *Akan Doctrine of God* (1944). A book of particular value from a Christian perspective is the doctoral dissertation of a Methodist missionary, S.G. Williamson, entitled, *Akan Religion and the Christian Faith* (1965). K.A. Busia, an Akan sociologist, is also a well known writer of repute.

Rattray showed conclusively that the Ashanti not only believe in a Supreme Being but nearly "every compound in Ashanti contains an altar to the Sky God, in the shape of a forked branch cut from a certain tree..." (Parrinder 1961:15) Decorated temples are erected in honour of Nyame (Onyame), the Supreme Being, and priests, elaborately dressed, serve him.

Parrinder claims, "The Ashanti are united in West Africa not in honouring a Supreme Being, but in having temples, priests, and altars to Him. In fact, over the whole of tropical Africa the only other people who seem to give similar attention to God are the Kikuyu of Kenya." (Parrinder 1961:15)

The Ashanti have sometimes thought of Nyame (Onyame) as both male and female. The female principle is symbolized by the moon which created man with water. The male principle is symbolized by the sun. The sun shot life-giving fire into the human veins and made man live. The Supreme Being is known as "the First, the Creator of all things," "the Eternal One," "the Powerful One," and "the Wise One."

The world is full of spirits among the Ashanti. The Supreme Being created a pantheon of divinities known collectively as *abosom*. These divinities "come from him and are parts of him." They derive their power from him and serve as his ministers and mouthpieces in this world. Below the divinities are the lesser spirits which dwell in trees, animals and inanimate objects. Then there are the ancestral spirits which are found everywhere.

Asase Yaa is the earth goddess among the Ashanti, sometimes thought to be a consort of Onyame. Busia denies that Asase Yaa is an earth goddess since she has no priests, nor is she consulted for divination like the other gods. Nevertheless, libation is poured and sacrifices made to her like the other gods. She is considered the creator of the underworld and the mother of the dead. She has a special day, Thursday, set aside for her. No farmer dare till the ground on Thursday. Before any farmer tills the ground, he must first ask permission from Asase Yaa. At the time of the rains, a fowl is killed, the blood poured on the ground and the remains cooked with rams which are then scattered in all directions. Likewise, before one can dig a grave, permission of the earth must be asked. Although there are no temples or priests connected with her, the influence and power of this deity are felt in many parts (1961:38).

The most powerful divinities are those spirits of the rivers. Even as women bear children, so the rivers and the lakes are said to bring forth many divinities. The second son of Nyame (Onyame) is said to be Tano. Though Bia, the first born, was Nyame's favourite son, Tano cheated his brother of his inheritance. Thus, Tano became the river god of the fertile land west of Ghana, while Bia became the river god of the barren lands of the Ivory Coast. The chief temple erected for him is elaborately decorated. Many others are scattered around, especially beside the rivers.

These divinities are actively worshipped. Rites and practices are performed for the Abosom. These divinities are known as the children of Onyame and serve as His spokesmen. Like the official speaker in the court who speaks on all public occasions as the representative of the king, so the Abosom are the ears and mouthpiece of Onyame. The priests for the various divinities believe they have been chosen directly by his particular divinity to serve him.

It is commonly reported that the pantheon of gods is increasing in numbers among the Ashanti. As the divinities increase, the worship of Onyame is on the decrease. For it is apparent that the Ashanti worship Onyame less frequently today than during the days of Rattray's investigation.

The Akan also believe in evil powers. Chief among them is Sasabonsam, a forest monster with long hairy legs and backward pointing feet. He sits on silk cotton trees and catches innocent travelers. He works in close relation to the witches and sorcerers and all workers of black magic.

Ancient Egyptians

The pantheons of divinities in West Africa have a striking parallel in many other parts of the world. Ancient Egypt is an exact parallel of West Africa. They had a belief in one eternal Creator, along with a host of other gods. In fact, so prolific were the Egyptian divinities that many scholars have concluded that the ancient Egyptians were pure polytheists. But the *Book of the Dead* reveals that belief in Neter, the Supreme Being, was a form of monotheism.

Observe some of the noble statements made about Neter collated from the *Book of the Dead*.

> God is One and only, and none other existeth with Him. — God is the One, the One who hath made all things. — God is a spirit, a hidden spirit, the spirit of spirits, the great spirit of the Egyptians, the divine spirit. — God is from the beginning, and He hath been from the beginning. He hath existed from of old, and was when nothing else had being, He existed when nothing else existed, and what existed He created after He had come into being. He is the Father of beginning. — God is the eternal One, He is eternal and infinite, and endureth for ever and aye (Budge 1960:106).

However, the Egyptians like their counterparts throughout the world, seem to have thought that God was too great and too remote to concern Himself with the problems of men. Instead, He committed the management of the world to a series of gods or spirits whom it was necessary to worship and propitiate. Many gods are worshipped and served. Tem (or Atmu) is the oldest of the gods. He is frequently called, "the self-created," "the maker of the gods," and "the creator of men." His centre of worship was Heliopolis. The female counterpart of Tem was Temt (or Temit). But in the 4th Egyptian Dynasty, Ra, the sun god, usurped the place of Tem. Ra was the first being created by Tem. Sacrifices are offered to him as the great god of this world. The sun is his emblem. Nu is the name of the great mass of waters in primeval times which were located in the sky. In this fathomless depth of water, the seeds of all life were found. Nu became personified as "the Father of the gods."

In the opinion of Budge, a long time student of Egyptian antiquities, "the truth of the matter seems to me to be that the Egyptian religion never wholly lost the monotheistic element which was in it. It existed in the earliest times, and it frequently appears in the early religious texts." (Budge 1960:115) He conjectures that the gods are a later development of the various priests of competing Egyptian cities. The priests of Heliopolis claimed the Sun god, Ra, was the greatest of all gods. In competition the priests of Memphis claimed their god, Ptah, was the creator of heaven and earth and all other gods were formed from him. The priests of all the other Egyptian cities claimed absolute sovereignty for their own gods. And thus developed polytheism along side of monotheism. Divinities proliferated in addition to the Supreme Being, Neter.

EXAMPLES OF DIVINITIES AMONG EUROPEANS

Before the preaching of the Gospel, the Europeans were also worshippers of many divinities. One of the oldest gods of the Teutons (a European tribal group including the Anglo-Saxons who settled in the British Isles) was *Ziu* (or *Tiu*). Originally, he was the shining sky who later became the god of war. We still honour him by our day, *Tuesday*. The god of war was *Wodin* (or *Odin*). His spear never missed. He also became the god of prophets and poets for he knew all things and saw everyone. *Wednesday* honours him. The red-bearded god of thunder and rain and the god of agriculture was Donar (or *Thor*). Throughout the world of the Teutons, he was pictured as a man carrying a hammer in iron gloved hands, riding a sky chariot drawn by two he-goats. He was honoured by *Thursday*. *Friday* was considered the luckiest day, for it commemorated the Scandinavian goddess of love known as *Frigg*. *Saturday* is the only day of the week in English named for a Roman god, *Saturn*. The sacred day of the Teutons was *Sunday*, the day of the *sun*. *Monday* was reserved for the *moon*. Thus, the names for each day of the week in English are derived from the European divinities prior to the coming of Christianity (*The New Webster's Dictionary of the English Language*:1981).

THEOLOGICAL PERSPECTIVE

How shall we then interpret these African divinities? Idowu maintains that Olodumare among the Yoruba is the supreme Creator, first cause of all that exists. The divinities are merely the ministers of Olodumare, exercising authority over the world under the direction of Deity. Idowu affirms, "All the indications which have come down to us are that they [divinities] were brought into existence by Olodumare that they might be His ministers in carrying out, each in his own office, the functions connected with the creation and theocratic government of the earth." (Idowu 1962:18) Olodumare is thus "supreme over all in an absolute sense; and His authority cannot be questioned by any one of the divinities, or by all of them together. He is in full control of all issues; and the divinities have executive powers only in so far as He permits them." (Idowu 1962:54).

Idowu surveys the "facts" concerning divinities among the Yoruba, the various myths and ritual associated with them. He acknowledges that to the "casual observer" the primary attention of the Yorubas is devoted to the many lesser gods (1962:107).

> Truly, to the cursory [casual] observer, the 'gods many and lords many' which form
> the Yoruba pantheon are, to all intents and purposes, sufficient for the needs of the
> people: to these the Yoruba address their worship and prayers as a general rule. It seems,
> therefore, that Olodumare is a remote Deity who could be thought of or called upon
> very occasionally. (Idowu 1962:48)

In fact, he himself devotes 32 pages to the description of worship of the divinities but only 1 page to the cult of Olodumare (1962:142). Furthermore, he admits, "The Yoruba appear to be quite satisfied with the divinities with whom they are in immediate touch." "But," he maintains, "this is only because they believe that once the divinities have been offered their worship, the divinities in their turn will transmit what is necessary of it to Olodumare. It is left to the divinities to take what belongs to them by virtue of their position as authorized by Olodumare and remit to Him all that is His whether to receive or to execute." (1962:142) Idowu, like the other apologists (defenders) for the ancestral cult, uses the social structure of the Yoruba to explain the relationship of Olodumare to the "indefinite" numbers of divinities and to the Yoruba peoples themselves (1962:141). Social custom considers it improper for a younger or inferior person to approach an older or superior person directly. Access to those in superior positions must be done through intermediaries. Thus, Idowu maintains, the Yoruba approach Olodumare through his ministers. However, when crises occur, the Yoruba may bypass the divinities and address themselves directly to Olodumare.

We observe that although many priests serve regularly at the temples erected for the divinities, no priest officiates at any temple for Olodumare for no temples have been erected for Olodumare. Though worship of the divinities takes place every morning at the shrines and though in some communities there is "ritual celebration going on almost all the time" for the divinities (1962:111, 112), we are made to understand by Idowu that this worship is all directed ultimately to Olodumare. Thus the apparent absence of worship of Olodumare among the Yoruba is only the conclusion of those with "incomplete" knowledge. In fact worship is directed to Olodumare through the worship of the divinities who pass on their worship to the Creator.

Idowu rigorously rejects the notion that the Yoruba are polytheists in any sense. The Yoruba "may appear to live their lives in absolute devotion to the divinities," Idowu declares, "but underneath all their acts of worship is the deep consciousness that Olodumare is above all and ultimately controls all things." (1962:50)

> The keynote of their life [the Yoruba] is their religion. In all things, they are
> religious. Religion forms the foundation and the all-governing principle of life for them.
> As far as they are concerned, the full responsibility of all the affairs of life belongs to
> the Deity; their own part in the matter is to do as they are ordered through the priests
> and diviners whom they believe to be the interpreters of the will of the Deity. Through
> all the circumstances of life, through all its changing scenes, its joys and troubles, it is
> the Deity who is in control...man is in the hands of the Deity whose dictate is law, and
> who is waiting on the other side of this life to render to him as he deserves (Idowu 1962:5).

Nevertheless, Idowu acknowledges elsewhere that "the cults of the hitherto ever-increasing intermediary divinities who for practical purposes often become ends in themselves have had an insidiously detrimental effect on His cult as a regular, objective phenomenon in the religious activities of the Yoruba." (1962:143) He thus admits that the divinity cults have the potential of harming the cultic worship of Olodumare.

Whereas, the Yoruba have not made an image of Olodumare, they have fashioned countless images of their divinities. Yet Idowu contends that the Yoruba do not bow down *TO* the wood and stone but only *BEFORE* the wood and stone which are emblems of the divinities. Idowu admits, however, that there is "grave risk" in doing so since the images could cease being a means to an end and become an end in itself. This would be idolatry if devotees actually bow down *to* images of the divinities. But Idowu contends that generally, for the most part, the Yoruba do not bow down *to* these images. "Whatever may be the momentary attitude of the Yoruba to the emblems of their divinities, if the question is put to them whether those were in reality the divinities or not, their answer will be an emphatic negative, because 'the home of the divinity is in heaven.'" (1962:66)

There are two aspects to the question before us. One aspect concerns the religious phenomena among the Yoruba, the myths, the cultic rites and practices, and all the materials used in the Yoruba worship of the divinities. The second aspect, however, deals with interpretation. The handling of the "facts" can lead to different interpretations and understandings of the religious phenomena.

We may then raise the question, "Are these divinities real entities in themselves?" From the biblical perspective, has God in fact created ministers to rule the earth in theocratic form through delegated authority? If indeed He has done so, are these myriads of divinities of His origination?

Idowu contends that many of the divinities are in fact "no more than conceptualizations [ideas or concepts] of some attributes of Olodumare...to those who worship the divinities and derive succour from belief in their existence, to such they are real: but to those who have outgrown them, all reality is concentrated in the Deity." (1962:63) Thus it would appear that Idowu is declaring that the reality of these divinities is resident in the mind of the believer alone. They have no external existence apart from the beliefs of the Yoruba. If the divinities are real to the Yoruba, then they are real to them. But if the Yoruba have outgrown the divinities, then to them the divinities are not real.

This general approach to West African divinities is also reflected in the writings of Ezeanya when speaking of the Igbo-speaking peoples of Southern Nigeria, though he makes some candid admissions (Dickson 1969:30-46). He affirms that the Supreme Being has created the various divinities and charged them with specific functions for man and society. When worship is offered to the divinities God's name may not ever be mentioned. "But whether he is mentioned or not, he is generally believed to be the 'ultimate recipient of offerings to lesser gods, who may be explicitly referred to as intermediaries.'" (Dickson 1969:37)

But then Ezeanya comments, "The point has been made that these spirits are agents of the Supreme God; actually, this is so more in theory than in practice. These spirits, it appears, are self-sufficient and do not therefore have to receive gifts from the Supreme God in order to distribute such to humans. They can bestow these gifts *of themselves*, [emphasis original] thereby acting independently of the Supreme God...They have their resources and have full powers to act without consulting God or asking for his permission." (Dickson 1969:42)

One may ask, whose "theory" is this that the spirits are agents of the Supreme Being? Is this the theory of academic scholars studying ATR or is this a pervasive reflection of traditional belief? It would appear that many devotees of these divinities do in fact attribute their origin and powers to a Supreme Being. But we must be fair and let the facts stand for themselves. And our conviction is that traditional belief is far less uniform and consistent than what is often suggested by scholars today. Mercier would concur with Ezeanya when he writes of the Fon of Dahomey, "Evidence is, however, provided by the existence of many groups of gods who, in spite of their subordinate status in relation to the dual creator, enjoy a high degree of independence in their use of the natural forces which they control." (Mercier 1954:229)

Furthermore, we must distinguish between theoretical polytheism and practical polytheism. Even if the general agreement among a peoples is that the Creator is the Supreme Being, underived and sovereign over all other creatures, we must inquire whether in practice the peoples live that way. For what people profess may be different from what they practice.

Adeyemo points to the polytheistic nature of ATR. In contrast, he observes that Mbiti and Idowu attempt to refute the idea of idolatry in order to emphasize monotheism in ATR.

> Idowu, in an attempt to refute the idea of idolatry and to uphold monotheism, has devised the term 'Unity in diversity,' describing God as One working through many divinities, the powers manifested in the natural phenomena (Adeyemo 1979:22).

Scholars have observed that human beings prefer to conceive of ultimate reality in terms of plurality rather than unity. As we survey the world religions we find evidence that among a large number of peoples there is a tendency toward pluralism. This is even evidenced among the Roman Catholics with their devotion to Mary and the saints.

Thus we find that Ezeanya, instead of "cleaning the deck" and restoring belief in the Supreme Being to a pure monotheism, he recommends the substituting of angels for the minor divinities and the Communion of Saints for the ancestral cult. The tendency toward pluralism seems to be prevalent everywhere, obscuring the pure worship and devotion of God.

Why is this a common tendency among humans? The conclusion of this study will await our investigation of the remaining topics of ATR. But some fundamental questions must be asked by evangelicals. From whence have come these divinities? Are they truly from God? If not, from whence have they come? Do these divinities have independent existence in and of themselves? Are they the mere creation of the imagination, brought about by a people during a lower level of development, only to be discarded when they are no longer believable? Have any peoples anywhere bowed down to wood and stone and served idols instead of God? Or have all peoples, once we truly understand them, had a "truer," "more spiritual" insight into ultimate reality then we have previously realized due to our lack of knowledge? Are these divinities merely the fragmentation of the Creator

God so that the peoples can conceptualize or visualize various attributes of God more concretely?

Accurate interpretation requires more than a knowledge of "the facts." Accurate interpretation requires a biblical world view which understands all of life through the filter of biblical revelation.

REVIEW QUESTIONS FOR CHAPTER 8

1. What is the one belief that makes ATR in West Africa and some other parts of the continent so different from most other parts of Africa?

2. Discuss some of the divinities (or lesser gods) found among the Yoruba, the Ewe, and the Akan.

3. What evidence can you find to support the statement that many West Africans are polytheists?

4. Were the ancient Egyptians truly monotheists or polytheists? Discuss, showing the parallel with West African religions.

Suggested Reading and Thought Questions for Advanced Study:

Argyle, W.J. *The Fon of Dahomey*, 1966, pp.174-200.

Field, M.J. *Religion and Medicine of the Ga People*, 1961, pp.4- 90.

Herskovits, Melville. *Dahomey, An Ancient West African Kingdom*, 2 vols., 1938.

Idowu, Bolaji. *African Traditional Religion: A Definition*, 1973, pp.165-173.

Idowu, Bolaji. *Olodumare: God in Yoruba Belief*, 1962, pp.57-106.

Lienhardt, Godfrey. *Divinity and Experience*, 1961, pp.56-170.

Mbiti, John. *African Religions and Philosophy*, 1969, pp.75-78.

Metuh, Emefie Ikenga. *God and Man in African Religion: A Case Study of the Ibo of Nigeria*, 1981, pp.85-104.

Parrinder, E.G. *African Traditional Religion*, 1962, pp.43-54.

Parrinder, Geoffrey. *West African Religions*, 1961, pp.26-85 .

Rattray, R.S. *Ashanti*, 1969. pp.146-212.

Talbot, P. Amaury. *Tribes of the Niger Delta*, 1967, pp.19-31.

Uchendu, Victor. *The Igbo of Southeast Nigeria*, 1965, pp.94-102.

Consider the ethnographic data, either from your own observation among your peoples or from some recommended books given above. Ponder over the following questions.

1. What evidence can you find that the peoples actually did believe in one Creator God who was self existent and uncreated? Describe the characteristics and activities of God.

2. Describe some of the divinities also feared among these peoples. What are their characteristics and their activities?

3. Are the people clear in their thinking that the divinities are creatures of the

Supreme Being, dependent upon Him and subservient to Him?

4. Do these divinities seem to have powers and authority in and of themselves or do they always rely upon the power and authority of God?

5. How do the divinities seem to be related to the Supreme Being? Is this usually clear in the minds of the people?

6. Who receives the most devotion and worship, divinities or the Creator? Discuss.

Chapter 9

SPIRITS IN AFRICAN TRADITIONAL RELIGION

Care must be taken when generalizing the beliefs of a whole continent. All African peoples believe in the Supreme Being, the spirit world and mystical powers, while some believe in divinities and others do not. But as we have observed before, the unique contribution of each ethnic group is the manner in which they have emphasized or de-emphasized some of these distinctives of ATR. In this chapter we shall focus on the spirit world with particular emphasis on the ancestral spirits. Many Bantu peoples major on the living-dead with much time and labour expended in appeasing them. Fear is a dominant feature.

The main part of the traditional religion of the Toubouri peoples in Chad was belief in the spirits which animate everything, including trees, stones, grass and water. The Toubouri seek to gain the favour of these spirits, either avoiding their anger or calling upon them to do evil to their enemies. Moreover, each man who founded a family became a kind of "god" to his living children when he died. The ancestral spirit of this father may ask for food by sending sickness to the family members. Offerings and prayers are essential for veneration of these ancestral spirits. Ceremonies are held each year for the ancestral spirits lest they become angry (Interview with Daidanso ma Djongwe of Chad who grew up in his African traditional religion:1988).

However, there are others who, though they believe in ancestral spirits, generally ignore them and surely do not fear them. The Murle of southern Sudan are a case in point. The Murle do not fear the spirits nor do they seek their blessing or help. When people die they descend into a hole in the ground and live in a shadowy world. But the ancestral spirits do not return to haunt the living. The Murle have no word for possession for spirits do not do things to people. Those who appear to be spirit possessed are said to be sick in the head. They, like the Nuer and Taposa, are a very practical people. Everything has a very practical, rational answer. In contrast the Kichepo living only a few miles from the Murle on the Ethiopian and Sudanese border have spirit possession (Arensen:1988).

Hence this chapter must be understood with that thought in mind, that there is a great range of variation in ATR.

KINDS OF SPIRITS

Broadly speaking, there are two different kinds of spirits: the ghosts of those who were born as human beings and those spirits which were created as spirits.

Ghosts of Human Beings.

The majority of spirits are thought by most people to be the spirits of departed human beings. These ancestral spirits are divided into two categories by John Mbiti: those ancestors who have died recently up to five generations ago, and those ancestors whose names and identity have been forgotten because they died more than five generations ago.

Traditionally, writers have referred to the spirits of the departed dead by the expressions, "ancestors," "ancestral spirits," or "dead ancestors." Mbiti objects to these ascriptions, since they are "misleading terms." He observes that this category of beings may include those who are technically not "ancestors," for example, the spirits of children, brothers and sisters. "One would strongly advocate the abolition of the two terms 'ancestral spirits' and 'the ancestors,' and replace them with 'spirits' or 'the living- dead' whichever is applicable." (Mbiti 1969:83)

One advantage of the term, "living-dead," is that it expresses the living relationship between the living and their dead ancestors. For the ancestral spirits are "the living-dead" and not the "dead ancestors." The living-dead for five generations enjoy a state of personal immortality while they are being personally remembered by name by their living descendants. "...their process of dying is not yet complete." (Mbiti 1969:83) They are partly spirit and partly human, with one foot in the spirit world and one foot in the world of the living. When the last person dies who could remember them, however, the living-dead have then completed the dying process and moved into the past (*zamani*) as impersonal spirits and become mere "Its."

Thus Mbiti calls the ancestors whose names are remembered, "the living dead." Whereas, the older ancestors, whose identity is lost in antiquity beyond five generations, Mbiti calls "spirits." These "spirits" have lost their "personal immortality" because the living no longer remember them by name. They leave the present (*sasa*) period with continuous involvement in family affairs and slip back into the past where they become impersonal "Its," unknown by name.

"Man does not, and need not, hope to become a spirit; he is inevitably to become one, just as a child will automatically grow to become an adult under normal circumstances." (Mbiti 1969:79)

Other scholars of ATR, however, continue to refer to the departed by the term, "ancestors" and "ancestral spirits." We recognize that some evidence supports Mbiti's analysis. However, we also contend that Mbiti's distinction between the living-dead (recently deceased) and the spirits (those ancestors deceased more than five generations ago), is an academic distinction which is often not reflected either in the vernacular vocabulary or in traditional thinking.

Among the ghosts of human beings are some with distinctive characteristics. Various African peoples believe that some people who die are not permitted into the realm of the ancestral spirits. These rejected ghost-spirits include people who were not buried properly, those who died an unhappy death by hanging, drowning, being struck by lightning, or in pregnancy. People who were accursed while living are also rejected. They will wander aimlessly, haunting such areas as forests, rivers, mountains and rocky ravines. They may enter animals. Their general aim seems to be molesting and harming people (Idowu 1973:174,175).

Another category of ancestral spirits is that of kings and heroes. Some peoples like the Baganda, Kalabari and Banyoro believe in spirits of legendary heroes. Among the Anyoro of Uganda, traditional religion does not centre on the ancestral cult but upon a pantheon of hero-gods called the Cwezi. Bunyoro was once ruled by a people who possessed much wisdom and power. When they disappeared from the country, they allegedly left behind ten Cwezi spirits, around whom the spirit mediumship cult centred. These spirits possess marvelous power like the former rulers and are still associated with quasi-historical figures of the past.

These ghosts of legendary heroes are sometimes merged with spirits of nature which were never human. Thus the Cwezi spirits of the Banyoro are also associated with natural phenomenon like thunder, lightning, the sun and moon. In this way the ghosts of the ancestors merge with the spirits created as such in the beginning.

Created Spirits

Many peoples believe in spirits which are not the ghosts of former human beings. They may be spirits which bring disease like the plague or smallpox. Others associate forces of nature with spirits. There are spirits which dwell in trees, mountains, rivers or other mighty forces of nature. Some believe that charms possessing magical powers have spirits living in them.

Idowu mentions one category of spirits among the Yoruba whose origin is uncertain. They are called "abiku" in Yoruba, that is, "spirits 'born to die'." "The belief here is that there are wandering spirits who specialize in the sadistic mischief of finding the way into wombs to be born in order to die." (Idowu 1973:175) Through divination, men can learn whether a child has such a spirit. Various medicines and magic are used to prevent further maltreatment.

CREATED SPIRITS

Dwelling Places of the Spirits.

Generally speaking, spirits are found everywhere. They especially like the woods, bush, forest, rivers and mountains. In each part of the country, certain places are especially regarded as the haunt of the spirits.

They may take up their abode in animals and birds. If some strange animal leaves its normal habitat and approaches a village, the local people believe that some spirit must dwell in the animal. For why would this normally aloof animal approach the habitat of men?

Some believe the realm of the spirits is below the earth. Others think it is above the earth in the sky. Spirits may also possess human beings. In most areas there is at least one person who may be seized by a kind of madness when possessed by a spirit. Spirits may also appear to people in their dreams.

Wherever the spirits may be, they are never far from man. In fact, Mbiti observes that the traditional African would be uncomfortable if the spirits would depart. "This would mean upsetting the balance of existence, and if that balance

is upset, then men make sacrifices, offerings and prayers, to try and restore it."
(Mbiti 1969:80)

Attitude Towards the Spirits.

Whether these spirits were created as spirits or whether they are nameless ghosts from antiquity past, their relationship with the living is very similar. They are nameless, unknown spirits, mere strangers to the living. They are unpredictable and frequently dangerous. Since spirits cannot be seen, and yet they can strike anywhere and at any time, they are feared. Whereas the living-dead are held in both fear and affection, the spirits are mostly feared.

Almost always the spirits appear to attack, molest, destroy and harm the living peoples. Since they are unpredictable, the safest thing is to remain far away from their places of abode. Any tragedy of illness, insanity or epilepsy may be blamed on them.

The conclusion of the book, *Spirit Mediumship and Sorcery in Africa*, is that "while some spirits are thought to be wholly malevolent, no spirits are thought to be beneficient all the time although the ancestral ghosts...are believed to be so as long as they receive attentions that they need." (Beattie 1969:xxi) Briefly, then, the attitude toward the spirits is mostly fear.

ANCESTRAL SPIRITS

Among many African peoples the vast majority of known spirits are ancestral spirits, that is, the ghosts of the dead, whether they are the recent dead (living-dead) or long since dead (spirits). It, therefore, seems appropriate for us to delve more deeply into the ancestral spirits. Only a few troublesome questions arise concerning traditional belief in non-human spirits. But much controversy has arisen on the subject of ancestral spirits.

Therefore, most of this chapter will focus on the more prominent aspect of traditional belief and practice, namely, the living-dead.

Continuation of Life after Death.

Belief in life after death is found among most African peoples from earliest times. *The Book of the Dead* represents a system of theology "derived from the primitive indigenous, and probably predynastic, Egyptians." (Budge 1960:1) The many burial customs and funerary rites found in this ancient book confirm that "the belief in immortality among the Egyptians is one of the oldest of their religious beliefs...The attainment of renewal of life in the Other World was the aim and object of every Egyptian believer." (Budge 1960:66)

Among the Bantu, "survival after death is not a matter for argument or speculation; it is an axiom of life." (Willoughby 1928:66) The same is true among other African peoples. Mbiti affirms, "Without exception, African peoples believe that death does not annihilate life and that the departed continue to exist in the hereafter." (Mbiti 1970:264)

Abode of the Ancestral Spirits.

Some believe that they live underground where they are buried. The Becwana say the old man is buried inside the cattle-pen "so that he may hear the tramp of his cattle as they go out to graze in the morning and return for safety at sundown." (Willoughby 1928:57) The underworld of the dead is a common belief among many.

At the same time, many believe the departed ascend to the sky to live somewhere above the world. The sky is the place where God now lives and the destined locality of the ancestral spirits.

Wherever the realm of the living-dead may be, the ancestors are closely associated with the place of burial and with their former home. Speaking of the Bantu, Willoughby asserts,

> The ancestral spirits are where their descendants are...Distance does not hamper their movements as it used to do before they discarded their tenement [body] of flesh...It seems certain, however, that spirits find no difficulty in being present at two or three places at the same time...They wander over the world, wherever their relatives go, helping or hindering them (Willoughby 1928:71).

Wherever the living-dead are, their abode is modeled after the pattern of the living. The herd-boy herds the goats and sheep, the women hoe their gardens and reap the crops, the men delight in their cattle, the villagers gather for discussion in the evenings, the drums beat and the dances follow. One major difference, however, is the absence of any form of marriages.

There is no division of the dead on the basis of character. Apart from witches and outcasts, all the living-dead, good and bad, live together in the world of spirits. Their character is much the same as in this life, partaking of jealousies and offended feelings like the living.

Although the ancestral spirits partake of increased power and knowledge, the state of the ancestors is nothing to be desired. The Tschwis say that the underworld is dimmer and a mere shadow-land of the present joys. A Tschwi proverb states, "One day in this world is worth a year in Srahmandazi (the underworld)."

Relationship of the Living with the Living-Dead

An essential element of ATR is the inter-dependence of the living and their ancestors. They live in intimate association, and are interdependent, each communicating with the other. Though a veil does separate the two, it is not an iron curtain. Each communicates with the other and each is dependent upon the other.

The Role of the Living-Dead Among the Living

The living-dead serve in various capacities as they relate to the living.

1)As senior elders of the clan, the ancestors function as the guardians of the family traditions and life.

Basic to the understanding of their function is the concept of seniority. A man's prestige increases as he grows older. Speaking of the living elders, Kenyatta remarks, "It is his seniority that makes an elder almost indispensable in the general life of the people. His presence or advice is sought in all functions." (Kenyatta n.d.:253) The ancestors are then the eldest of the senior elders. Even as the youth look to the living elders for direction, so the whole living clan looks to their living-dead for guidance.

2)When the living fail to follow the customs of the fathers, it becomes the duty of the ancestors to correct their errors.

Virtually every crisis that develops, whether it is drought or pestilence, sickness or death, may be attributed to the displeasure of the ancestors. By these means the living-dead make known their will and seek correction of the wrong.

In this respect, the direction of the people is turned back to the traditions of the ancestors. Since *zamani* [past] is the focus of concern, there is a reluctance to innovate and change direction.

3)As elders, the ancestors serve as the owners of the land, fertilizing the earth and causing the food to grow. The land becomes "sacred" in the sense that it binds together the living with their ancestors.

4)The living-dead receive the requests from the living.

The living may implore, beg, request or ask their ancestors for assistance. Fertility is of greatest interest to the living-dead, since without a continual reproduction of children, they will lack descendants who can continue to remember them and supply necessary sustenance. Thus, people often request their ancestors for help in bearing and preserving children.

Since the ancestral spirits may be the cause of trouble among the living because of some offense, requests and offerings are often made to the living-dead. The medicine man frequently identifies a particular ancestor who has been offended and who needs to be propitiated in order to restore peace and prosperity.

5)The ancestral spirits may also serve as intermediaries between man and God.

Being close in time to the living, the living-dead can best understand man's needs. Being closer to God, they have "full access to the channels of communicating with God directly."

A skillful hunter among the Tonga in Zambia found that his fortunes in hunting began to wane. Upon seeking the advice of a diviner, he was advised to sacrifice to the living-dead. Not satisfied, he inquired,

How is it that we folk are always worshipping the "mizimu" [ancestors]? Why not approach Leza [the Supreme being] direct?" To which the Diviner replied, "Because the ancestral spirits are subordinate chiefs under God, the Supreme chief. Just as in our human courts of justice you first take your affairs to a subordinate official, and he is able to take them to the higher chief, so also the ancestral spirits play a similar part in relation to Leza. We approach them first and they lay our affairs before God (Smith 1966:68).

However, as we shall see later, many people approach the ancestral spirits without any knowledge that they are merely intermediaries between God and man. John Mbiti goes beyond the bounds of reasonableness when he contends, "God is the ultimate Recipient whether or not the worshippers are aware of it." (Mbiti 11969:58) When we study ATR we must learn what in fact the peoples traditionally believed and practiced and not what we as academic scholars think they ought to have believed and practiced.

6) The living-dead become a source of comfort to the living who are always conscious of their presence. There is an inner sense of relief for traditional Africans when they are assured that their ancestors are continually with them.

7) The living-dead communicate with the living by revelations.

Whenever the living-dead seek to help their living kin by forewarning them of future dangers, or rebuking them for some transgression of tradition, or rebuking them for some offense, there are several methods available whereby they can communicate with the living.

Dreams. Like many other peoples, the Africans consider dreams a method by which the ancestral spirits can communicate with the living. The warnings, cautions and hints derived from dreams are taken seriously. If admonished to pluck leaves from a bush for use in herbal medicines, they will arise in the middle of the night and do it, immediately after seeing the dream. If a dead father appears in a dream, the living will seek the advice of a diviner and offer a sacrifice. If men desire to retain a good dream in their memory, some may spit on the floor; but if they desire a bad dream to vanish, they may sneeze and chew some medicine. Dreams are usually taken seriously.

Calamity. Whenever some crisis occurs, be it personal illness, tribal disaster or death, the diviner is consulted to ascertain whether some ancestor is seeking to make known his displeasure. Accidents which are too trivial to be considered disasters are looked upon as warnings from the spirit world.

Ecstasy and Trance. Certain people are subject to periods of emotional disturbance, excitement or unusual changes in their normal personality. true.
In Ukambani before this century, one Mukamba received the revelation that the Masai would be severely stricken with smallpox and that they would subsequently settle among the Gikuyu as a result. Shortly afterwards, this actually happened. This same Mukamba foretold that a white race would enter the country and live side by side with the Akamba and Gikuyu. This vision occurred before European colonization. Again, he was seized by the spirits and predicted the great famine of 1900 before it happened.

Possession. The living-dead are thought to enter individuals and use them as mediums of communication with the living. Every village is full of vivid accounts of people possessed by the spirits. When in this state of possession, they receive special revelation from the spirit world.

Prophets. An African prophet is one who can foretell some future event, as was illustrated above. This prophecy may be through a variety of means, including dreams, spirit possession or by the ability to interpret the signals of the living-dead in calamities. The difference between a possessed man and a prophet is that the former delivers messages of local importance, whereas the latter addresses a larger group with wider implications. "The impressive feature of the 'prophet' is that he uses no argument and appeals to no authority but that of the spirit which inspires him. It is the Bantu equivalent of 'Thus saith the Lord'... (Willoughby 1928:115)

Divination. A diviner is consulted when the living-dead reveals himself through dreams or calamity in order to determine its true source and meaning. This diviner or medicine man is in fact a medium who is able to communicate with the ancestral spirits.

Obligations of the Living to their Ancestral Spirits

Throughout life, there are many occasions for remembering the living-dead. These obligations which, if omitted, may bring wrath down upon the living.

Daily at Home. As the elder members of the family, the ancestral spirits are shown signs of hospitality as a matter of course. Customary household rites include giving a pinch of snuff, a swallow of beer, a whiff of pipe smoke, a portion of spittle, a taste of food. Since the living-dead complain easily when ignored, their presence is continually acknowledged in every part of daily life.

The Cycle of Life. Periodic remembrance of the living-dead occurs at significant points in the cycle of life. At child birth, puberty, marriage, birth of offspring, sickness and death, the living-dead are specifically remembered, for they are intimately involved in the continuation of the ancestral line. Some believe that apart from the special work of the ancestors, no child can be conceived. The living and the dead meet together at marriage, for apart from marriage and birth of children, the living-dead have no one to remember them. Ceremonies and requests to the living-dead are necessary at death in order to guarantee a peaceful entrance into the spirit world.

The ancestors are remembered in various ways.

Birth. Water is sometimes blown from the mouth, accompanied by requests to the ancestral spirits. Beer is poured on the ground as a libation or offering in a private family gathering, as prayers of thanksgiving are offered. A goat is sacrificed with prayers for the welfare of the mother and child.

Marriage. Sacrifices to the living-dead are often necessary in order to obtain their agreement for the marriage when the bride price is given. At the marriage itself, some animal may be sacrificed with portions given to the ancestral spirits. The man and woman are smeared with the gall and entrails of the animal. Wristlets or necklaces from the animal are made with special medication applied. And the living-dead are asked to care for the newly married couple.

Sickness. Among most African peoples, there is a remembrance of the living-dead in times of illness, even though the ancestors may be neglected at other times. If, through divination, the family learns that the sickness has come through some offense against the living-dead, sacrifices are offered and prayers made. As among the Zulu, a cow is sacrificed and offered to the living-dead with this request:

> We offer unto you, spirits of our departed relations, this beast, in order that you, who are the chief relations of this patient, may invite all your other spiritual relations to partake of this beast offered unto you, even as you did on earth while alive, in behalf of the patient; satisfy yourselves and show kindness unto this patient, your relation, by giving him good health (Willoughby 1928:190).

Death. The living are responsible to give their dead a proper burial, according to the customs. If some crisis occurs after death, the living quickly conclude that their departed ancestors may be displeased with some aspect of the burial. No stone is left unturned until the wrong is made right, even if they must re-bury him again.

The Cycle of Seasons. Throughout the year, there are special occasions determined by the seasons, when the living-dead are specially remembered.

Times of Rain. Rain rites are common around the world, especially among those peoples living in dry regions where the rains frequently fail. Among the African peoples, God alone is the source of rain. However, prayers for rain may be made to the living-dead and thanks for rain afterwards may be directed to them. In fact as we shall see later, many people seem to assume that the ancestral spirits are in and of themselves empowered to send the rains.

Times of planting, growth of the crops and harvest. These three great events in the cycle of the agricultural year are marked by rites among most African peoples. Libations, prayers and offerings are given to the ancestors at these times.

Times of hunting and fishing. Rites and ceremonies often, though not always, accompany the beginning of hunting and fishing expeditions. Before the people of Thongaland go fishing, someone must spit into the water, saying, "Let fish abound! Let them not hide in the mud! Let there be enough of them to satisfy everyone." Elsewhere the spirits are invoked by throwing beer and tobacco into the water. Similar offerings and prayers are made to the ancestral spirits before a hunt.

Other Special Occasions. Every ethnic group has rites that are unique to them. The Ashanti of Ghana observe special ceremonies every three weeks. The living-dead are represented by a stool which they used during life. These stools are kept in a stool-house. Every three weeks the ancestors are called upon. Water is poured on the ground so that the living-dead can wash their hands, food is given them and a sheep is sacrificed and smeared on the stool.

Among the peoples of West Africa, human sacrifices were made upon the death of a king, in order to provide him with servants in the spirit world. This is very similar to the practice of the ancient Egyptians. Sir Richard Burton estimated that about 80 human beings were offered annually in Dahomey as a continuing supply of servants for the departed royalty. Human sacrifices were offered at various times in Uganda to ward off sickness, to cure disorders of the land and to mark the accession of a new king. Others, like the Akamba, offered human sacrifices in times of critical drought.

Attitude Toward the Living-Dead

An ambivalent attitude is manifested.

1. On the one hand, there is an attitude of affection and respect because the ancestral spirits are in fact their own family members, as they understand these spirits. Lindblom observed of the Akamba that "he feels a close bond between himself and his dead, and the latter often come at night to visit their old village. They can be talked with, though they are not visible." (Lindblom 1920:211) Their ancestral spirits show "a certain friendly interest in their descendants." (1920:214)

2. Yet on the other hand, the living-dead are dreaded. The ancestors are feared. When death occurs, a barrier is erected between the living and the living-dead which creates anxiety and fear.

Mbiti observes that the living-dead are not really welcomed by the living. The two gestures of hospitality are greetings and food. Yet no one ever passes on greetings to the departed when the living-dead are thought to pay a visit. Neither are they welcomed and invited to wait until food is prepared. "The food and libation given to the living-dead are paradoxically acts of hospitality and welcome, yet of informing the living-dead to move away. The living-dead are wanted and yet not wanted." (Mbiti 1969:84)

The ancestral spirits tend to be unpredictable and easily offended so that the people live in fear and apprehension. Speaking of the Akamba, an anthropologist observed,

> The most characteristic feature of the conception of 'aimu' [ancestral spirits] is, however, that they are considered to expect constant attention from their living relations, in the form of sacrifices. The sacrifice is a gift which the 'aimu' need; by it also the connection with them is maintained and strengthened. The least inattention in this respect is avenged by the sending of all sorts of misfortunes down upon the negligent one, such as diseases of both men and domestic animals, and even death. Therefore, when an accident happens, it is feared that it is caused by the 'aimu.' The result of these beliefs is that the natives never know whether they have sacrificed enough, and so they live in a constant state of anxiety lest they shall incur the displeasure of the jealous and capricious [changeable] spirits [italics mine] (Lindblom 1920:214).

The Tallensi of Ghana are said to wage a constant struggle with the living-dead. "Men try to coerce and placate their ancestors by means of sacrifices. But the ancestors are unpredictable. It is their power to injure and their sudden attacks on routine well being that make men aware of them rather than their beneficient guardianship." (Parrinder 1968:59) Parrinder continues to write, that in

Ghana "no man is half so much afraid of his gods as a man is of his ancestors...the ever-present watchful dead and their power to smite or bless the living."

Thus the traditional attitude toward the ancestral spirits is simultaneously attraction toward them and repulsion from them. Summarizing this ambivalent attitude of the traditional African towards his ancestors, Taylor writes that they have a "strangely mingled sentiment of awe, anxiety and affection which the living feel toward the ancestors." (Taylor 1963:152)

Deceitfulness is Displayed

Even though the living-dead are thought to have an ever present knowledge of the events occurring on earth, they can be deceived. For instance, a mother may name her child, 'hyena,' a most loathsome animal, in order to deceive the living-dead into thinking she does not love the baby. This is done to ward off further attacks of the ancestral spirits after several infants have died in the family.

Scolding and Mockery are Manifest

It is not uncommon for the living-dead to be scolded, rebuked, threatened and reprimanded. In fact, it is this feature that frequently distinguishes the requests to the ancestors and the prayers made to God.

Prayers to the departed ancestors may contain an element of scolding like this example. "You are useless, you gods. You only give us trouble. For although we give you offerings you do not listen to us! You so-and-so are full of hatred. You do not enrich us." (Smith 1968:25) Such scolding is not frequently found in prayers directed to the Supreme Being.

CONCLUSION

An academic understanding of ATR is inadequate. One must try to walk in the shoes of a traditional African and learn to feel the way he feels. Genuine empathy is required. Perhaps the closest we can come to a genuine feeling of ATR within the confines of a book is to reflect on the poetry written. For poetry expresses the feelings of the people, not merely their intellectual formulations.

Perhaps the most vivid portrayal of the living presence of the ancestors among the traditional Africans in poetic form has been penned by Senegal's poet, Birago Diop.

Forefathers

> Listen more often to things rather than beings.
> Hear the fire's voice,
> Hear the voice of water,
> In the wind hear the sobbing of the trees,
> It is our forefathers breathing.

The dead are not gone forever.
They are in the paling shadows
And in the darkening shadows.
The dead are not beneath the ground,
They are in the rustling tree,
In the murmuring wood,
In the still water,
In the flowing water,
In the lonely place, in the crowd;
The dead are not dead.

Listen more often to things rather than beings.
Hear the fire's voice.
Hear the voice of water.
In the wind hear the sobbing of the trees.
It is the breathing of our forefathers
Who are not gone, not beneath the ground,
Not dead.

The dead are not gone forever.
They are in a woman's breast,
A child's crying, a glowing ember.
The dead are not beneath the earth,
They are in the flickering fire,
In the weeping plant, the groaning rock,
The wooded place, the home.
The dead are not dead.

Listen more often to things rather than beings.
Hear the fire's voice,
Hear the voice of water.
In the wind hear the sobbing of the trees.
It is the breath of our forefathers. (Hughes 1961:184,185)

REVIEW QUESTIONS FOR CHAPTER 9

1. Generally speaking, what are the two different kinds of spirits in ATR?

2. Explain the difference Mbiti makes between the living-dead and the spirits. Is this kind of distinction made among your peoples? Explain.

3. Where may spirits be found?

4. Describe the attitude of people towards the spirits.

5. Discuss the various activities which the living-dead perform on behalf of the living. Illustrate this from your own personal knowledge.

6. How do the living-dead communicate with the living? Illustrate this from the stories you have heard yourself.

7. Discuss the obligations that the living have toward the living-dead. What

customs do your own peoples have in remembering the dead?

Suggested Reading and Thought Questions for Advanced Study:

Adggbola, E.A. Ade. *Traditional Religion in West Africa*, 1983, pp.128-136.

Idowu, Bolaji. *African Traditional Religion: A Definition*, 1973, pp.173-189.

Mbiti, John. *African Religions and Philosophy*, 1969, pp.78-91.

Parrinder, E. G. *African Traditional Religion*, 1962, pp.57-66.

Parrinder, Geoffrey. *West African Religion*, 1961, pp.115-127.

1. Do your people believe in spirits who are different from ancestral spirits? If so, describe them, giving their names, origin, nature, habitat, powers and activities.

2. Talk to someone who has communicated with the ancestral spirits. Describe their seance: who initiated the communication, under what circumstances and how was this done, what was said etc. Do you believe these spirits are real or imaginary? Give reasons for your answer.

3. What obligations do the living have toward their ancestors?

4. How pervasive is the belief of spirits among your people? What occupies the thought and activity of the traditionalists more: mystical powers, spirits, the living-dead or the Supreme Being? Justify your answer with reasons.

5. Discuss Mbiti's distinction between "personal immortality" and "collective immortality." Is this distinction made by your people in the vernacular? Discuss.

CHAPTER 10

CASE STUDY OF THE AKAMBA

IMPORTANCE OF ANCESTRAL SPIRITS

The spirit world is most important among the Akamba. "The bulk of Akamba religious ideas and practices is to be found in connection with the 'spirits' of the departed, or *aimu* (*iimu*, singular). Concepts regarding *aimu* are more fully developed than those regarding God or the universe in general." (Mbiti 1971:10)

The spirits pervade the whole of Akamba life. The whole world of the Akamba was inhabited by the spirits. No single part was without them. Everywhere one moved, the spirits were present. People were ever conscious of the spirits.

Spirits could be heard or seen in the hills, beside the rivers, within stony areas, among the fig trees. The Akamba could hear sounds of the spirits in the morning or evening. Cheers of dancing, people preparing food, cows, chickens and goats making their noises, women milking cows, babies crying – all could be heard from the spirit world. As the spirits drove their cattle home at night, they could all be heard with the accompanying whistling and singing.

Spirits were especially found near the shrines. One Mukamba who passed a shrine saw the appearance of a person at the centre of the traditional shrine (*ithembo*). She trembled in fear for the person had the appearance of her dead uncle. She tried to call him but no sooner had she raised her voice than he disappeared in a big cloud of smoke. She nearly fainted but gained sufficient strength to return home.

Sometimes the spirits would appear in the form of a snake. One grandmother spoke of a python which regularly appeared in their home to bless them. When the python appeared every day he was fed with milk, fat and blood. It could rest at the fireplace for a long time. No one dared to play with the snake for it was treated with great respect. The python, the embodiment of a family ancestor, brought peace to the household. The python would sometimes crawl all around the house, even on the roof and fall onto a bed. But the children were taught never to interfere with the presence of the python and to remain quiet when it came.

The spirits would possess people, especially women, during their dances. When the Akamba were possessed they could stand on burning charcoal without being burned. They could take red hot metal rods and place them in their mouths without harm. When a person was possessed in a dance, everyone knew it. All noise subsided. The drums and the pattern of dancing would be patterned after the one possessed. Many times the spirits overpowered the possessed one so that she would fall down.

Having demonstrated the importance of the ancestral spirits among the Akamba, let us examine some of the traditional beliefs concerning these ever present spirits.

ROLE OF THE ANCESTRAL SPIRITS

Senior Elders

As we have observed before, the Akamba community includes the unborn, the living and the living-dead. The dead are in fact not dead, but as Mbiti calls them, the "living-dead." Thus the ancestors are involved in the community life of the living, communicating with them, appearing to them, directing their lives and maintaining the traditions of the fathers.

The meaning of age is important for our understanding of the activities of the *aimu* among the Akamba. A person's prestige and honour increases as he grows older. A man's reputation depends in part on his experience as he rises through the traditional stages of maturity. As one grows older he has more children, gains more wealth, and marries more wives. An elder with great respect is one with well controlled children. From earliest years the children learn that they are not the centre of the universe. They learn the chain of command, the younger always revering the elder. Each generation reminds the younger generation of their inferiority through greetings. In response to the greeting, *Wakya*, the younger replies, *Aa*. A man fifty years old answers the salutation of an older person in the same way a child does. This simply reinforces the authority and position of the older person. The more wealth one acquires the more people become obligated to him. The Akamba are very generous. They find it difficult to say "no" to anyone making a request. The more one possesses, the more he is able to give, and consequently, the more people will become obligated to him. Prestige and honour grows for wealthy elders, for they acquire more power and influence. They are able to give animals for the elders to eat during traditional feasts. Thus age, with the associated experiences, provided the elders with great influence traditionally.

The living-dead are the elders of the senior living elders. The *aimu* have more experience, have seen and known more than any of the most senior elders among the clans. The *aimu* have more power and prestige, being in the spirit world.

Therefore, proper attention and honour must be given to the living-dead. Any inattention or neglect will result in punishment. Careful attention to the traditions of the elders will result in favour from the *aimu*. But any deviation from tradition will bring wrath of the *aimu* upon the living. Therefore, the ancestral spirits are the guardians of tradition, the senior elders who maintain tight control on the activities of the living.

When the living fail to follow the customs of the fathers, the ancestors will punish them and lead them back to the traditions. Virtually every crisis that develops, whether it is drought or pestilence, sickness or death, may be caused by the angry ancestors. By means of trouble the *aimu* make known their will through the medicine man so that correction can be made. In this respect, the direction of the Akamba is turned back to the traditions of the fathers. Since *zamani* [the past] is the focus of concern, there is reluctance to innovate and make changes.

Muange told of an experience in which a medicine man overcharged a woman who came to him sick. The next day the medicine man himself became sick with the same disease which she had. The medicine man sent his two wives to two different medicine men to inquire about the reason for his illness. They both reported back that the living-dead had revealed that his sickness was due to him overcharging his client, the sick woman. Thus the ancestors had become angry. So he appeased the ancestors by returning the goat to the woman who had been sick. The medicine man also slaughtered a goat for his living-dead.

As the senior elders among the Akamba, the living-dead play a crucial role in the social unity of the peoples. The ancestors help to unite the people together and bind them to the traditions of the fathers.

Jacobs contends that,

> The central feature of the Kamba culture is the mystical union of the tribe. This binds all of the tribesmen together, whether they be the living, the dead, or those yet unborn. A Mukamba's security, both in this life and in the life to come, depends upon how he relates himself to the mystical tribe (Jacobs 1961:98,99).

Harmony must be maintained with the living-dead. When trouble comes the medicine man is the specialist who communicates with the ancestral spirits, pours libations, and speaks soothing words. The final act of the medicine man re-establishes the harmony among the living and the dead. The living direct their attention to their senior elders, the living-dead, in order to maintain unity and harmony (Ndeti 1972:118).

As the senior elders, the living-dead relate to the living in a manner that reflects the social structure of the Akamba.

As we have seen, the smallest social unit among the Akamba is the *musyi* or homestead. Special attention is paid to the ancestral spirits of the homestead who are also known as "the gods of the homestead" (*ngai sya musyi*).

In addition to the immediate ancestors in general, each home has a *muithi*, a shepherd who is responsible for the home. The medicine man informs the family of the name of their shepherd. Before any journey, beer is poured out to their shepherd (*muithi*), beseeching a safe journey. They ask him for health and protection.

Usually, there is a goat dedicated to the *muithi*, though not frequently done these days. This is known as "the goat of the ancestors." Whenever a person becomes sick or members return home from a long journey, they lead this goat around the homestead so that the shepherd can protect the home. The second major social unit of the Akamba is the *mbaa*, a larger social unit extending five generations back. For instance, the *Mbaa Mbuu* is the family unit traced back five generations to Mbuu, the founding father. Philip whose name is Nyamai, traces his ancestry through his father, Muia, grandfather Ng'ata, great grandfather Nduva, and his great great grandfather Kivindyo whose elder brother, Mbuu, gave his name to Philips's *mbaa*.

Every *mbaa* has their *kimoi*, the one who began their family and to whom offering and sacrifices are given. If the *kimoi* (the founding father of the family) was a medicine man or priest, a tree is planted for him as a shrine. Each traditional *mbaa mbuu* looks to *Mbuu* for protection and help. They reciprocate by giving him sacrifices and offerings.

Larger than the *mbaa* is the *mbai*, the clan. The chief clan ancestors remembered are the *kimoi* of the various branches of the clan. Thus the clan has many ancestral spirits remembered by the pouring of drink and the giving of food. To these ancestors the Akamba look for protection and assistance.

At the family shrine, the centre pole of the house, the father always gives offerings to his immediate forefather and asks him to pass it on to his forefathers. Men never give offerings to women ancestors. But women may also give offerings to female ancestors.

Sacrifices given to the living-dead at the public shrines, however, may not necessarily be family or clan members. The offerings are given to the living-dead to whom the shrine is dedicated. The ancestor may have been noted for special powers, usually a medicine man or medicine woman. Therefore, the ancestral cult observed at the public shrine does not necessarily involve a member of the *musyi* (homestead), the *mbaa* (five generations in the family) or the *mbai* (clan). The Akamba gave sacrifices to that deceased former Mukamba leader, not because of family relationships, but because he or she is able to help them in a particular need.

Thus the Akamba traditional relations with their ancestors reflect the social structure among the peoples. These ancestors are looked upon as the senior elders who deserve honour and are capable of giving practical assistance in life.

Since the role of the ancestors is to serve as the senior elders who are frequently consulted, regularly appeased and gratefully honoured, the living-dead serve as the social bond among the Akamba. As Mbiti writes, "They strengthen ties, and to some extent they are the guardians of family solidarity." (Mbiti 1966:15)

Benefactors

Even as all kinds of trouble are blamed on the *aimu*, so every kind of blessing is attributed to the ancestors. One Mukamba said, "The ancestors are responsible for every good thing that comes to us and we must offer gifts and sacrifices to them as thanksgiving."

Healing sickness and protecting from sickness are major benefits. "If the ancestors are treated well," say the Akamba, "they can protect people." For example, if a child is sick, then the medicine man is consulted. He will announce what the ancestor wants. Then the father will pour libation to the ancestors, find a goat for them and the child will be well. One Mukamba said, "Yes, it is true, the ancestors do benefit the living. They do bless their people only if the living do sacrifice to them according to their will. The blessings may be giving the children good health, health to the cattle and prosperity in the gardens."

Although the ancestors normally speak to the common people through the mediums, such as the medicine men, they can and do communicate directly to the people at times. For example, one Mukamba reported this.

I was very sick, in a critical situation. I had stayed for three days without knowing what was happening to me. People had no hope. They knew I was dying. Then all of a sudden I sat up in bed where I was laid. Then I saw my mother-in-law and my father-in-law (who had died about three years back) appear at the door of the hut. My father stood right at the door supporting himself with a walking stick which he used to have when he was alive. He said nothing to me, but my mother-in-law proceeded and came and stood beside my bed, having in her hands the handwork she used to do, making Akamba baskets. Then I knew beyond doubt that they were the ones. Then my mother-in-law said to me, "Ma Mwee, I was at Kangundo and there were people coming for me, but now, you are going to be well." After my mother-in-law said these words to me she left me and was led by my father-in-law and I watched them disappear.

In this instance the living-dead appeared to the person, communicated good news of physical recovery which led to restoration of health and vigour.

Protection from danger was another benefit from the *aimu*. The ancestors were beseeched for safety in the home and safety on a safari. As one person said, "The ancestors can bless the living if the ancestors are given what they ask for. They can bring wealth, health to the sick, and protection from danger."

One vivid example is reported. "When my father died," Ngei informed me, "at our home came a black snake which used to coil itself on the wooden gate, hanging down near the gate. When our cattle wanted to be moved out, my mother used to speak to this snake and request it to allow the cattle to go out, which it used to do even in the evening when the cattle were coming back." This snake was interpreted as an ancestor who came to be with the family and to protect them from danger.

"The living-dead are able to bless their people," another person said. "I personally know this practically. Once upon a time I wanted to have a wife. I went to a medicine man who told me that my brother who was dead wanted me to marry a certain small girl. This is still my beloved wife up to this day."

The *aimu* have a personal interest in benefiting their descendants for only then will their descendants in return favour the *aimu* with sacrifices. This reciprocal relationship is reflected in the comment made by another Mukamba. "The ancestors bless their living. Because if the ancestors do not do so, where would the *aimu* expect to go and ask for food and drink when their friends are going in their own homes?"

The living-dead can protect their living descendants from unjust neighbours. Mailu said, "Young man, let me tell you, when Mbova was rude by refusing us permission to graze our cattle without a good reason, we reported this to our ancestral spirits by pouring beer on the ground where they are. Within days he died."

Foretelling the future was a common benefit from the ancestors. For example, the grandfather in one family directed the living how to lead the family. He foretold of famine through dreams so that the family could prepare for it. During some of the great famines their family did not suffer because the dead grandfather informed them what types of crops to plant in anticipation of the famine.

Ancestors guide the living through omens. If you set out on a journey and you hear a particular kind of bird (*ngoma-komi*) which sits in the tree and sleeps most of the time, the ancestors are thereby informing you that your journey will be successful. If, on the other hand, you meet a woman or girl on the journey, this was a bad omen meaning misfortune.

In fact, every conceivable blessing can come from the ancestors. "*Aimu* can help one in whatever he is doing," said a Mukamba. "For example, if your child is in school, you can commit that work to the *aimu*."

A Mukamba from Kitui replied, "The ancestors do bring blessing, for example, in the form of rain. When a certain ancestor appears to someone and the *kilumi* dance is played, they can bring rain." While some Akamba insist that only God can bring rain, others clearly assert that the *aimu* are responsible. While the Akamba recognize that rain comes from God, they also believe the ancestors have the knowledge and power to bring rain. As one person stated, "The ancestors do bless the people and all things are done by the power of the *aimu*." Kathila is the name of one *iimu* in Kitui who is responsible for bringing rain. When one *iimu* fails, the Akamba turn to other *aimu* for help. The ancestors inform the living of the impending rain through the medicine man of the kilumi dance.

Mediators

Most contemporary writers of African Traditional Religion refer to the ancestors as mediators between the living and their Creator. Ndeti represents this line of interpretation. "Another significant role of *aimo* [*aimu*]," Ndeti writes, "is to mediate the affairs of the living to *Molungu* [*Mulungu*] (Creator). The position of *Ngai* is such that the Akamba avoid direct contact with him." (1972:175)

Many Akamba in fact do refer to the intermediary role of the living-dead. The following comments are representative of the responses given by various Akamba. "There were no other gods except God the Creator," said another. "The Akamba had to pray through the living-dead as their mediator. I pray to God through the ancestors," said Muia, "just because I found my fathers doing the same thing." Muia declared, "I cannot pray directly to God at any time. What I do is to pray to the ancestors who in turn derive power from God to provide me with what I need." Another said, "God cannot in any way speak to the living apart from using the dead. Nor would the living dare approach God apart from going through their ancestors."

Various Akamba speak of the ancestors being nearer to God and, therefore, possessing better knowledge of God and access to Him. They go so far as to say that no one can approach God directly but must pass through the ancestors, reciting the names of all those forefathers who have gone on before. They in turn intercede with the more remote forefathers, those who are now nameless spirits, who will do the same until the message is given to God. Thus the living-dead pass on the messages from the living to the spirits who will not refuse to pass on the message direct to God.

The ancestors thus form a chain of communication through whom the living relay their prayers to God. This concept of the mediating role of the living-dead is reflected in the social relations among the Akamba.

A daughter would never approach her father directly, but first presents her needs to the mother who then approaches the father. Even a younger son does not normally approach the father directly, but first makes known his need to an elder brother who then serves as a mediator with the father. The word of the father is final. This decision is then mediated through the mother or the first born son who then relays the message to the child concerned.

People are normally afraid to approach the Chief of the area directly. They prefer to go through the Sub-Chief who then relays the request to the Chief.

Sending a mediator is indeed traditional among the Akamba. Traditionally, whenever a person wants to negotiate with another, he sends an elder on his behalf. If you desire to make right a wrong after some argument, you send another to intercede on your behalf. Even in the case of a man seeking a wife, another goes on his behalf to make those arrangements.

Therefore, many Akamba reason that the living approach God in the same manner through the ancestors who serve as mediators. Other Akamba intermediaries include the priests (*athembi*), prophets (*athani*), diviners (*andu awe*) and rain makers (*eti ma manzi*).However, one is not fair to the evidence if he insists that all the Akamba believe that the *aimu* are intermediaries between God the Creator and mankind. Mbiti appears to impose this interpretation of traditional beliefs on all Africans when he states, "God is the ultimate recipient *whether or not the worshippers are aware of it*." (1969:58) Whether or not the Akamba believe that the ancestors are intermediaries is important. And it would appear that many are not at all clear about this.

A practicing medicine man stated, "The *aimu* answer my prayers when I pray and there is no need to pray to God." Mutua claimed, "I do not pray to God. I pray to the *aimu* and they help me." Another medicine man said, "I pray to the *aimu* directly and I don't pray to God."

Inquiry done in some places did not disclose anyone who represented the *aimu* as mediators between God and the living. "Ancestors were at the centre of the Akamba's life," said one person. "They were consulted for anything that happened in the family. Ngai was hardly consulted for anything, and in fact, not at all. Except that when the Akamba sacrificed they would place some food, beer and blood for God separate from the *aimu*." However, they knew that the work of creating and shaping the world was through God, and not through the *aimu*.

One old lady, over 80 years of age, said that the Akamba never pray to the ancestors so that they in turn will pray to God. Instead, people pray to God to remove the ancestors when they become too troublesome. This lady had been to church only once and stopped going when the *aimu* troubled her too much because of her attendance.

"I never heard the Akamba refer to the *aimu* as intermediaries with God. The *aimu* deal with people, not with God. The Akamba know of God, the Creator, but they have no dealings with God. The people communicate with the *aimu*." (Arms, Jack and Lolly:1982) As missionaries for 32 years among the Akamba at grassroots level in the remote parts of Kitui, Rev. Jack Arms and his wife, Lolly Arms, could say, "We have never run across the idea among the heathen Akamba that the *aimu* are intermediaries with God."

As we have seen before, there are differing opinions held by different people in different locations. So what may be true in one area is not necessarily true in another area.

We conclude that for many Akamba an important role of the *aimu* is a mediatory role between the living and God. But for many others the ancestors are prayed to as ends in themselves. They are expected to help the living through their own powers without intercession made with God.

COMMUNICATION

Communication is a major aspect of the relationship between the living Akamba and their ancestors. The ancestors seek to communicate with the living through various means and the living reciprocate. There are many different ways of communicating.

Apparitions

On infrequent occasions the *aimu* appear in non-material but visible form. At night the ancestors may appear in the house which is flooded with light. The living can recognize the form of his ancestor by his appearance and clothing. They may manifest themselves near the shrines. But if the people draw near, the spirits may chase them, sometimes by throwing stones or throwing their torches. Or the ancestors may suddenly disappear. The *aimu* can be seen moving from one shrine to another in the form of great lights. Great flames of fire, reaching to the sky, or a one legged man stretched upward to the sky may be seen moving from one shrine to another.

Dreams

A more frequent way of communication is through dreams (*ndoto*). The ancestor appears to the living while he is sleeping, usually though not always at night. While sleeping, he dreams that the ancestor awakes him. Sitting up in bed the Mukamba is informed by the *iimu* what should be done.

For instance, one Mukamba said. "When I was lying outside being sick with malaria, I saw an ancestor who beat me with a branch of the 'Mutundu' tree and said, 'Wake up and go. If you do not, you will die.' I awoke and went to the house and after some time I gained my health."

In most cases it is the male living-dead who appear to the living, not the women. In most cases the living-dead are the leading men of the family, not merely anyone.

If a woman ancestor does appear in a dream, she may demand a certain kind of cloth, usually a traditional cloth with mixed threads of colour, or she may demand the slaughtering of a goat. When the Mukamba awakes in the morning, he is required to share with the family members what he saw in the dream and what the ancestors required.

While the Westerner may be skeptical as to the reality of this form of spirit communication, it is known that the living can do something to prevent this type of appearance in dreams. Such dreams stop when people become Christians. These dreams appear to be a real method of spirit communication. One old woman, a former leader of the *kilumi* dances before her conversion, reported this. "The spirit of my grandfather, Muinde, appeared to me and showed me a certain herb. I was told to get it and I poured it for my child who was sick. When I did what I was told, my child became well. In that dream I was shown the herb to use and the place where my child was sick."

Sometimes the appearance of living-dead is more like a vision than a dream.

One Mukamba reported, "Concerning rainfall, I am always shown this. I am translated to a sea and then I see the water splash up. That means there will be rain. But if it doesn't splash, that indicates there will be no rain and hence little harvest."

Dreams are said to fall into two categories, good and bad. If a bad dream of death or disaster is dreamed, in the morning the Mukamba takes a small gourd of water and pours it on burning coals of fire. "At the same time praying to the *aimu* not to let the dream become a reality." (Beresford- Stooke 1928b:176)

If the dream is good, dealing with riches or blessings, the Mukamba fills half a gourd with milk and water and pours it slowly on the ground outside his house, "at the same time praying to the spirits of any near relatives who have died, with the words, 'Drink this milk and water and send me the good things you showed me last night'." (Beresford-Stooke 1928b:177)

Fire

The appearance of the living-dead in fire occurred mostly at the traditional altars where special libation was poured, namely, at the altars of the elders (*thome wa atumia*), the places where men used to warm themselves by fire outside their houses and where they would celebrate and fellowship.

According to tradition, when fire appeared at these shrines, everyone stayed silently in their houses. The elders ensured that they had done everything that they should have done.

If the flame of fire was red, the Akamba believed that the living-dead were warning of some pending tragedy. When the red flame was observed, the living could also see in the flames and hear cows mooing, children crying, women drumming and passing by their homes. A green or a blue flame meant that the family would have peace and prosperity, peace with the ancestral spirits and prosperity from them.

When this fire was observed at one home, the grandfather went out to throw some porridge there and pour a libation of beer. The next morning he slaughtered a goat so as to give the ancestors blood for the security of the family.

Trouble

A more common way by which the *aimu* reveal themselves is through sickness, death, famine and trouble. Cattle may begin to die, or children become sick. Such trouble may be a signal from the living-dead that they seek to communicate to the living. As one Mukamba said. "The *aimu* reveal themselves in sickness and in cattle dying."

When trouble occurs the person must go to a medicine man for consultation to learn from the medium what the *aimu* are trying to communicate. The ancestral spirits can sometimes disclose a person's need to the medicine man before the client arrives. "When we start to inquire what the cause of sickness is, the medicine man will disclose to us what the ancestral spirits had previously told them," as one person said. He may request, for example, the sacrifice of a white goat and the pouring of some beer to the *aimu*, so that the sick will be healed.

This usually happens, but not always.

To obey the demands of the ancestral spirits as made known through the medicine man is the way of wisdom. One Mukamba told of his mother who died because she persistently bit her tongue. The father refused to pay the bull which was demanded by the *aimu* through the medicine man. Consequently, the mother continued biting her tongue until she painfully bled to death.

Spirit Possession

A major way by which the ancestors communicated with the living was through possession. (The primary research for the following discussion on spirit possession was done by Jonathan Musango in Kitui. See acknowledgements.) One traditionalist described spirit possession in this way.

> During the time of possession, one loses his own being, his senses are gone, he is transformed physically and psychologically and becomes simply a tool of the spirit in him. Without his realization, he acts and speaks according to its wishes. Though not hurting himself, he can lick a red hot iron bit with his tongue until it cools off without burning his hand or tongue. When a person is a medium, you can see him breathing very hard, his arm muscles stiffen considerably and he makes a beastly sound. Then the spirit shouts through him, giving out its message or judgement.

The act of being possessed is called *kukwatwa*. This has the idea of something entering the person.

Spirit possession usually begins by someone starting to cry for no reason. Or he may have an abnormal sickness, like a headache which is accompanied by loud crying or running away from home.

There is general agreement that during the transition period, as the person passes into the state of possession, there is a feeling of going numb throughout the whole body. The person becomes weak as his bodily strength declines. Darkness grips the mind.

When one is fully possessed, he demonstrates the powers of the *aimu*. He demonstrates unusual physical strength. One famous spirit medium in Kitui runs very fast on one leg towards some distant hill to which she has been called. Or the possessed may walk on fire without being burned, cut himself without being hurt or eat dangerous fruits without being sick.

Kinds of Possession. There are basically two different kinds of spirit possession among the Akamba in which the spirits seek to communicate with the living: the unexpected spirit possession and the induced spirit possession.

1. Unexpected Possession. Anyone can be possessed at any time or any place. Maithya narrated the following.

> When I was coming from the forest where I went to collect fire wood, I was caught in a thorn bush from which I could not remove myself. This was the start of my discipline. I was possessed and saw myself in the thorn bush from which I could not remove myself. I started screaming until family members came and when they arrived they heard me conversing with the voice of my grandfather. They offered sacrifices to appease the ancestor' wrath. After awhile I was released from the thorn bush and we went home.

Sometimes, the ancestor who died without wives, known as *mivau*, returns to his family and causes trouble. The spirit may not only torment the person but the tormented person beats others in the family and chases them. He may be given an appetite to eat certain types of food. Every two or three days he may require a goat to be slaughtered for him. He may not sleep long at night. His behaviour disturbs the family. Consequently, the possessed person may be driven out of the home to live in the wilderness or bush. When such symptoms occur, the family consults the medicine man. He may divine that an unmarried ancestor has returned to the family. The only solution is to slaughter a goat for the ancestral spirit. The possessed person then wears a goat skin from the animal sacrificed in order to ward off the *iimu* (*mivau*). Failure to do this will only cause the family to suffer endlessly. On the other hand, if the family is on good terms with their living-dead, the diviner may conclude that the problem is the result of witchcraft.

On other occasions a Mukamba may see spirit children playing. He becomes sick, is unable to sleep and hears the noise of the spirit children (*Mbaa Mutile*) playing. He may eat a lot but is never satisfied.

If the medicine man divines that the spirit is *Mutile*, he advises the family what is needed to satisfy *Mutile*. They shall buy a white sheet with red lines and bushy ends, a black sheet with red lines across it and a small basket with a chain and beads.

These together with four hens are brought to the medicine man who then gives the items to the possessed person in response to *Mutile*'s request. The next morning the medicine man takes the heads and feathers of the four hens to the path which divides, as a Y, and deposits them there. When *Mutile* has thus been given what she wanted, and she and her children are escorted down the path, the possessed person is healed. To refuse *Mutile* her request may lead to death.

All the Akamba spoken to in one area of Kitui declared that all the spirits who possess people unexpectedly are dead relatives, such as husbands, sons, daughters or grandparents. The people always listen to these living-dead and seek to fulfill their wishes. These spirits possess the living because they have been forgotten or neglected. They possess in order to request things such as a special cloth or a goat dedicated to them.

Strange spirits, unknown to the people, do possess them at times. They simply wander from place to place because no one remembers them. Thus they threaten the living and compel them to offer gifts to them. These unknown spirits are usually harmful. The people merely give them what they want in order to send them away so they will not return.

2. Induced Possession. Normally, people must prepare themselves for spirit possession, apart from the unexpected variety. Certain ones are more likely to be possessed than others. These are said to have "soft bodies." Women are possessed more often than men.

Induced possession is of two types: that which is experienced by the *mundu mue* and that which is experienced at special dances.

Possession Experienced by the *Mundu Mue*. The most frequently possessed Mukamba is the medicine man or woman who induces the *aimu* to possess him or her in order that they might communicate their advice and information to the diviner.

Each *mundu mue* has a particular spirit who helps him or her. For instance, one *mundu mue* in Kitui has two spirits from Machakos who help her. You can identify those spirits because of their Machakos accent and their Machakos names.

The *mundu mue* induces his own spirits to possess him by playing his bow and singing. When he is possessed he falls prostrate on the ground, writhing and foaming at the mouth. After some time he would receive the information desired. He might even obtain knowledge of a new way of treating a certain disease troubling the client.

The work of the medicine man is closely linked with his intimate relationship to the *aimu*, and therefore, spirit possession is a frequent experience. For it is the ancestral spirits who impart to the medicine man his special powers of *uwe*.

Spirit dances are the second kind of induced spirit possession. In the traditional relationship of the Akamba with their ancestors, "dancing is an important feature" in order to communicate with the *aimu* to obtain information desired. "In dancing one gets into the ecstatic condition [highly emotional] in which one comes into communication with the spirits more easily. The ecstasy is certainly brought about principally by the music which accompanies the dancing..." (Lindblom 1920:230)

Thus the places where the people are most likely to become possessed are the dancing grounds (*ituto*) and the places where the harvest is prepared (*ivuiyo*). The younger women are taught to know the importance of these places for they are most conducive to spirit possession. At the *ivuiyo* the women danced, singing and praising the ancestors and God for giving a good harvest. Women dancing at the *ivuiyo* sought possession, as they sang and danced for the *aimu*. But the *aimu* would choose where and when to possess a particular person.

Certain kinds of songs made people become possessed by certain kinds of ancestors. These songs had distinctive beats which induced the ancestral spirits to come and heal the sick.

There are basically two kinds of dances which have the specific intention of inducing spirit possession. The first is the *kilumi* dance. Only the medicine man (*mundu mue*), the older women and a few elders may dance the *kilumi*. During this dance the living-dead, those ancestors who once lived and whose names are remembered, are the ones who clearly possess the people. These are the *aimu*. Subsumed under this broad category of *kilumi* dance are different kinds of dances, all directly related to the living-dead. There were so many songs and dances with their distinctive beats, each in honour of a different ancestor. These songs, sung in honour of the spirit possessing, were sung to induce a spirit to possess them. The purpose of the *kilumi* dance is to appease the spirits. In parts of Kitui the *kilumi* dance is intended to inquire about the rain and seek help against cattle epidemics.

The dance is led by a special *mundu mue* who plays a drum made from the hollow trunk of a tree with one side covered by a hide. This *mundu mue wa kilumi* is a woman, for the *kilumi* dance is intended primarily for women. She leads in songs which she has learned from the ancestral spirits. Other women attend the dance but the main purpose is to induce the *aimu* to possess the *mundu mue* so she can gain information from them useful to the people. In the process of dancing other women may also become possessed. The possessed person is the property of the ancestors and is called *mundu wa aimu*, "the person of the ancestor."

The characteristics of one becoming possessed at the *kilumi* dance are as follows. She begins to dance very vigorously and continuously, rolling on the ground with the body trembling all over. She may begin to display unusual behaviour, acting like an elephant digging water, or a German soldier marching, or like another *iimu*.

The tone of her voice changes. She may speak in a different language. One *mundu mue* reportedly speaks Italian, another Arabic.

When possessed these women can foretell the future, interpret the cause of sickness and give instruction how to cure illness. She may foretell the coming of rain, how much it will rain and what should be planted.

When the *mundu mue wa kilume* is possessed she takes the drum, sits on it to show that they need not continue dancing anymore since the *iimu* has already come. She then proceeds to give the required information. The ancestor states whether there will be rain or what should be done concerning the cattle sickness.

At times a person being called to become a medicine man is possessed at the *kilumi*. When such a person enters the dancing ground he appears oppressed and begins to tremble. Seated on his stool, his eyes roll back and forth uncontrollably. He appears to struggle with unseen forces. Because he is in training, his assistants help him to his feet, paint his body with white clay and adorn his body with a cloth. Then for hours he dances about vigorously. He is under the complete control of the *aimu*. He dances extra ordinarily. Such a person, being chosen by the ancestors to be a medicine man, is said to be called. During the time of his vigorous dancing and possession he seems to manifest different personalities, determined by the different *aimu* which possess him. At the conclusion of the possession, the *aimu* shouts to the people through the mouth of the possessed the message to be delivered. When this is done, the person collapses from exhaustion and the *aimu* leave him. He then stands up and appears as if he has just been awakened from sleep.

Such a person undergoes a series of possession during his training period. At the conclusion the person promises to accept that particular spirit for whom he will serve as a medium. He cannot complain about any discomfort or displeasure he may experience through the possession. He is bound to serve as the medium of the *aimu*.

The second type of "spirit dance" is the *ngoma*. This dance differs from the *kilumi* dance in that normal drums are used during the *ngoma*. The purpose is to deal with a stubborn spirit which has possessed someone. The *ngoma* is arranged on the advice of the medicine man. While the main concern is the sick person, other people may become possessed during the *ngoma* dance.

One Mukamba described spirit possession at the *ngoma* dance.

> One goes to the ngoma to participate with the others. As she dances she acquires a strange feeling which runs throughout the whole body. She may say, 'How am I feeling? I want to sit here.' Others then recognize the sign of potential possession as they sing

the song which is associated with the spirit which is known to possess her. She dances to the satisfaction of the spirit. Then she is interviewed and the spirit bids her farewell.

In these dances the participants all change their dancing style the moment they recognize that someone is being possessed. They recognize the kind of spirit which is possessing her, they understand the type of dancing which that particular spirit enjoys, and so they all change the drum beat and rhythm to agree with the spirit's preference. The spirits enjoy dancing through the living and thus they possess people at the dances to enjoy the drum beat and rhythm.

The people recognize the identity of the spirit in various ways. The voice may give him away. The kind of demands made by the spirit may be indicative. For instance, if one spirit complains that a goat formerly dedicated to him has been sold, then the living know which ancestor this is. The spirit frequently identifies himself by giving his name. The strange behaviour of the one possessed may resemble the unique behaviour of an ancestor. The very type of dance which is danced by the possessed may be the revealing clue, for it is the same type of dance he loved when still alive.

The sick person, for whom the *ngoma* has been arranged at the direction of the medicine man, is placed in the centre of the dancing ground. As the women dance around, dancing with the rhythm of the drum, a certain point is reached when the sick person or someone else dancing is moved with emotional excitement and starts speaking in the name of an ancestor in his or her family. In the name of that ancestor, the sick person requests certain things in order to heal the sick one. If all the requirements are met, the sick person is healed completely. If all the demands are not met, worse things may take place. When the sick person is possessed, the ancestor usually identifies himself by giving his name. The medicine man inquiries of the spirit what demands he is making. When the demands are met, the medicine man asks the spirit to leave the victim in peace.

The medicine man pulls the middle finger of the victim and each other finger at least once. He then smacks the face of the person, blows his breath on the person and calls her by name. When she answers, this indicates that she has returned to normality.

Assessment of Spirit Possession. All the Akamba spoken to on one occasion agreed without hesitation that possession was not pleasant. The one possessed rolled in the dust, making himself dirty. During that time they displayed their nakedness. Violent behaviour often led to personal harm. They tore off their ornaments which they normally loved. Because of their excessive use of energy, they became excessively weak and exhausted afterwards. Ndeto who runs rapidly into the hills on one leg is compelled to remain in bed for days afterwards because of extreme exhaustion.

The only one who is pleased with possession is the medicine man, for he acquires wealth and fame through his communication with the *aimu* during possession.

In all these dances the people believed the *aimu* were present because they enjoyed dancing too. When the women danced, little was attributed to God. Their total devotion was given to the ancestral spirits. When someone became possessed, she would start dancing in a particular style. The spirit world would reveal to another woman dancing which ancestor had possessed that other person. She would inform the others dancing so that they could all change their style of dancing to conform to the style of the one possessed. Thus they would dance in honour of that ancestor.

Spirit possession is always a temporary experience, though it may be a repeated one. Everything is done to satisfy the demands of the *aimu* in order to appease him and be released from the possession. Offerings and sacrifices are made in accordance to the requests of the ancestor in order to appease him and be freed from possession. To be sure that the *aimu* will leave for certain, "the Medicine-Man sends it into an animal, such as a goat or a sheep." (Lindblom 1920:233). The ear of the animal is cut off while the animal is still living and it is hung around the person. Food is offered in the hut. The *mundu mue* says, "'This goat is yours. Stop troubling N.N. further, and go into the goat.' This method of procedure is said to have a speedy result." (Lindblom 1920:233)

CONCLUSION

As the senior elders among the Akamba, the living-dead serve both as the benefactors and disciplinarians of the living. They communicate in the day through apparitions and at night through dreams. Trouble of any kind is not by chance. There must be a reason and one possible reason is the displeasure of the living-dead. The medicine men are the mediums through whom the living-dead disclose their demands to the living. Spirit possession is, therefore, a profitable business for the professionals but a source of discomfort for the others.

No one can doubt the importance of spirits in Ukambani. As Parrinder says, "There is no doubt that ancestral spirits play a very large part in African thought...The ancestors are part of the social group." (Parrinder 1962:57) The Akamba are no exception.

REVIEW QUESTIONS FOR CHAPTER 10

1. Describe the kinds of spirits among the Akamba, their habitat and their relationship with the living.
2. Discuss the various roles which the living-dead play among the living Akamba.
3. How do the living-dead seek to communicate with the living Akamba?
4. Describe the various kinds of spirit possession among the Akamba.
5. What kind of attitude do the Akamba living have toward their living-dead?

Suggested Reading and Thought Questions for Advanced Study:

Field, M.J. *Religion and Medicine of the Ga People*, 1961, pp.92- 109, 196-206.

Evans-Pritchard, E.E. *Nuer Religion*, 1974, pp.28-122, 144-176.

Gelfand, Michael. *Shona Religion*, 1962, pp.1-178.

Kenyatta, Jomo. *Facing Mt. Kenya*, n.d., pp.253-258.

Marwick, Brian Allan. *The Swazi*, 1966, pp.231-234.
P'Bitek, Okot. *Religion of the Central Luo*, 1971, pp.88-120.
Rattray, R.S. *Ashanti*, 1969, pp.86-138.
Read, Margaret. *The Ngoni of Nyasaland*, 1970, pp.157-204.
Setiloane, Gabriel. *The Image of God Among the Sotho-Tswana*, 1976, pp.64-76.
Talbot, P. Amaury. *Tribes of the Niger Delta*, 1967, pp.32-107; 258-271.
Wilson, Monica. *Rituals of Kinship Among the Nyakyusa*, 1957.

1. Do research on spirit possession among two other African peoples (from the books recommended above or from field research among your own people). Compare the similarities and differences of these beliefs and practices with those mentioned here for the Akamba. How does this illustrate either the diversity or the similarity of African religions?

2. Talk to five different African traditionalists to learn their feelings and attitudes towards their living-dead. Observe what their practical relationships are with them. Is their attitude ambivalent (both fear and affection) or is it different from the Akamba traditional attitude?

3. Among your own people (or among those researched in the books above) are the living-dead as prominent traditionally as among the Akamba? If not, do they play the same roles? That is,

a. Do the living-dead communicate to the living through the medicine man and/or their appointed mediators?

b. Do the living-dead bring sickness and trouble to the living when they are offended?

c. Do the living-dead seek to preserve the traditions of the ancestors and thus resist change and innovation?

d. Are the living-dead resentful when the living neglect them?

e. Do the living-dead frequently visit the living through dreams, possession or other means?

f. Are the living responsible to remember the living-dead and honour them? If yes, when and how is this done?

g. Do the living benefit from a good relationship with the living-dead? How?

4. Study the different kinds of spirits among two different peoples researched in the above books. Discuss their identity, activities and relationship to the peoples. How are these spirits similar or dissimilar to the spirits among the Akamba?

as the postcards. One book had never been removed from the book shelf since it had been bought. Pictures disappeared, blank stationary mysteriously appeared, things were in disorder, windows were opened, clothes misplaced, a mirror mysteriously moved before their very eyes. All of these, in one way or another, reminded them of the Bishop's late son.

The final incident was the discovery one morning that all the milk in the refrigerator had turned sour, even the milk bought that morning. They recalled the belief that the presence of witches can curdle milk.

Even though Bishop Pike did not believe in the biblical doctrine of the immortality of the soul, he decided that his late son must be trying to communicate with him. So he consulted a medium.

Several meetings were arranged with a Mrs. Twigg. On each of these occasions, the medium spoke in the first person as if it were Jim speaking. Various statements were made that made James Pike believe it was really his son. It is interesting to note that Jim urged the Bishop to continue his campaign against Christian doctrines. He stated that he had seen nothing to make him "any more inclined to believe in God."

All these meetings with Mrs. Twigg occurred in London. Just before his departure for the United States, he inquired from his late son how he could be contacted in the States. The strange answer came in four phrases: "Spiritual Frontiers — A Father Rauscher — priest of the church — in New Jersey." After hearing from his son, the Bishop asked Mrs. Twigg about the meaning of "Spiritual Frontiers." Mrs. Twigg looked blank and said she had no way of interpreting it. In a remarkable turn of circumstances, James Pike was led to a spirit medium in the United States. By chance, he spoke with someone who, he discovered at the last moment, was a member of an organization called "Spiritual Frontiers Fellowship," which was presided over by a Father Rauscher who lived in New Jersey. Through this connection, he was led to have further alleged contacts with his late son, Jim.

During this new series of seances, Jim expressed concern for the Bishop who was facing charges of heresy. But the late son assured his father of help in his fight. Thus, the Bishop was encouraged to go on in his battle against orthodox Christianity. Jim also said that he had heard nothing about Jesus since his death and none of his companions talked about him. But he admitted he was in the sphere reserved for those who had made "mistakes."

CONCLUSION

We may observe in conclusion that throughout the world in space and time there has been a persistent belief, not only in the immortality of the soul and life after death, but in a continued relationship between the living and the dead. What the living do may either appease the dead or offend them. Mediums are a primary means of communicating with these ancestral spirits. Much of life is determined by the dictates of the ancestors. In practical terms the ancestral spirits become a primary focus of the religious belief and practice of mankind.

REVIEW QUESTIONS FOR CHAPTER 11

1. Is the African traditional belief in spirits unusual and unknown in the rest of the world? Explain.

2. Where and when throughout the world have others had similar belief about spirits?

3. Discuss the belief in the living-dead found in many places in Europe and Asia.

Suggested Reading and Thought Questions for Advanced Study:

Ancient Egyptians
> Budge, E.A. Wallis ed. *The Book of the Dead*, 1960.

Confucianism
> Noss, John. *Man's Religions*, 1963, pp.335-341.

Folk Religions
> Howells, William. *The Heathens: Primitive Man and His Religions*, 1948, pp.145-213.
> Lessa, William and Evon Vogt. *Reader in Comparative Religion*, 1965, pp.466-495.

Islam
> Zwemer, Samuel. *The Influence of Animism on Islam*, 1920.

Religions Worldwide
> Hastings, James. *Encyclopedia of Religion and Ethics*, 1909, Vol.I,425-467.

1. Discuss the influence of animistic spirit beliefs on the religion of Islam. To what extent does fear of spirits dominate the practical lives of Folk Islam? (see Zwemer 1920)

2. Discuss the complex ancient Egyptian beliefs of life after death. What similarities can you find between those beliefs and the traditional beliefs of your own people? Discuss the differences (see Budge 1960).

Chapter 12

THE SPIRIT WORLD IN BIBLICAL PERSPECTIVE

As evangelicals, we weigh the African traditional world view of the spirits in the light of God's Word. But secular western scholars and all who learn at their feet have embraced a naturalistic world view. So widespread is this anti-super-natural, non-biblical world view, that many churchmen and theologians have shaped their own presuppositions with a naturalistic bias.

For the evangelical, who by definition accepts the absolute authority of the Scriptures, the reality of the spirit world is a *sine qua non*. In fact, the evangelical alone can approach ATR with respect and wholesome acceptance. In biblical perspective, we can accept as real what the traditional African accepts as real. The powers and influences experienced in traditional Africa are not mere superstition and imagination. They are not the reflection of childish understanding. For the Scriptures teach the reality and activity of unclean spirits. More than that, the Gospel brings good news of deliverance from the fear of those evil spirits through the blood Jesus Christ.

What then is the biblical perspective of the African traditional world of spirits?

BIBLICAL TEACHING OF THE SPIRIT WORLD

Biblical View of Demons

The belief in the spirit world among traditional religions is both degrading and exaggerated. We find in Africa, as in other places, that the Creator, who is powerful and good, does not effectively control or limit the activities of the spirits. As a result, the spirits are a cause of continual fear. The Arabs see demons everywhere in the desert. There are so many spirits that they must apologize before throwing any object, lest they hit a spirit and offend him. The spirits in ancient Babylon swarmed everywhere, creeping under doors, hiding behind walls and filling every crevice. The Chinese hear their voices in the strange sounds of the night and the traditional African sees the activity of the spirits in everything that is unusual and different. Therefore, fear of spirits is found everywhere.

In contrast, the Bible teaches the reality of spirits within the framework of the sovereignty of God. In Scripture, the wide spread fear of spirits cannot be found. Their existence is acknowledged. But God is sovereign. Though evil spirits exist, there is no need for fear since God is all-powerful. Belief in spirits is exaggerated.

Spirits do not dominate and pervade all of life. The faith of Israel was higher and purer in its teachings of demons. While the neighbouring peoples of Israel had an exaggerated and pervasive consciousness of evil spirits, the Hebrew faith was restrained and reserved in its acknowledgement of demonic spirits. In Scripture God, is truly sovereign and the activities of the spirits are under His control. Speaking of biblical revelation in the Old Testament, Merrill Unger writes,

> Its purity consisted in its clear-cut separation to the one true God in the midst of universal idolatry (Deut. 6:4; Isa. 43:10-12). Israelite religion began as pure monotheism, in a radical and complete purge [removal] from polytheism, and the genius of it lay in its perpetuation as such by rigid and uncompromising isolation...Yet it is to be observed that not even in its monotheism does the religion of Israel show a loftier [higher] elevation from the faiths of the surrounding peoples than in its demonology [italics mine] (Unger 1952:22).

Description of Unclean Spirits

Nevertheless, the Bible recognizes and affirms the reality of the powers and principalities, the demonic spirits who together with Satan rebelled against their Creator. During the life time of Christ these unclean spirits were particularly active. Let us see their description.

a. They are active spirits who can influence mankind. They have a spiritual nature (Mt. 8:16; Lk. 10:17; Eph. 6:12). Yet, they can make their presence known. Scripture says little of the manner of their appearance to man, though it does allow for the possibility of their tangible appearance. We may imply this from the ability of the angels to appear with a visible body (II Kings 6:17; Acts 5:19; 27:23,24). Thus evil spirits may do the same (cf. Rev. 9:1-11; 16:13- 16).

b. They oppose God and all that is good. Their moral character is described as "unclean," (Mt. 10:1; Mk. 1:27; 3:11; Lk. 4:36; Acts 8:7; Rev. 16:13). The very name, "Satan," means "adversary." Not only does Satan oppose God (Job 1:6ff; Mt. 4:1ff), he seeks to corrupt the people of God (I Pet. 5:8). Since evil spirits are subject to Satan, they are also enemies of God and His people (Mt. 12:26).

c. They are powerful creatures who can oppress men. They bring blindness (Mt. 12:22), insanity (Lk. 8:26,36), personal injuries (Mk. 9:18), physical defects and deformities (Lk. 13:11-17), and dumbness (Mt. 9:32,33). They may give men a desire to kill themselves (Mk. 9:22). Their power can enable those whom they possess to do superhuman acts (Lk. 8:29).

d. They provide the dynamic of heathen worship. Contrary to the will of God, Israel "mingled with the nations, and learned their practices." Consequently, they "served idols...they sacrificed their sons and their daughters to the demons, and shed innocent blood, the blood of their sons and their daughters, whom they sacrificed to the idols of Canaan." (Ps. 106:35-37) Here, demons are intimately associated with idolatry. Though Scripture teaches that idols are nothing (I Cor. 8:4), these demons are recognized as the real spiritual beings behind the idols. While idols are lifeless representations of heathen gods, demons are the spiritual powers behind the idols which inspire and motivate heathen worship. Paul likewise teaches this in I Corinthians 10:20 (see Deut. 32:17)

The classic passage which identifies heathen gods with demons is Psalm 96:5 (LXX 95:5). "For all the gods of the peoples are idols ['ililim in Hebrew, *daimonia* in the Septuagint], but Jehovah made the heavens." The Hebrew word, *'ililïm*, is the plural of the adjective meaning, "of nought, empty, vain." Though heathen gods are "vain and empty," behind them and through them is the activity of the demons, drawing away the worship of people from the true God to the actual worship of demons (cf. Lev. 17:1-7). These unclean spirits also lead people away from the truth of God (I Tim. 4:1,2; I Jh. 4:1-6).

e. They can possess a person. This is vividly portrayed in the Scriptures given below. The basis of our belief in spirit possession is found in the very teachings of Christ. On the basis of His authority, we must accept the possibility of men being possessed by evil spirits. This was also taught by the early church and taught in the Acts of the Apostles and the Epistles.

Spirit Possession

References to demonic spirits and spirit possession are frequent in the Gospels. The Greek word for demon occurs 52 times in the Gospels and eight times in the remainder of the New Testament (four of which are in I Cor. 10:20,21). For this Greek word, the Authorized Version always translated it "devil," except in Acts 17:18 where it is translated, "gods" of the Athenians. These demonic spirits are also spoken of as "unclean spirits" or "evil spirits." Altogether the word "spirit," is used 43 times in the New Testament for demons. "To be demon possessed" occurs 13 times in the Gospels and nowhere else in the New Testament. Clearly then, the Gospels are the focal point for the biblical teaching of demon possession.

An integral part of Jesus' ministry was the casting out of demons. Summarizing Jesus' ministry after John the Baptist was imprisoned, we read that "he went into their synagogues throughout all Galilee, preaching and casting out the demons." (Mk. 1:39) When Jesus chose his twelve apostles and commissioned them to minister, we are told, "He appointed twelve, that they might be with Him, and that He might send them out to preach, and to have authority to cast out the demons." (Mk. 3:14,15) On their tour of ministry, commissioned by Christ, the twelve not only "preached that men should repent," but also "were casting out many demons and were anointing with oil many sick people and healing them." (Mk. 6:12,13; see Lk. 9:1,2; Mt. 10) The same is true with the ministry of the seventy. When they returned from a period of service, they "returned with joy, saying, 'Lord, even the demons are subject to us in Your name.'" (Lk. 10:17)

Symptoms of Spirit Possession. There are several passages which treat demon possession at some length: the Capernaum Demoniac (Mk. 1:21-28; Lk. 4:3137); the Epileptic Boy (Mt. 17:14-20; Mk. 9:14-29; Lk. 9:37-43); the Syro-Phoenician Girl (Mt. 15:21-28; Mk. 7:24-30). The most extensive description of a demon possessed person in the Gospels is the Gerasene Demoniac which we shall examine more carefully (Mt. 8:28-34; Mk. 5:1-7; Lk. 8:26-37).

a. He was possessed by "an unclean spirit." (Mk. 5:2) This is indeed the essential feature of demon possession: an alien spirit being with personality and powers who normally resides elsewhere, enters into the human being, taking possession and effective control of that person. As McCasland comments,

> The most decisive mark by which the phenomenon called demon possession is
> known is the change of personality which takes place, in which the normal self of the
> human being appears to be replaced by that of a demon who has overcome him. This
> change of personality is the key to the present study (McCasland 1951:5).

In fact, this is the chief distinction between those definitions of demon possession given by evangelicals and non-evangelicals.

According to one evangelical, Merrill Unger, "Demon possession is a condition in which one or more evil spirits or demons inhabit the body of a human being and can take complete control of their victim at will. By temporarily blotting out his consciousness, they can speak and act through him as their complete slave and tool." (Unger 1952:102)

This definition by Unger is fully supported by Scripture and illustrated in our present text (Mk. 5:2). It is in sharp contrast to the definition given by Raymond Firth and followed by John Beattie and John Middleton. They affirm, "Spirit possession is *a form of trance* in which behaviour actions of a person *are interpreted* [italics mine] as evidence of a control of his behaviour by a spirit normally external to him." (Beattie 1969:xvii)

Unger accepts the reality of spiritual beings residing in a person. Firth only accepts this as the interpretation given by people. But by implication he does not believe in the validity of that interpretation. The first definition is biblical; the second one is not.

b. He possesses unusual powers. In the case of the Gerasene Demoniac, he possessed such unusual strength that he could break any chain binding him, thwarting all those who sought to control him (5:4). He was apparently not always fierce. At times he was mild mannered and allowed people to shackle him. Violence and excessive strength are not always present, but when the demon enraged the man, he was capable of breaking in pieces the shackles which bound him.

He also demonstrated supernatural powers of knowledge, for he ran toward Jesus and cried out with a loud voice, "What do I have to do with You, Jesus, Son of the Most High God?" (5:7) This knowledge of Jesus' identity frequently occurs in other cases recorded in the Gospels. The slave girl in Philippi had a spirit of divination which enabled her owner to gain much profit through the spirit's supernatural ability to foretell (Acts 16:16ff).

c. He resists the things of Christ (5:7). A demon possessed person will resist in a variety of ways, either with active opposition or passive inattention.

In Dr. Koch's counseling throughout the years, he has seen that demon possession always displays the same characteristics. One characteristic is that the person resists the Gospel. When one prays with him or counsels him concerning Christ, he becomes angry and violent. He may curse and blaspheme. But he will always oppose the Gospel. Another characteristic, according to Koch, is that the person becomes unconscious during prayer. He becomes unconscious as the Word of God is preached. Either passively or actively the possessed person resists the things of Christ.

d. He shows signs of disintegration, a splitting of the personality, for he runs toward Jesus for help, and yet cries out in fear (5:6,7). A "normal" response would be either to run away because of fear or to approach Jesus for help. But in this case he appears to do the two things at once, showing a disintegration of his personality.

At times he is calm and under self control. At other times he enters an abnormal or unusual state (Mk. 9:18) and falls into a fit of rage and tears apart the chains which bind him (Mk.5:4). He may fall to the ground and foam at the mouth (Mk. 9:18; Lk. 9:39:42).

At times he talks normally. At other times he changes his whole personality and becomes something which he is not normally. The new personality shows characteristics that are strange to the person in his normal state. Many times this includes tendencies of immorality (see Lk. 8:27). The possessed person's voice may change so that a male voice is spoken by a female, or the possessed person speaks with a foreign accent. In the case of the Gerasene Demoniac his voice changed in speaking, as "a legion" of demons spoke through him.

Or the possessed person may speak foreign or unknown languages. Dr. Koch personally observed a Philippine boy who knew only poor English and one other language. But when he became possessed, he was capable of speaking ten different languages including Russian. This strongly argues against the idea that spirit possession is only a mental illness.

These very same symptoms are found today among those possessed by spirits. Dr. John Nevius, a former medical missionary to China for 38 years, said that his careful study of many mental cases over the years provided strong evidence that demon possession existed in China. He further pointed out the similarities between the New Testament account and his own experiences.

And our own study of possession by ancestral spirits in Ukambani concurs with these observations. Possession is often induced through the rythmic beating of the drums. When someone is possessed, he displays unusual powers, his personality changes, and he comes under the total control of the spirit possessing him.

A Caution is Given. It is very easy to fall into the temptation of blaming anything and everything on demon possession. Whether the problem is a headache or a belly ache, the problem is diagnosed as demon possession. But caution needs to be exercised. With all of Dr. Koch's vast experience, he has never felt able to tell a man, "you are demon possessed."

> One cannot approach the world of evil spirits and demons in such an off-handed way. It cost Jesus His life when He made an end to the powers of darkness on the cross. And who are we compared to Him? He must be very careful not to start jumping to conclusions in this area, and thereby become the victims of a kind of occult neurosis. We need not blame demons immediately something goes wrong in our own lives, and we should guard against calling others as demon possessed when we have no proof of the fact that they are. All too often people call events as demonic for which there is a quite natural explanation (Koch 1970:64).

Counseling Those Who May Be Possessed. Several suggestions are here offered. Exorcism is as much an art as it is a science. Though there are guiding principles, there must be divine wisdom through the guidance of the Holy Spirit to know how to approach each situation in the will and power of God. Exorcism in the Name of Christ is not a kind of magic with fixed rules and formula. Counseling and helping those possessed by evil spirits requires patience, spiritual understanding and divine guidance.

Deliverance is always and only possible through the Name of Jesus Christ. Christ demonstrated His power over all the evil spirits during His earthly ministry. And he declared, "If it is by the finger of God that I cast out demons, then the kingdom of God has come upon you." (Lk. 11:20) Even today the unclean spirits are subject to the authority of Jesus Christ when the demons are commanded in Jesus' Name. Commanding the spirits in Jesus' name has great power when spoken by one who is cleansed by the blood of Christ.

Permanent deliverance, however, depends on complete breaking of all ties with everything associated with those spirits. Every object of sorcery or spiritism must be destroyed. It would appear that the evil spirits are closely identified with certain objects. These should be destroyed completely if deliverance is to be complete. Friendship with mediums must also be broken. Friends who may have contact with the spirit world may have demonic influence over a person. Those friendships must be broken, even if they are close relatives.

The formerly possessed person must confess his sins, including specific repentance for sins of the occult. He must denounce Satan specifically and renounce all relationship with the evil spirits. A person who has been a slave to some spirit has been a possession of Satan in a unique way. It is, therefore, desirable to reject all evil powers.

Sometimes exorcism (the casting out of the demons) requires extra ordinary power through united prayer with others. One individual is too weak to combat the Devil. The team-work of other Christians provides divine power. And this may require prayer with fasting.

The Christian who engages in exorcism, casting out demons, must find his own protection in the blood of Christ. Living in sin will only open him up to the attack of the Evil One. But when cleansed by the blood of Christ and invoking the protection from the blood of Christ, this is the Christian's perfect weapon. Nothing causes the unclean spirits to tremble more than the use of the Name and the blood of Jesus Christ.

Jesus Christ is sovereign. He has overcome the Devil (I Jn. 5:8). Those who would engage in combat with the spiritual powers of darkness must find their power and refuge in Jesus Christ and in Jesus Christ alone (Rom. 8:31-39).

Conclusion.

We conclude that *the activity of evil spirits is real*, and is witnessed both by Scripture and the experience in traditional religion.

Both Hobley and Lindblom report frequent "disturbances of a religious character like epidemics" which swept over Ukambani among the Akamba in Kenya. One such disturbance was the "Kiesu" in 1906. It began in Mukaa when medicine men taught people a new religious dance which they said was commanded by the spirits. The dance spread like wildfire. Symptoms consisted of people going into fits at the sight of a European or pith helmet or a red fez. "The afflicted one fell to the ground, writhing [twisting] as if suffering from violent cramp, moaning and groaning." (Lindblom 1920:239) The Akamba tried to avoid these attacks by wrapping their blanket around their head when seeing a European. The meaning of "Kiesu" is not clear, though some, including Lindblom, believe it is connected with the name, Jesus. On one occasion, Lindblom recorded some of the words of the "Kiesu" dance and several times the name, "The Lord Jesus," was mentioned. It may have arisen from the teaching of the missionaries, Lindblom suggested.

We may be sure that the Kingdom of Darkness does not remain passive when the servants of the King invade with the Light of the Gospel. Opposition of a violent nature can be expected. But thank God, we need not stop here.

We may also affirm, that *the power of the Gospel of Jesus Christ can overcome darkness.*

It is a known fact that in lands where the Gospel is preached and believed, the open activities of demons has been quieted. In western nations today, where the peoples are turning their backs on the Word of God, there is a renewed interest and involvement in spiritism.

Experience with evil spirits decreases with the coming of the Gospel. Lindblom again makes this interesting comment back in the first decade of this century.

The Akamba themselves said in 1920 that the spirits did not appear nearly as often since the arrival of Europeans in the country. The American mission station at Machakos is built on an old place of sacrifice, and the *aimu* [ancestral spirits] are said to have been specially troublesome just there before the arrival of the missionaries, while they have now completely vanished (Lindblom 1920:216).

Our Lord declared, "I will build My Church and the gates of hell shall not overpower it." Thus we find that, although the Bible recognizes the existence of Satan and his legions of fallen angels, Jesus Christ is Lord and through His death on the cross the powers of the Kingdom of Darkness have been vanquished.

ANCESTRAL SPIRITS AND THE BIBLE

A Problem to Some Christians

We have seen that the African traditional belief in spirits is a problem not only to those educated in western oriented institutions immersed in the naturalistic world view, but is also a problem to many professing Christians today. Among a people who have traditionally maintained an intimate relationship with the departed spirits, communicating with them, honouring them with offerings, depending upon them for guidance, and reckoning on their presence, the teaching of the Christian church concerning the ancestral spirits has brought distress to the inner soul of many Africans.

This problem, though not equally experienced or expressed by every African church member, is widely proclaimed these days. This may be evidenced by the numbers of African Christians who resort to the traditional customs regarding ancestral spirits, despite the teaching of their churches; by the numbers of Africans who remain outside the fellowship of the Christian church because of their commitment to their ancestors; by the various African Independent Churches which have restored some of the traditional ways; and by the African theologians who are addressing this question.

A Suggested Solution

John Taylor is one example of many who suggest that the solution for the African Christian Church is in the doctrine of the communion and veneration of saints.

Taylor says, "Is it not time for the Church to learn to give the Communion of Saints the centrality which the soul of Africa craves?" (Taylor 1963:158)

He then recommends prayer for the dead as the "tender bridge" which should unite the living and the dead with Christ.

> To ask for the prayers of others in this life, and to know that they rely on mine, does not show any lack of faith in the all-sufficiency of God. Then, in the same faith, let me ask for their prayers still, and offer mine for them, even when death has divided us. They pray for me, I may believe, with clearer understanding, but I for them in ignorance, though still in love (Taylor 1963:160).

Raising the question whether such communion should be limited to the Christian dead, he responds, "That must remain a crucial question for Africa, awaiting the study of her future theologians." He then proceeds to suggest his own answer in these words:

> The words, 'in Christ all...' cannot include less than that in life. The genealogies in the Gospel linking Christ Himself with the unnumbered multitudes of the dead are a symbol of the unbroken cord with which God will finally draw Adam back to paradise. The Christian's link with his pagan ancestors, in remembrance and unceasing intercession, may be part of that ultimate redemption [italics mine]: for as Ceasaire the Martiniqean poet puts it, 'there is room for all of us at the rendezvous [the meeting place] of victory.'" (Taylor 1963:163)

Today, many of Africa's theologians are following this suggestion of John Taylor in developing the doctrine of Communion of Saints with an emphasis on universalism. All the ancestors, whether Christians or not, are in the great body of Saints. The liberal teaching, that all men will be saved, whether or not they have personally accepted Christ by faith, is appealing to men today.This subject deserves extensive treatment which will hopefully be forthcoming in another separate volume. But for our purposes in this survey of ATR, we shall make a few observations concerning the relevant biblical teaching.

1. Necromancy Forbidden

The practice of communicating with the ancestral spirits is explicitly and repeatedly forbidden in Scripture. The manner in which this practice is forbidden is so strong and repeated that the Christian Church is alerted to a fundamental problem with any association with necromancy.

The chief word in the Hebrew Bible for necromancy is *darash*, the root appearing 165 times in the Old Testament. *Darash* simply means "seek," "ask," and "inquire." The context must determine the precise meaning on each occasion. In a large number of cases *darash* means to "inquire of God," to "consult Yahweh" or ask the prophet who serves as the mediator for God. The predominant use of *darash* in the Old Testament is in the context of seeking or asking God.

But many passages refer to an abuse of *darash* by asking other gods or the spirits of the dead. A classic text in which *darash* is accompanied by other words denoting cultic activity is Jeremiah 8:2. "And they will spread them out to the sun, the moon, and to all the host of heaven, which they have *loved* and which they have *served*, and which they have *gone after*, and which they have *sought* [*darash*], and which they have *worshipped*." The acts of loving, serving, seeking and worshipping, which should be directed to the Creator, have instead been directed to the creature. God's judgment is this: "They will not be gathered or buried; they will be as dung on the face of the ground." The objects of this illegitimate seeking include: the Baals, the gods of the nations, the gods of the sons of Seir, Baalzebub, the god of Ekron, the dead (*methim*), the mediums, the shades (*repha'im*), the gods of Edom, idols, the wizards, the sorcerers, the sun, the moon, and all the host of heaven (see Wagner 1974).

Isaiah 8:18-20. This passage uses *darash* in two ways, referring to legitimate inquiry and illegitimate inquiry. That which makes inquiry illegitimate is the object. "And when they say to you, 'Consult (*darash*) the mediums and the wizards who whisper and mutter,' should not a people consult (*darash*) their God? Should they consult the dead on behalf of the living? To the law and to the testimony!"

During the days of Moses, God had redeemed Israel from Egyptian slavery. At Mount Sinai they were formed into a nation with a unique relationship with God, their Redeemer. Israel was chosen in the words of God, to be "My own possession among all the peoples for all the earth is Mine." (Ex. 19:5) Any "seeking" or "inquiry" by Israel was to be directed to Him alone. This exclusive relationship between God and His people was for the glory of God and the good of Israel.

Israel was in crisis during the period before their captivity. The Assyrian threat in the eighth century was real. Pekah of North Israel and Rezin of Damascus desired Ahaz, king of Jerusalem, to be an ally with them against Assyria. When Ahaz rejected their proposals, and preferred friendship with Assyria, the Syro-Ephraimitic uprising occurred in 734 B.C. in which Pekah and Rezin joined hands to fight Ahaz, hoping to replace Ahaz with a king disposed to their desires. In panic Ahaz appealed to the king of Assyria (Isa. 7:1-9). Though God intervened and saved the southern kingdom, terror and fear prevailed among the Jews because of Assyria. When Tiglath-pileser marched south, over throwing the king of Samaria, destroying Philistine cities, it appeared as though Judea would fall (Smith 1927:125).

During those critical days, filled with fear and terror, the children of Israel turned to the mediums and wizards who communicated with the spirits. They forsook God and turned toward pagan religion.

The medium was one with "a familiar spirit" (*ob*). The basic meaning of *ob* is "a leathern bottle" used for water or wine. *ob* also came to mean "necromancer, sorcerer, a conjurer who professes to call up the dead by means of incantations and magic formulas, in order that they may give response as to doubtful or future things." (Gesenius 1868:ad loc) Thus the medium is like a leathern bottle, filled with a spirit, from whose belly comes gurgling sounds of the one possessing him.

The Septuagint used the Greek word, *engastrimuthos* meaning "ventriloquist," to translate *ob* (Lev. 19:31; I Sam. 28:3-9). Thus the person with an *ob* who used the techniques of necromancy was labelled a ventriloquist.

But the meaning of ventriloquist has changed through the centuries. Today, ventriloquism is a purely natural phenomena in which a person projects his voice so that it appears that the voice proceeds from some other person or puppet or from some other place. Our contemporary definition of ventriloquism should not mislead us to think that the translators of the Hebrew Bible considered the technique of necromancy a merely clever, natural technique of ventriloquism as we know it today. Ventriloquism among the Greeks involved the presence of spirits. "It cannot be too strongly emphasized that such a conception is far removed from the ideas of peoples of the ancient world. By them it was firmly believed that persons so designated were actually 'pregnant' with a god or spirit." (Langton 1942:178) Plutarch states that one of the factors present in the operation of the Delphic oracle was the activity of demons. "Among the ancients this power of ventriloquism was often misused for the purposes of magic...As to the connection between these two significations of *bottle* and *necromancer*, it probably arose from regarding the conjurer, while possessed by the demon, as a *bottle*, i.e. vessel, case, in which the demon was contained." (Gesenius 1868:20) In other words, *ob* and *engastrimuthos*, among the ancients, signified a medium who became possessed by a spirit. Customs among the nations differed. But the basic element of contact with the spirit world was always present.

The other specialist whom the Jews consulted was the "wizard," the translation of *yidd'oni*. The wizard was,

> primarily the possessor of a prophesying or soothsaying spirit...and then the soothsaying spirit itself (Lev. 20:27), which was properly called yidda'on (the much knowing), like daimon, which according to Plato, is equivalent to daemon. These people, who are designated by the LXX, both here and elsewhere, as eggastromuthoi, i.e. ventriloquists, imitated the chirping of bats, which were supposed to proceed from the shades of Hades, and uttered their magical formulas in a whispering tone (Delitzsch n.d.:I,240).

These mediums and wizards are said to have whispered and muttered, referring to the way in which the familiar spirits chirped and twittered while the specialists were their mouth pieces. These were the ghosts who were alleged to have knowledge of the future, "ghosts of knowledge" (see Lev. 19:31; 20:27; Deut. 18:11). Reference to muttering and whispering may have a broader meaning than the manner in which the familiar spirits spoke through the medium. It may be a polemic against the untrustworthiness of the message given. God disparages the reliability of any message given by the dead, through the inaudible and indistinct words of the medium.

How shameful for the people of God to turn to mediums and wizards for a prophetic word concerning the future. Under the Old Covenant, God's people were to consult the prophets. "In these latter days, God has given to us His infallible Word, the Bible. When we wish to consult Him, let us turn to the Bible, for its words are the words of God Himself." (Young 1978:319) In contrast to the consultations with the dead, God commands us, "To the law and to the testimony!" Sinful man, yearning for knowledge that God has not willed to grant him, unwilling to trust and obey the One who created him, turns from God's Law and the Testimony to seek answers from the dead. For those who inquire from the mediums and wizards, God declares the morning light has not broken upon them. They remain in darkness of sin. "Necromancy...is a most gloomy deception." (Delitzsch n.d.:I,240) Nor will the light ever dawn upon them until they turn to the Law and the Testimony. From there the light shines.

Leviticus 19:26-31. Chapter 19 contains a series of commandments which are not logically related to one another. We have previously examined several verses from this chapter concerning mediums. Our attention is now drawn to the warnings against necromancy.

One of the commandments concerns the honour given to elders. "You shall rise up before the grayheaded, and honour the aged, and you shall revere your God; I am the Lord." (vs. 32) God wants His people to give proper respect and honour to the aged, those elders among us who through their years of experience deserve our deference. The fifth commandment is important.

But the elders to whom God commands us to give honour, are the *living* elders. There is nothing wrong with honouring those who have died, so long as it is appropriate according to the Scriptures. Proper burial and memorializing of the dead are fitting. But the command in the Bible to honour our parents and to honour our elders and those who have the rule over us is honour directed to the living, not the dead.

It is, therefore, significant that contiguous to verse 32 is the command *not* to consult the dead. "Do not turn to mediums or spiritists; do not seek them out to be defiled by them. I am the Lord your God." (vs.31) The mediums and spiritists, as we shall see below, were unquestionably acquainted with necromancy (Keil n.d.:II,425).

No only are mediums and spiritists outlawed in Israel on the pain of death, but various practices associated with the dead are forbidden. "You shall not make any cuts on your body for the dead, nor make any tattoo marks on yourselves; I am the Lord." (vs.28) The children of Israel were to abstain from all idolatrous practices. They were forbidden to disfigure their bodies on account of the dead. During the passionate outbursts of mourning among the nations in the East, they would commonly scratch their arms, hands and face. Tattoo marks were made, some think, in association with the custom of making expiation for the dead. They cut the hair from their head and beard (vs.27) with reference to the dead. These customs were carried on by the Babylonians, Armeneans, ancient Romans and Arabs. Despite the prohibitions in Israel, these customs, related to the honouring of the dead, persisted in Israel (see Jer. 16:16; 41:5; 47:5). (Keil n.d.:I,423f)

Deuteronomy 18:10,11. Previously we have examined this most comprehensive passage in the Old Testament concerning the prohibition of pagan practices as found in Deuteronomy 18:9-14. We shall only remind ourselves concerning its teaching on necromancy.

In verse 11 he forbids approaching a medium or a spiritist and one who calls up the dead.

The spiritist (*yidd'oni*) is the wise and knowing person who is acquainted with the secrets of the unseen world (Brown 1983:ad loc). The word is translated by the Authorized Version as "wizard" meaning, "the knowing one." Formerly, the "wizard" was the male and the "witch" was the female, both of whom practiced divination by similar means. The Hebrew word actually means "familiar spirit," indicating the close association which this specialist had with the spirit world. This word has already been studied in passages formerly considered, such as I Sam. 28:3,9; Isa. 8:19; and Lev. 19:31. In all these places the spiritist is linked with the medium.

The medium is a "consulter with familiar spirits," "a *pythoness*, one who inquiries by the means of one spirit to get oracular answers from another of a superior order." (Clark n.d.:ad loc) There is no essential difference between a medium and a spiritist. To make fine distinctions between these various words is futile. The evident purpose of this multiplication of words is to make a comprehensive statement concerning the forbidden practices. "The author almost exhausts the Hebrew vocabulary in order to designate various types of superstitious practice." (Wright 1953b:446) Moses is piling up term after term to include all those practices from pagan religion which were excluded from genuine faith in the Creator God.

The Authorized Version translates this, "necromancer," the only time that word occurs in the King James translation. The basic Hebrew word for "inquire" or "seek" (*darash*) is here used, the same word used for seeking and consulting God. While Israel was commanded to "consult" God, they were forbidden to "consult" the dead.

Conclusion. We conclude from these verses that God has forbidden all contact of any sort with the spirit world, whatever may be the nature of those spirits. Communication with the spirits of the dead is specifically prohibited. Punishment for such a practice in the Old Testament was death. Capital punishment was executed upon necromancers because it constituted idolatry. For these sins God punished the Canaanite nations. Because Israel followed after these idolatrous acts the wrath of God was poured out upon them also, resulting in captivity. Communicating with the dead is spiritual harlotry, betraying one's trust in the living God.

2. Prayers to, for and by the Dead are Unbiblical

Certain elements within Christendom promote prayers to, for and by the dead. They believe that in this way the felt needs of many Africans will be met after they become Christians. If we base our theology on church tradition, then indeed there is much support for these prayers. Tertullian in A.D. 211 was the first to mention prayers for the dead in public, as Christians prayed for their dead on the anniversary day of their death. Many such examples may be cited in church history.

However, if we rely exclusively on the Scriptures for our final authority in faith and practice, then we have no basis whatsoever for these prayers. Roman Catholics and others who advocate prayers for the dead refer to the apocryphal writings, such as II Maccabees 15:12ff. However, the apocryphal writings are not part of the canonical Scriptures. Our Lord Jesus Christ quoted from Moses, the Writings and the Prophets, but He never quoted from the Apocrypha. The fact is that II Maccabees is full of historical errors. Hence, we cannot acknowledge the authority of such quotations. Moreover, the passage cited above is even contrary to Roman Catholic teaching. For Roman Catholics teach that we ought not pray for those who have died in idolatry. Yet this is exactly what the Maccabean Jews had done.

The fact is that Scripture is silent on the church tradition of praying to or for the dead. We cannot help but believe that this unbiblical practice has creeped into various Christian denominations through accommodation and compromise. This tradition is the result of syncretism in the past whereby pagan traditions were introduced into church theology and practice in order to accommodate the desires of those new converts. But evangelicals who desire to be faithful to the Scriptures and the Scriptures alone, cannot accommodate such traditions, no matter how ancient, respected from age or widespread they may be.

Towards a Biblical Solution to the Problem of Ancestral Spirits

There is a great need in Africa for the Christian believers to remember their departed ancestors. Memorializing the dead has precedent in the Scriptures and is surely sanctioned by the Bible. Whether this be through the naming of children after their forefathers, or erecting monuments, or through the dedication of articles of furniture in the churches to the memory of dead loved ones, the Christian church needs to assist the believers in memorializing the dead in some satisfactory way. This needs to be done creatively and collectively by the African believers in ways that are not offensive to the community of believers.

Apart from creative and indigenous efforts to keep the memory of the dead alive among the believers, following are some broad guidelines for the basis of an evangelical solution to the problem of ancestral spirits.

We suggest that any solution must include the following truths which we have clustered together in one phrase: *FAITH IN THE LIVING GOD WITHIN THE COMMUNITY OF BELIEVERS ACCORDING TO THE SCRIPTURES*. If the Christian church in Africa is to replace the ancestral cult with the Christian faith, pastors and teachers, missionaries and evangelists must equip the saints with these basic truths for the work of building up the Body of Christ (Eph. 4:11,12).

The Living God. Within this "vale of woe" in which people are the objects of temptation and attack from the Evil One, there can be no refuge or security apart from the pre-eminence given to the living God. While traditional religion reflects a certain knowledge about the Creator God, the Christian Church must strengthen that knowledge through biblical teaching and go beyond that by promoting a personal knowledge and trust in the living God through faith in Jesus

Christ.

God as the sovereign Lord must be made real in the daily lives of men and women. When God is removed from the daily concerns of people, other sources of refuge are sought. Jesus Christ, God come in the flesh, must be presented as the Lord who has power over all things. His abiding love for His people and His supreme victory over the forces of darkness must be stressed constantly. The blessed work of the Holy Spirit, the Comforter, should be proclaimed equally. To the impoverishment of many believers, the Church has often neglected the vital ministry of the Holy Spirit in the lives of believers — comforting, rebuking, encouraging, strengthening, correcting, teaching and protecting.

When anyone resorts to the ancestral spirits or traditional help in time of trouble, he reflects a failure to allow God His rightful place in his life. God is all that we need. He must be made real to the people. The riches of Scripture concerning the work of the Father, Son and Holy Spirit, in and for the believers, must be researched and imparted to the peoples so that the Creator God of whom the peoples of Africa had a partial knowledge might be brought close to the believers through Christ and the blessed Holy Spirit.

Faith. There are two kinds of faith: assent to the Christian creed and personal trust and confidence in the living God. While the first kind of faith is important, it has no saving value. Many people profess to be Christian, are baptized members of a church, attend the services and may even take leadership roles, but they do not know God. They believe the Christian faith but have never placed their personal faith in Jesus Christ.

Consequently, when these individuals face problems of life, having never known the power of Christ in their lives, they readily fall away from their Christian belief and resort to traditional help from the ancestors. In Africa where church growth has been phenomenal, many people give intellectual assent to the teachings of the church but they have never been born again. Living, personal, growing faith in Jesus Christ is the *sine qua non* for dealing with the ancestral cult. There is no substitute.

Within the Community of Believers. Earlier we stated that human beings are both spiritual and social creatures. As a spiritual being, he can never find fulfillment, never be what he was created to be, unless God has His rightful place in His life. But people are also social beings. Men and women were never intended to be isolated individuals. They are to be an integrated Body, socially inter-related with each other.

When the Christian church was formed within these traditional cultures of Africa, the Christians became part of a new community, the Church of Jesus Christ. While believers still retain their relationship with the extended family, clan and tribe, their new membership in the Christian Church takes on new and greater significance. The Church is the Body of Christ in which every member contributes his gifts to the building up of one another (I Cor. 12-14).

When seeking to deal with the problems of the ancestral cult among the true believers in Christ, the vital, functioning role of the Body of Christ is essential. Where there is a living faith in Jesus Christ and where the community of believers is functioning as they should, there will be great release from the temptations of traditional religion.

According to the Scripture. Scripture is the mediating channel through which we obtain personal faith in the living God and an active communal relationship within the Body of Christ. God breathes out His Spirit and grants people faith as they meditate upon the Word of God. The stress on literacy during the Reformation was for the purpose of helping each believer to read the Scriptures. The motive of primary school education wherever missionaries have gone was to give the Bible to the people. Every Christian is a priest before God. Every Christian has the right and obligation to know the Word of God. Prosperity and success were promised to Joshua if he would meditate on the Book of the Law day and night (Josh. 1:8). Those who delight in the Law of God and meditate in it day and night are promised prosperity (Ps. 1:3). There is no substitute.

Only as the Christian church continues to return to the Scripture and submit to its judgment, only as she continues to be judged and reformed by the Scriptures, can Christianity be God's answer to man's problems.

Traditional African belief in the ancestral spirits is one of those items in ATR which is totally incompatible with the Christian faith. Apart from memorializing the dead as mentioned above, there must be deliverance from traditional captivity through the blood of Christ. Daidanso referred to Jesus' words to Peter, "Feed my sheep." Daidanso contends that if the traditional African comes to Christ, he needs to be delivered. Jesus' words to the African pastor are, "Deliver my sheep." In Chad a new believer is asked if he has any object which has been in association with the spirits. If so, he brings them all out and they are burned while the Christians sing. This is a testimony of the new believer which requires courage. This act of burning those objects is a clear sign of his commitment to Jesus Chrtist for salvation and deliverance. If he refuses to burn the fetishes, this reveals fear within him. Many are saved out of ATR but remain bound to the occult. They need to be delivered by claiming the blood of Christ. If he exhibits continued bondage to the occult, sometimes the new convert is invited to stay and live with an older believer who helps him.

In addition to deliverance according to the Scripture, however, the believers must also be taught. "Feed my sheep." The African Christians need clear teachings from Scripture. Daidanso says that because people are not instructed in the ways of God, these immature Christians return to the spirits during times of sickness and death. ATR becomes a real problem to the African church when suffering comes. Sickness and death lead the people back to ATR. Thus the African pastor must both deliver and feed the sheep (Daidanso ma Djongwe:1988).

CONCLUSION

Divinities, nature spirits and ancestral spirits in various ways have detracted from the glory of God. These spirits have promoted an unlawful relationship with men and women contrary to the will of God. These spirits have possessed and enslaved human beings. In biblical perspective these are non other than the unclean spirits, the fallen angels who serve their master, even Satan. Nothing could be plainer in the Bible than the divine abhorrence and active opposition to any contact, communication or relationship with the ancestral spirits, divinities or other spirits. The living God created us for Himself and He alone is to be our hope and confidence and refuge. From God and His Word alone should we obtain guidance. As prophet Isaiah wrote,

> But people will tell you to ask for messages from fortunetellers and mediums, who chirp and mutter. They will say, 'After all, people should ask for messages from the spirits and consult the dead on behalf of the living.' You are to answer them, 'Listen to what the Lord is teaching you! Don't listen to mediums —what they tell you will do you no good.' (Good News Bible)

REVIEW QUESTIONS FOR CHAPTER 12

1. While Scripture teaches the reality of spirits, what is the difference in attitude toward spirits between the biblical viewpoint and many traditional Africans?

2. Discuss the different perspectives of spirit possession among many anthropologists, psychologists, theologians and among those evangelicals who seek to be faithful to the Scriptures?

3. How would you deal with someone who is possessed by a spirit?

4. Discuss the teaching of the Bible concerning the communication with the dead.

Suggested Reading and Thought Questions for Advanced Study:

Dickason, C. Fred. *Angels, Elect and Evil*, 1975.
Koch, Kurt. *Between Christ and Satan*, 1981.
Koch, Kurt. *Christian Counseling and Occultism*, 1981.
Koch, Kurt. *Demonology: Past and Present*, 1981.
Leahy, Frederick. *Satan Cast Out*, 1975.
Montgomery, J.W. ed. *Demon Possession*, 1976.
Summer, Montague. *The History of Witchcraft and Demonology*, 1969.
Unger, Merrill F. *Biblical Demonology*, 1952.

Check the following topics in various standard evangelical reference books on theology, in Bible dictionaries and encyclopedias: demons, demonic, demonology, demon possession, exorcism, familiar spirit, spirit, Satan, medium, death, spirit, necromancy, necromancer.

Baker's Dictionary of Theology, Everett Harrison ed.
Evangelical Dictionary of Theology, Walter A. Elwell ed.
The International Standard Bible Encyclopaedia, Geoffrey Bromiley ed.
The International Standard Bible Encyclopaedia, James Orr ed.
New Bible Dictionary, J.D. Douglas ed.
Unger's Bible Dictionary, Merrill F. Unger ed.
Wycliffe Bible Encyclopedia, Charles Pfeiffer ed.

1. Discuss the biblical teaching on the nature and activites of evil spirits. How does the biblical view differ radically from the western naturalistic philosophy? What evidence have you seen that these western naturalistic presuppositions are influencing the world view of many educated scholars in Africa today?

2. How does the biblical description of spirit possession compare with spirit possession in Africa? Compare and contrast the characteristics of the spirit possessed person in Africa and the characteristics of the possessed recorded in the Scripture.

3. How should the Christian church seek to deal with spirits in Africa today? What was the former approach by many earlier missionaries? Why do you think many missionaries formerly dismissed spirit activity as mere superstition? Why should we be cautious lest we become a victim of "occult neurosis"?

4. Why do you think the Bible portrays necromancy as such a wicked sin? Support your answer with biblical teaching.

5. How can the traditional belief in the spirit world serve as a bridge to present the truths of the Gospel? What positive truths can be found in the traditional spirit world that the Gospel can build on? Discuss.

6. How should the Christian church handle the traditional cult of the ancestral spirits? By repudiation, accomodation, transformation or substitution? Why do some Christians retain their former relationship with their ancestors while others do not? Discuss, seeking a biblical solution.

PART FOUR

THE SUPREME BEING IN
AFRICAN TRADITIONAL RELIGION

Chapter 13

SUMMARY OF BELIEF IN THE SUPREME BEING IN ATR

ATR traditional belief in God is both its great strength and its major weakness. We shall, therefore, devote much thought to this aspect of our study. Many books have been written on our topic. Some are ethnographic studies of individual ethnic groups in Africa, detailing the particular beliefs of a particular people. These studies derive their strength in being more comprehensive and detailed. Other books on ATR are broad, sweeping generalizations covering the whole continent. Their benefit is the possibility of summarizing traditional beliefs for the whole continent of Africa.

We shall follow our own practice of beginning with a general survey of traditional belief and practice in Africa, but we shall devote most of our effort to the examination of a particular case study, namely, the Akamba. Our general survey is derived from other general surveys of ATR. There are some excellent surveys and the reader is encouraged to consult these. But our examination of the Akamba is derived through personal conversations, investigation and consultations with various Christians and non-Christians among the Akamba and the reading of all the materials available on the Akamba over a period of eleven years. For we find that generalizations about Africa often overlook particular weaknesses and errors that are brought to light when one considers more carefully the particular beliefs and practices of a particular people.

Briefly, let us survey some of the traditional beliefs and practices concerning the Supreme Being.

THE ATTRIBUTES OF THE SUPREME BEING

1. God knows all things

Various authors object to any suggestion that the God of ATR was omniscient. Omniscience, they claim, is a Greek thought, not a traditional African thought. To them this is reading into ATR what is not there. Perhaps! But I have found no evidence that traditional Africans believe that God is limited in his knowledge. Perhaps they have not speculated abstractly to think that God has full knowledge of everything, everywhere, always and from eternity past and is therefore omniscient. But we do find universal confidence in the Supreme Being who knows everything about people and their activities and from whom we can hide nothing. We may deceive the ancestors but we cannot deceive God.

2. God is present everywhere

Though God may take up temporary abode in a particular place on earth while on a visit, He is truly everywhere in the sense that people can call upon Him wherever they are. Whether it is correct to speak of God's omnipresence (His presence everywhere), some may argue. But practically speaking, the traditional African believes that wherever a person may be, he may call upon God in times of crisis. Man cannot wander away from the presence of God. Whether African peoples approached God only in times of distress and as a last resort, God could be approached anywhere when people were in desperate need. And they did approach Him.

3. God is almighty

When all other assistance fails, including mystical powers, ancestral spirits and divinities, men may seek God who is able to do all things. If the prayers of people are not heard, it is not because of the weakness of God. Nothing is too hard for Him. There can be no objection to speaking of the almighty power of God among the traditional Africans. The peoples did not always believe that God would intervene on their behalf. But He was able if He so desired.

4. God is transcendent (extraordinary)

Like the first three attributes of the Supreme Being, the transcendence of God is widely and prominently held. God is highly exalted above the creature. He is the One High-up, He who has always been. He is without limitation and beyond human comprehension. No one can search and understand the ways of God. He is above and beyond.

Because God is so great and highly exalted, His ways are beyond our ability to understand. God is mysterious. He is incomprehensible. The mysteries of providence with pain, suffering and death, are beyond our ability to understand. Seldom is God blamed for trouble, though there are occasional indirect complaints. But in the midst of trouble, the traditional response is not complaint but resignation. Who can fathom the mysteries of life?

5. God is everlasting

Another attribute that sets God apart from all others is that He has had no beginning. Whatever one may say about traditional belief in ancestral spirits, nature spirits and divinities, they have all been created. They derive their existence from God. While the whole world has been created, God has not been created. He alone is eternal with the ground of His Being within Him.

6. God is spirit

God has no body. He is invisible. Africa has never practiced the kind of idolatry which was common among the Europeans and Asians. Only one idol of the Supreme Being is known among all the African peoples. God is spirit and He is transcendent so that no attempts have been made to fashion any representation of God out of wood or stone.

7. God is kind, merciful and good

The former attributes are rather well documented. But we can also say that traditional belief to some extent also embraced the mercy, kindness and goodness of God. The giving of rain, birth of children and the healing of the body remind the peoples that God is good. Whatever tragedy man may experience is blamed on witchcraft or the living-dead. But God is seldom charged with wrong doing in Africa, though there are exceptions.

Very few African peoples speak of the love of God. But in fact, the peoples of Africa seldom speak of human love either. Instead, "a person shows his love for another more through action than words." (Mbiti 1970:33)

For two reasons we would agree with others that the Supreme Being traditionally was regarded as kind, merciful and good. First, various blessings in life occasionally led people to remark about the mercy or goodness of God who provided them with rain and food. Second, we find little evidence that traditional Africans blamed God for not being kind, merciful or loving. Anticipating what we shall say later, the fullness of knowing the love and mercy of God awaited the coming of the Gospel. But the Gospel did not introduce a surprise or a contradiction to their former understanding.

8. God is holy

By inference we conclude that God is considered holy, both in the sense that He is separate from His creatures and and in the sense that He is separate from wrong doing. He not only is Wholly Other, the uncreated creator who is transcendent above the world. He is also above any fault and beyond reproach of men. He never lies and can always be trusted. There is little direct traditional teaching concerning the holiness of God as understood from biblical revelation. But we can affirm that the nature of God in all of His holiness as traditionally understood by Africans is compatible with biblical revelation which fills more complete their basic perception.

9. God is unique

There is no one that can be compared to the Supreme Being in ATR. He is unique. No one can draw an image of God for God is incomprehensible. He is unlike anything or anyone we may know. Unlike the creatures, God has no limitations. Unlike creation, God had no beginning. Thus God is transcendent and beyond our ability to comprehend Him.

SUMMARY: THE SUPREME BEING IN ATR   191

THE WORKS OF THE SUPREME BEING

1. God created the world

The belief that God created the heavens and the earth is widespread all over Africa. The names attributed to God reflect this basic understanding. He is known as the Excavator, Hewer, Carver, Creator, Originator, Inventor and Architect. And many traditional stories narrate the order and procedure which God followed in placing man upon the earth.

2. God protects and saves

A great mistake was made in past studies of ATR. Students of ATR concluded that Africa's traditional concept of God was similar to that of the Deist. The Deist acknowledges God as the Creator. But he taught that the world was so created that it would be self-sufficient, containing all the laws needed for operation. Thereafter, God removed Himself from active participation in the sustaining and guidance of the things upon the earth.

However, the Deist's view of providence is quite different from that of the traditional African. For ATR recognized the continued involvement of God in the maintenance and operation of the world. God is the One who provides food, sunshine, rain, children, health and protection. These are gifts from Him.

As Supreme Ruler over the earth, God is known as King, Lord and Judge. His will is absolute and He rules with power.

Whereas, earlier studies erred in claiming that God had virtually, for all practical purposes, abandoned the earth. Many current studies seem to err in the other direction, suggesting a fullness of revelation in ATR which is comparable to biblical revelation. The fact is that God is involved in this world. People can and do call upon Him for help in times of dire distress. The fact also is that the ancestral spirits, spirits and divinities have clouded the picture of traditional belief and worship of God.

THE WORSHIP OF THE SUPREME BEING

In discussing the worship of African peoples, Mbiti defines worship broadly to mean, "man's act or acts of turning to God." (Mbiti 1970:178) For our present purposes we shall follow this broad definition.

Some Africans have traditionally prayed every day. Many observe religious rites during the four major periods in the life of the person, namely, birth, initiation, marriage and death. For agricultural peoples, religious rites may be performed at the time of planting and harvest. Hunters may seek God's help at the time of hunting. Warriors may seek aid during the time of war or cattle raiding. For many Africans the worship of God is mingled with petitions and sacrifices offered to the ancestral spirits so one may hardly speak of it as divine worship. And some African peoples do not offer any sacrifices or offerings directly to God at all. It is at times of distress, illness and calamity, that most Africans are found seeking God in prayer and sacrifices, but usually mingling their worship of God with their supplication to the living-dead.

Sacrifices and offerings are a common form of worship in Africa. The purpose generally is to restore the balance in nature that has been upset through the displeasure of the spiritual beings. When crises occur the people traditionally conclude that the reason is either witchcraft or the wrath of the ancestors and/or God. Thus sacrifices and offerings are intended to re- establish the balance which has been upset.

Prayers are by far the most common means by which men approach God. Most prayers are brief, however, and to the point, beseeching Him for some particular need. The prayers are practical and are primarily brief, to the point, requests for health, protection and guidance.

Worship may be formal by religious specialists and on special occasions. Or worship may be informal, as when the head of the family offers thanks and petitions. Worship may be on a regular basis, such as every sunrise and sunset. Or it may be irregular in times of crisis.

The times of worship most typically were in times of personal, communal or national need — times of drought, famine, disease or during warfare. But worship could also occur during the daily routines of life. Prayers and sacrifices were frequently offered during the seasons of the year, at the time of planting and harvesting.

Worship, defined as any act of turning toward God, could occur anywhere and at any time. But the more formal and communal worship took place in a special grove of trees or under a particular kind of tree, such as a fig tree. The temples and cathedrals of Africa were under the celestial roof and nearby some unique place in nature. One should not imagine that permanent buildings or shrines were erected for worship in ATR, though some mud temples were erected in some places. Since the peoples were often nomadic they could not erect any permanent structure.

Anyone could pray or offer sacrifices. But in many places there were religious specialists who officiated for the community. These were elders, known for their experience, character and wisdom. Their age enabled them to be much closer to the living-dead and the spirit world. These elders had gained the respect of the community.

But the worship of the Supreme Being was not always separate from and distinct from the veneration given to the living-dead as we shall see. Somehow the worship of God was frequently mingled with prayers and sacrifices given to the ancestral spirits. Furthermore, the worship of God was utilitarian, seeking God for the help they might receive, rather than extolling the greatness and goodness of God. ATR worship was anthropocentric.

CONCLUSION

There are both strengths and weaknesses in the ATR knowledge and worship of God as we shall see. Truth and error are co-mingled together. But we can affirm that the ATR notion of God in many ways forms a continuity with biblical revelation. Through general revelation truth has been disclosed. And through the fall of man, error has clouded and perverted that knowledge. But despite the clouded and confused vision, God has not left Himself without a witness.

REVIEW QUESTIONS FOR CHAPTER 13

1. Describe the characteristics of God as He is known in Africa. Discuss the knowledge of God as found in your own area.

2. What are the works of God according to traditions in Africa? According to the traditions in your area?

3. When, where and how did Africans traditionally worship the Supreme Being?

4. How close was God to man after creation according to many African traditions? How close is God to man today? What brought the change?

Suggested Reading and Thought Questions for Advanced Study:

Adggbola, E.A. Ade. *Traditional Religion in West Africa*, 1983, pp.338-366.

Idowu, Bolaji. *African Traditional Religion: A Definition*, 1973, pp. 140-165.

Kato, Byang. *Theological Pitfalls in Africa*, 1975, pp.27-46 "African Traditional Religions: A Case Study".

Mbiti, John. *African Religions and Philosophy*, 1969, pp.29-74; *Concepts of God in Africa*, 1970.

P'Bitek, Okot. *African Religions in Western Scholarship*, 1970, pp.80-89.

Parrinder, E.G. *African Traditional Religion*, 1962, pp.31-43.

Parrinder, Geoffrey. *West African Religion*, 1961, pp.13-25.

1. Research the traditional belief in God among your own people. Then compare your findings with Mbiti's summary for all of Africa (Mbiti 1970:3-42). To what extent do your findings agree with or disagree with Mbiti's generalizations?

2. Read P'Bitek 1970:80-89. To what extent do you agree or disagree with P'Bitek's following assertion: "The African deities of the books, clothed with the attributes of the Christian God, are in the main, creations of the students of African religions." (p.88) Justify your answer with specific personal observations of your people's traditions.

3. Read and compare the perspective of Kato and Idowu (Kato 1975:27-46; Idowu 1973:140-165) When there are such great differences of opinion between African scholars and theologians (eg. Kato versus Idowu, P'Bitek versus Mbiti), how can we arrive at a firm understanding of what the actual traditional belief in God was? Whom do we believe? Why? Discuss thoughtfully.

4. How can we be assured that ATR's belief in God today is static and representative of ATR's belief 75 years ago? What profound influences have been operative to modify and alter traditional belief over the past 100 years? How then can we be assured of the accuracy of our own observations and the inaccuracy of the observations made by professional anthropologists 50 years ago?

Chapter 14

CASE STUDY OF THE AKAMBA: THE SUPREME BEING

UNDERSTANDING TRADITIONAL BELIEF

The early students of Akamba traditional religion were perplexed about the Akamba traditional belief in God. Even today the Akamba themselves convey contradictory notions about the Supreme Being.

Mbiti states that "The Akamba recognize *Mulungu* as God, the Creator and Preserver of all things. He gives them children, rain and food, but nobody knows where and how He lives, or what He looks like." (Mbiti 1971:9) Mbiti thus implies by that statement that *Mulungu* is personal. Whereas, Ndeti states that *Mulungu* is impersonal. "The notion of a personal God is extremely naive and does not make sense in the Akamba belief," he declares (1972:175). Another Mukamba, Muthiani, writes,

> To some degree the Akamba are monotheists in that they have the concept of the one Supreme Being they call Mulungu; on the other hand, their religious practices revealed a belief in three gods — the 'Creator,' the 'Splinter,' and Mulungu. They rationalized that the job of the Creator was to create man and everything else, the Splinter would come along and split the limbs, fingers, branches and leaves of plants and anything that gives form to anything that exists. But the Splinter and the Creator are Stewards of Mulungu (Muthiani 1973:98).

Thus we may expect differences in viewpoints. There appears to be a wide range of differences among the individuals and localities in Ukambani. To present Akamba traditional belief in simple, straightforward doctrinaire perspective is to misrepresent reality. ATR is more complex. ATR lacks the uniformity that is presented in broad sweeping summaries of traditional belief and practice.

NAMES FOR THE SUPREME BEING

One approach to the study of Akamba traditional belief in the Supreme Being is to examine Kikamba names for God. Such a study clearly confirms that traditional Akamba did believe in God as the Supreme Being, the Creator and highly exalted one.

One of the most traditional names for the Supreme Being is *Mulungu. Mulungu* was the more common name back in 1910, according to Lindblom (Lindblom 1920:243). The name, *Mulungu*, and various derivations, are found in more than forty Bantu languages. *Mulungu* is closely related to *Mungu*, the Supreme Being in Kiswahili. *Mulungu* refers to the "one Supreme Being." (Muthiani 1973:98) This name seems to denote the fear and awe accorded to the Supreme Being and the consequent honour that is His.

Another old name for the Supreme Being is *Mumbi*, meaning "the Creator." The verb form from which *Mumbi* is derived, means, "to create" or "to bring into existence." Lindblom says that the Akamba speak of *Mulungu* as "the creator of all things and therefore call him *Mumbi* (the one who fashions)..." (Lindblom 1920:244) *Ngai Mumbi* is the powerful God whose power is manifest in creation.

Associated with the name, *Ngai Mumbi*, is a name used less frequently, *Mwatuangi*, which means "the cleaver." The verb form means literally "to split into halves" with an ax. *Mwatuangi* can refer to the splitting of a stool from a log of wood. It denotes the act of splitting. *Ngai Mwatuangi* is the one who splits the fingers, toes, eyes and mouth of created beings. When God first created man out of clay he was a mere chunk of earth. *Mulungu* is not only the One who is the most powerful and who alone created, He is *Ngai Mwatuangi* who shaped man with his various parts. He forms the baby in the womb today.

Two lesser known names for God are *Mukunoku* and *Ngai Mwiyumbi*. *Mukunoku* signifies God's ability and mighty hand in doing things which men cannot do. *Mukunoku* is associated with earthquakes and thunderstorms. *Mwiyumbi* means "self-caused" and "self- existing."

Today the most common name for God is *Ngai*. The evidence suggests that *Ngai* is not an indigenous Kikamba term. Mbiti claims that he has not found *Ngai* in any accounts of Akamba life prior to this century (Mbiti 1971:9), though we must add that Lindblom found it in use in 1911 (Lindblom 1920:243). The neighboring Masai call their Supreme Being, *Engai* (see Lindblom 1920:247; Munro 1975:19) The neighboring Kikuyu, more influenced by the Masai than the Akamba, have also adopted the name Ngai for their Supreme Being. The name, *Ngai*, can be used independently. But it is frequently affixed to another name for God, such as *Ngai Mwatuangi*, or *Ngai Mumbi*.

Ngai is also used of lesser "gods" or ancestral spirits. Traditional Akamba speak of "gods (*ngai*) of the family," "traveling gods (*ngai*)," (that is, those spirits not of a particular home, but those who pass by, bringing calamity and passing on), "mountain gods (*ngai*)", "the gods (*ngai*) of the Akamba Diviners who consult the spirits." These "gods" are also spoken of as *aimu*. One recent convert said, "These gods (*ngai*, referring to the *aimu*) were feared very much because they were able to bring about any kind of calamity, even death."

This use of the word, *ngai*, for lesser creatures can bring confusion. After one is rescued from danger, the Akamba say, "Your *ngai* is so good." Various Akamba in doing research recognize a problem in understanding which *ngai* this has reference to. The Mukamba will say, "My *ngai* came to me when I was sleeping or when I was walking." When rejecting Christianity some Akamba will say, "All I know is that my *ngai* is my mother and father." Children are admonished, "Do not despise your parents. They are your *ngai*." This of course does not mean confusion between *Ngai Mumbi* and the gods (*ngai*) of the home. The parents and the ancestors of a home simply possess certain qualities similar to *ngai* in that they protect and help them. These gods of the home bear a similar relationship to their posterity as *Ngai* maintains with them. This way of speaking, however, sometimes brings confusion and misunderstanding as to which *ngai* is really referred to. One Mukamba researcher commented, "The interpretation has been hard to reach as I have been researching. I am as confused as many others. All I can say is that the *aimu* are not God in any sense."

Indeed, this is the main point. Whatever reason the traditional Akamba had in calling the *aimu* "god," they all recognize a very definite difference between *Ngai Mumbi* and the gods of the home who are the *aimu*. While *Ngai* can be used in the plural form when referring to other spirits, *Ngai Mumbi* or *Mulungu* can never be in a plural form. The phrase, "their gods (*ngai*)," is used frequently. But this is found in the context where spirits are being referred to. Though *ngai* may refer either to the Supreme Being or lesser spirits, there is no confusion between the two categories. When one Mukamba was asked, whether he worshipped one God or many, he categorically replied, "We knew only one God." *Ngai Mumbi* is the Creator God, while the "gods" are the gods of the family, the ancestral spirits who are of a totally different category of being, for they are created beings, finite in their powers. Only *Ngai Mumbi* is the Creator. *Ngai Mumbi* has the most power. All Akamba believe this.

In the course of time the early missionaries chose the word *Ngai* for the name of the Christian concept of God, rather than *Mulungu*. The probable reason for rejecting the name, *Mulungu*, was the rather distant and impersonal nature of *Mulungu* among the Akamba. While the *ngai* are near the people, *Mulungu* is removed and relatively unknown. "Among the Akamba, *Mulungu* is a conception which, both as regards meaning and name, corresponds to what is known from so many other Bantu peoples, viz. a divinity that seems almost impersonal, since there are no conceptions – or very vague ones – of its being and characteristics." (Lindblom 1920:243)

In retrospect one could argue that the early missionaries erred by adopting another name, *Ngai*, which was less clearly associated with the Creator God, and which was frequently used of their ancestral spirits. Nevertheless, we find today that the name, *Ngai*, has triumphed. Not only is this word used to translate "God" in the Kikamba Bible. *Ngai* has become adopted by the non-Christian traditionalists. Thus the Christian teaching has infused into an alien and impoverished word all that God has revealed about Himself in Scripture. *Ngai* is the name for God most frequently used by Christians today.

We may say through this initial study of the Names of God that the Akamba, beyond dispute, have believed in the Creator God who shapes and fashions the world by the power of his might. As Mbiti affirms, the Akamba "simply knows and acknowledges the existence of God who is known as *Mulungu*." (Mbiti 1966:14) There is no need for any apologetics to prove the existence of God for the Akamba. Nor was there ever a need for missionaries to teach creation as a novel idea. The Akamba begin where the Bible begins, "In the beginning God created the heavens and the earth." (Gen. 1:1)

CHARACTERISTICS OF THE SUPREME BEING

God is Transcendent and Mysterious

One of the most pronounced characteristics is that God is transcendent (extraordinary) and mysterious. *Mulungu* is "the one who stays alone." He has no other companion. God is basically unknowable for He is mysterious and distant from people. The Akamba say, "*Ngai* does not eat ugali." *Ngai* does not fellowship with people but stays alone. He thus cannot be known. Traditionally, the Akamba did not conceive of any personal relationship with *Mulungu*. In areas of Ukambani where Christianity is influential today, there is a noticeable change in the thinking of traditionalists. But Jack Arms, who worked in the remote parts of Eastern Kitui for 30 years, said, "I do not recall any heathen approaching God in times of distress." Among those Akamba, "God is not conceived as a person, someone with whom you can talk and have personal relationships. The people believe that God creates, sees and knows, but they have no concept of a personal relationship with Him." (Arms:1982)

In fact, so mysterious, distant, great and awesome is *Mulungu*, that many have thought He is impersonal. This debate, whether *Mulungu* is a personal God or an impersonal force, has raged from the beginning of the century (see Lindblom 1920:244; Jacobs 1961:76). Even today a Mukamba university professor affirms that *Mulungu* is *not* personal (see Ndeti 1972:175).

To what extent we may legitimately call *Mulungu*, "personal" or "impersonal," is beyond the limits of this chapter. The author believes that we are not true to the facts if we describe *Mulungu* merely as impersonal. In many important ways the traditional concept of God among the Akamba is personal. The significance of this whole discussion, however, is that *Mulungu* does not develop personal relations with his creatures, except as they are mediated through the spirits or on rare occasions. Ndeti states, "Thus *Mulungu* is an extremely impersonal force which is rarely mentioned or called upon for personal gains or triumphs... One of the reasons for avoiding direct contact with *Ngai Mumbi* (Creator) is that the Akamba are very strict monotheists. *Mulungu* stays above and beyond the Universe in a place called *ituni*" (Ndeti 1972:175) "The word *ituni* has no specific locality, unlike cloud or sky. The word means 'above and beyond.'" (1972:176) "The Akamba go to extremes to avoid direct dealings with *Mulungu*." (1972:178)

One may try to magnify the virtues of traditional belief by saying *Mulungu* refers to ultimate reality which is beyond any personal intellectual formulations. One may insist that *Mulungu* is so great that we cannot confine him to any ontological category known to men, such as spirit or person. But the end result is the same. The traditional Akamba generally avoided God, seldom had communion with him, and were preoccupied with the *aimu*. The Akamba knew *Mulungu* as the originator of everything but did not know Him as One who would personally sustain and guide them day by day.

In this framework we can understand better this basic characteristic of the Supreme Being among the Akamba. *Mulungu* is so great, so mysterious, that He is feared above all other beings. The most feared person among the Akamba is the medicine man. But *Mulungu* is more greatly feared. For the medicine man dies, while *Ngai Mumbi* does not. The Akamba recognize the limitations of the Diviner. The *aimu* are also feared, but God is feared above them. No one has ever seen *Mulungu*. Though the *aimu* are spirits, these ancestors can appear to people in dreams, or in bodily form such as a reptile. But God has never been seen for he has no body and dwells in the heavens. No images of the Creator have ever been made by the Akamba. "He is invisible, or at least it is not known what He looks like or exactly where He lives; these being questions with which the Akamba do not bother." (Mbiti 1966:14)

Therefore, it seems unwise to describe *Mulungu* as imminent. He is definitely near the people in the sense that the Akamba may call upon Him at any time and anywhere when in critical need. The traditional Akamba perception of God is certainly not similar to that of the Deists. The Akamba do not consider God to be totally uninvolved in the affairs of men. When people reach their limits, having first sought the assistance of the medicine man without finding help, they reply, "Now, the remaining part is for God to play." When the Akamba are rescued or their lives have been spared, the traditionalist expresses thanks to God. "God saved us with his hands," they reply. Yet we should observe that this was not always done directly but through the ancestral spirits.

The overwhelming evidence simply does not point to a balanced emphasis on the remoteness and nearness of God as Mbiti would imply. Even Mbiti concedes in another place, "For most of their life, many African peoples place God in the transcendental plane, making Him seem remote from their daily affairs," though Mbiti still maintains that "they know He is imminent." (1970:18) *Mulungu* is near in the sense that He is always accessible to the Akamba when they call on Him in prayer. But he is not near in the sense that He is actively involved in the affairs of the people. Nor do the traditionalists seek fellowship with Him.

God Knows All Things

The Akamba believe that *Mulungu* sees and knows everything. Though one can deceive the *aimu*, no one can deceive *Mulungu*. "God knows everything, we cannot hide anything from him," the Akamba say.

God Can Do All Things

Mulungu is also believed to have great power. Nothing is too hard for him. *Mulungu* is the one who gave wisdom to select men, a knowledge of *uoi* (evil powers used by witches) and the knowledge of *uwe* (good powers to counteract witchcraft). The *aimu* can do nothing without permission from the Supreme Being. God may allow the *aimu* to kill or injure without necessarily approving of the action. The *aimu* cannot kill anyone unless God permits it. When there is a severe drought, people are heard to say, "God will help us, there is nothing to defeat him."

God is Present Everywhere One Goes

Mulungu is also present wherever people are. A Mukamba cannot travel any place where he is unable to call upon *Mulungu* in times of dire distress. Of a person who escapes from danger, the Akamba remark: "He is a man of God!" or "God was with him.!" The person himself proudly tells his experiences, emphasizing that "Except for God's presence, I would be dead now." The obvious implication is that God's presence shields people from danger. Similar expressions are used when a person prospers or succeeds in hunting, finding a wife, or breeds cattle well. "The Akamba thus conceive of God's presence in terms of blessings and their welfare are concerned." (Mbiti 1970:6)

God is Morally Good, Kind and Loving

Concerning the moral character of *Mulungu*, we are assured that the Christian concepts of the love, mercy and kindness of God are not opposed to the traditional concept of *Mulungu*. The biblical teaching of justice, righteousness and holiness of God is not alien to the Akamba. But neither should we impart to *Mulungu* all the biblical riches of Christian theology.

The traditional beliefs are being modified today through Christian influence. Whatever an expatriate missionary or anthropologist wrote some decades ago, can be readily dismissed today by many as an inadequate etic perspective. Fortunately, we have an emic perspective of the Gikuyu through the late Jomo Kenyatta who wrote in the 1930's. Some contemporary Gikuyu are inclined not to accept his perspective of a distant Creator, unwilling to be disturbed. But who are we to challenge his perspective? How are we able to disprove some observation made by an anthropologist 75 years ago? No doubt attempts can be made through careful research. But in the flux and flow of rapidly changing cultures, we find it difficult to sort out what is genuinely traditional and what is the result of Christian influence.

No one will likely challenge the assertion that the Christian concept of the goodness of God is compatible with the Akamba beliefs. But can we legitimately say that the Akamba traditionally taught that God is good? By implication, God is good for he gives the rains. When writing of the goodness of God, Mbiti says, "the Akamba say that 'God does no evil!" (1970:34) Since "God does us no evil," by implication, Mbiti concludes that the Akamba traditionally believed in the goodness of God. The Akamba certainly did not believe that God was **NOT** good. Christian teaching elevates and fulfills traditional belief that "God does us no harm." But we must be careful not to read back into the traditional Akamba beliefs what is now held by the Akamba through Christian teaching.

The same thing can be said about the love of God. The Akamba never believed that *Mulungu* was a hateful being who maliciously and unpredictably harmed people. That might be a description of the *aimu*, but not of *Mulungu*. The Christian concept of the love of God is compatible with the Akamba traditional concept. The Biblical teaching fulfills, that is, fills full the genuine revelation which God had given to the Akamba through nature and conscience.

As one Mukamba said, "If God had hatred, he could not give us anything." A good harvest, the sending of rains, the protection from danger are all signs that God sustains them and provides for them. By implication God loves them. But Mbiti verifies that "We do not have any examples in which people talk about the love of God" in Africa. (1970:33)

This is not due to the fact that the Akamba denied the goodness and love of God, but that the living, loving reality of God's presence was not among them. They did not perceive God as taking a personal interest in people.

When Mbiti describes the concepts of God in Africa, we do not object on the basis that the Supreme Being is in actual fact the opposite of what he declares. But he seems to infer a fullness of revelation which is exaggerated. Kato comments, "After reading the book, *Concepts of God in Africa*, one cannot but wonder what missionaries came to do in Africa. African understanding of God seems to be complete and does not need any further light from elsewhere. African Religions appear so systematic." (Kato 1975:69)

Take the example of the righteousness of God. The Akamba did not believe in an unholy and unrighteous God. They believed in the Creator who is in many ways quite compatible to the Christian concept of a holy God. While people may blame and accuse the *aimu* for maltreatment, the Akamba do not normally blame *Mulungu* for evil. The Akamba blame the hare and the chameleon for having transmitted death to people. They do not blame God. In other myths the Third Party mediates between man and God. If the request was denied, the Akamba blamed the Third Party, not God (Ndeti 1972:178). A Mukamba said, "*Mulungu* has mercy and does no harm." Campbell has suggested that the Akamba name for God, *Mulungu*, means "the Righteous One," being derived from a root meaning "to be right, straight, righteous." Young believes *Mulungu* is derived "from a verb which conveys the picture of one concerned with 'righteous' or 'undeviating direction.'" (Mbiti 1970:40) Whatever the accuracy of this etymological suggestion for *Mulungu*, there can be no doubt that the Akamba ascribe justice to God.

But that is not the full story. One could argue that the nature of God is neutral and not wholly allied with righteousness and goodness. *Mulungu* is the Creator of the powers of the *aimu*. Witchcraft originated from God. One Mukamba said, "God created the harmful herbs and he gave the medicine man the power to know them. Yet he gave the medicine man the power to know how to reverse the evil activity of witchcraft. All get their powers from God." *Mulungu* is, therefore, the one who has empowered the good *aimu* and the evil *aimu*. This, in the opinion of Sila, is a deep mystery. "No one is able to resolve it for you." But he continued to speak of God mysteriously. "People could do *Ngai* good, but he refuses to do good." Another traditionalist replied, "There was uncertainty. *Ngai* was not known or predictable."

Yakobo, an aged man of 95 years old and a former specialist in traditional religion, gave his testimony as a Christian. According to him, he enjoyed great acclaim as a traditional song composer and dancer. On the dancing ground, he won applause and was able to frustrate other song leaders who could not match his ability. Due to this ability, he recalls the great immorality into which he was plunged. He could always draw the affection of young girls to himself and he felt proud as a result. Yakobo claimed that while he was doing all of this he was in favour with *Ngai* and that he believed his power to entice the girls and win the applause of men came from *Ngai*. He became involved in much drinking and immorality. Now that he is a Christian, his perspective of Kamba traditional religion is this: "Kamba traditional religion has cooperation with Satan and demonic activity so that I don't see why I should have anything to do with it. In Jesus there is benefit."

If *Ngai Mumbi* is the source of this great power to dance, compose songs and seduce the women, as this Mukamba has testified, then we cannot state categorically that the Creator is fully righteous and holy. Some confusion and corruption has entered into this traditional concept of the Supreme Being.

There were many specialists among the traditional Akamba, including the medicine man (the diviner and mediator between the *aimu* and the living) and the witch (the sorcerer or wizard). While some Akamba claim they received their power from the evil spirits (*aimu*), Nzau, a present day specialist in traditional religion, asserts that the power for all specialists comes from *Ngai Mumbi*. Nzau was cross examined and he steadfastly insisted that the power for both the medicine man and the witch came from God. Thus a certain balance is maintained, *Ngai* providing the witch the knowledge and power to exercise evil and, at the same time, granting powers to the medicine man in order to reverse the effect of the witch. Thus we could argue that *Ngai Mumbi* of the Akamba is neutral, striking a balance between good and evil.

Kimatu is both a seer (*mwoni*) and a medicine man, still an active practitioner today at the age of 100. He complains that the present generation has distorted Kamba traditional practices. He maintains, "I still worship and please the spirits and do everything that they desire." Kimatu claimed that he has supernatural powers to know the future. For him it is important to please both *Ngai Mumbi* and the living dead so that they will approve of him. His power comes from both God and the living dead.

We conclude that all of Akamba life was in some way associated with *Mulungu*. Both the good and evil practices owed their explanation and their powers to him. *Mulungu* among the Akamba is associated with magic, sorcery, and divination, practices which are hated by the God of Scriptures. *Mulungu* empowers the spirits to do their work. *Mulungu* through the *aimu* has commanded extra-marital sex in purification and acts of worship. This factor must surely enter into our understanding of *Mulungu*. How do we respond to the claim that *Mulungu* is the "the Righteous One"? The dialectical "yes" and "no" is the only way to respond. "Yes," the Akamba see in *Mulungu* enough of the righteousness of God that the Christian concept of God does not sound strange and foreign. "No," we dare not suggest that *Mulungu* is the pure, holy and undefiled Creator, separate from sin, as we read in the Scriptures. Otherwise, we overlook some of the evidence that implicates *Mulungu* in practices which, from the Christian perspective, are not merely less than Christian but contrary to the Gospel.

WORSHIP OF THE SUPREME BEING

Frequency of Worship

First, we observe that many writers, some themselves Akamba, declare that God received very little worship.

Lindblom declared,

> Mulungu is not worshipped at all (or at least extremely seldom) by offering

sacrifices, nor in any other way. He dwells in the skies at an indefinite distance, is held to be well-disposed towards human beings, but beyond that has nothing to do with them. 'Mulungu does us no evil so wherefore should we sacrifice to him?' says the Akamba characteristically (Lindblom 1920:224).

At times Mbiti seems to echo the same refrain. "Except among Christians, communication between human beings and God is very rare, and only in times of dire need, e.g. after a prolonged drought, in times of epidemics, or in sudden danger. Then a short prayer, addressed to God, is offered or uttered, but there is no general ritual to be followed." (Mbiti 1966:14) He acknowledges that the Akamba, God's children, "are used to living almost unconsciously without Him." (1966:14)

Elsewhere Mbiti contends that "In the strict Christian sense, worship is almost unknown in traditional life." (1972:91) He then lists various activities, such as offerings, sacrifices, and prayers which "are in the nature of worship." But these are seldom addressed to God. Referring to the various ceremonies and rites in Akamba life, Mbiti states that "God is rarely brought into the picture, except on major occasions when people solicit His intervention and assistance. And even on such occasions, it would be incorrect to assert that the people experience spiritual fellowship with God. God is 'utilized' rather than 'worshipped'." (1972:95)

We have also found that an amazing number of traditionalists claimed they never prayed to Ngai Mumbi. A practicing medicine man said, "I do not pray to God at all. I pray to the living-dead and they answer my prayers." Another said, "We never pray to God at any time."

We may say confidently that the Akamba normally did not worship Him as individuals but only as a community. Furthermore, the Akamba traditionally worshipped Him only two or three times annually when all went well, namely, before the rains and after the harvest. During the drought or life threatening plagues such as caterpillars or war, they would worship Him more often. The Akamba say, "People do not go to the traditional shrine without reason." "God is never prayed to for nothing." Unless there is a serious crisis threatening the whole community, or unless there is need to thank Him for a good harvest, there is no need to bother Him. When there is peace and plenty, the Akamba are reluctant to disturb Ngai Mumbi for they believe He is pleased with them.

It is only at times of great trouble, such as epidemics, boils or ticks, or when there are a large number of deaths, or during drought and after a good harvest that the people resort to Ngai Mumbi.

Drought is the most serious problem facing Ukambani. Famine is a periodic experience. In 1897 and 1899 when the Europeans first came to Kenya, there was a serious drought lasting two years. The Akamba cooked their old sleeping skins for food. Reports are given that people began eating one another. Many Akamba deserted their land. Women married Masai and Gikuyu who had food.

After the Council of Kisuka sacrificed many cows, goats and sheep to no avail, the medicine men said that God wanted to drink human blood. So the Akamba began sacrificing young children, ages 8 to 10. The people living in Kivauni Location were the most notorious for sacrificing their children. The medicine men informed the elders that a particular child was wanted by God. He gave the sex, name of parents and the name of the child. The elders of the Council of Kisuka dug a deep hole beside the tree at the community shrine. They brought the child to the traditional shrine where the people remained silent.

The elders prayed. *"Ngai Mumbi*, we have given you the greatest sacrifice of a child. We have sacrificed the child whom you have requested from us so that you can bless us with rain." The people responded by saying, "Let that be done." The senior elders were assisted by the junior elders who covered the child with soil. The people then departed in silence, eating nothing.

Normally, when the Akamba face drought they supplicate *Ngai Muthiambi*, *Ngai Muviti*, *Ngai Mumbi* and the *aimu* at the *kilumi* dance. This was done at the instructions of the medicine man. They danced for the *aimu* and offered sacrifices for them at the the traditional shrine (*ithembo*) in order to appease them. Drought and epidemics were said to be due to the displeasure of the ancestral spirits. The women stayed at the home of the medicine man, dancing the *kilumi*. When the medicine man became possessed, he gave instructions what to do. Upon receiving these instructions the women would dance one more day at the house of the medicine man, followed by two more days of dancing the *kilumi* dance at the traditional shrine. Following this they returned to the house of the medicine man for another day of dancing when the medicine man would be possessed again and prophesy about the coming of the rains.

The women always took the seeds for planting to the medicine man who first planted the seeds. Then the medicine man gave the women planting seeds which were to be planted before the women reached home. This always involved a form of worship for they would spend the night dancing the *kilumi*, pleading for the rains to come.

A day was set aside when no work was to be done. On that day the rains were to fall and the planting of the gardens proceeded the following day.

If the rains ceased and the crops began to wither, they went to the medicine man to plead for rains. He informed them of the problem which had caused the drought. The goat was slaughtered with food and tobacco offered to *ngai*. The women spent the night there dancing the *kilumi*.

One Mukamba gave a practical example when she and two others took food and tobacco to the traditional shrine to pray for rain. "We went to worship and we carried food for an offering. We ate and danced. Then before long we saw clouds coming so we departed for home. On the way we met a man whom I knew. He was in his sugar cane garden. One of us requested that he give us some sugar cane to plant, and if not, some to eat. But he refused by hiding. When we arrived home it rained heavily, even throughout the night, heavier than it had ever done in previous years. To our surprise all his sugar cane was carried away by the flood."

But if the drought persisted, the Akamba stopped sacrificing to *Muviti* and *Muthambi* and turned their attention to *Ngai Mumbi*.

Thus the traditional Akamba worship of *Ngai Mumbi* was strictly utilitarian and infrequent. Basically, desperate need determined the frequency of worship.

Officiating Elders for Worship

The Council of *Kisuka* officiated in the offering of sacrifices and prayers to the Creator God. This council is composed of three groups of people: elders of the *mutwe*, elders of the *syaao*, and elders of the *angi* (or *anake ma kisuka*). Membership in the Council of *Kisuka* is determined by age and contribution of animals to the Council. These animals may not be given all at once, but time must elapse between each contribution. This is the process whereby a man is admitted into the lower ranks of the Council and by which he is elevated from rank to rank.

The elders of *mutwe* are the highest rank of elders, being well advanced in years and having given at least ten goats and two bulls to the Council. There are not many elders of *mutwe*, sometimes only one or even none in a village.

These elders have the final authority in religious matters. They are seated in order by rank. The best meat and beer are given to them. The elders of *mutwe* are highly honoured, though they are not paid. One of these elders is the leader of the Council of *Kisuka*.

The elders of *syaao* are the assistants to the elders of *mutwe* in the worship of the Creator God. They will eventually take the place of the highest rank of elders when they die. These elders of *syaao* are trained for their work by their senior elders. Most members of the Council of *Kisuka* are the younger members, married men who have contributed at least one goat to the Council. They are called elders of the *angi* (or *kisuka*).

Their task is to perform the menial work of preparing for sacrifice. They gather the sacrifices, skin the goat, collect the blood in a half gourd, mix the intestines of the goat with fat, roast the meat, and mix the blood with salt so that it will not clot. These younger elders are sent by the senior elders as messengers to inform the community of a planned sacrifice and instruct the people what to bring.

The women were likewise organized in a Council of Elders. These old women have passed the age of giving birth to children. They have also paid a number of goats for the process of being made a woman elder. Their function is to locate milk and various kinds of foodstuffs for the sacrifice.

Example of Worship at the Shrine

During the sacrifice at the traditional shrine, the Council of *Kisuka* sit close to the shrine in order of their rank. The senior elders sit nearest the food at the shrine, with the elders of *angi* and the women elders sitting furtherest away. The majority of the people sit quietly at a distance from the shrine. The senior elder leads in the ceremony, assisted by the elders of *syaao*.

Musyoki gave the example of what happened in his place. Before the beginning of rain all five villages of his location gathered to worship and ask the Creator God for rain. Each village brought a goat, certain foodstuffs and beer in a small gourd. This beer had been brewed in the house of one of the elders. Only a small amount was placed in a gourd for the ceremony with most remaining at home in the large calabash. The leading elders of *mutwe* for each village were invited to participate in the worship.

At the shrine the goats were slaughtered by the junior elders. The blood of the goats was mixed with the contents of the intestines and poured at the foot of the sacred tree at the traditional shrine. Also poured was fresh milk from a cow and beer. Cow fat and the contents of the goat's intestines were smeared on the tree. The head and the hooves of the goat were buried there.

As they poured offerings, the leading elder prayed to the Creator God. For instance they might pray, "*Ngai Mwatuangi*, who created us, we have sacrificed to you so that you can give us rain and food." Another example is here given. "*Ngai Mumbi*, we are sacrificing to you blood, food, meat and milk from cows, so that you can bring us rain. If we die, who will sacrifice to you?"

During the ceremony the beer is shared by a few of the elders who drink from the same half-calabash gourd. Representatives of the elders of *syaoo* and the elders of *kisuka* are given a swallow of the beer.

When everything is about to conclude, the elders of *mutwe* inform the crowd to be prepared to shout loudly together. In unison the women shout, "*kisiilila*," a shrill cry marking the conclusion of the ceremony.

Thereafter, the people departed and returned to their homes. While the women go hurriedly to their homes, carrying pieces of meat shared at the traditional shrine, the elders of *kisuka* return to the house of the elders of the *mutwe* to drink the remaining beer. Rain may fall shortly thereafter as they reach their homes.

Places of Worship

There are two different kinds of shrines, places for the Akamba to worship: the family shrine and the community shrine.

But most shrines are located at a certain type of tree. These are generally a kind of fig tree which does not shed leaves quickly. The chief trees for the shrines are: *mumbu*, *mukuyu* and *muumo* fig trees. *Muambwa*, another type of tree with hard wood, is also used for the shrines. These trees can grow into the oldest, tallest and most impressive trees in the community. These trees selected for the community shrine are not planted by the people but have grown up naturally.

The family shrine may be a tree which has grown from a stem taken by the family elder from the community shrine. This tree may be planted at the grave of the grandfather of the home. Or the people may use the center post of the house where the offerings are poured.

At these family shrines worship is offered to God the Creator, the ancestral spirits, *ngai Muviti* or *ngai Muthambi*. This is done whenever the family faces a problem and they fear they have wronged some spirit. The family ceremony of worship is led by the elder of *Kisuka*. One medicine man said he hung his equipment over a certain post in his house. At the foot of this post he would pour libations of milk, beer, snuff and bits of food for the ancestral spirits.

The community shrine is more sacred than the family shrine. Hunters are not allowed to kill animals hiding there for the shedding of blood would anger *Ngai*. Thieves are known to hide at the shrine for they could not be attacked by their enemies. Children are warned not to graze their cattle at the traditional shrines, nor could firewood be gathered from there, lest the *aimu* be angered. Anyone breaking this taboo is fined a goat by the Council of *Kisuka*. This goat is for the cleansing of the shrine. If a man refuses to pay the goat, the ancestral spirits would soon visit him and kill some of his animals until the man agrees to cleanse the shrine.

No one dare cut down the tree lest a curse come upon him. They are protected by law even as church buildings today. However, in the early days various shrines were cut down by Christians and to the amazement of the people no harm came upon them.

The community shrine is chosen by a medicine man. It is never planted by a person but has grown naturally. Traditionally, there has been a community shrine in every sub-location, though in these days they are becoming scarce in parts of Ukambani. The community shrine is not a place for an individual to worship alone. It is intended for the benefit of the whole community. Many of these old trees were hollow and very imposing from a distance. Small huts were often built at the foot of the tree as a dwelling for the spirits and a place where offerings could be placed.

Means of Worship

Sacrifices. The most common animals sacrificed are cows, sheep and goats, all without spots. For instance they may sacrifice a goat being totally black and without any spots. The animals were strangled to death so that the blood could be collected and poured as a libation from a half gourd at the foot of the tree. The animals were then roasted over the fire. Seven pieces of meat were placed at the foot of the shrine by the senior elders, together with the blood collected in the gourd.For instance, Kisina gave his experience. When three of his children became sick, he was told by the medicine man to offer a sacrifice which is given for all new born children. So he killed a goat, gave some of the uncooked blood to his children and poured the rest on the ground "so that these *ngai* may be appeased."

> After I did all what was expected of me from these gods through the medicine man, my children recovered rapidly. Therefore, I know for sure that after the people die they become gods, because they have power of healing. The power of these gods used to be great in the past. But now they don't have power over me because I am a Christian and I have nothing to do with them.

Offerings. Offerings which were bloodless sacrifices were of two types: beverages and food.

Libations were made of beer, honey, porridge, milk, blood, or water. Offerings of food included maize, millet, cassava, nuts, eggs and sorghum. Tobacco was also offered.

When making these offerings at the community shrine the women elders, those old women who have given the Council of *Kisuka* a goat to be introduced into the Council of Women Elders, are the ones to bring the foodstuffs to the shrine in order to hand it over to the senior elders.

The offerings are token gifts for the spirits. For instance, only a small portion of beer is actually poured at the shrine while the large amount remaining is intended for the people to consume.

Offerings are given at different times. Before the Akamba set out on a hunting trip, they offer tobacco and food to their *ngai*. Their bows and arrows are then placed at the shrine for blessing. Only then do they proceed for the hunt. Before setting out on a journey, tobacco and beer are offered, asking for a safe journey.

Prayers. Prayers are the most common form of worship. They are said when giving of sacrifices and offerings. Prayers are said with the eyes wide open and usually said by the elder who leads, usually by the oldest elder. During the *kilumi* dance, prayers are accompanied by music, and the rhythmic movements of the dancers.

There were basically two types of prayers: family prayers and community prayers.

Family prayers are conducted usually when someone is sick. The owner of the home takes water or beer and slowly pours it on the ground, beseeching the ancestors by name to take the drink and heal the sick. A sample prayer is this. "You, Mulwa (one of the ancestors), this son is yours. Heal him and ask whatever you want and it shall be given to you." Such prayers must be done willingly from the heart and not in a quarrelsome spirit. The Akamba believed the ancestors ate the food at night and had fellowship with the other members of the family. If the person does not recover, the next step is to inquire from the medicine man who will either inform them that the illness is from bewitching or from some ancestors. Other such prayers are the following. "Nganga (an ancestor), that is your food, take it and do stop troubling us. Here is your water." "Muoki and our respected ancestors, So-and- so, here is your beer and blood. Take them and release for us our dear son bound with sickness."

Community or public prayers are usually done when something affects the whole village, such as drought. During times of community calamity the people consult the medicine man

CONCLUSION

Missionaries have remarked about the readiness of Africans to hear of the God of Scripture. Dr. Henri A. Junod, a pioneer missionary remarked, "It is wonderful to notice how early the idea of the Christian God is accepted by the Bantus." (Smith 1966:133)

One cannot help but think that the belief in God found among the Akamba has the marks of the "decayed remnant of a clearer monotheistic faith." (Smith 1966:133) The Creator has not left Himself without a witness. Truth about God is known among the Akamba so that the messengers of the Gospel find here a point of contact in communicating the Word of God. As Mbiti states, "African peoples are not religiously illiterate." (Mbiti 1970:XIII)

But the evidence does point to the fact that these beliefs are "a *decayed remnant* of a clearer monotheistic faith." (italics mine) Though *Mulungu* is on the lips of the Akamba, they do not worship him or sacrifice to him with any frequency. He is the ultimate explanation for all things, but the peoples do not traditionally live in communion or fellowship with Him.

The traditional Akamba belief in *Mulungu* corresponds to that of the Gikuyu traditional belief expressed in this saying, "*Ngai ndegiagiagwo*," (God must never be pestered) (Kenyatta 1938:227). That is, when sickness comes, the people use ordinary medical knowledge. Should herbal medicines fail, they consult the spirits through the medicine man. When everything else fails, the head of the family appeals to *Ngai*. Thus the Creator is not bothered with worship when things go well. Nor is he approached for minor problems. Only as a last resort is God sought.

REVIEW QUESTIONS FOR CHAPTER 14

1. What are the names for God in Kikamba and what do they tell you of traditional belief in God?

2. How is the Creator God (*Ngai Mumbi*) related to "the gods of the homes"?

3. What evidence points to the remoteness of God among the Akamba, and what evidence points to the nearness of God? Assess.

4. Describe the characteristics of God according to the Akamba traditional religion.

5. To what extent do the characteristics (attributes) of God among the Akamba compare or contrast with the biblical teaching?

6. How, when and where did the Akamba worship?

Suggested Reading and Thought Questions for Advanced Study:

Danquah, J.B. *The Akan Doctrine of God*, 1944.
Evans-Pritchard, E.E. *Nuer Religion*, 1974, pp.1-27.
Idowu, Bolaji. *Olodumare: God in Yoruba Belief*, 1962.
Kenyatta, Jomo. *Facing Mt. Kenya*, n.d., pp.222-253.
Lienhardt, Godfrey. *Divinity and Experience*, 1961, pp.28-55, 171-319.
Marwick, Brian Allan. *The Swazi*, 1966, pp.228-230.
Melland, Frank H. *In Witch-Bound Africa*, 1967, pp.154-182.
Metuh, Emefie Ikenga. *God and Man in African Religion: A Case Study of the Ibo in Nigeria*, 1981, pp.1-59.
P'Bitek, Okot. *Religion of the Central Luo*, 1971, pp.41-87.
Rattray, R.S. *Ashanti*, 1969, pp.139-144.
Setiloane, Gabriel. *The Image of God Among the Sotho-Tswana*, 1976, pp.77-86.

1. Compare Mbiti's understanding of the nature of God in Akamba traditional religion with Ndeti's (Mbiti 1971:9,138; Ndeti 1972:175,176). How can you explain such divergent opinions by two Akamba scholars concerning their own traditional religion? Why do you think they differ in their interpretation?

2. Research the traditional belief in God among two other African peoples (from the books recommended above or from field research among your own people). Compare the similarities and differences of these beliefs and practices with those mentioned here for the Akamba. How does this illustrate either the

diversity and/or the similarity of African religions?

3. To what extent is the African concept of God's transcendence and His immanence similar to or dissimilar to the Old Testament concept? (see Ex. 19,20; Deut. 4-6) Also, compare the African and the Israelite experience with God.

4. In what sense was God traditionally involved in the daily affairs of the Africans you have studied and to what extent was He not?

Chapter 15

THE SUPREME BEING IN TRADITIONAL RELIGION WORLDWIDE

The evidence worldwide from all the peoples is overwhelming. Man is not merely a religious animal with religious cults everywhere. A knowledge and belief in God or divinities is found in every continent and virtually in every corner of our globe. To be sure, we also find everywhere evidence of man's attempt to escape from God and replace God with idols. Man's knowledge of God has often been so corrupted that there is little similarity with what we know of God from the Scriptures. Nevertheless, we discover in the sands of history the footprints of God who continually seeks after a sinful and disobedient people. For the Christian who believes in natural revelation, such evidence is not unbelievable.

Wilhelm Schmidt gathered evidence supporting a universal belief in God or many gods among the traditionalists throughout the world and he compiled the evidence and published an English translation under the title, *The Origin and Growth of Religion: Facts and Theories* (London, 1931). Rationalists dismissed his evidence, attributing such beliefs to the work of missionaries. However, such an unfair treatment of the evidence cannot be sustained in our day. We owe a great debt to him and others for providing us with solid evidence that Africans are not alone in their united belief in the Creator God. The concept of God may vary greatly throughout the world. Nevertheless, man cannot escape God though man tries to escape from His rule.

A few examples will illustrate the principle. Africans are not unique in their belief in deity. Such belief is found universally.

CHINESE

The Chinese from earliest days were very religious according to our earliest accounts. In the earliest of Chinese ancient writings, we find reference to Shang Ti, the Supreme Being. He is always portrayed as the personal, majestic and glorious being. Shang Ti is the Supreme Ruler and the One who imparts morality. Through the course of the centuries reference to Shang Ti decreased and T'ien, the more impersonal name for Heaven or Providence, became predominant.

As Shang Ti became more impersonal and distant, the ancestral cult developed more strongly. Confucious himself used the personal name for God, Shang Ti, only once in all his recorded teachings. Ancestor worship became the binding force that united the Chinese Empire together. By teaching the children to obey their parents, follow the family teaching, respect the older generation, including the ancestors, the Chinese Emperors were able to govern the vast Empire. This became prominent especially during the Shang dynasty.

> Shang religion was inextricably involved in the genesis and legitimation of the Shang state. It was believed that Ti, the high god, conferred fruitful harvest and divine assistance in battle, that the king's ancestors were able to intercede with Ti, and that the king could communicate with his ancestors. Worship of the Shang ancestors, therefore, provided the powerful psychological and ideological support for the political dominance of the Shang kings (Keightley 1978:213).

The social order of the Chinese Empire was a definite hierarchy, ranging from the Emperor down to the lowly peasant. Gradually, there developed the notion that it was improper for a man to worship and sacrifice to a spirit being of higher rank. Thus only the Emperor could worship the Supreme Being while the peasants could only worship their own ancestors.

> In China, therefore, from about the second century B.C. on, it became the settled practice for the common man to worship only his ancestors and such household and personal spirits as the guardians of the door and of the stove and the gods of health and luck; he let the feudal lords or their officers worship the hills and streams of the province for him...And of course the Emperor alone addressed Shang Ti, or the sublime T'ien, in the ceremonies at the Altar of Heaven outside the capital of the empire (Noss 1963:342).

Thus we see that the belief in the high god from antiquity became overshadowed by the ancestral spirits. Shang Ti became removed from his preeminence in the practical daily life of the Chinese.

ROMANS

Ancient Roman religion was eclectic, that is, selecting various doctrines and practices from various religions, whatever pleased them. The Romans included religious elements from many different peoples. As they conquered one nation after another, they absorbed more gods into their pantheon (hierarchy) of deities (Noss 1964:93-107).

The basic belief of the Romans from the beginning was a kind of animism, that is, a form of religion with the belief that men, animals, plants and stones are inhabited by souls which may exist separately. The Romans had the belief in nature spirits. Those most prominent were the spirits related to the family, for Roman religion was communal with strong emphasis on the family. "Vestra" was the spirit concerned with the hearth fire in the home. "Lares" was the spirit responsible to guard the home and land holdings. "Janus" was the spirit of the door which was thought to possess magical powers. "Penates" guarded the larder. In each home there were found tiny metal images representing the spirits of the home. Every time the family ate, "bits of food were burned in receptacles [containers] as offerings to the departed." (Hadas 1966:123)

Throughout nature were spirits which affected the well being of people. These spirit powers were identified with every phase of life. Nothing in nature was conceived as being natural only. Springs, woods, burial places and strange objects drew the worship or veneration of the Romans.

Certain high gods were held in veneration from the beginning. Jupiter, the sky god (similar to the Greek god, Zeus), was in some sense superior to the other gods and associated with lightning and weather. Mars was the god of war who also defended agriculture. Diana, later identified with the Greek goddess Artimis, was the goddess of women, to whom they prayed when wanting children. Juno, a warlike goddess, had the chief function of supervising the women, especially in their sexual life. Minerva functioned as the god of craftsmen. Hercules, a Greek god adopted by the Romans, was venerated for his many journeys and labors, and his ability to avert evil. Apollo was the sun god and the supreme dispenser of agricultural wealth.

Thus we find another variation in religious belief among the Romans. There is no evidence of monotheism among them. But neither were they atheists. The high gods were numerous and the nature spirits abundant. The Creator God had been exchanged for a plurality of nature gods, each concerned with a different area of life.

INDIANS

Early Hinduism among the Indo-Aryans likewise had a belief in many gods. The Rig-Veda, a collection of religious poetry compiled in ten books, contains hymns addressed to one god, or often two or more gods. These stanzas of praise to the deities originated in antiquity, being first placed into writing about the 8th century B.C. (see Noss 1964:126ff)

Their religious beliefs are shared by the Iranians, Hittites, Greeks and Romans. The early Indo-Aryans worshipped Dyaus Pitar or Father Sky (Zeus among the Greeks and Jupiter among the Romans), Prithivi Matar or Mother Broad-Earth (Gaia Mater of the Greeks), Mitra (Mithra of the Iranians) who was perhaps the sun god originally.

But these gods were only conceived of vaguely and appealed to seldom. Displacing them were the nature gods who achieved pre-eminence over those high gods. These nature deities included Indra, the god of storms; Vritra, the drought dragon; Rudra, the mountain god; Vayu, the god of wind; Ushas, the god of the dawn; and Yama, the god of the dead (who himself was the first man to die) who became the judge and ruler of the ancestral spirits.

Hinduism evolved over the years with a multiplication of deities and a change in emphases. Janism and Buddhism sprang up in reaction to the ethical laxity and religious perplexity of Hinduism. One might characterize these heresies of Hinduism as atheistic ultimately. The Jains for instance maintained that there is no Supreme Ruler of the world to whom one may pray. There are higher beings whom we might describe as gods. But they are also finite beings and subject to death as men are. Thus praying to gods is of no avail (Noss 1964:152-250).

ARABS

Prior to the Islamic revolution under Muhammed, the Arabians followed a semitic religious faith which included belief in various deities (see Noss

1964:716ff). They had a vague conception of a creator, a remote high-god known as Allah. But the Arabians also worshipped local gods and goddesses. In Mecca, the Arabians worshipped three goddesses considered to be the daughters of Allah. Their idols formed the centre of pagan worship with emphasis on fertility, using the sexual organs as symbols. There was also a veneration of certain astral deities.

Muhammed became dissatisfied with the idolatrous polytheism, together with such practices as drinking, gambling and dancing. He called for the worship of the Creator. According to the famous Muslim creed, "There is no God but Allah and Mohammed is His prophet." This one God, according to Muhammed, is unique and supreme. He knows all things, can do all things, and is present everywhere.

While Islam stands with Judaism and Christianity in its emphasis on monotheism, the remnants of the pagan past still cling to Islam (see Zwemer 1920).

CONCLUSION

On the one hand, belief in gods, spirits, divinities and deities is a universal phenomena. ATR simply reflects the religious nature of mankind who has the law of God written on his heart.

On the other hand, man has to one extent or another suppressed that knowledge of God and exchanged it for some varied lie. We may say that the adherents of folk religions (sometimes called Animists), the traditionalists throughout Africa and throughout the world, have a clearer concept of the Supreme Being than some other peoples, such as the Hindus, Buddhists and Janists. It may very well be that this is part of the reason why the adherents of the folk religions worldwide, have responded to the Gospel more readily than many others.

REVIEW QUESTIONS FOR CHAPTER 15

1. To what extent do peoples around the world have the concept of a deity or many deities?
2. Is the African traditional belief in God unique, unknown or unusual in the rest of the world?
3. Discuss the evidence that Orientals, Europeans and Africans have shared together something of the knowledge of the Supreme Being, albeit often mixed with divinities and other gods and spirits.

Suggested Reading and Thought Questions for Advanced Study:

Confucianism
    Noss, John. *Man's Religions*, pp.324-334.
Folk Religions
    Howells, William. *The Heathens: Primitive Man and His Religions*,

    1948, pp.215-258.
Hinduism
    Noss, John. *Man's Religions*, pp.278-297.
Islam
    Noss, John. *Man's Religions*, pp.730-731.
    Spencer, T. *Islam in East Africa*, 1964.
Shintoism
    Noss, John. *Man's Religions*, pp.429-432.
World Religions
    Hastings, James ed. *Encyclopedia of Religion and Ethics*, 1909. vol.VI,
    "God", pp.243-306; vol.XII, "Worship", pp.752-811.

1. Study the traditional belief in the Supreme Being or in many deities in one of the world religions of the East. Enumerate the similarities and differences between their beliefs and those of ATR. Which traditional belief in God seems to be closer to the biblical view of God? Discuss.

2. Study the pagan background in which Muhammed was born and the Muslim concept of Allah. To what extent was Muhammed influenced in his teaching of God and idolatry by Judaism and Christianity? What elements of animism still cling to Islam? (see Spencer 1964)

Chapter 16

TRUTH IN
AFRICAN TRADITIONAL RELIGION
IN BIBLICAL PERSPECTIVE

We have spent considerable effort probing the raw data of ATR, the generalizations that can be made for ATR as a whole and the particular study of the Akamba traditional belief in the Supreme Being. What can we now say concerning all this from a biblical perspective? As we have noted earlier, traditional belief in the Supreme Being is both the great strength of ATR and its most serious weakness. We shall, therefore, examine the positive aspects of traditional belief, the truth which has been derived by common grace given to all men through natural revelation. And then in the following chapter we shall examine the negative judgments that must be made on the authority of God's Word.

A perusal of *African Ideas of God* edited by Edwin W. Smith and *Concepts of God in Africa* written by John Mbiti impresses one with many of the truths and spiritual insights which traditional Africans held before the coming of the Gospel. Since all truth is God's truth, we readily acknowledge with gratitude the gracious work that God has done by His Spirit before the preaching of the Gospel in Africa.

KNOWLEDGE ABOUT THE SUPREME BEING

Let us note some of the beautiful expressions made about God. Among the Zulu, a very powerful and warlike nation, God is conceived as "He who roars so that all the nations are struck with fear." (Mbiti 1970:9) Among the Yoruba God is known as "He who sees both the inside and outside (of man), the Discerner of hearts." (Mbiti 1970:3) Many peoples acknowledge that God is everywhere at once and He meets you everywhere you are. The Gikuyu say that God is "all alone," without father or mother and without companions. To the Tonga God is "the Ancient of Days," "the Limitless One who fills all space." (Mbiti 1970:12,14) The Akan respond when asked, "How are you?," with these words, "By God's grace, I am well." (Smith 1966:249) The Gikuyu say that God "is the same today as he was yesterday," and that He is neither a child nor an old man (Mbiti 1970:28).

A beautiful traditional hymn of the Pygmy says,

In the beginning was God,

Today is God
Tomorrow will be God.
Who can make an image of God?
He has no body.
He is as a word which comes out of your mouth.
That word! It is no more,
It is past, and still it lives!
So is God. (Mbiti 1970:23)

Knowledge of the Supreme Being, the Creator of heaven and earth, the Governor of the universe, was indeed a valuable heritage of traditional Africa. Let us never assume that missionaries preached the Gospel to empty heads or to people living without a knowledge of God. Through God's prevenient grace the Creator had made known to the Africans a true knowledge of God.

KNOWLEDGE OF CREATION

The belief that God created the heavens and the earth is common all over Africa. Nearly every African people has some tradition of creation. H. Baumann has recorded 2,000 such myths from Africa. So the truth that God is and that He has created this earth with man upon it, is not news to the African. He knows this well (Mbiti 1969:92-95; 1970:161-170).

KNOWLEDGE OF THE ORIGINAL STATE OF MAN

The Africans have various traditions of an original state of happiness, child-like innocence and immortality. However, we must hasten to say that these traditions are by no means found among most Africans. At least the evidence has not been seen.

The Acholi say that God gave man all the necessary things, including the art of making beer. The Azande say that among the gifts of God is the art of magic and the knowledge of medicines. The skills needed in life were learned from God, including farming, cooking, hunting and building houses.

Most significant is the tradition among some Africans that God was in close fellowship with man at one time. As these few African peoples look back into the golden age of the past, their ideal life is that which is lived close to God. During this time men lived without dying. They had all the provisions needed and lived in happiness. Some peoples say that God visited them frequently and even lived among them. "It was like a family relationship in which God was the Parent and men were the children." (Mbiti 1969:96)

KNOWLEDGE OF
THE SPIRITUAL NATURE OF MAN

Nowhere do Africans traditionally conceive of man as mere matter. Man is a spiritual being with both body and soul. "Although he has a body, yet it is inconsequential to define with precision how it came into existence. It is a temporary residence which gets its significance from its unity with that which dwells within it. The body is the oil-container of the lamp..." (Dickson and Ellingworth:1969:100; see Willoughby 1928:7ff)

Whatever this spiritual part of man is, it may be variably called heart, head, judgment, mind, reason, soul or breath while it remains in the body. But when the spiritual part leaves the body, it is spoken of as a shadow, ghost, spirit or soul.

Many African peoples believe that man is made of two parts, body and soul, the latter becoming the ancestral spirit upon death. The Gikuyu of Kenya believe that man's soul, *n'goro*, which is the individuality and centre of the person, becomes the *n'goma*, the ancestral spirit when the body dies (Routledge 1910:239). The Tiriki of Kenya believe the same (Sangree 1966:42).

Others, however, believe man is composed of three parts. The Bena of Tanzania, for instance, think of man as tripartite: the *muwili*, or body, which decays at death; the *mtima*, or life giving spirit, which also ceases to exist at death; the *kiboka* is the spirit or soul which remains immortal (Culwick 1935:101).

KNOWLEDGE OF THE LOST PARADISE

The traditions vary as to the reason why God and man became separated. Some, like the Ashanti, picture God living close to man in the heavens. When the woman ground the grain with a pestal, she bumped against Him, so He moved far away up into heaven. The Mende say that God broke His fellowship with man because people asked Him too many questions. Others say that God withdrew because the smoke from grass fires irritated His eyes. According to the Bambuti, Banyarwanda, Barotse, Bushman, Chagga, Elgeyo and others, God gave to man a particular law to obey. When man broke that law, God separated from them.

Whatever the reasons, these Africans believe that God moved away from man. Death came and man lost his first state of happiness and peace. It would appear, however, that most African peoples do not have these traditions of God living in close fellowship with man followed by separation. But whatever tradition the peoples may or may not have, there is a general sense of broken fellowship and a distant relationship with God.

GOD'S COMMON GRACE IN ATR

But there is much more than a knowledge about God. There are many other evidences of God's prevenient (common) grace operating among traditional Africans. There is a recognition that God is deserving of honour and worship. Blood sacrifices and the offering of the first fruits are a means of worshipping God. People in need, when all else has failed, may turn to God wherever they are to seek His help. God has written in the consciences of men and women a sense of right and wrong. They recognize that any failure to do what is right may lead to retribution from the spiritual world. And they believe that wrong doing requires sacrifices to restore harmony once again. The dominant place that the supernatural has played in ATR has opened the door for people to understand and believe the Gospel.

Generally, the Bible translators have adopted the African names for God in the translations of Scripture. Problems have arisen, of course. Some ideas associated with the traditional African belief in God do not apply to the God and Father of our Lord Jesus Christ. Nevertheless, there has been sufficient basic similarity between the two concepts that the Christian Church has been able to purge away the error and give biblical meaning to the names for God.

This in fact has been the general policy of the Christian Church from the beginning. When the Apostle Paul preached to the Lycaonians, bathed in animistic superstitions, and to the Athenians with their Greek philosophies, Paul spoke of God as *Theos*. Whatever these pagans understood by the term, *theos*, it surely was not the same as that which Paul meant. Nevertheless, the early Christian Church used an expression associated with non-Christian nuances and breathed into it a meaning derived from biblical revelation.

The same is true of the missionaries to the Europeans. The Teutonic peoples served many gods, such as Wodan, god of the dead; Donar, god of thunder and the sky; Tyre, god of war. The Christian missionaries used a class-word, "god," to refer to the God of Scriptures. "God" for the Teutonic peoples meant "a superhuman person who was worshipped as having power over nature and the fortunes of mankind; and also an image or other object which was worshipped." Christianity, therefore, remodeled this word, removing the false and breathing into it new meaning.

The fact is that every place where people are found, you find traces of the presence of God. For within everyone are the sin stained remnants of the image of God. Through God's gracious revelation in conscience and nature, people know intuitively that God is and that they are responsible to Him.

ATR, A PREPARATION FOR THE GOSPEL

It becomes quite evident that the grace of God has penetrated the hearts of the Africans with a knowledge about Himself. And this measure of truth has served as a royal road by which we may communicate the Gospel to traditional Africans. The hearts of Africans have been prepared for the Gospel through God's prevenient grace that has been operating among traditional Africans prior to the Christian era.

A thoughtful reflection on all that has been said about African traditional belief and practice reveals much in common with the Christian faith. Many of the basic beliefs are harmonious with the teachings of Scripture. Through these beliefs and practices God has prepared the peoples to hear and receive the Gospel.

God the Creator and man the creature are basic truths. We have seen that some African peoples even believe in a pristine original state in which there was fellowship between man and God who lived in proximity. There is a recognition that this original state has been changed for one reason or another and that God is somewhat distant from man, though man can always call on God's help wherever man may be.

Here we find vital points of contact, truths known by God's grace and capable of being utilized for the Gospel. Undoubtedly, these basic truths were not always understood so clearly by all the African peoples. This is one problem in generalizing. We overlook the particulars and obscurities and make some broad, general observations. We should not dismiss too quickly the comments made by Okot P'Bitek. For he could argue that his people were atheists in the sense that their concept of God was radically different from the concept of God in Scriptures. Many have felt that the broad summary of ATR by John Mbiti obscures the differences between ATR and Christianity by making plain what is in fact more obscure.

Nevertheless, we find that the basic world view of the Africans is essentially compatible with the Christian Gospel. Could it be that communication of the Gospel with the traditional African is easier than with the Hindu or the Buddhist because of the difference in their world views? Africans have traditionally recognized a Supreme Being who is the Creator of mankind.

Moreover, man is composed of body and soul, a material part which dies and decays and a spiritual part which continues to live on immortally. Hence the traditional African believes in the spiritual world, a world of spirits and ancestors. He believes in life after death, the immortality of the soul. Living man is affected by what takes place in the spiritual realm.

Despite the many differences between ATR in practice and the Christian faith, there are many similarities, points of contact, which can be used as bridges for the Gospel. These include: God the Creator who can communicate with mankind, man with body and soul, immortality, life after death, the spiritual world, the supernatural, the sense of right and wrong — the moral ought, the necessity of doing what is right to avoid punishment from the unseen world, blood sacrifices and many more.

Throughout our study of ATR, however, we have found one major significant void: the absence of any traditional hope or provision of deliverance. Nothing in traditional religion supplies the remedy for the loss of that first fellowship with God. Indeed, for many peoples death is inevitable and what has always been will always be.

John Mbiti concludes his discussion with a significant observation.

> Yet behind these fleeting glimpses of the original state and bliss of man, whether they are rich or shadowy, there lie the tantalizing and unattained gift of the resurrection, the loss of human immortality and the monster death. Here African religions and philosophy must admit a defeat: they have supplied no solution. This remains the most serious cul-de-sac in the otherwise rich thought and sensitive religious feeling of our peoples. It is perhaps here then, that we find the greatest weakness and poverty of our traditional religions... (Mbiti 1969:99)

God in His grace has prepared the soil in Africa for people to hear the Gospel and believe. The Holy Spirit has been at work in the hearts of the Africans as we have indicated earlier. The Gospel of Jesus Christ provides that answer through repentance from sin and faith in Christ who alone can forgive sins and grant eternal life.

Yet one could observe that there seems to be no concept of sin or eternal punishment as understood biblically. Though some people have myths concerning a lost paradise, a lost fellowship with God the Creator, these are by no means prevalent throughout Africa. Indeed, for most Africans the good is defined in terms of physical well being, material prosperity and social prestige, while evil is defined as the opposite. The good is compliance with the traditions of the forefathers and evil is disregard for the traditional. Though people may fear death there is no sense that death is the result of sin against God. What people yearn for is power in this life so that they may prosper materially and socially and be preserved from sickness. What kind of Gospel can we then preach?

Admittedly, the African concept of sin and salvation is rudimentary at best. In fact the biblical doctrine of sin is in sharp contrast to ATR. Nevertheless, even here we find points of contact which are useful in communicating biblical truths.

We believe the traditional African belief in God and worship has served as a definite point of contact, an invaluable stepping stone in preaching the Gospel. We need not introduce the Africans to the concept of God. Nor should we begin with the story of Jesus. We must begin where every good communicator begins. We begin with the known and proceed to the unknown. We begin by speaking of the Creator God. We may speak of His power, wisdom and goodness. From that point we find some avenue to launch into the Gospel. Perhaps we can use a traditional concept of uncleanness, or the wrath of the spirits because of wrong doing. Perhaps we could refer to the blood sacrifices which were necessary to be reconciled with the spirit world. We may appeal to the people's inner sense of right and wrong, to their need for a sense of well being, or the need for love. There are literally dozens of points of contact within traditional religion which can be used to introduce the Gospel of Jesus Christ. The wise communicator of the Gospel will be alert to the many traditional beliefs and practices which may serve as bridges into the hearts of traditional Africans. For God has not left Himself without a witness.

CHRISTIAN WORSHIP AND ATR

There are also many areas where the Christian church may use the traditional culture for the glory of God. One rather strategic area these days is Christian worship. God desires above all else a people who are *worshipping* Him from their heart. Not only has the architectural designs of cathedrals and churches been imported from overseas, our forms of worship have been designed outside the continent. And we rigidly hold to these forms as though they had divine origins.

I suggest there must be a healthy balance between form and freedom, between liturgy and spontaneity. Development of liturgy can provide people with rich biblical content so that our worship is truly Christian. Spontaneity of praying, sharing and exhorting allows for the freedom of the Spirit. Thus a form , wor ship that includes opportunities of spontaneous expressions of worship is biblical.

There is a real need for a spontaneous sharing within Christian worship. The believers need to become a community which knows and loves one another, shares and prays for one another. The traditional church service imported from the West does not meet that need. The writer of Hebrews exhorts, "not forsaking our assembling together, as is the habit of some, but encouraging one another..." (Heb. 10:25) In a formal worship service with its one-way communication, from pulpit to pew, there is little opportunity of "encouraging one another."

From the experiences of many people, we can say that generally speaking Christians do not find in the Sunday morning worship service the time when they are most helped spiritually. The greatest help is found in the small groups where Christians pray together and share together. They grow together as a nucleus of God's people. Perhaps the Sunday morning worship service can never take the place of small groups. But surely something should be done to make the Sunday service more worshipful and more meaningful. And this could be done in part by adapting more to the traditional patterns and forms of worship.

Singing has always been one means ordained by God for worshipping and praising Him. If that is true of all peoples, then it is doubly true of Africa. For Africans are a singing people. They love music and find great entertainment through singing. Yet the singing in churches is pathetically uninspiring. Singing in African churches cannot hold a candle to the singing in American churches. The reason is evident: the music is foreign. When you invite the peoples to sing certain kinds of Christian songs, such as choruses, they light up and throw themselves into the singing with all their might. Yet tradition shackles the churches so that they continue using foreign hymns instead of developing a church hymnody that is rich in biblical content and written with the African style, melody and rhythm. God can only be truly worshipped in spirit and in truth when God's people express their praise naturally. And that involves the use of music that is authentically African.

Thus we find in mission founded churches a well established tradition of singing western type hymns that have been translated from European languages. But the singing is usually dull, without any enthusiasm. One can hardly say the music is attractive or inspirational.

What a contrast to the Murle church in Sudan. After just two short years of planting the church, the young believers write their own praise songs to Jesus Christ for their salvation. Traditionally, they had sung praise songs to their goats. Now they use the same rhythms and melodies to praise the Lord. So attractive are these contextually relevant hymns that non-Christians sing the Christian hymns all the time (Arensen:1988).

However, it would appear that once an African people learn western type hymns and appreciate pop music or pan-African music, they can never go back to African traditional music. Thus time brings changes. Culture is not static and the peoples continually learn new songs. This should also be increasingly true in Christian churches where people need to be helped to sing joyfully and enthusiastically in worship and praise to God from their heart by singing contextualized music.

Worship cannot be restricted to the Sunday service. Worship should describe the whole of the Christian life in which nothing is secular but everything is sacred. Traditionally, Africans have been extraordinarily religious, bringing their religious beliefs into every aspect of life. By contrast westerners compartmentalize their lives into the secular and sacred. African Christians can teach western Christians much about the integration of the Christian faith into every aspect of life. But alas! As in so many areas, the westernization process taking place throughout Africa is breaking down that continuous dependence upon the spiritual realm. And the Christian church has failed to capitalize on this traditional heritage of religiosity.

The African Christian church must think through creatively the various ways and times when God's people should worship. The Murle of Sudan were never taught that worship is for Sunday only. Thus the Murle Christians meet and sing every night when in camp. Traditionally, special prayers were said during times of planting, harvesting, hunting and fishing. Traditionally, periodic acknowledgement of dependence on the spiritual realm and the giving of thanks took place during the high points in the life of a person — during puberty, marriage, child birth and death. How has the Christian church related the Gospel to this African tradition? Various constructive efforts have been made here and there to one degree or another. But much more effort should be expended so that our faith in the living God through Jesus Christ is experienced in every aspect of our lives.

CONCLUSION

Much more could be said about the positive role that ATR has played and should play in the Christian Church. Biblically speaking, we know that God has not left any peoples without a witness of Himself. God has not totally abandoned anyone but continues to disclose Himself through nature and conscience. As such we find that ATR has been used of God to prepare traditional Africans for the Gospel.

However, we ought not overrate ATR, for the traditional religion in Africa is representative of natural religion throughout the world. God's revelation in nature points to God the Creator. God's revelation in conscience shows man that he is a sinner. But God does not disclose the way of salvation through nature and the conscience.

While there is no message of hope and salvation in ATR, there is a preparation for the Gospel. Through God's revelation in nature and conscience as reflected in ATR, God has prepared Africans for the Gospel. They know much truth about God.

They have learned that they have a desperate void: alienation from God. God is distant and remote with resulting futility and despair. The reality of God's distance rather than His presence is portrayed vividly by an old pagan who spontaneously told this story to Edwin W. Smith (Smith 1966:33,34).

An old woman who lost all her relatives was destined to live the rest of her life in solitude. She determined to search for God to demand a reason for her inexplicable loss. She attempted to reach heaven by building a tower but failed. She visited country after country, asking everywhere for God. When she explained her affliction they replied, "In what do you differ from others? *Shikakunamo*, the Besetting One, sits on the back of everyone of us, and we cannot shake him off." She never found God. And the narrator said sorrowfully, "since her day no man has ever got an answer to her question — Why?"

Sadness, grief, perplexity, bewilderment, sorrow and a keen sense that God is not near. And yet, paradoxically, the African recognized that God was near. He "sits on the back of everyone of us." But fellowship with God was unknown. God's presence was not a living reality. There was a sense of despair.

Thus through one means or another God has used ATR to prepare the peoples for Himself. In many cases the torment and fear of the spirits has driven people to embrace the Gospel as the answer for their needs. God who is traditionally known as the all powerful one could not or did not protect the Africans from the torments of witchcraft and malicious spirits. Whatever the reason may have been, people lived in fear of the spirits rather than in the security of the Creator. Thus ATR has proved to be God's providential preparation for the Gospel.

REVIEW QUESTIONS FOR CHAPTER 16

1. Discuss the truth known about God in Africa. If you are able, supplement the suggestions in this book from your own observation.

2. How do you explain the beautiful and true things known about God in Africa?

3. In what way is the traditional belief in God a point of contact in the preaching of the Gospel? What do we mean by "point of contact"?

4. What are some of the features in African traditional worship that can be adopted in the Christian form of worship?

5. Enumerate other truths (besides the knowledge of God) known in ATR which have proved to be valuable points of contact for the Gospel?

Suggested Reading and Thought Questions for Advanced Study:

McVeigh, Malcolm J. *God in Africa*, 1974.
Mbiti, John. *Concepts of God in Africa*, 1970, pp.1-90.
Smith, Edwin. *African Ideas of God*, 1966.
    pp.36-58,   Peoples of Malawi by T. Cullen Young.
    pp.135-161, Ovambo in Namibia by G.W. Dymond.
    pp.162-179, Ngombe of Zaire by J. Davidson.
    pp.180-200, Peoples of Burundi by Rosemary Guillebaud.
    pp.224-240, Yoruba and Ewe of West Africa by E.G. Parrinder.
    pp.241-259, Akan of Ghana by H. St John T. Evans.
    pp.277-297, Mende of Sierra Leone by W.T. Harris.

Study the biblical teaching of natural revelation in standard evangelical reference books.

For example:

    Elwell, Walter A. ed. "Revelation, General," pages 944-945 in *Evangelical Dictionary of Theology*, 1984.

    Warfield, B.B. "Revelation," pp.2573-2582, Vol.IV, in *The International Standard Bible Encyclopedia*, James Orr ed., 1952.

1. What beliefs or practices in African traditional culture have been either ignored or misrepresented or misunderstood in the past but could be utilized in developing a Christian faith clothed in African garments? Research and discuss thoughtfully.

2. Why do you believe so much truth and virtue can be found in ATR? Is this because of borrowing, diffusion, African originality, genius or what? Study the biblical teaching of general revelation to help in your answer.

3. Why do you believe many of these truths and virtues in ATR were overlooked or unnoticed in the earlier years? (or were they overlooked?) Do you believe that African apologists of ATR today (eg. Mbiti and Idowu) see "the facts" in a more objective light than former students of ATR? Discuss.

4. Select three different African peoples reported in Smith 1966 above. Discuss the beautiful and true insights they have expressed concerning the Supreme Being.

Chapter 17

ERROR IN ATR
IN BIBLICAL PERSPECTIVE

The truth in ATR, discussed in chapter 16, is only half the truth, as we seek to evaluate traditional religion in biblical perspective. If we neglect to emphasize this providential aspect of the truth in ATR, we err. But the other half must also be emphasized. And the second half is the error we find in ATR.

We have previously pointed out the errors of mystical powers, divinities and the relationships with the dead. But what of the traditional belief in the Supreme Being? Is this not the strength of ATR? Indeed, it is. But we believe that from a biblical perspective, it is also the most serious error of ATR.

There are twin errors in traditional belief and practice related to the Supreme Being, each error being the opposite side of the same coin. In brief, they are that: 1)God has been removed from the centre of life, and 2)Idolatry has been fostered.

GOD HAS BEEN REMOVED FROM THE CENTRE
OF LIFE

Conflicting Opinions

Diedrich Westermann, an acknowledged authority on Africa and Christianity a generation ago, writes thus: "The high-god is, as a rule, not the object of a religious cult and is of small or almost no significance in practical religion. People acknowledge him, but neither fear nor love nor serve him, the feeling towards him being, at the highest, that of dim awe or reverence." (Westermann 1937:65)

Fifteen years later St. John T. Evans, the late archdeacon of Ashanti, concluded his brief study of the Akan doctrine of God by observing, "It should now be clear that even so recent and authoritative a writer as D. Westermann was in error so far at least as the Akan are concerned, when he declared that Africans 'acknowledge him (the High God), but neither fear nor love nor serve him...'" (Smith 1966:255) Evans affirms that *Nyame*, the Akan name for God, is honoured, his presence acknowledged and his blessing sought in all crises of life. Further, he is thought to be eternal, omniscient and loving-kind. He has his own worship, temples and priesthood.

In his book, *African Traditional Religion*, E. Bolaji Idowu quotes the same passage from Westermann. Anyone, Idowu claims, who has made a careful study of African Traditional Religion will see this is a sweeping statement that cannot be taken seriously today. The cause for Westermann's misunderstanding, according to Idowu, was due to the absence of proper sources of African beliefs and practices. Westermann was no doubt limited and his understanding inadequate. That can be said of any one of us. But what is the evidence as we know it today?

Africa is an immense continent with over 1,000 peoples, diverse from one another. A broad, sweeping statement about Africa in general is indeed a dangerous step. So it would be well to consider some of the particular peoples themselves and their beliefs concerning God to judge for ourselves whether we can any longer state that God has been removed from the centre of life and replaced by the creature.

Ethnographic Evidence

The late Mzee Jomo Kenyatta, the eminent statesman in Kenya and a pioneer among African anthropologists, wrote an ethnographic study of his people, the Gikuyu in the 1930's, entitled, *Facing Mt. Kenya*. In this book he observes that the Gikuyu usually called upon God during the times of crises: at birth, initiation, marriage and death. On some other occasions also they may call upon God, as for instance when a taboo is broken.

However, Ngai is "a Distant Being and takes but little interest in individuals in their daily walks of life" (Kenyatta n.d.:225). The affairs of individuals do not concern God, only those of the community. "God lives in the heavens and does not bother with the work or affairs of one man alone. He looks after the whole people or homestead group. There is no one man's religion or sacrifice."

More important, Mzee Kenyatta writes,

> So far as people and things go well and prosper, it is taken for granted that God is pleased in the general behaviour of the people and the welfare of the country. In this happy state there is no need for prayers. Indeed, it is inadvisable, for Ngai must not needlessly be bothered. It is only when humans are in real need that they must approach him, without fear of disturbing him and incurring his wrath [italics mine] (Kenyatta n.d.: 227).

The significance of this statement is two fold: it was written by a Gikuyu himself and written in the 1930's. Such an explanation of traditional belief might easily be dismissed if uttered by a European. But Kenyatta spoke of what he knew. Moreover, he spoke of what he knew in the early part of the century. Many changes have transpired in ATR in the past century. Without question the Christian Gospel has brought many revolutionary changes to Africa, even within ATR. But what Kenyatta affirmed represents traditional belief as he understood it to be in the early part of the century.

The beliefs and practices of the Turkana have not been studied nearly as much as the Gikuyu and the Akamba. But it is known that they believe in a Supreme Being called, *Akuj*, the same word for "sky." He is a person who owns a large homestead with many cattle grazing on ever green pastures.

Yet P.H. Gulliver reports that *Akuj* is only "potentially" supreme "because, although omnipotence is attributed to him, yet in practice only certain powers are expected of him." (Gulliver 1951:230) Everyone says God is omnipotent but no one expects Him to work any miracles. He has great power if only one can induce Him to work on man's behalf. In practice they do not depend on Him for much. If Akuj answers prayer, no one gives Him thanks or shows Him honour. Likewise, if He does not answer prayer, this is also taken as a matter of fact. One can go for weeks, it is reported, without hearing His name.

The Wazigua of Tanzania believe that God was an "awful, unapproachable Power, contact with whom must be maintained through a medium. Like the Pare, they chose the spirits of their ancestors to act as mediators and like the Pare they chose the spirits only of elder males as efficient to act." (Baxter 1943:4)

Speaking of Ruwa, the God of the Chagga of Tanzania, we read that "The truth is that Ruwa has long ago ceased to mingle with and care for his creatures, and they on their side seek succour from him only in extreme distress, sacrificing to him at rare intervals just such animals as he has provided them for the purpose." (Dundas 1924:107)

God among the Sukuma of Tanzania is called *Likuube*. Cory says *Likuube* can be explained in terms which are used by a great many East African Bantu for *Mulungu*.

> He is the very remote supreme being, who created the world. 'Likuube' is so remote and exalted that he cannot be expected to interfere with the fate of an individual. No sacrifices and prayers can reach him; he has done his work but he is not working any more because all that is, has never changed (Cory 1960:15).

Though the Sukuma mention *Likuube* in their prayers, it is only by way of introduction while the prayer itself is directed to the spirits nearer to men. The same kind of sentiment is expressed by the Swazi (Marwick 1966:228).

Parrinder, who has a helpful discussion on this topic, refers to various peoples. The Mende of Sierra Leone believe that God retired to the heavens after creation and is little concerned with the activities on earth. He can be approached in times of distress, but normally people use the intermediaries, the divinities and the ancestors. The Leza of Zimbabwe have no ceremonies for God who is considered too far away and fearful, though they may approach God directly in times of great need. Normally, they pray to the lesser divinities who serve as intermediaries. Parrinder concludes by saying, "In many parts of Africa one finds the strange phenomenon that God is believed in yet, is thought of as so great and remote that He is offered no regular worship." (Parrinder 1962:38)

John Taylor focuses on the paradox of African belief and practice, that God is both far away and near. The Dinka sing a song underlining this paradox.

> Great Deng is near, and some say 'far' O Divinity.
> The Creator is near, and some say 'he has not reached us.'
> Do you not hear, O Divinity?
> The black bull of the rain has been released from the moon's byre,
> Do you not hear, O Divinity? (Taylor 1963:79)

Among the Nupe of Northern Nigeria, "the most common and strongly emphasized comment on the nature of the deity is, 'soko Lokpa.' God is far away, yet in a different sense, more mystic sense He is present always and everywhere." (Taylor 1963:78) Concluding the chapter Taylor writes,

> But while everywhere there seems to be an underlying conviction that such a God

ERROR IN ATR

is, it is accompanied, and usually overwhelmed, by the pragmatic knowledge that such a God has gone away. The African myth does not tell of man driven from Paradise, but of God disappearing from the world. It is men, not God, whose voice calls through the desolate garden, where art thou? (Taylor 1963:76)

John Mbiti recognizes this paradox in traditional religion. Mbiti writes, "For most of their life, many African peoples place God in the transcendental plane, making Him seem remote from their daily affairs. But they know that He is immanent." (Mbiti 1970:18) Speaking of the Africans' knowledge of God, Mbiti writes,

It is a paradox that they 'know' Him, and they do not 'know' Him; He is not a Stranger to them, and yet they are estranged to Him; He knows them, but they do not know Him. So God confronts men as the mysterious and incomprehensible, and as indescribably and beyond human vocabulary. This is part of the essential nature of God. (Mbiti 1969:35)

These words of Mbiti are profound and true. Yet we feel constrained to go beyond them in biblical perspective. The peoples of Africa are in solidarity with the human race. The human nature of Africans is identical to the nature of mankind, because all men partake of the nature of Adam, the father of the one human race. According to Scripture, all men have been given a knowledge of God in nature but all men have rejected Him.

For even though they knew God, they did not honour Him as God, or give thanks but they became futile in their speculations, and their foolish heart was darkened. Professing to be wise, they became fools (Rom. 1:21,22).

Harry Sawyerr wrestles with the question among West Africans, whether they believe in God. He observes that the Akan are among the few peoples in West Africa who have built temples for the worship of God and assigned priests to offer regular sacrifices to Him. Instead of worshipping God,

we meet a whole array of lesser gods and the long line of ancestral spirits to whom prayers are offered and who are, indeed, regarded as the more responsible for the day-to-day factors of life. It is in this context that we have to inquire whether the African does in fact 'believe in God'. We recall the remark made earlier that God is thought to be far removed from the affairs of man. And yet, men do always appeal to Him in times of crisis. How then can we reconcile these two contrary attitudes? (Sawyerr 1970:6)

His response is that "the African's attitude to God is a reflection of his experience and his relationship with his chiefs." Chiefs or kings traditionally ruled the peoples in Africa and these chiefs or kings were approachable only through intermediaries. "For all practical purposes, the chief is distant from ordinary men. He is addressed only through the intermediary and, in turn, he addresses his petitioners only through the intermediary." (Sawyerr 1970:7)

Perhaps if this notion of the distance of the early ancestors were to be combined with the attitude of aloofness noticeable among the chiefs, we may be able to find a probable source of the notion of the remoteness of God. God is like the chief and is, indeed, the chief Sovereign. He rules the world and administers justice and equity. He is a distant ancestor who has a direct interest in the well-being of man and could be directly approached by anyone in times of danger or crises. Does a personal relation exist between God and man under these circumstances? (Sawyerr 1970:9)

He replies that, although God is transcendent, He can and does hear the cry of his children wherever they are. His omnipresence is assumed. Furthermore, whenever they participate in the worship of the cultic and nature spirits, they are confronted with "concrete manifestations of the power of God." Furthermore, these divinities maintain the moral standards of life. Hence they know that since the ministers of/God are concerned with morality, so must God be. Since ATR is primarily a communal religion, God also relates Himself primarily with the community. However, God is also a personal God who relates to individuals.

Such an explanation for the distance of God in Africa is far from satisfactory. In fact, it is distressingly unsatisfactory. Sawyerr wrestles with the evidence. God is indeed removed from the centre of life. While the divinities are worshipped regularly and while the ancestors are the prime factors influencing the lives of the Africans, God is in fact not worshipped in the same manner.

Sawyerr finds solace in a sociological understanding of the African peoples. The religious beliefs of Africans are a reflection of the sociological structure of the African community. This may be good anthropology, but it is bad theology. How should we understand ATR from a biblical perspective? Sawyerr never touches the question even though he is a Canon of St. George's Cathedral, Freetown. But it is a central contention of this book that we cannot truly understand or interpret ATR from God's point of view unless we examine ATR through the spectacles of biblical revelation.

Moreover, Sawyerr's interpretation, however deficient it may be, only confirms the fact that God has been removed from the centre of life. Even as the chiefs and kings were distant from the peoples, generally beyond personal fellowship or communication, so God is likewise removed. But whereas Sawyerr finds a sociological explanation for this removal, we find a theological reason.

A study of African Traditional Religion, like the study of history, is a narrative of God seeking and calling men to Himself, but men rejecting His love and grace. Instead, God is only the last resort in time of trouble. As the leader of a hunting expedition said after two weeks of bad luck, "I am tired of asking the shades, let us pray to God." (Taylor 1963:80) Africa has known *ABOUT* God but they have not known Him personally. The presence of God is not practiced among the people traditionally because they have been alienated from God through sin.

As Rosemary Gullebaud says of Imana, the name of God among the peoples of Ruanda and Burundi, "Imana is the great Creator, the First Cause of all good. He does not enter into daily life at all, in a practical sense, and yet is continually in the peoples' thoughts...The name of Imana is constantly in the life of the people, even though they do not worship Him." (Smith 1966:186, 188)

Conclusion

Thus we believe that it is true, both from the Scriptures and from a study of world cultures, that the Africans in solidarity with the human race, have traditionally removed God from the centre of their lives. He is neither worshipped nor honoured as God should be. In practice He does not have first place, the pre-eminence, even though He may have pre-eminence in theory. This is indeed the first step toward idolatry and can be observed among "Christians" who have been catechized and baptized. God looses His pre-eminence among them. In the following generation the "Christians" are only Christian in name but in practice they do not know God. Nor is He the Lord of their lives. Though in theory they still acknowledge God as Lord.

IDOLATRY IS FOSTERED IN ATR

The first error in ATR concerning their belief in God is that the Creator has been removed from the centre of their lives. That is the converse of the second error, namely, that in the place of God men have elevated idols which receive their trust, dependence, honour, and homage which is due to God alone. In the first place, God is either ignored or removed from the vital and central place in the lives of men. In the second place, men have elevated the creature to the place of idolatry.

Atheism is the denial of the existence of God. Idolatry is the worship of substitutes instead of the only true and living God. Like many Europeans, the African peoples are not atheists in their beliefs, though they may live as if they can get along without God most of the time, except in times of crises. Nor do Africans traditionally bow down to wood and stone. No one today in Europe or America bows down to a cultic object of worship either. But in fact, all men have removed God from Lordship and have become idolaters by substituting the creature for the Creator as their daily source of dependence. The African experience is not unique. It is indeed representative of what has taken place among all mankind throughout the world.

Biblical Teaching

What does the Scripture teach concerning idolatry?

The Greek word, *eidolon*, comes from a word, "to see," and means "a picture" or "a copy." *Eidolon*, when referring to the figure of a man, means a copy of the man, not the man himself. A work of art may be called an *eidolon*, since it is a copy of the living being, not the person himself.

In the Septuagint, the Greek translation of the Hebrew Old Testament, the word *eidolon* is used to translate many different Hebrew words. Some of these Hebrew words are as follows (see Unger 1960:511):

Awen is used in many places to mean "nought, vanity, iniquity and wickedness." It is used only in Isaiah 66:3 for an idol. Thus an idol is empty, nothing, vain, false and wicked.

Shiqqus refers to filth and impurity. In particular, it refers to the immoral rites associated with idolatry and hence to ceremonial uncleanness (Ezek. 37:23; Nah. 3:6).

Gillulim originally meant droppings of dung. Ezekiel uses this word over 38 times to describe the false gods and their symbols (eg. Ezek. 6:4-6, 9, 13).

Bosheth means a shameful thing. It describes the filthy and immoral worship associated with the Baal cult.

Elil means a thing of nought, something that does not exist. This word is not only used for the images but for the pagan deities themselves (I Chron. 16:16; Ps. 96:5; 97:7).

These different Hebrew words are translated into the Greek Septuagint by the word, *eidolon* (from which we derive our English word, idol). The Hebrew prophets thus poured contempt and scorn on heathen idolatry by using these Hebrew words.

Kittel makes this important comment.

> Behind the usage there is obviously a polemic [arguments] against paganism. The presence of images as the focus of worship is used to emphasize the unreality of heathen belief and the heathen gods. For the Jews, idols and heathen deities are identical, and they prove that the heathen have images but no true God. Thus, 'copy' (as distinct from the reality) is the word for both images and gods. The word 'idol' in its emphasis is often laid on the idea of an object of false worship rather than on that of something without reality which fools have put in the place of the true God. In its strict sense the idol is not merely an alternative god; it is an unreal god, and therefore false as distinct from true and real (Kittel 1964:377).

Two great truths are recognized in the Old Testament concerning idolatry: first, the idol is nothing; but secondly, there is nevertheless a demonic spiritual force represented by that image.

Idolatry is generally associated with images in the Old Testament. Isaiah and the other prophets ridiculed and scorned the vanity and emptiness of bowing down before images of wood and stone (Isa. 2:8; 40:18-26; 41:6,7; 44:9-20; 46:1,2; 50:18-20; also see Ps. 115:4-7).

But while recognizing the falsehood and emptiness of the idols, the prophets also acknowledged that spiritual powers behind the image made the worshippers unclean. To follow after these idols is to commit spiritual adultery (Deut. 31:16; Judg. 2:17; Hos. 1:2). Because of the spiritual powers represented by the idols, the images were an abomination to the Lord (Deut. 7:25) and filthy, rejected things (Deut. 29:17).

The New Testament rests on the revelation of God given in the Older Testament and the Septuagint translation into the Greek language. Like the Old Testament, Paul taught that the heathen gods were false in comparison to the true and living God (I Thess. 1:9; I Cor. 12:2). In the words of Paul, "We know that there is no such thing as an idol in the world, and there is no God but one" (I Cor. 8:4). Idols were only products of human sin and folly (Rom. 1:23; Gal. 4:8).

And yet behind the very images which are "nothing," lay the power of fallen spirits, demons who are serving Satan and hostile against God (I Cor. 8:5,6; 10:14-22). They could not be dismissed as mere foolishness, for they made the worshippers unclean (Acts 15:20) and enslaved the people (Gal. 4:8). The worship of images which could not see nor talk was closely connected with the worship of demons (Rev. 9:20).

For our purposes of evaluating African Traditional Religion in the light of Scripture, we need to stress the new feature of the New Testament teaching on idolatry. In the New Testament, the term, idolatry, is "used figuratively of undue obsession [intense desire] with any object less than God." (Buttrick 1962:II,675)

"The idol is whatever claims that loyalty which belongs to God alone." (Is.42:8) (Douglas 1962:553). "In general sense idolatry is the paying of divine honours to any created thing; the ascription of divine power to natural agencies." (Unger 1960:512) "In the New Testament, idolatry came to mean, not only the giving to any creature or human creation the honour or devotion which belongs to God alone, but the giving to any human desire a precedence [priority] over God's will." (Orr 1952:III, 1448)

Riches are considered an idol by the Lord Jesus when a person gives his primary affection, devotion, time and attention to them, rather than to God. "No man can serve two masters; for either he will hate the one and love the other, or he will hold to one and despise the other. You cannot serve God and Mammon." (Matt. 6:24)

Covetousness is idolatry because a covetous person is seeking to possess something which God has not given to him. He prefers his own will to the will of God. "For this you know with certainty, that no immoral or impure person or *covetous man, who is an idolater*, has an inheritance in the Kingdom of Christ and God." (Eph. 5:5) "...and greed, which amounts to idolatry." (Col. 3:5) In the context, the covetous man appears to be the lustful person whose inner thoughts are filled with sexual desire forbidden by God. But whether covetousness is sexual lust or a lust for position, power or material wealth, covetousness is a form of idolatry.

Participation in heathen feasts amounted to idolatry (I Cor. 10:14-22)

Immorality has always been closely associated with idolatry. Sexual impurity has been the appeal of idolatry in the past (cf. I Kings 14:23; Amos 2:7, 8; I Cor. 10:7, 8). It is, therefore, not surprising that idolatry is frequently associated with warnings against immorality in the New Testament (I Cor. 6:9; Gal. 5:20; Eph. 5:5; I Pet. 4:3; Rev. 21:8).

Conclusion

From this survey of biblical teaching we conclude that the heart of idolatry is the removing of God from His rightful position as Lord. For the creature to have any desire, treasure any thing or seek any object outside the revealed will of the Creator is to commit idolatry.

The popular notion that idolatry is only the worship of images is not the biblical teaching. True, idolatry has often been associated with material objects, icons that are worshipped. But idolatry is more. It is giving personal desires first place above the will of God. It is giving honour to the creature which alone belongs to the Creator.

For all people, even for Christians, there is a real danger of falling away from the true God and giving undue homage, honour and devotion to an idol, whatever form that may take. In our spiritual life, "Our struggle is not against flesh and blood, but against the rulers, against the spiritual forces of wickedness in the heavenly places." (Eph. 6:12) Therefore, the Apostle John closes his first Epistle with these words, "Little children, guard yourselves from idols." (I Jn. 5:21) And the Apostle Paul exhorts the Corinthian believers, "Therefore, my beloved, flee from idolatry." (I Cor. 10:14)

If Christians need to be on the guard against idols coming between God and themselves, how much greater is this danger among unbelievers. As a matter of fact, the Bible shows that all men, apart from the grace of God, are idolaters. They have rejected the knowledge of God and honour the creature rather than the Creator (Rom. 1:18-32; Eph. 2:1-3; I Pet. 4:3).

Nothing could be plainer in Scripture that idolaters shall not inherit the kingdom of God (I Cor. 6:9; Gal. 5:19-21; Eph. 5:5; Rev. 21:3; 22:15).

CASE STUDY OF IDOLATRY IN AFRICA

We now move from the pages of Scripture to an examination of a case study in ATR. We believe that the ethnographical studies of the African peoples (studies made of African cultures by anthropologists) demonstrates that they, together with the whole human race, have removed God from the centre of life and have worshipped and served the creature rather than the Creator who is blessed forever.

Preliminary Observations

But first it is necessary to make two preliminary comments. First, we reject any attempt to enter into judgment of individuals. That is the right of God alone. Only He knows the hearts of men. Only the Judge of the whole earth can determine whether or not a particular individual is an idolater. However, God has given us His revelation in the Bible. And the teachings of Scripture are uniformly pessimistic about mankind in general apart from Christ. That is, the Bible sees all men lost in sin apart from God's grace operating through the Gospel. But the assessment of individuals in the sight of God is beyond our own ability to judge.

Second, much more needs to be learned about the religions of all the peoples of Africa. John Mbiti used all the written sources available to him when he wrote, *The Concepts of God in Africa*. Yet he could only refer to 270 peoples out of the 1,000 ethnic groups throughout the continent. And many of those 270 ethnic groups have very inadequate study made of their traditional religion. Much more field research needs to be done before we can reach any final conclusions about the whole continent. Furthermore, our attention has been drawn repeatedly to the fact that the African peoples vary greatly in their religious beliefs. Therefore, what may be true of one, is not necessarily true of all others.

Nevertheless, there seems to be a general agreement in the broad outlines of belief throughout Africa. Most, if not all, African peoples acknowledge the existence of God the Creator who Himself had no beginning. But the question arises, what have the people of Africa done with that knowledge of God? Idolatry is not merely a matter of doctrine but of practice. We believe that the ethnographical evidence (studies made by students of culture) points to the fact that Africans stand in solidarity with the whole human race; that God's judgment of mankind as a whole applies likewise to the peoples of Africa.

> For even though they knew God, they did not honour Him as God, or give thanks; but they became futile in their speculations, and their foolish heart was darkened. Professing to be wise, they became fools (Rom. 1:21,22).

Theologically, we maintain that all religions, being the creation of fallen men, are guilty of idolatry. But idolatry may take various forms. Materialism is predominant in the West. Covetousness (which is idolatry) and greed are rampant among many professing Christians. India is filled with idols of their multiplied millions of gods. Divinities (lesser gods) in many corners of the world, including West Africa, detract from the glory of God and His pre- eminence.

Daidanso reports that all Chadians believe in a Supreme Being who created the world and everything in it. In this sense they are theists. However, they do not know how to approach Him. God remains for the Chadians a far god, far from them. He is not near the people. In place of this invisible Creator the Chadians have placed visible divinities which are more visibly present because they can send sickness among the peoples. But are the Chadians in fact aiming their worship to the Supreme Being through the divinities and spirits? In the opinion of Daidanso, they are not. The Chadians have a knowledge of the Supreme Being but since they cannot see Him, He sees far away, so they have turned to the creatures which they can see and understand (Daidanso ma Djongwe:1988).

One prominent feature of African Traditional Religion that suggests idolatry is the traditional relationship with the ancestors. We must observe, however, that "ancestor worship" is surely not a problem for all of Africa. The ancestral cult plays a very insignificant part in many parts of the continent, particularly among the Nilotic and Nilo Hamitic peoples. However, we believe that wherever the ancestral cult is prominent, as among the Bantu, idolatry is a living danger.

In times past anthropologists and missionaries readily referred to "ancestor worship" among African peoples. Lindblom, for instance, divides his treatment of Religion among the Akamba into two topics: "1) A developed worship of the spirits of their ancestors (*aimu*) and, 2) A vague belief in a Higher Being (*Mulungu, Ngai*)." (1920:209).

Today the pendulum has swung in the other direction. The late Rev. T. Cullen Young, the late missionary of the Livingstonia Mission of the Church of Scotland, declared that "ancestor-worship" is a "highly misleading term. Carrying, with us, a reference to existence of a different kind from that of man on earth, it immediately parts company with the African View." (Smith 1966:39) A majority of African writers today would support this opinion. Referring to the Gikuyu, the late President of the Republic of Kenya, Mzee Kenyatta, affirmed in his book that "from practical experience," he knows that the Gikuyu did not worship their ancestors. "They hold communion with them, but their attitude towards them is not at all to be compared with their attitude to the deity who is truly worshipped." (Kenyatta 1938:255)

Parrinder in his helpful discussion on this subject quotes J.H. Driberg as saying, without question,

No African prays to his dead grandfather any more than he 'prays' to his living father. In both cases the words employed are the same: he asks as of right or he beseeches, or he expostulates with [demands], or he reprimands...but he never uses in his context the words for 'prayer' and 'worship' which are strictly reserved for his religious dealings with the Absolute Power and the divinities. The Latin word 'pietas' probably best describes the attitude of Africans toward their dead ancestors, as to their living elders. (1962:64)

Many writers of African culture, therefore, discuss the ancestors under such topics as "Man's Society" rather than his religion. For instance, K.A.Busia, a sociologist from Ghana, discusses the living-dead under the heading, "Political Organization," instead of under his first heading, "A World of Spirits." Relations with the ancestral spirits are treated as a social phenomena (object of experience), not a religious phenomena.

Idowu seems to have a more balanced perspective. On the one hand he correctly repudiates those who reduce ATR to mere ancestor-worship. Writers in the past have exaggerated and distorted ATR, he maintains, making the ancestral cult the basis of ATR and *the* religion of Africa (Idowu 1973:180).

On the other hand he questions those who dismiss the possibilitiy of ancestor worship in Africa. Those who say categorically that Africans do not worship their ancestors are forgetting the complex nature of the working of the human mind. Worship and veneration [respect mingled with awe]...are psychologically closer than next door to each other: the emotional indicator is always trembling between the two, swinging to the one or to the other in accordance with the emotional pressure or the spiritual climate of the moment. This is something that happens anywhere, everywhere, in the world, and with peoples at every level of development (Idowu 1973:182).

Idowu then refers to those churches which seek to distinguish between worship and veneration and observes.

> It is however, needless to say that between worship and veneration [respect mingled with awe] in religious buildings or precincts [immediate surroundings], the dividing line is often a hair's breadth, the human mind being what it is. Anybody who has watched with discernment this type of 'veneration' in the Roman Catholic Church, the Russian Orthodox Church, or at Westminster Abbey, or at a household or wayside shrines in Europe, will appreciate this fact (Idowu: 1973:180).

We would support Idowu in his contention that we must be open to the possibility that people anywhere and everywhere may give undue homage to their ancestors or dead "saints." That is a possibility that must be seriously considered.

Kivuto Ndeti, while rejecting the notion that ancestor-worship is the essence of Akamba religion, correctly assesses the situation when he says, "This [ancestor worship] is an inadequate interpretation of a very complex phenomenon." (1972:174) And with this we agree.

Idolatry Among the Traditional Akamba

For our case study we shall examine the question of "ancestor worship" among the Akamba. We need to pick our way through this thorny issue which is admittedly "a very complex phenomenon." Our approach here will be to let the Akamba speak for themselves.

The Akamba conceive of the *aimu* as their ancestors, and therefore, express a certain honour for them. The living share a respectful relationship with their departed relatives and friends since biological death cannot separate the living from their ancestors. In this context we understand the "communion" and communication which takes place between the living and their ancestors. According to a popular interpretation such a relationship cannot be spoken of as worship but rather a form of veneration in which the living show honour and respect to their ancestors. Mbiti affirms, "The acts of pouring out libation (of beer, milk or water), or giving portions of food to the living-dead, are symbols of communion, fellowship and remembrance. They are the mystical ties that bind the living-dead to their surviving relatives." (Mbiti 1969:26) In other words, the relationship between the living and their ancestors is a continuation of a family relationship. "There is nothing here," Mbiti maintains, "about the so-called 'ancestor worship,' even if these acts may so seem to the outsiders who do not understand the situation." (Mbiti 1969:26)

In their thinking the Akamba have always distinguished between *Ngai Mumbi* (God the Creator) and the *ngai* (gods) of the family. *Mulungu* alone has all power. *Mulungu* alone cannot be deceived. The ultimate explanation for everything, including the *aimu*, is the Creator God.

In contrast the ancestors are created by *Mulungu*. While the living possess enhanced powers after their transition into the spirit world, they are still finite creatures who can be tricked. The ancestors can be reprimanded and sharply criticized.

Many traditional Akamba do believe that they honour God more than the ancestors. Musya declared, "God is honoured more than the ancestors, even though I sacrifice to the *aimu*. I have never said, 'that if it were not for the ancestors I could have had an accident,' but I always praise God for all the good I see." Another said, "God has all powers and responsibilities over all the spirits and the living creatures. Therefore, we do first give God priority over the ancestors." Other knowledgeable Akamba agree. Though the first fruits of the harvest are given to the *aimu*, thanks is given to God. Though the Akamba sacrifice to the *aimu*, seeking safety from danger, they speak of God as the one who saved them from harm. With their mouths they thank God, while they offer sacrifices to their ancestors. As Kitheka stated, "I honour God very much and I sacrifice to the *aimu*." Another Mukamba explains the reason sacrifices are rendered to the ancestors while the Creator receives only verbal thanks. "The greater honour is given to God but God does not ask me to give him anything."

Part of this apparent contradiction, that actual deeds of honour are rendered to the *aimu* rather than the Creator, may be explained by the belief of many Akamba that the ancestors are intermediaries between God and man.

However, we must insist that the relationship between the living and their ancestors is "a very complex phenomenon," as Ndeti has maintained. To explain the relationship only in the terms of the nature of man, as Ndeti has done, is to overlook other evidence.

The problem is that in practice there is very little to distinguish the honour given to God and the honor given to the *aimu*.

The prayers offered in the home during the pouring of the libation, the intercession at the shrines when sacrifices are offered, the religious rites and ceremonies which occur during the cyclical events of the year and the rites of passage, the prayers and sacrifices offered under the direction of the medicine man, all intermingle the honour given to the Creator God and to the ancestral spirits.

The following collection of prayers will exemplify this assertion. These two prayers are said when offering libation in the home.

God the Creator, who created and divided the fingers of people (Ngai Mwatuangi), drink this water; and you, my father and grandfather, drink this water.

Kyunda, drink this wine and give to Mutyanyungu; and Mutyanyungu, give Isenge; and you, Isenge, give Mundo; and you, God who is the shepherd, also drink this wine; and all of you, preserve the family because if you let it be destroyed where will you be coming to visit?

Prayers for divine assistance can be addressed to the ancestral spirits without referring to the Creator God. Before going on safari, a Mukamba prays, "Father, grandfather, and my mother's brother and the rest of the family, drink this wine and protect me on the way." When praying for milk to be given by cows, a Mukamba says, "Father and mother, we give milk and then give us more milk for this cow does not have any."

The evidence shows that the Akamba confessed to the ancestors when they failed to give the ancestors their due respect; they praised the ancestors during time of abundance; they offered prayers of supplication to the ancestors when sickness or famine occurred.

For example, when a good harvest was reaped, the Akamba prayed, "Father and the rest in the family (those who have died), thanks for the harvest which you brought and then have this cow (it was slaughtered and the blood poured) or bull or ox. And continue to bring more harvests and I will continue to give you something like a goat."

There simply is no difference in the way sacrifices and prayers were offered to God or the ancestors. Prayers offered in the home intermingled God the Creator and the ancestral spirits. Another prayer is as follows:

Our ancestors, drink from there with our father, mother, grandmother, our daughters, the one who perished with the bow and arrows, then pass it to all those who disappeared, and are forgotten; and you, those who died without wives, drink from there, then let the bowl go because it is not yours; God the Divider, Kathambi, and Muviti, drink or eat our food from here; receive yours, then, Ngai Mwatuangi, drink yours together with the others.

God is plainly and unmistakably associated with all the other spirits in equal fashion. They are all treated the same as in this prayer: "God (*Ngai Mwatuangi*), we pray to you and to our ancestors, and also to Kathambi and *Muviti*, we want you all to...for us."

One word for worship in Kikamba as we have seen is *kuthemba*, to offer a sacrifice. *Nthembo* is a sacrifice of any kind, including food, beer, blood, drink or animal sacrifice. This sacrifice was never given to the living but restricted to God and the ancestral spirits. *Kuthemba* is used of the giving of offering in the Christian church today.

This sacrifice is given to the ancestors primarily, with God being seldom honoured by offerings. There is no clear distinction made between God and the ancestors with reference to sacrifice at the traditional shrine.

As one Mukamba remarked, "Some of the ancestors (*ngai*) were worshipped by having their offerings taken to the shrine, while others received their worship through sacrifice offered right at home. The only difference in the worship of the gods was that the gods of *Muviti* (ones who pass by) could not come home or enter any house. So their sacrifices had to be taken to the shrine. The gods whose sacrifice was given right at home were those who were relatives to the family."

The description of sacrifices made at the shrine was made earlier. In the opinion of many Akamba, those who are generally traditionalists to this day, and those who were converted to Christ out of an active worship in Akamba Traditional Religion, the ancestors were indeed worshipped.

As one Mukamba remarked. "The ancestors were the ones worshipped. There were no other gods like them. These were worshipped in two different ways: the traditional dance and sacrifices."

Some would argue that the Akamba's attitude toward the ancestors has been misinterpreted because the *aimu* are greatly feared. They are not worshipped but appeased out of fear.

The Kikamba word used here is *kikio* which means to respect or to fear. This conveys the concept of fear mixed with respect and honour. People respect others because they fear their authority and not because they respect their character. Fear and honour are intertwined. The *aimu* are respected and honoured in this negative sense of fearing retaliation and punishment. Therefore, it can be argued, that the Akamba attitude toward the *aimu* is not of worship in the highest sense but showing honour out of fear.

Indeed, the ancestors are greatly feared. Since they are unpredictable and very dangerous, they need to be appeased. One Mukamba said, "If you see these people on the way, you had to hurry back home to find some food for them in order to appease them. Then the food should be taken outside the house in order that they eat from there, for no one wanted them to enter their houses."

If the dead requested a goat in Kitui, they would take an iron bar and repeatedly strike the neck of the goat, causing blood vessels to burst. They continued to beat the goat until it died. This torture was a way of showing great honour and respect to the ancestors. One medicine man said, "These *aimu* are not grateful at all. They molest and torture the one who sacrifices to them."

Therefore, it could be argued that the Akamba attitude toward the *aimu* is one of appeasing, not of worshipping. Only God is trusted and worshipped.

The response of Akamba Christians is a very striking contrast to that of the traditional Akamba. When Christians are asked, "Do you worship your ancestors?" they respond uniformly in the following ways. "No, I stopped that long ago after believing in Jesus Christ." "Formerly, I used to worship them. But now I have entered into Christianity. I don't worship them through pouring down beer and libations." "I used to worship them there before, so that they could reveal to me what ought to be. But now I worship God the Father of the Saviour, Jesus Christ." "Now I don't worship that way anymore. I worship God, the Father of the Saviour, Jesus Christ. At night I do pray to God, even when I am on my journeys."

In contrast the traditional Akamba uniformly agreed that they did worship their ancestors. "I worship my ancestors. I sacrifice goats to them and give them some blood. When I do this, I pray what I want from them." "Yes, I have to worship the *aimu*. Since they care for me and give me anything good that I ask them. They are the source of every good thing that comes to me." "I worship the *aimu* by giving them beer and pouring water for them and if there was anything bad, it goes away."

One could dismiss the comments made by the traditional Akamba as a misinterpretation of what they meant. For they are simply using Kikamba words which express the rendering of honour to their ancestors. As we have seen before, many traditional Akamba believe that greater honour is rendered to *Mulungu*. Therefore, one could assert that the honour rendered to God is worship and the honour rendered to the ancestors is veneration.

The following comments by traditional Akamba might be taken to support this contention. Mbithuka says, "The honour I give to God is superior to that of ancestors because He is the one who enables me to do anything I ask from them." A medicine man replied, "God is the one who gives the *aimu* power to meet my needs. So it is God to whom I give higher honour. For example, the gifts of food are in the form of bulls, while those of ancestors are in the form of goats." Another Mukamba said, "God is the one who is great. He is the one who gave the *aimu* the power to live."

But one must also assess the response of the Christians. For some reason they uniformly reject all "worship" of the ancestors. One must conclude that in the consciousness of the Akamba Christians the honour rendered to the ancestors is unfitting and unchristian. A former leader of the *kilumi* dancers and now a recent Christian convert, said, "I am now in another state. I don't worship as I used to do before. I give God full respect. When the *aimu* come, I refuse their requests. That which profits me is only Christ. If they were really truthful, they could have revealed clearly whatever they desired of me that I may know."

Salalah concludes his study of the Basukuma in Tanzania in much the same way.

> Although Mbiti and Pritchard claim that African peoples worship or sacrifice to God when they sacrifice to the spirits, the Basukuma practice seems to be too evasive for one to come up with an unequivocal [clear] view. There are no shrines devoted to God, neither are there priests set apart for Him. He is recognized as the Creator of all things and is not put on the same level with ancestors. However, when it comes to the question of actual worship and sacrificing to Him, evidence seems to be inconclusive (1981:53).

He questions Mbiti's assumption that the ancestors are always and only intermediaries between God and man.

> The Basukuma monotheistic concept cannot be affirmed without some qualifying statements. God's place in their religion is obscured by ancestral spirits, who are the center of worship in people's daily lives. Mbiti's contention that ancestors are intermediaries between God and man, and that people worship Him through ancestral spirits, does not appear to be apparent among the Basukuma (1981:61).

We may conclude by saying that there is no possibility of making a sweeping statement as many do that the Akamba only worshipped God as God and they only venerated their ancestors as ancestors. The picture is far too complex to make a statement like that.

For the traditional Mukamba, he makes a distinction in his mind between the Creator and the ancestors. They are entirely separate categories of beings. Yet in their practice, the Akamba do not demonstrate a sharp distinction between the honour they give to God and the veneration they give to the ancestors. For the Christian Akamba, as we have seen, there is a turning away from the traditional veneration offered to the *aimu*. The traditional system of worship appears incompatible and irreconcilable to the Christian's new relationship to Jesus Christ.

CONCLUSION

We conclude our study of traditional belief in God with the observation made by the Apostle Paul. What Paul said concerning mankind as a whole is likewise true of the peoples in the great continent of Africa.

> That which is known about God is evident within them; for God made it evident to them. For since the creation of the world His invisible attributes, His eternal power and divine nature, have been clearly seen, being understood through what has been made, so that they are without excuse (Rom. 1:19,20).

To a wonderful extent the traditional religious belief of Africa demonstrates that God has not left Himself without a witness among the peoples. Many true insights into the nature of God have been provided. This can only be explained from a biblical viewpoint by the activity of God among the peoples.

With these truths known by the traditional African peoples, the missionaries of the Gospel may find points of contact, royal roads into the lives of the Africans. Because the African culture has the marks of common grace within it, the Christian Church may use much within the African cultures to build a truly biblical and yet an authentically African Christianity.

But the Apostle Paul does not stop with the positive. He continues.

> For though they know God, they did not honour Him as God, or give thanks; but they became futile in their speculations, and their foolish heart was darkened. Professing to be wise, they became fools, and exchanged the glory of the incorruptible God for an image in the form of corruptible man and of birds and four footed animals and crawling creatures. For they exchanged the truth of God for a lie, and worshipped and served the creature rather than the Creator, who is blessed forever, Amen (Rom. 1:21-23,25).

Though something of the splendor and majesty of God was revealed, men have substituted the creature for deity. The form of those idols varies greatly from one culture to another. Africans have never worshipped birds or four footed animals and crawling creatures. But neither have the Americans or Europeans. One can look in vain for such evidence of idolatry in the West and find none. Yet Americans and Europeans are not exempt from the sin of idolatry. The lust of the flesh, the lust of the eyes and the pride of life have all taken the place of the pre-eminence of God the Creator. Materialism, sensual lust, greed, pride of class and status, and a host of other vices substitute the creature for the deity. And in Africa idolatry has included among other things the ancestral cult which draws men in dependence and obedience to the creature rather than the Creator.

What has taken place in Africa is by no means unique. It is in fact representative of what has taken place among all men, in all places, in all ages, apart from the grace of God revealed in the Word of God. In the Gospel of Jesus Christ we are invited to draw near to the Creator through the Son in living obedience and fellowship.

> Therefore, remember, that formerly you, the Gentiles in the flesh...were at that time separate from Christ, excluded from the commonwealth of Israel, strangers to the covenants of promise, having no hope and without God in the world. But now in Christ Jesus you who formerly were far off have been brought near by the blood of Christ (Eph. 2:11-13).

We concur with Idowu that many Africans like the Akamba make a distinction between the Supreme Being and ancestors. Akamba theology recognizes the pre- eminence of the Creator God. But in daily life the relationship between the Akamba and their ancestors frequently verges on idolatry. Idowu writes,

> Our conclusion is that while technically Africans do not put their ancestors, as ancestors, on the same footing with Deity or the divinities, there is no doubt that the ancestors receive veneration that may become so intense as to verge on worship or even become worship (Idowu 1973:186)

Moreover, traditional African worship of the Supreme Being is idolatrous for it is utilitarian, anthropocentric and mingled with the veneration or worship of the ancestral spirits. We concur with Adeyemo who writes,

> In the New Testament, both Jesus Christ and His apostles taught and demonstrated that only God is to be worshipped...Any attempt to worship anyone else besides the tri-une God is a perversion of truth. This is Satan's avid effort to secure for himself what belongs properly to God alone (Matt. 4:9)... Undue deference paid to men verges at times on worship and this is resisted by the disciples (Acts 10:25,26; 14:11-14)...Explicit commands are given in the Bible not to worship any other, be it celestial body, natural phenomena, or ancestors, except the Living God (Exod. 20:3; Deut. 4:14-20; Job 31:24-28; Col. 2:18). In the light of this sharp distinction, this writer understands worship in the traditional religion as idolatry with the best commentary in Romans 1:21-25 and I Corinthians 8:1-7.

In one way or another the traditional African through his traditional religion removed God from practical pre-eminence in his life and worshipped and served the creature rather than the Creator. In this the traditional African stands in solidarity with the whole human race.

REVIEW QUESTIONS FOR CHAPTER 17

1. Name the two main errors in African traditional belief and practice concerning the Supreme Being.
2. Discuss the evidence presented which illustrates the statement that God has been removed from the centre of the African life.
3. Is idolatry only the worship of images? What is idolatry according to the Scripture?
4. According to the Scripture, are all peoples idolatrous or not? Explain. Do Christians face the danger of idolatry? How?
5. Discuss the evidence presented which illustrates the statement that not only has God been removed from the centre of the African life, but that idolatry is practiced in Africa.

Suggested Reading and Thought Questions for Advanced Study:

Kato, Byang. *Theological Pitfalls in Africa*, 1975, pp.27-46.
McVeigh, Malcolm J. *God in Africa*, 1974.
Smith, Edwin ed. *African Ideas of God*, 1966.
     pp.36-58, "Peoples of Malawi" by T. Cullen Young.
     pp.135-161, "Ovambo in Namibia" by G.W. Dymond.
     pp.162-179, "Ngombe of Zaire" by J. Davidson.
     pp.180-200, "Peoples of Burundi" by Rosemary Guillebaud.
     pp.224-240, "Yoruba and Ewe of West Africa" by E.G. Parrinder.
     pp.241-259, "Akan of Ghana" by H. St John T. Evans.
     pp.277-297, "Mende of Sierra Leone" by W.T. Harris.

Study the topic of idolatry, using standard evangelical reference books. See the suggested reference books found in chapter 12.

1. Study your own people's traditional religion, either through books or in field research. To what extent do you agree or disagree with the main thesis presented in this chapter, that ATR has removed God from the centre of life and elevated some "idol" in God's rightful place of pre-eminence? In your answer use both ethnographic material and biblical teaching to support your thesis.

2. The Old Testament condemnation of idolatry usually focuses on the worship of images. Discussion of idolatry in Africa usually focuses on divinities and ancestors. Discuss the biblical teaching of idolatry and explain how all peoples everywhere (whether they believe in ancestors, divinities or image- idols or not) in fact fall into the temptation of idolatry.

3. There is a sharp reaction by African scholars against the former consensus that God in Africa was remote and distant, "a high god." (eg. Idowu 1973:140-148; Mbiti 1970:12-18). Compare their comments with several ethnographic presentations found in Edwin Smith's book, *African Ideas of God*, 1966.

Discuss the factors which you must consider when evaluating the opinions of various authors. How can we arrive at a knowledge of the truth concerning African traditional belief in God?

4. The Bible teaches that the sovereign Lord causes even the wrath of men to praise Him (Ps. 76:10). Describe how God has been pleased to use even the errors of ATR to bring men to a personal trust in Jesus Christ.

PART FIVE

CONCLUDING OBSERVATIONS

Chapter 18

THE RELATIONSHIP OF BIBLICAL CHRISTIANITY TO AFRICAN TRADITIONAL RELIGION

In recent years there has been a great surge of interest in the field of interpreting the world religions and their relationship to the Christian faith. Down through the Christian centuries there have been a variety of ways in which Christianity has been interpreted in its relationship to other religions. Categorizations usually tend to be simplistic, ignoring the small differences and shades of interpretations of different scholars. In many ways there is a continuum, a series of theological viewpoints as in a line, stretching from those who emphasize an extreme form of exclusivism (that God has not granted revelation to other peoples and nations, but only to the prophets and apostles of Judaeo-Christian faith) to an extreme form of pluralism which sees all religions as adequate revelations from God by which men may be saved.

However, for our purposes we shall reduce this wide range of interpretations to three in number: those scholars who stress the *continuity* between Christianity and other religions, those who emphasize *discontinuity* and those who teach *a biblical continuity-discontinuity*. Within each of these categories there is great variety. Unanimity does not prevail. But in general they are united by focusing either on continuity between other religions and Christianity, discontinuity or by emphasizing a biblical continuity-discontinuity.

CONTINUITY

Throughout most of Church history, *continuity* between Christianity and world religions has *not* been the emphasis. The goal of missions was to preach the Gospel, call people to repent, baptize converts, build churches and extend the lordship of Christ over the peoples of the world. The Christian church taught the uniqueness of Jesus Christ and the uniqueness of biblical revelation. The emphasis was more on discontinuity than on continuity.

However, with the development of humanism in the 15th and 16th centuries, followed then by the Enlightenment, and with the development of evolutionary theories in the 19th and 20th centuries, absolutism was replaced by relativism. A tolerance was developed, rooted in skepticism. Having lost faith in the exclusive claims of Christ and the Bible, these individuals began to stress continuity between the world religions and Christianity.

Furthermore, with the development of a global village with an increasing cross fertilization between peoples, cultures and religions of the world, there is a growing attempt to understand one another with sympathy and mutual respect. Under these conditions and with a loss of conviction in the final authority of Scripture, there is a deluge of scholars and their writings who stress continuity.

A wide range of individuals today stress continuity between Christianity and world religions. They range from humanists to liberal Protestants and Roman Catholics. Indeed, they represent the majority of those scholars writing on the subject today. They do not deny differences between Christianity and the religions. They may not even deny the revelatory character of Christianity or the centrality of Christ. But for one reason or another they believe that the relationship with world religions is best characterized by continuity.

Some teach that every religion says basically the same thing. All religions deal with ultimate reality. Others teach that world religions are all a manifestation of the Divine Life and that they represent the religious development of the human race, with Christianity at the apex of the evolution of religion. Many theologians believe that world religions are preparatory for and lead to the Christian faith. Others believe that Christianity shares with all other religions something of divine revelation and man's response to that revelation. Some emphasize the relative value of each religion for each adherent. And still others admit that while there are serious differences between world religions, they all stand side by side in their practical religious experience. Let us examine some of these opinions.

Historians and Philosophers

Hegal. The view taught by Hegal was that Christianity is the flower of the Divine Spirit, the ultimate manifestation of the Spirit of God unfolding Himself. In various ways God has in various parts of the globe disclosed Himself in different ways. In this universal process of the unfolding of the Spirit within the human race, there is gradual assent in humanity's perception of the Spirit. Christianity is the crown of this manifestation of the Spirit. While this older view of Hegal relativized Christianity (stating that qualitatively Christianity is no different from other religions), it maintained the superiority of Christianity. Other religions contained truth but Christianity had succeeded in achieving the highest and best formulation of that truth.

Ernst Troeltsch. Ernst Troeltsch claims that all religions are expressions of the religious consciousness of differing cultures and civilizations. Christianity is the way God and his revelation has been received by much of the western world. It is the manifestation of the Divine Life in man in certain western cultures. Troeltsch claims, "We cannot live without a religion, yet the only religion that we can endure is Christianity, for Christianity has grown up with us and has become part of our very being." (Troeltsch 1980:25)

Yet other people have grown up with different religions which they themselves cannot forsake for similar reasons. These world religions do for them what Christianity does for us. All religions are mere expressions of the religious consciousness of different cultures. The Divine Life is experienced by people in different ways. Differences in world religions are due to the individual differences in race and culture.

But Troeltsch distinguishes between higher religions and lower religions. It is probable, he claims, that the various civilizations and higher cultures with their own individual religions will remain distinct. We can all learn from one another in our contacts with one another.

> The heathen races, on the other hand, are being morally and spiritually disintegrated by the contact with European civilization; hence they demand a substitute from the higher religion and culture. We have a missionary duty towards these races, and ours is likely to meet with a success amongst them (1980:27).

Thus it would appear that for unstated reasons Troeltsch has determined that all "higher religions" are of the same essence and to be tolerated, while the "lower religions" should be replaced by "higher religion" through missionary enterprise. Exactly, what his criteria is which determines higher and lower religions, he does not say. And why he thinks one should be treated differently from the other, he does not explain.

Troeltsch thus emphasizes continuity and relativity, with his peculiar distinction between higher and lower religions. All religions must renounce self-will and the tendency to dominate. We all can learn from one another. All religions are expressions of the spiritual life within each given culture and civilization.

Arnold Toynbee. Arnold Toynbee believes that "God has revealed Himself to some extent in each religion." Therefore, Christianity must purge itself of the traditional belief that Christianity is unique. To teach that Christianity is unique is to teach selfishness and pride. What Christians must do is to maintain their own beliefs while recognizing, "in some measure, all the higher religions are also revelations of what is true and right. They also come from God and each presents some facet of God's truth." (1957:100) Thus there is continuity between Christianity and other religions because God has revealed Himself in some measure to each. They are all positively related.

Once again we find this world historian distinguishing between higher and lower religions. For Toynbee, all higher religions must unite together in a crusade against "collective self-worship," "the worship of collective human power, armed with weapons." By this he means primarily Fascism, Nazism and Communism which uses modern technology to enforce the worship of collective human power. But he includes with these "isms" "primitive religion" which he says focuses on Man. Man worship is found in both "primitive religion" and in collective human power with secular states.

Thus Toynbee sees affinity and continuity between the higher religions which enables them to join together to fight their common foe. "Primitive Religion" appears to be of a different kind and ought to be replaced.

Wilfred Cantwell Smith. Smith, the historian, does not believe there is a unity in the religions of the world, for they are exceedingly complex and diverse. In order to understand the adherents of other religions we must understand people with sympathy and imaginative perception. Religion is more than doctrine and practice. We cannot truly understand religions by observing externally and objectively their beliefs and behaviour. We must understand the consciousness of religious people who are participating in their religion in time and space.

> The question of their truth or falsity must be set forth in more historical terms...They can be seen as less or more true in the sense of enabling those who looked at life and the universe through their patterns to perceive smaller or larger, less important or more important, areas of reality, to formulate and to ponder less or more significant issues, to act less or more truly, less or more truly to be (1981:94).

Thus we do not judge by external theological standards. There is no external criteria by which we ascertain truth and error. Instead, we understand the meaning and significance of a man's beliefs and practices by seeing things through his own eyes. For instance, we cannot conclude that a Hindu is an idolater who bows down to wood and stone. Objectively, this may be correct. But this is ignoring his own perception, his own consciousness of what he is doing.

The accent of Smith is on continuity and relativity. For he believes that God has spoken through many diverse means through the centuries. Each person has a faith that is particular and personal, understood best as the participation in the on-going historical process. Faith has different forms and by these different faiths people are saved from self-destruction and alienation.

Liberal Christian Theologians

There is considerable difference between the historians and philosophers we have considered and the liberal Christian theologians we shall now consider. For these Christian theologians generally see Christ as the crystal clear revelation of God who is the measure of all truth. For many there is a finality in the Gospel of one sort or another. However, they also emphasize continuity. Instead of confrontation and exclusivism, these liberal theologians emphasize inclusivism. In every way they seek to avoid confrontation with world religions. Moreover, the philosophical approach of Toynbee, Troeltsch, and Hegal form the background and foundation for the interpretation of liberal theologians. This liberal trend toward continuity is found both within the Roman Catholic Church and the Protestant main line denominations.

Vatican Council II, 1963-1965, is a watershed in the Roman Church. There we find many of the seeds which have blossomed in the post Vatican II era. The older Roman Catholic Church taught "no salvation outside the church." Vatican II signaled a change from this ecclesiastical exclusivism to an inclusivism which finds continuity and hope in other religions. (see Flannery: 1975) Preceding Vatican Council II the Protestants also began switching from discontinuity to continuity. Instead of teaching "Christ the only way of salvation," they have begun finding hope in other religions. In many ways the liberal Roman Catholics and liberal Protestants feed one another with this surge toward inclusivism.

Karl Rahner. Karl Rahner is the major Roman Catholic proponent of continuity since Vatican II. On the one hand, he believes that Christianity is the absolute religion for all men and he cannot recognize any other religion beside itself as of equal right. On the other hand, he believes that,

Until the moment when the Gospel really enters into the historical situation of an individual, a non-Christian religion (even outside the Mosaic religion) does not merely contain elements of a natural knowledge of God, elements, moreover, mixed up with human depravity which is the result of original sin and later aberrations. It contains also supernatural elements arising out of the grace which is given to men as a gratuitous gift [freely] on account of Christ. For this reason a non-Christian religion can be recognized as a LAWFUL religion (although only in different degrees) without thereby denying the error and depravity contained in it... (Rahner 1980:61).

Thus Rahner believes that "the supernatural elements" in world religions, the gratuitous gifts of Christ even though mixed with error, can enable these world religions to be God's way of salvation. So that adherents of these religions are in fact "anonymous Christians."

We find in various other Roman Catholics a similar emphasis on continuity (Schlette 1966; Hillman 1968). In fact a large number of Roman Catholics have an optimistic view of human nature and find in Christianity a fulfillment of the world religions. These world religions are not so much wicked revolt against God but "factual incompleteness." Schlette concludes his study with these words, "If general sacred history can and must be held to be positively willed by God, then non-Christian religions also have to be considered to be willed and sanctioned by God." Thus the social structures represented by the various religions "represent a historically tangible expression of God's universal salvific will." (1966:78) Non-Christian religions form the "ordinary way of salvation."

John Mbiti. Mbiti is a scholar holding to such a view of continuity.

The old nonsense of looking at African background as devilish, and fit only to be swept away by Euro-American civilization, is or should be gone by now. African religious background is not a rotten heap of superstitions, taboos and magic; it has a great deal of value to it. On this valuable heritage, Christianity should adapt itself and not be dependent exclusively on imported goods (McGavran 1972:147).

Mbiti goes on to say that ATR should be considered a preparation for the Gospel. Traditional Religion is fulfilled in Christianity. While ATR can only listen to the New Testament in silence with a spirit of learning, Mbiti contends that "in the area of the Old Testament a certain amount of give- and-take or mutual enlightenment can be carried out." (McGavran 1972:152)

Bolaji Idowu. Bolaji Idowu also stands in solidarity with those who stress continuity between ATR and Christianity. He teaches that all worship is valid before God, that the impulse to worship comes from God and thus the resulting practice of worship is Yahweh's (Kato 1975:96, 97).

Idowu's basic premise is that there is only one God who reveals Himself in different ways to all races and creeds. This one God reveals Himself "in the way which each understands." All religions are, therefore, the result of God's loving activity among all the peoples of the world.

... surely, God is One, not many; and that to the one God belongs the earth and all its fullness. It is this God, therefore, Who reveals Himself to every people on earth and

According to Idowu's understanding, the supersensible world eludes our human ability to comprehend it, even though man feels a compulsive need to understand it. As feeble and poor as our minds may be, we can only search out the ultimate reality as best we can. Our ability to comprehend spiritual reality varies.

It is to each according to his own ability. To the reflective, contemplative or speculative, the method of abstraction may lead to the goal of spiritual satisfaction. But they are a minority. To the remaining majority, fundamental truths can only be grasped when they are presented in descriptive patterns —in pictures; in something concrete, at least palpable... (Idowu 1962:65)

Hence, *Each With His Own Brush,* may describe the various religions of the world, each one portraying to others what they themselves have apprehended of the supersensible. What has been described as polytheism in West Africa, Idowu would describe as "Implicit Monotheism" or "Diffused Monotheism." What others have called crude and absurd images are for Idowu mere symbols of ultimate reality, reflecting divine revelation to a given people in a given time and culture. The many gods have become concrete concepts of the one eternal God.

Thus, according to Idowu, we find in ATR and other world religions a continuity with Christianity for the only true and living God has disclosed Himself to all peoples in diverse ways.

This sentiment of continuity was expressed over a generation ago when W.C. Willoughby gave this warning.

One of the dangers that threatens Africa is that Africans may come to regard Christianity as a white-man's religion. It is of paramount importance, therefore, that the religion of Jesus should be presented to them as the full expression that for which their fathers groped (Willoughby 1928:xx).

Thus we find in Africa the stress on continuity, finding in African Traditional Religion elements of truth, practical evidence that the Eternal Logos has been lighting the peoples of the world. They do not deny that error may exist in ATR. No one who holds to continuity denies the existence of evil in the various world religions. But the emphasis is on finding truth, not error. The relationship is positive, not negative. The relationship of ATR to Christianity is that of law and grace. Just as the law prepared people for the grace of Christ manifest in the New Testament, so ATR has prepared men and women to embrace Jesus Christ.

Conclusion

There are various aspects of truth in this emphasis on continuity which we shall mention later. But here we observe some of the serious problems.

First, the Scriptures simply do not stress the positive relationship between biblical faith and other religions. While the Bible recognizes the witness of God among the non-Christians through revelation in nature and conscience, the response of mankind is disobedience and rebellion against God.

Even those proponents of continuity recognize that the biblical emphasis is not on continuity. Schlette acknowledges that the interpretation of Scripture played a major role in causing Christians to pass a negative judgment on non-Christian religions (Schlette 1966:25). The fact is that only by taking verses from their context and reading into the Scripture that which is not plainly taught, ignoring the analogy of Scripture, can come up with anything that resembles the emphases these days on continuity.

Second, converts from non-Christian religions do not recognize that their old religion prepared them for Christianity. Nor do the adherents of other religions acknowledge that their religions are a preparation for conversion to Christianity. Adherents of other religions and Christian converts from those religions see discontinuity, not continuity.

The third fundamental problem with the school of thought emphasizing continuity is that this extreme emphasis on continuity is contrary to the orthodoxy of the historic Christian church. The theology of continuity is rooted in the skepticism of the modern era since the Enlightenment and is fostered by those who deny the uniqueness of Christ and biblical revelation.

DISCONTINUITY

As a result of the extreme form of continuity which prevailed in the early part of the 20th century, a reaction set in led by Karl Barth. Barth and the Neo Orthodox strongly reacted to the Hegalian notion of evolution in religion with Christianity being the most perfect religion. The Barthians taught that Jesus Christ is the sole criterion by which we can judge all religions.

Karl Barth

Karl Barth fathered the dialectical renewal of European theology. He taught "The Revelation of God as the Abolition of Religion" (*Church Dogmatics*, Vol.I,Part 2,Section 17). He contended that "religion is unbelief." All of man's religion is vain, even at man's best. For in religion man seeks after God, rather than God seeking men. Man talks to God, rather than God revealing Himself to men. The religious man gropes after God. Man's attempts in religion are all futile. In fact, no religion is true. Even the so-called elements of truth are a lie. Human religion is mere resistance to divine revelation.

Revelation is all by grace. Revelation is God's gracious self-offering. And revelation does not link up with human religion. Revelation contradicts religion and displaces it. Revelation presupposes that man is unable to help himself. Because human nature is unrighteous, it leads to damnation.

> Jesus Christ does not fill out and improve all the different attempts of man to think of God and to represent him according to his own standard. But as the self-offering and self-manifestation of God he replaces and completely outbids those attempts, putting them in the shadows to which they belong (Barth 1980:40).

Hendrik Kraemer

As the continental movement of dialectical theologians gained influence, Hendrik Kraemer wrote a classic, entitled, *The Christian Message in a Non-Christian World* (1963). In this book he contended that Christianity was unique, "absolutely *sui generis*." There could be no continuity between the religions and Christianity. For Christianity is not the story of man's pilgrimage toward God, but a record of God's sovereign acts of grace in redeeming mankind.

> Theologically speaking, 'nature,' 'reason' and 'history' do not, if we want to think stringently, afford preambles [an introductory portion], avenues or lines of development towards the realm of grace and truth as manifest in Jesus Christ. There are, to be sure, longings and apperceptions [clear understanding] in the religious life of mankind outside the sphere of the Christian revelation, of which Christ, what He is and has brought, may be termed in a certain sense the fulfillment. Yet, it is mistaken and misleading to describe the religious pilgrimage of mankind as a preparation or a leading up to a so-called consummation or fulfillment in Christ (International Missionary Council 1938:2,3).

Kraemer did not deny the presence of values in other religions or the longings on the part of the non-Christians. But Kraemer denied that these longings or apprehensions, though "*in a certain sense*" fulfilled in Christ, are simply perfected in Him. These values must be radically recast. And the longings frequently turn out to be blind and misdirected.

Christ becomes "the crisis of all religions." "...God as He is revealed in Jesus Christ is *contrary* to the sublimest pictures we made of Him before we knew of Him in Jesus Christ." (IMC 1939:4) If we accept the value of reconciliation, then the core of the Gospel is that "mankind in its totality is in a state of hostility towards God as *He really is*."

The fundamental discontinuity between non-Christian religions and Christianity excludes the possibility of natural theology, if by natural theology is meant an imperfection of the perfect revelation we find in the Gospel. This does not deny the truth that God has been working among men and women.

> Yet to represent the religions of the world as somehow, however imperfect and crude it may be, a ...schoolmaster to Christ, is a distorted presentation of these religions and their fundamental structure and tendencies, and a misunderstanding of the Christian revelation.

> Only an attentive study of the Bible can open the eyes to the fact that Christ 'the power of God' and 'the wisdom of God' stands in contradiction to the power and the wisdom of man (IMC 1938:5).

Conclusion

Thus the Barthians reacted against the theological liberals and turned the tables for three decades. Discontinuity between non-Christian religions and Christianity became the accent, instead of continuity.

BIBLICAL CONTINUITY-DISCONTINUITY

It would appear to us that biblically speaking, there is in fact a measure of continuity between ATR and Christianity which is ignored or down-played by the Barthians. But it would also appear to us that the discontinuity between ATR and Christianity is so great that we cannot truly speak of mere continuity between the two. We can only speak of a Biblical Continuity-Discontinuity. For unless we hold to the two aspects, we shall fall into an imbalance. Lack of balance leading to distortion of the full biblical emphasis is the root of all heresy.

A Biblical Discontinuity

The relationship between ATR and Christianity is not merely one of imperfection-and-perfection. Nor is it merely one of promise-and-fulfillment. We have seen that in so many ways Christianity is compatible with ATR. That is, biblical revelation completes that which is vaguely perceived, it corrects that which was partly understood though with distortion. But for us to reduce the relationship between ATR and Christianity as merely one of continuity, we are misrepresenting both ATR and biblical revelation.

1. THE THEOLOGICAL EMPHASES OF ATR AND CHRISTIANITY DIFFER.

a. ATR Focuses On Man While Biblical Revelation Focuses On God.

ATR is anthropocentric. The basic feature of ATR is "that it tries to make the divine powers an instrument of man's personal welfare." By performing his rites, his aim is to compel them into his service. The Alpha and Omega of a pagan's religious action and prayer is, "My will be done." (Westermann 1937:75)

An African church leader writes, "...the African peoples do not seek God for His own sake. They seek Him in worship for what they can get out of Him. Mbiti has rightly described their objective as utilitarian. It is a means to exploit rather than veneration." (Adeyemo 1979:47)

In sharp contrast, biblical revelation is theocentric, centring on God. Kraemer writes,

> In calling the Bible a radically Theocentric book, we simply mean to say that the Bible takes in a radically serious fashion, the fact that God is God, that He is the Absolute Sovereign and the only rightful Lord, with all the consequences that are implied herein for the world, human life and the position of man (Kraemer 1963:63).

The eternal and living God and His will for mankind is the essence of the biblical message. God is not only the origin of man, but He is the ultimate goal and purpose of man's life. "The chief end of man is to glorify *GOD* and to enjoy *HIM* forever." The whole Bible is the revelation of how God created man for Himself, how man rebelled against God, and how God is seeking to restore that unique and exclusive relationship with man. For the Christian, God's will and kingdom are supreme. His goal in life must be to "seek first the kingdom of God and His righteousness." His prayer must be, "Thy will be done."

This contrast between being anthropocentric and being theocentric is not a minor difference. It strikes at the very heart of ATR and the Christian faith. The central concerns of ATR and Christianity are poles apart. We cannot speak of this as continuity.

b. ATR Belief In Man And Sin Contrasts With Christianity.

Scripture teaches that man was made in the image of God and for His glory and fellowship. But through disobedience to God, man became separated from Him. The judgment of God which came upon man because of His sin is death.

To some people, this belief, that man is created in the image of God and yet is totally depraved, may seem like a contradiction. Biblical revelation provides the highest view of man found anywhere in the world religions. At the same time the Bible presents man as totally depraved. Because of the sin of Adam and Eve, the whole human race has become utterly sinful (Rom. 5:12-21).

The evil in man is not some general sickness. Scripture is clear in showing that man's basic problem is transgression of the law of God and rebellion against Him (I Jn. 3:4). Whereas, evil in ATR is basically that which conflicts with the interests of the community and the traditions of the past, sin in Scripture is always related to God. Sin is sin because it is contrary to the will of God and contrary to His very nature.

ATR takes a very different turn. Some Africans do speak of an original proximity between God and man followed by a separation. But few if any understand the real nature of the sin problem. ATR does not teach that sin is rebellion against God or the transgression of God's law. Instead, the traditional way of life is the best life which has been given by the ancestral spirits, the divinities and by God Himself. There is no understanding of a spiritual new birth, a need to grow and progress in the knowledge of God. Since the status quo is the best life, man's primary concern is material prosperity and prestige.

c. ATR Understanding Of Salvation Contrasts With The Gospel.

In biblical terms, salvation is the deliverance or release *from* sin and all its effects, *unto* a new life which is eternal in nature and duration. Salvation is unique in biblical revelation in two ways.

Salvation is past, present and future. Some religions stress entirely the present. In ATR the stress is upon a good life here and now. But the Christian faith focuses on the past, present and future aspects of our salvation. In the *past* when we first trusted Christ as our Saviour, He saved us from the penalty of sin (Rom. 8:1). In the *present*, while trusting in Christ, He is delivering us from the power of sin in our lives through sanctification by the Holy Spirit. And in the *future* we shall be saved from the very presence of sin when our bodies shall be changed and we shall be like Him (Rom. 8:23; I Jn. 3:1-3). More than that, God even now provides us with all things to enjoy (Ps. 16:11; I Tim. 6:17).

This salvation is by grace through faith alone. All other religions, including some Christian churches, emphasize human effort, good works, personal merit, keeping the commandments, obeying God and controlling the flesh in order to merit salvation. ATR is no exception.

Adeyemo points out that since ATR reduces sin to anti-social acts, the traditional concept of salvation is also in error.

> If an anti-social act is all there is to sin, salvation from sin would be in the same terms. Thus, it is plain in the oral traditions that to be saved primarily means to be accepted. One is first accepted to the community of the living by being good to one's neighbours, and secondly accepted among the community of the dead ancestors by remembering them through libations, prayers and offerings. An aspect of this acceptance is the struggle for power or 'vital force.' It is believed that one who excels his equals has been specially favoured by the ancestors and such an honour is indicative of salvation (Adeyemo 1979:93).

The good life is abundant in "vital force." A person in good health with a large and growing family, many possessions and increasing influence and power is enjoying a good life. This is the best that can be known for man. But when trouble strikes, he fears the evil influences of the unseen world. Therefore, he presents gifts, sacrifices and libations to keep away evil. A good life depends on his ability to keep on good terms with the powers that be.

The question of man's original rebellion against God and the essential, fundamental biblical doctrine of justification are foreign to their [African] considerations. Generally, the majority of African peoples claim that God punishes people and rewards them in this life. There is nothing awaiting them when they die, for sin is chiefly an offense against one's neighbour and is punishable here and now (Adeyemo 1979:70).

But biblical revelation is unique in that salvation is completely "a gift of God." The sacrifices in the Old Testament were not intended to please God through human merit. The focus of worship was both past and future: past, as a remembrance of what God had already done in Israel's history in visiting and redeeming the people of Israel from slavery in Egypt; and the future, as an expression of faith in what God would do in sending the Servant of God to die as the sacrificial Lamb (Isa. 53:6).

Nothing could be plainer in the New Testament than the nature of salvation: it is all by grace received through faith alone (Rom. 3:21-31; 6:23; Gal. 2:16; Eph. 2:8,9).

Salvation in ATR, however, is thought of in a different sense. Disruption of the status quo is the result of offended ancestral spirits or witchcraft. These evils may be removed by proper sacrifices and traditional rites. By satisfying the offended spirits, or by counteracting the powers of witchcraft with greater powers, man can restore a bountiful life with health, wealth and prestige.

d. The Relation Of Ethics And Religion Is In Sharp Contrast.

In biblical terms, ethical behaviour is rooted in God Himself. "The ethical is always in the Bible submerged in, derived from, and subordinated to, the religious..." (Kraemer 1963:63) That is, right living depends on a man's relationship with God. God establishes the standard of holiness and man through grace conforms his will to that of God. Right behaviour is rooted in God Himself. The standard of all right and wrong is God. He gives the Law and enables one to keep it. To break a commandment is to offend God. Before Him we stand guilty.

Since man is a sinner, the New Testament speaks of the new birth with the need for spiritual renewal and a change of a man's life. Jesus Christ becomes our righteousness in the judicial sense. He pronounces us righteous before God through faith. The Holy Spirit who lives within the believer gives him power to keep the commandments and live a holy life.

All this is foreign to ATR. The measure of right and wrong are the dictates of society and its traditions. There is no concept of an ideal life made possible by the divine entering into the human.

> Man, as he is, is man as the Creator intended him to be. The required life pattern for man in his society is set forth in the traditional cultural pattern which he shares...His moral horizon is never beyond his reach. His ethics are socialized ethics, sanctioned by spirit-ancestors and gods, but expressed through society and his own socialized personality (Williamson 1965:144).

To reduce the relationship between ATR and Christianity to one of imperfection and perfection is to distort everything. We cannot do justice to ATR by taking beliefs here and there from traditional religion and interpreting these in isolation to ATR as a whole. The basic thrust of ATR is in contrast to biblical revelation. Continuity is not the accent.

2. ATR IS A DEGENERATION OF BIBLICAL REVELATION.

The state of man outside of Jesus Christ is vividly portrayed in Romans 1-3. The extent of man's rebellion can best be seen in the light of the revelation given to all men and what men have done with that revelation.

In Romans 1:20, Paul teaches that two specific attributes of the Supreme Being are revealed in nature: "His *eternal power* and *divine nature*." But all non-Christian religions neglect either one or the other of these attributes, so that they in fact do not worship the true God as revealed to them in creation.

On the one hand, some world religions like ATR exalt God so highly above the world that God becomes remote and distant. He may not be inaccessible. He may be immanent in the sense that men can call upon Him in times of crisis. But communion with Him is severely restricted. God lives on the transcendent plane rather than the imminent. In this respect, they *deny the power of God* operative in their lives. We cannot say that ATR has pushed God out of daily experience and completely denied all divine power in their lives. But to a very significant extent, ATR has reduced His daily work in the lives of people.

On the other hand, some world religions *deny the divine nature* of the Supreme Being by reducing Him to an impersonal or vague force, a pervading power or influence within the universe. This not only can be illustrated by the religions of India, China and liberal theology. This can also be found in Africa. God has become so distant and remote that for some peoples the personality of God is not prominent.

In all non-Christian religions, we find man ever seeking for God and yet fleeing from Him, just as Romans 1-3 indicates. In man's religiosity, he cannot avoid some recognition of the Supreme Being. Yet in his rebellion he continually flees from Him.

Christianity, as an institutional religion, falls under the same judgment. Human nature is essentially no different, whether he is an adherent of ATR or a baptized member of a Christian church. Without genuine conversion and without a continuous work of sanctifying grace, a professing Christian will exhibit the same marks: denying the power of God in their lives. Much of western culture reflects this very thing even today. Various theologians have made God inoperative and inapproachable through their re-construction of the nature of God.

We have found in ATR much beauty and riches derived from God's common grace given to all men. But ATR is fundamentally more than a preparation for the Gospel. It is the result of man's fall away from God. As one missiologist has written,

> Heathenism is nothing else but having other gods before the only true and living God. Heathenism is nothing else but changing the glory of the incorruptible God into an image made like to corruptible man. It is the worshipping and serving the creature. It is rebellion against the Creator. That is what the Bible teaches us concerning the essence of heathenism (Bavinck 1948:101).

3. CONVERTS FROM ATR STRESS DISCONTINUITY, NOT CONTINUITY.

We not only have a theological problem. We also have a problem of one's relationship to traditional religion. Second generation Christians, like John Mbiti, simply do not see things in the same way as those converted right out of ATR. For a growing number of Africans today, their knowledge of traditional religion is not direct and intimate. They were not born in a home practicing traditional religion. They were never reared in such an environment. Nor did they practice ATR themselves. Instead, their knowledge of ATR is derived from detached observation, discussion and reading. Out of this experience is derived a more favourable impression.

Not so with the first generation Christians. From a collection of many testimonies by those saved out of traditional religion, we derive a picture that emphasizes discontinuity between the Christian faith and traditional religion. Sera from Kitui was formerly a diviner. She declared, "I am negative toward my former religion, believing that it did not prepare me to become a Christian." Today instead of giving her offerings to her ancestors, she offers them to almighty God. Lois who had been active in the *kilumi* dances and about to be chosen as a leader before her conversion, shared these thoughts. "My feelings and my attitude towards traditional religion are that it will not bring you closer to God, but will keep you away from Him all the time. It will cause you to stay in darkness while the light has come through Jesus Christ. It did you more harm than good."

Naumi observed, "I cannot see how traditional religion could have prepared me to become a Christian. All that I experienced tried to tear my life apart. If it were not for God's powerful hand I would have died." Explaining her negative thoughts, she said, "It made homes to be unhappy and without development. It made women quite inferior because we were regarded as useless things before the men. Christianity has made us feel like important human beings in the world..." Kalinda, another diviner before her conversion, stated that she hated traditional religion. If she would be given anything or everything in order to return to traditional religion, she would not agree. For she now feels free. Christ has set her free from the things which once bound her.

So many of these Christians speak of their poverty which they experienced by the constant demand of goats by their ancestors. The spirits continually troubled them, making incessant demands upon them. Because they had to give goat after goat, offering after offering, to satisfy the requests of the ancestors, they became poor. They saw in Christianity deliverance from the troublesome ancestors. Before his conversion Samson had been deeply involved in the traditional practice of communicating with the ancestors. He says, "Day and night I had to give my offerings or sacrifices to my ancestors." When he heard a pastor preaching the Word of God he decided to become a Christian. He observes, "I turned from Traditional Religion because it is the way of wasting my hens and goats and other things."

One of the great problems facing those who advocate continuity is that no practitioner of his own religion will ever acknowledge that his religion is preparatory for faith in Christ. They see discontinuity, not preparation. And those converted out of African Traditional Religion see the same. David, a converted medicine man, says that "Traditional Religion is opposed to the Christian faith for it is based on spirits of the dead, while the Christian faith is based on the living God."

Joseph, a former medicine man, portrays his feelings towards his former religious beliefs. "It is a dark cave full of poisonous snakes; a home for the worried and disabled people under the bondage of Satan. I do not have any positive feelings towards Traditional Religion because it is not one which prepared me to become a Christian."

Rev. Daidanso, reared in ATR, declares that ATR is a religion of fear. Traditional Africans, faced with numerous spirits, did not always know their will. Hence, the traditional African lived in fear that he might provoke their anger. Thus the traditional African involved himself in many taboos to protect himself from their displeasure. It may have been this fear (a negative feature of ATR, not a positive one) which led many Africans to receive Christ as their Lord and Saviour (Daidanso ma Djongwe: 1988).

Nothing that has been said should be construed to mean that these Christians do not value anything from their past traditions. Quite the contrary. There are many things which they appreciate. They recognize that the traditional belief in their "gods" with worship directed toward them enabled them to understand the biblical teaching of Jehovah. The diligence and faithfulness in traditional worship is admired. Traditional family counseling with the males being taught separate from the females is valued. Marriage arrangements were better than today, for the parents participated, resulting in few divorces and broken marriages. The old men were respected. Any older person was empowered to discipline a child who was misbehaving. There was strong discipline among the people which was helpful.

But the plain fact is that they do not "feel" positive toward their traditional religion as a whole, nor do they consider it preparatory for their Christian faith. The most one can hear is the statement by Noah. "I believe that Traditional Religion helped me to some extent to become Christian. Some of the basic aspects taught in Traditional Religion such as the requirements of young people are also taught in Christianity."

As theologians we acknowledge that there is an element of continuity between traditional religion and Christianity. General revelation in nature and conscience brought these peoples to some basic conclusions which prepared them to hear the Gospel (Acts 14:17; 17:23). It is essential for the health of the church that we acknowledge God's work of grace among the peoples, preparing them to hear and believe the Gospel. There were certain virtues and values treasured in the past which are passing away these days under the impact of westernization. The religiosity of African Traditional Religion, permeating every area of their lives, is something which should be sanctified and transformed into a deeply, pervasive Christian faith and life of obedience. We may praise God that due to His prevenient grace there are significant elements within traditional culture which can and should be preserved within Christianity so that African Christianity will be distinctive and unique, truly Christian and truly African.

Therefore, the Kingdom strategy of "standing firm against the schemes of the devil" will incorporate many of the virtues and values in traditional culture which are compatible with the Gospel. These distinctively African cultural traits form the bedrock of what will become African Christianity. The process of "Africanizing Christianity" is the careful selection of those traditional practices which reflect the grace of God in the pre- Christian culture. We agree with Mbiti when he rejects that perspective which sees African Traditional Religion only as "a rotten heap of superstitions, taboos and magic." We agree that there is "a great deal of value in it."

At the same time, the Bible teaches and African converts from Traditional Religion testify that there is a basic discontinuity between the two. As Kabuba said, a former practitioner of traditional religion and now a born again Christian,

> Biblically, there was no benefit to worship our traditional gods. The God of Israel commanded that we should not have any other god besides Him. Visiting the diviner or any other person who communicates with spirits is idolatry. We should bear in our minds that Christ's power has defeated that one of African Traditional Religion.

Nathan gave his testimony. "The influence which led me to accept Christ was that I saw how the Christian men living with me maintained such good behavior, not being troubled by the evil spirits. That led me to receive Christ as my personal Saviour." With such experiences they focus on the discontinuity. They even have difficulty comprehending how Traditional Religion prepared them for Christ. For these converts the need for a total break with the past is evident. There needs to be a turning away from their Traditional Religion.

4. CHRISTIANITY IS *NOT* A FULFILLMENT OF ATR.

We shall demonstrate shortly that there is a certain measure of continuity between ATR and Christianity. But it is not the kind and measure of continuity so often stressed. In trying to support their view, these proponents of continuity refer to various proof texts which they lift out of the biblical contexts in order to serve their own purposes. Does Scripture support those who say that Traditional Religion is fulfilled in Christ? Let us examine some classic passages.

Matthew 5:17. "I did not come to abolish, but to fulfill."

A fair understanding of this phrase is governed by the context. This has direct relationship to the Law of Moses and the prophets of Israel. The phrase, "the Law and the Prophets," was frequently used to refer to the whole Jewish sacred canon of writings (see Mt. 7:12; 22:40; Lk. 16:16; Acts 13:15).

Christ did not come to destroy those writings in the sense of abolishing them. He came to fulfill them. This probably refers both to the ceremonial and moral aspects of the Old Testament Scriptures. In Christ's life, He fully obeyed all the commandments. More than that, He fulfilled in His person all the prophetic types. In this particular context, the emphasis is upon the moral teachings which He filled out, expanded and to which He gave a deeper and more spiritual meaning. The passage immediately following is a case in point in which Christ enriched the Old Testament law with a deeper and more spiritual meaning.

The whole emphasis of this text, however, is upon the Law of Moses and the prophets of Israel. No other religion of any kind is in mind here. Israel held a unique position in salvation history which is unparalleled anywhere (cf. Rom. 9:3-5; 10:4; Gal. 3:13). The older covenant has a relationship with the new covenant that is unique and unparalleled. We cannot quote this reference and apply it to ATR. The context will not allow it.

Colossians 1:16. "For in Him all things were created, both in the heavens and on earth, visible and invisible, whether thrones or dominions or rulers or authorities – all things have been created through Him and for Him."

This text is often quoted to show that all of man's experiences with other spiritual beings may be included in Christianity. Since Christ is the Creator of all invisible powers, we are told, they may be included in the Christian faith.

But this text teaches the very opposite. The Epistle was written to deal with compromise within the church. Christ was lowered and angels were elevated. This seems to reflect syncretistic tendencies which later developed fully in the second century.

To reject this false teaching, the Apostle teaches us that Christ is pre- eminent (1:15,18). The worship of other spiritual beings is forbidden (2:18). The text in question (1:16), is only introduced for the purpose of explaining the final source of Christ's power over all these spirits. He is pre- eminent because He created them (see Jn. 1:1-14). This text cannot be used to support the inclusion of ancestors, spirits or divinities into Christianity. To do so is to be dishonest with the text.

Acts 17:16-34. This text is more complex and requires more detailed attention. The point at issue is Paul's reference to "An Unknown God," worshipped by the Athenians. Paul writes, "What therefore you worship in ignorance, this I proclaim to you." (17:23) Exactly, how is the "Unknown God" related to the God and Father of our Lord Jesus Christ? Is it a relationship of promise and fulfillment? Is it a relationship of imperfection and perfection? The Athenians knew something of God. Did they simply need more education, more instruction and more information? Did Paul merely add further light to the little light which the Athenians already had?

On the whole, Paul is quite negative towards other religions throughout his writings (see I Cor. 10:20, 21). His initial reaction to the Athenians is no different. Athens was a beautiful city and the cradle of democracy. But Paul was not stirred by these positive thoughts. Instead, "his spirit was being provoked within him as he was beholding the city full of idols." (17:16) That is, he became upset and indignant. As Lange phrases it, he "suffered a moral shock."

As he preached in the market place concerning Jesus Christ, he was invited by some philosophers to address them at the Areopagus. Like any good speaker, he seeks a point of contact whereby he may relate his message to that which is known by the people. He chose the image erected, "To an Unknown God."

Now it is significant that this "Unknown God" was not found in the main stream of Greek religious tradition. In one sense, this altar was the lowest level of pagan belief in Athens. Benjamin Warfield comments,

> For what could be worse than the superstitious dread which, after cramming every corner of the city with altars to every conceivable divinity, was not yet satisfied, but must needs feel blindly out after still some other power of earth or air or sky to which to immolate victims or before which to cringe in unintelligent fear? (Warfield 1952:564)

Their worship of him was "in ignorance." This surely is not a compliment. This can only remind us of Jesus' own words to the woman of Samaria, "You worship that which you do not know; we worship that which we know; for salvation is from the Jews." (Jn. 4:22)

When Paul speaks of God being near them, he quotes two of the Greek poets in 17:28,29. This at first sight may seem like truth being plucked from Greek philosophy. In actual fact, Paul greatly changed the original meaning of the phrases. The Greeks believed that man is integrated into the universe which is permeated by the divine spirit. By "the divine element", the Greeks meant a universal divine reason which is impersonal. But Paul takes these quotes and imbues them with a radically new meaning. He speaks of a personal relationship with God, a concept wholly alien to the Greeks. What may appear as approval, turns out to be conversion, changing the very meaning of the quotations.

Yet not all is negative. Paul finds in this image, paradoxically, "the least degraded expression of the religious aspirations of the Athenians." There was no specific degrading content associated with the altar "To the Unknown God." Paul recognized and acknowledged a reality and value of religion among the heathen. "Enshrined within his general condemnation of the heathenism of the Athenians there lies thus a recognition of something not to be condemned — something worthy of religion." (Warfield 1952:564) Man is endowed with an inescapable sense of dependence and this truth is reflected in man's religiosity. Paul uses an aspect of their religion as a basis for an appeal to them.

Paul introduced his message with the observation, "I observe that you are very religious in all respects." Though the Greek word for "religious" is translated in the Authorized Version, "superstitious," it means nothing but "divinity-fearing." Though it can be used in a negative sense to mean superstitious, it is frequently used in the good sense. In this introductory remark, Paul is not setting off on the wrong foot, condemning them for superstition. He is simply recognizing a religious disposition. The term is non-committal in character since it does not really say, "God-fearing." Though not an outright commendation, neither is it a condemnation. In the words of Warfield, Paul chose a word "by which he expresses at least no active disapproval and even a certain measure of active approval. Paul, in fine, commends the religiousness of the Athenians." (Warfield 1952:564)

In this passage we find a "certain recognition to the religion of the heathen." But Warfield stresses that it is not a recognition but "a *certain* recognition." "The heathen religions are uniformly treated as degrading to man and insulting to God...Nevertheless, alongside of and in the very midst of this sweeping and unmitigated condemnation of the total religious manifestation of heathendom, there exists an equally constant and distinct recognition of the reality and value of religion even among the heathen." (Warfield 1952:565)

Yet we need to be careful of overstating this positive element. Nowhere does Paul suggest that if the religion of the Athenians would be left alone it would blossom into an acceptable way of life. Nor does he suggest that by adding some new truths to their already basic knowledge they would arrive at a true knowledge of God. Paul's word of application is this: "God is declaring to men that all everywhere should repent" because of the day of judgment coming (17:30, 31). Some did believe and joined him.

The implications of this sermon are clear. Conversion to Christ is necessary to be saved from the last judgment. "It is clear, that the relation between the worship of the unknown god and the worship of the Father of Christ is not that of fragment and fullness. Luke rather dialectically states: 'What you have worshipped in ignorance, that we proclaim unto you.'" (Wille 1970:2)

A Biblical Continuity

This author is neither satisfied with the proponents of continuity nor discontinuity. There is truth in both which must be maintained in biblical balance.

On the one hand, there is radical discontinuity between ATR and biblical faith. Man by his sinful nature is in rebellion against God and fleeing from God. Man in his culture and religion has sought to deify man and remove God from His rightful pre-eminence. Repentance and conversion are required. This is biblical truth.

On the other hand, the discontinuity is not so radical that the Gospel is preached in a vacuum. Despite man's rebellion, God in His grace pursues men and women, seeking them out and disclosing something of Himself and His will for them. Thus there is a measure of continuity.

1. Christian Faith is a Fulfillment of Mankind's Desires.

Though the Gospel is not a fulfillment of ATR in the same sense that the Old Testament was, the Gospel does fulfill in a different sort of way.

Because of the nature of man, he has an inner hunger and thirst that cannot be met apart from a personal faith and trust in God through Christ. Sometimes this sense of need may be verbalized as a desire for God. Other times the sense of need may be less articulate.

Westermann says of the African what can be said of all mankind outside of

Christ, that he "suffers from a constant feeling of insecurity. Part of this needed security he derives from his social environment, the shelter of the home and the use of his own skills." But,

> man wants something more powerful to supplement his own activity in order to overcome those adversities which are beyond human aid. This craving for power is the driving force in the life of African religion. It has its origin, not in logical reflection, but in a feeling of incapacity and in an obstinate desire to overcome it...Man is weak and what he needs is increased strength. The world about him is powerful...The absorbing question for him is how to acquire some of this power so that it may serve for his own salvation or that of the group for which he is responsible (Westermann 1937:84).

Thus there is a void within the heart of men and women which cannot be satisfied with ATR. ATR may itself be a reflection of this yearning. But ATR is incapable of meeting that human need. From Scripture we know that all seeking in natural religion can only lead to disappointment. Only through personal faith in the living God can a person find rest, security and power needed for life.

Therefore, the continuity is "based on a relation of hope and fulfillment between traditional African religions and the gospel." (Wille 1970:12) The Christian faith fulfills that for which people yearn in their hearts.

2. ATR Provides Valuable Points of Contact.

While we agree that religion is unbelief, religion is more than unbelief. It reflects something of that general revelation which has filtered through man's depraved understanding. Karl Barth's denial of natural revelation resulted in his extreme view of discontinuity. While he rightly rejected the liberal's teaching on natural theology, he erroneously minimized the importance of natural revelation in the development of ATR.

The Gospel is not preached in a vacuum, to people without religious knowledge. The evangelist begins with what is already known. Paul wrote of the Gentiles, that God "did not leave Himself without a witness." (Acts 14:17) In the words of Alan Tippett,

> I believe that there are basic values and convictions in animist thought that made possible their hearing of the gospel when it was preached to them, that permitted them to understand it, and to accept it (McGavran 1972:132).

We need not be an Arminian to believe that. God and God alone by His sovereign grace enables man to understand and accept the Gospel. But the evangelist uses language that communicates. Language is a mirror reflection of any culture. There are in fact within every culture beliefs and practices which serve as bridges for the Gospel. Such beliefs as the Creator God, man as body and soul, a sense of right and wrong, belief in the supernatural, spirit world, life after death, sacrifices, ritual defilement and many other religious beliefs serve as windows into the hearts of the people.

This should not be misunderstood. We do not believe it is possible to move from partial understanding through natural revelation to a fuller understanding in the Gospel, as if we were proceeding on a continuum. Conversion, a turnabout, is required. Repentance is called for. Furthermore, we must consider

ATR as a system of belief and practice. We cannot do justice to ATR or any other religion if we consider an isolated belief or practice detached from the whole fabric of that religion. We do not become a Christian by transcending that which went before through a path of continuity.

We therefore, reject the kind of thinking expressed by A. Hetherwick a generation ago. Instead of seeing non-Christian religions as "wholly erroneous," Heatherwick enjoins missionaries to "look for elements of truth among these non-Christian faiths and to utilize them as foundation stones on which to build the fabric of truth he has come to teach." (Heatherwick 1932:100,101). The notion is expressed that just as Jesus took the five loaves and two fish from the little boy and blessed them, so we must take the fragments of truth and with the blessing of the Lord pass them back, enriched by the fuller revelation of divine truth in Christianity.

J.H. Bavinck warns against this tendency by some who "mistakenly suppose that somewhere within non-Christian religions, perhaps in a hidden nook or cranny, there lie hidden moments of truth and that it is to these that one should join his own argument." (Bavinck 1960:135) There are indeed moments of truth which point to God. God's revelation in nature and conscience is not so totally hidden or distorted that men are lost in total darkness. ATR does have positive elements as we have seen.

However we must not forget that there is a vast gulf of discontinuity that separates biblical Christianity from ATR. What may appear at first to be particles of "truth" are often encased in such wrong understanding that even the "truth" must be purged from error. As Bavinck says, the Gospel does not simply grow out of ATR as in a continuum. Because of God's special revelation to the Hebrews, written on parchment by the inspiration of the Holy Spirit, Christ could say that He came to fulfill the Old Testament law. But God's revelation through Moses and the prophets is a world apart from God's general revelation through nature and conscience which has become corrupted by sin. We cannot be fair to ATR by abstracting "moments of truth" from the whole fabric of traditional religion. The basic thrust of ATR is anthropocentric. Even worship is utilitarian and man-centred. Belief in man's soul, life after death, the necessity of sacrifices and offerings to appease the anger of God, are all part of the total fabric of ATR which is a distortion of divine truth. The Gospel cannot be said to be a fulfillment of ATR in the true sense of the word.

But having affirmed that, Karl Barth can hardly be correct when saying that mission work occurs "in a void." The very fact that communication of divine truths is possible in the vernacular language, reveals the fact that God has been working. As we have previously seen, Paul's message at the Areopagus (Acts 17) reveals that despite the great darkness and misconception on the part of the Athenians, there was within man that "semen religions," that seed of religion, which can become a bridge of communication. ATR does have positive elements which can be used as analogies in communicating the Gospel.

Let us just remind ourselves of the Akamba whom we have studied. We remember that the Akamba understanding of the Supreme Being is far from biblical. So much contradiction and mystery surrounds the essential nature of God, that scholars, including the Akamba themselves, have claimed that God is not even personal. A personal God makes no sense to the Akamba, the Akama themselves say.

Nevertheless, Linnell Davis, a retired missionary to the Akamba and himself orn in Ukambani, writes, that from his own experience, the Akamba

> concepts of God as creator, as the high One in the heavens, as being essentially good have enabled them...to readily understand the biblical concepts of God and His personality. Many Kamba friends have shown by their intimate fellowship with God and their joyful devotion to Him that there is a reality in their understanding, and that their background has not been so far removed that communication had been very difficult (Davis 1968:43).

We conclude with Bavinck, therefore, "It is...impossible to preach without ome 'contact.' No one can be reached in a vacuum." That point of contact is ound primarily within the people themselves, and secondarily, within various lements of ATR.

CONCLUSION: AN HISTORICAL PERSPECTIVE

Our contention has been that a truly biblical perspective of our subject at and will include both continuity and discontinuity with balanced emphases. No oubt evangelicals will vary in some of their insights. But an evangelical perspec- ve of the Bible cannot be either one of continuity alone or one of discontinuity 'one. We believe that a survey of what evangelicals have said throughout the past entury will support this affirmation.

During the Centenary Conference in London, 1888, many missionaries spoke n many subjects. Let us listen to their opinions. Rev. G. Mackenzie Cobban of ae Wesleyan Missionary Society in Madras declared, "Everything non- Chris- an is not of the devil. God and spiritual truth are not shut up in the Hebrew and hristian sacred books; they are outside these as well as inside." Though the elegates were uncertain how these spiritual truths entered India, "we all agreed at every fragment of spiritual truth came from God." (Johnston 1888:89)

Yet there was some disagreement over the value of other religions. Rev. Prin- pal Brown of Aberdeen commented,

> The question is not how many good beliefs these people have, for there are elements of true religion all over the world which require only to be developed in order to show that there is a spark of truth in them. But what I want to know is, Is there anything saving, anything quickening, anything elevating, anything purifying outside of Chris- tianity? My friend Mr. Swanson who has been speaking with great power today and has known China for nearly thirty years, once said to me, Say what men will, nothing lifts humanity out of the dregs and dirt into which it has been plunged in heathen lands, but the Gospel of Christ; there may certainly be a great many elements of truth, but because they want that which is saving and quickening in it, they do nothing whatever to ac- complish the great object that God has in view: there is no salvation for the human soul in them (Johnston 1888:95).

The argument was closed by this observation. When an esteemed missionary is asked, "What do you think of the condition of the heathen outside Chris- nity?" he replied, "Ask a converted heathen what he thinks of the state he was when he was an unconverted heathen, and I leave the question there." ohnston 1888:95)

During the Ecumenical Missionary Conference of 1900 in New York, simila discussions were held.

George Robson of the United Presbyterian Church of Scotland affirmed,

> Every fragment of truth imbedded in those erring and imperfect religions, every germ of spiritual insight however distorted, every motive of moral origin however misguided in operation, every yearning proper to a human heart however faint and uncertain, the Son of Man regards as part of the inheritance to be rescued, conserved, purified, and perfected in himself (Ecumenical Conference 1900:357).

Yet Robson could also state, "The actual task of the missionary implies a dea ing with men who are not simply erringly or defectively religious, but who are a tagonized by sin to true religion." (Ecumenical Conference 1900:365) Samue Macauley maintained that the true conception of non-Christian religions is thi that originally they had "more or less revealed truth in them" but gradually be came mixed with error. Rev. A.C. Dixon maintained that even as the Lord flun Satan out of heaven like lightning, so in this world "we need lightning as well a light; light for the man that is in error, and lightning for the error."

The World Missionary Conference in Edinburgh, 1910, was a landmark i missionary history. Extensive preparation was made for the document on the mi sionary message in relation to non-Christian religions. A set of questions was se to missionaries all over the world. The Report is a compilation of the answe: returned from 200 missionaries representing all the fields and most denomina tions.

This report advised that the missionary should demonstrate "sympathy towards the animist. "He should esteem the heathen's faith as a religion." H should rejoice in every element of truth and goodness found among the animist The missionary must avoid all contempt and vehement denunciation and all u bearing manners. Patience is required. "Many evil customs exist to meet great evils in the social life of the people, and it is dangerous to displace them until yo have given a substitute which they can accept intelligently." (World Missiona Conference 1910:21)

> As to the crucial question of the attitude to be taken up towards Animism, any difference of opinion that may exist is apparent rather than real. It is held by the majority that there is a modicum of truth in all religious systems, God not having left Himself without a witness in the peoples. 'The animistic religions present certain points of contact for the preaching of the Gospel.' (World Missionary Conference 1910:22)

Yet there was an acknowledgement that "animists" are not only in error b are "slaves." "Fear is the moving power of animistic religion, in Asia as in Africa Conversion was required and syncretism was to be avoided.

Thus we find that in the great evangelical Edinburgh World Missionary Co ference of 1910, the accent was both on continuity and discontinuity. While sor stressed one or the other, the accent was on what we have called, a biblical co tinuity-discontinuity.

The liberal trends within the western churches, begun in the later part of t 19th century, began to penetrate the missionary societies during the early part the 20th century. Consequently, by the time of the Jerusalem Meeting of the I ternational Missionary Council, 1928, liberalism dominated the scen liberalism, dominated by the comparative school of religions, saw Christianity as merely the fulfillment of the elements of value and truth in the non- Christian religions. Continuity between world religions and Christianity was the accent. Through the social gospel, these liberals expected to build the kingdom of God. The concluding document of the Jerusalem Conference included this statement on the relationship with non-Christian religions.

> To non-Christians also we make our call. We rejoice to think that just because in Jesus Christ the light that lighteth every man shone forth in its full splendor, we find rays of that same light where He is unknown or even is rejected. We welcome every noble quality in non-Christian persons or systems as further proof that the Father, who sent His Son into the world, has nowhere left Himself without witness (International Missionary Council 1928:Vol.I,410).

This document in fact was carefully crafted because of the dissenting Barthians who were a minority at Jerusalem. These continental theologians prepared their own paper in which they expressed concern for Jerusalem's drift to syncretism. They maintained, "It is the main task of missions to work for the conversion of men, that is, their conscious break with their past life, the New Testament *metanonia* required of all Christians." These Barthians contended,

> In view of these facts, though fully acknowledging the spiritual values in the non-Christian religions, we are disquieted by the question whether the offer of salvation to non-Christians can be made by setting over against one another the spiritual values of the non-Christian and the Christian religions, the scheme followed by most of the papers presented.

> Further, we do not believe that the central task of the Christian missions can be accomplished by a so-called 'Social Gospel!' banding together all men of goodwill across the boundary lines of different religions in a common warfare against the evils of the world, indispensable and urgent though this warfare is (International Missionary Council 1928:348).

By the time of the next International Missionary Conference held at Tambaram, Madras, in 1938, the Barthians had taken over. Instead of continuity, they stressed discontinuity. In preparation for the Madras Conference, Hendrik Kraemer wrote his book, *The Christian Message in a Non-Christian World*. He coined the phrase, "biblical realism," to refer to the absolutely unique revelation Christ. He maintained that the Bible is not a tale of man's pilgrimage toward God, but a record of God's sovereign acts in saving men. Therefore, these Barthians said there cannot be continuity between the religions and Christianity.

Kraemer maintained that there were only two possible positions: continuity a theology of fulfillment, or discontinuity with its rejection of natural theology and general revelation. Furthermore, he maintained that if we accept the reality reconciliation, then the core of the Gospel is that "mankind in its totality is in state of hostility towards God as He really is."

Gradually, over the following decades the Barthians lost their influence and through the merger of the International Missionary Council with the World Council of Churches, the pendulum has swung to the other extreme of continuity. At the time of the Assembly of the Commission on World Mission and Evangelism of the World Council of Churches in Bangkok, 1973, humanism was the moving spirit. "Humanization" became the goal of missions. Even today the ecumenical churches are emphasizing the continuity between non-Christian religions and Christianity.

Continuity, therefore, has its roots in a low view of Scripture and a high opinion of man's moral character. Discontinuity in its Barthian form is a reaction to continuity of liberal theologians. A biblical continuity- discontinuity seeks to maintain both emphases of Scripture with a proper balance. There must be discontinuity because of man's sinful rebellion against God. But there must also be some measure of continuity because of general revelation given to all men through nature and conscience. This is not only good theology, this accords with experience.

REVIEW QUESTIONS FOR CHAPTER 18

1. Explain the three different views of the relationship between Christianity and non-Christian religions.

2. Disucss the contrast between African Traditional Religion and Biblical Religion.

3. What evidence supports the belief that ATR is a degeneration of the True Faith? Evaluate in the light of God's Word.

4. When men teach that Traditional Religion is fulfilled in Christianity the quote such verses as Matt. 5:17, Col. 1:16, Acts 17:16-34. What do these verses really teach?

5. In what way is Christianity a fulfillment of ATR? Evaluate.

Suggested Reading and Thought Questions for Advanced Studies:

Anderson, J.N.D. *Christianity and Comparative Religion* (or the revised edition of the same book, *Christianity and World Religions: The Challenge of Pluralism*, 1970.

DuBose, Francis ed. *Crucial Issues in Missions Tomorrow*, 1972, "Mission Encounter with Non-Christian Religions," pp.358-375.

Freytag, Walter. *The Gospel and the Religions*, 1957.

Hick, John and Brian Hebbeltheaite eds. *Christianity and other Religions*, 1980.

Keeley, Robin ed. *The Lion Handbook of Christian Belief*, 1982. "God in Other Religions" by Stephen Neil, pages 191-203.

Knitter, Paul F. *No Other Name? A Critical Survey of Christian Attitudes Toward the World Religions*, 1985.

Kraemer, H. *The Christian Message in a Non-Christian World*, 1963.

Newbigin, Lesslie. *The Finality of Christ*, 1969.

Parrinder, Geoffrey. *Comparative Religion*. London: Sheldon Press, 1976.

Race, Alan. *Christians and Religious Pluralism*, 1983.

Tippett, Alan. "Possessing the Philosophy of Animism for Christ," *Crucial Issues in Missions Tomorrow*, Donald McGavran ed. 1972, pp.125-171.

Tisdall, W. St. Clair. "Comparative Religion," *International Standard Bible Encyclopedia*, James Orr ed., 1952, Vol.II,pp.691-694.

Verkuyl, J. *Contemporary Missiology*, 1978. "Trends in the Theology of Religions", pp.341-372.

1. Evaluate the adequacy of the proposal given by the author, entitled, "A Biblical Continuity-Discontinuity." Wherein do you agree or disagree? What may be lacking or overstated? Support your answer with biblical teaching.

2. Make a biblical study of the word, *kosmos* (world), in the Johannine writings (using a concordance to study each occurrence in the context). What light does John's teaching on *kosmos* shed on the question of continuity versus discontinuity between ATR and Christianity?

3. Research the *Logos* theology based on John 1:9, both historically and exegetically. How does Jn. 1:9 harmonize with the rest of Scripture dealing with natural revelation and the spiritual condition of "the heathen"?

4. Read Harry Sawyerr, *Creative Evangelism: Towards a New Christian Encounter with Africa* (London: Lutterworth Press, 1968), pp.66-117. What presuppositions seem to underlie his theses? Does he stress continuity, discontinuity or biblical continuity-discontinuity between ATR and Christianity?

5. Read Byang Kato, *African Cultural Revolution and the Christian Faith* (Jos, Nigeria: Challenge Publications, 1976; "The Meaning and Content of Culture," pp.8-31). What presuppositions seem to underlie his theses? Does he stress continuity, discontinuity or biblical continuity-discontinuity between ATR (and African culture) and biblical Christianity?

6. Where does Lesslie Newbigen (*The Finality of Christ*) seem to fall in the question of continuity, discontinuity, and biblical continuity- discontinuity? In light of his stated beliefs on revelation and salvation, is this a biblically balanced continuity-discontinuity?

7. Discuss your understanding of the relationship between ATR and biblical Christianity, giving biblical data to support your answer.

Chapter 19

SYNCRETISM

INTRODUCTION

The goal of planting the Church of Jesus Christ in Africa is to make Christ incarnate among the peoples to the glory of God the Father. Jesus Christ, in the words of Chalcedonian creed, is "the same perfect in Godhead and also perfect in manhood; truly God and truly man of a reasonable soul and body." Christ's incarnation took nothing away from His deity nor did it make Him less of a man.

Even so we believe that the Gospel of Jesus Christ must remain pure within every culture but at the same time clothed with indigenous garments. The Gospel must be contextualized in such a manner that the eternal truth of the Gospel remains unchanged. Yet the embodiment of the Gospel becomes truly "native," contextualized fully within the cultural forms of the peoples.

Because God has not left Himself without a witness but has been continually at work among all peoples, culture can be redeemed, even as people made in the image of God can be redeemed. But because man has fallen, all of culture is permeated by the transgression and rebellion of man. Consequently, culture must be transformed.

This missiological concept of transforming cultures to conform to the will of God has been called by various names: adaptation, accommodation, possessio or transformation. The proponents of each particular viewpoint have their own unique approach to cultural transformation. Roman Catholics with their Thomistic view of sin and salvation speak of accommodation to culture (see Luzbetak 1970). Many Arminian Protestants tend to ally themselves to the school of accommodation. Reformed theologians with their concept of sovereign grace speak of "possessio," God sovereignly possessing culture which has fallen from grace (see Beyerhaus 1975). Various linguists prefer the notion of transformation of culture from within (Kraft 1979). Delving into the nuances of each view is not our present purpose. We simply observe that the goal of all Christian missiologists, to one degree or another, is to incarnate the Gospel in every culture, transforming and possessing the culture for God's glory.

Failure to incarnate the Gospel will lead to one of two errors: planting a foreign church which is not truly contextualized, or planting a syncretistic church which compromises the truth of the Gospel.

We have all too many examples of foreign based churches. When Christianity brings to another culture all the problems and questions of a foreign culture and fails to address itself to the issues and needs of the new culture, that Christianity will remain foreign based. When Christians of one culture seek to express their

Christian faith in foreign forms, the Gospel fails to become rooted and indigenously established.

However, we also have all too many examples of Christopaganism, churches which have lost or distorted the truth of the Gospel. Syncretism has been a problem among God's people throughout the ages and is a growing problem in Africa and the world today. What is syncretism and how should we deal with it? This is our topic for this chapter.

MEANING OF SYNCRETISM

Root Meaning of Syncretism

The English term, "syncretism," comes from the Greek word, *synkretismos*. This word is said to have come from a custom of the ancient Cretans. They had a habit of fighting fiercely among themselves, but combining resolutely against their common enemies. This expediency of uniting quarreling factions was called *synkretismos*, which in turn was derived from the verb, *synkretizein*, meaning "to combine." Plutarch used the word for the uniting of quarreling brothers in face of common enemies (see Harrison 1960:510).

Therefore, according to the historical and etymological derivation of the word, syncretism refers to the joining together of quarreling brothers. Syncretism is the attempt to unite together those elements which are incompatible.

Definitions of Syncretism

Reference books on the subject define syncretism along similar lines. According to the English dictionary, syncretism is "The combination or reconciliation of differing beliefs in religion, philosophy, etc. or an attempt to effect such compromise." The *Evangelical Dictionary of Theology* says syncretism is "The process by which elements of one religion are assimilated into another religion resulting in a change in the fundamental tenets or nature of those religions. It is the union of two or more opposite beliefs, so that the synthesized form is a new thing." (Elwell 1984:1062)

Tippett defines syncretism "as the union of two opposite forces, beliefs, systems or tenets so that the united form is a new thing, neither one nor the other." (Yamaori 1975:17)

CHARACTERISTICS OF SYNCRETISM

Cultural adaptation is not necessarily syncretism though it may be. The absorption of cultural ideas and practices in a local Christian community need not be syncretistic. If these ideas and practices are consistent with the Scriptures and do not conflict with the essential message and world view of the Bible, then syncretism is not a problem.

Negatively, we may say that syncretism is the denial of any unique revelation or exclusive faith. Syncretism is rooted in the belief that all theology is relative and biased. A. Oepke says, "Real syncretism is always based on the presupposition that all positive religions are only reflections of a universal original religion and show therefore only gradual differences." (Anderson, 1970:12)

Positively, syncretism is the attempt to unite, harmonize or fuse together the diverse beliefs of one religion with the conflicting beliefs of another. Syncretism is essentially unfaithfulness to one or the other religion. The problem is not the adaptation of items by one religion from another religion or culture. The problem is that of taking something which is incompatible and irreconcilable from one culture or religion and trying to incorporate that into the other religion.

Summarizing these characteristics, J.N.D. Anderson writes, "The syncretistic approach may be defined as 'the view which holds that there is no unique revelation in history, that there are many different ways to reach the divine reality, that all formulations of religious truth or experience are by their very nature inadequate expressions of that truth and that it is necessary to harmonize as much as possible all religious ideas and experiences so as to create one universal religion for mankind.'" (Anderson 1970:12)

Syncretism generally has a negative connotation when referring to the Christian faith. It implies compromise. Hence, few people ever believe that they themselves are falling into syncretism. Therefore, we need to weigh the evidence before we can determine whether syncretism has taken place or not.

KINDS OF SYNCRETISM

There are different kinds of syncretism. We may divide syncretism into two types: that which is conscious and deliberate and that which is spontaneous.

Conscious and Deliberate Syncretism

Syncretism which comes from the top leadership within the churches is often conscious and deliberate in seeking to accommodate the Gospel to other religious faiths or cultures. While the proponents usually do not intend to compromise the Gospel they in fact seek to accommodate the Christian faith in order to make it more appealing and relevant. Thus they assimilate various practices and beliefs which in fact are incompatible with the truth of the Gospel. This is the eclectic approach in which the various noble teachings and practices of all religions are blended together and joined in a world religion. This view has been championed by William Ernest Hocking in his book, *Living Religions and a World Faith*. This has been the view of various theologians in the ecumenical movement. The call is for people to become Christian Buddhists, Christian Muslims and Christian Confucianists.

This deliberate and conscious form of syncretism may also be represented by many of the African Independent Churches. In their dissimulation from the mission founded churches they deliberately choose to retain some of their traditional culture. They may be unawares of the incompatibility of the many elements in the traditional culture with the Gospel. But they consciously choose to retain elements of magic and divination which are contrary to the Bible. They may equate the work of the ancestral spirits with the work of the Holy Spirit, thus intermingling the Holy Spirit with traditional spirits. Thus they are knowingly engaged in syncretism through deliberate actions on their part (see Sundkler 1961).

Spontaneous Syncretism

Most syncretism, however, is spontaneous without anyone seeking intentionally to combine conflicting elements of different religions. This spontaneous syncretism usually takes place at the grass roots level by people who unknowingly mix things which do not mix. The resultant mix is sometimes called split level Christianity or two-storied religion. This is a compromise between the truth of the Gospel and some of the traditional customs and beliefs.

For instance Christians may seek prayers and spiritual help from the church and pastor for a sick family member. But when that fails they seek traditional help from the medicine man. Christians may bury their dead loved ones through the church and the pastor, but then at night seek out the counsel and help from the traditionalists. Thus there are two levels of Christianity, the ideal which operates in the day through the church and is publicly professed, and the real practice which takes place at night, secretly and beyond public knowledge.

Various forms may also be combined which unintentionally are syncretistic. A song with solid biblical content may be sung to the chant and drumbeat which was traditionally used for inducing spirit possession. Thus the meaning and message conveyed is syncretistic.

SYNCRETISM IN HISTORY

Although the word, syncretism, does not occur in the Bible, the problem of syncretism has been with the people of God from Old Testament days through the church age until the present. We shall look at the tendencies toward syncretism in the Old Testament, in the early church age and in contemporary times.

Syncretism in the Old Testament

The whole history of Israel is the story of conflict between God and Satan, between the purity of divine revelation and the corrupted Phoenician-Canaanite fertility cult of Baal. Beyerhaus points out that God's strategy to counteract the danger of syncretism was segregation, eradication and adaptation (Beyerhaus 1975:127). Israel was commanded to eradicate the Canaanites, segregate herself from the Gentiles but she was allowed to adapt what was not contrary to the essence of God's divine revelation.

God had called Abraham out of his native land for the very purpose of separating him from the idolatrous contamination of Mesopotamia. His own father, Terah, served "other gods." (Josh. 24:2,3) But even during those early patriarchal days in the land of Canaan, there was evidence of syncretism through the assimilation of pagan customs of their neighbours (Gen. 31:19,30,34; 35:4). Hence God gave to the sons of Abraham various laws which segregated them from their Canaanite neighbors. Intermarriage was totally forbidden (Gen. 24:1-

9; Ezra 9). They were to be a holy race, separated unto God from the peoples, forbidden to follow the customs of the Gentiles (Lev. 19,20; especially 20:22-26).

When Yahweh led the people of Israel out of Egypt into the Promised Land, she was explicitly told to slay the wicked nations, lest their presence should become a source of temptation (Exodus 23:20-33, especially vss.32,33; Deut. 7:1-26; 9:4,5; 20:16-18; see Judges 2:1-4). Some have questioned the morality of this eradication of the Canaanites, but recent archaeological evidence points to the utter depravity of these people. A brief survey of the Canaanite religion is profitable as a background to the syncretistic trends.

The Supreme Deity among the Canaanites was El, the generic name for god sometimes used in Scripture. The root meaning is "to be strong, powerful." Thus El was "The Strong One." El was the head of a pantheon of gods. He was married to three wives who were also his sisters. El was a bloody tyrant, terrifying other gods, taking the throne from his father, murdering his favorite son, cutting off the head of his own daughter. A Ugaritic description of his uncontrolled lust in seducing two women is "the most sensuous in ancient Near Eastern literature." (Unger 1952:171) Despite this, El was considered "the exalted father of years," "the father of man" and "the father bull." He was likened to the bull in the midst of the cows.

Baal was the son, the pre-eminent king among the gods. He was conceived as the god of the rain and storm and "the Lord of heaven." As the giver of fertility, Baal is prominent in the struggle with drought and adversity. In Canaanite mythology, Baal struggles with Mot (death) and is slain. Thereafter, a cycle of seven years of scarcity follows. But the goddess, Anath, the sister and lover of Baal, searches for his body. When she finds Mot, she slays him. Baal is then brought back to life, ensuring seven years of plenty.

The three prominent wives of Baal were Astarte (Ashtoreth), Asherah and Anath. Asherah is prominent in the Old Testament as the goddess beside Baal. Most biblical references to Asherah are of some cult object of wood which could be cut down and burned (I Kings 15:13; II Kings 21:7). Vessels were dedicated to her (II Kings 23:4) and prophets served her (I Kings 18:19).

These goddesses were associated with sex and war. In her role of sacred prostitution, Anath is perversely called "virgin" and "The Holy One." Anath was pictured as a naked woman riding a lion with a lily in one hand and a serpent in the other. The lily symbolized grace and sex appeal while the serpent depicted fecundity.

Sacred prostitution of both sexes debased pagan worship of the Canaanites. References to the male prostitutes are usually translated "sodomites" in Scripture (Deut. 23:18; I Kings 14:24; 15:12; 22:46). The females are also mentioned (Deut. 23:18; Hos. 4:14). The Canaanite temples were centres of legalized prostitution in the name of religion.

From biblical perspective, the extermination of the Canaanites is justified on two counts: they were hopelessly wicked, deserving the judgement of God. And their presence among the Israelites would have badly corrupted the true faith.

But despite the divine command to abolish all pagan remnants in the land, Israel compromised. The consequence is found in the book of Judges, one of the most dreadful accounts of repeated apostasy in the Word of God. Judges 2 is the sad summary of the whole sequence of events. They did not drive out all the inhabitants nor break down all their altars (2:1-5). Consequently, they lapsed into paganism, serving Baal and Astartes (2:6-15). The wrath of God fell, the people repented, God in mercy raised up judges to redeem them, but after the death of the judge, the children of Israel lapsed into paganism again (2:16-23; see 10:6-16).

This apostasy occurred intermittently throughout Israel's history. Solomon, at the end of his reign, turned to other gods, with the result that God tore the nation of Israel into two kingdoms.

The whole northern kingdom adopted syncretistic practices. Beginning with Jeroboam they professed to serve Jehovah under the guise of two golden calves. Whatever Jereboam's specific intent, the similarity of the golden calves to the images of Baal in the form of a bull was very close. Israel fell into idolatrous pollution as a result. Fertility cult groves were introduced (II Kings 13:6) and high places for licentious rites of the Canaanite agricultural gods were established (I Kings 12:31). The period of Ahab and Jezebel was specifically marked by the Baal cult. In this crucial period, God sent forth the prophets, Elijah and Elisha, to call people to repentance (I Kings 16:29- 22:53). After the downfall of the northern kingdom, a lamentable commentary is recorded, giving the reasons for their fall (II Kings 17:1-41). Compromise in the form of syncretism and idolatry resulted in the wrath of God.

By far the greatest crisis in the southern kingdom, which eventually led to the fall of God's judgement and the exile of His people, transpired during the last century prior to the Exile, between the fall of Samaria and the fall of Jerusalem, 722 B.C. to 605 B.C. Most of the prophetic literature in the Old Testament is concerned with this time. All the major prophets and most of the minor ones wrote during this period.

The role of the prophets was to call Israel back to true fidelity to her God. God had entered into a covenant relationship with Israel. "I will be your God and you shall be my people," said the Lord. But Israel persisted in her wayward tendency toward syncretism.

Manasseh (687-642 B.C.), one of the longest reigning monarchs in Judah's history, perverted the faith of Israel and introduced a thorough-going syncretism. By reputation, Manasseh was "the most wicked king of Judah" (II Kings 21:1-15; II Chron. 33:1-20) because of his total compromise with heathen religions.

He raised up altars to Baal (II Kings 21:3). The "high places" on wooded hilltops were again erected where the worship of Baal was mixed with gay licentious dances. Images of Asherah, the female consort of Baal, were also placed beside the pillars of Baal (II Kings 21:3).

Asherah, Anath and Astarte were symbolized as pregnant "virgins" whose presence signified the licentious immorality performed in the name of religion. Further abominations included the star and planetary worship (II Kings 21:3,5), the worship of Moloch, an Ammonite deity, whose worship included child sacrifice (II Kings 21:3,5). Archaeological investigation has revealed piles of ashes and infant skeletons near the heathen altars, pointing to widespread abominations of this nature. The cult of Moloch was closely connected with astral divination (astrology) as well (Amos 5:24,26; Acts 7:41-43). Manasseh also engaged in witchcraft, divination and spiritism (II Kings 21:6).

Throughout this period the Bible reflects a repeated and continuous return to the religious practice of Gentile nations. The worship of the sun with sun-chariots is mentioned (II Kings 23:11). The Queen of Heaven, the Mother Goddess representing life-giving Nature, was worshipped (Jer. 7:18; 44:17). Tammuz, the Babylonian god who died and rose, was wept over (Ezek. 8:14). Pagan deities were worshipped in and around the temple. Within the temple itself heathen prostitution took place (II Kings 23:7).

A major problem was political. The kings of Judah were faced with political realities of powerful nations whose hostility threatened the very survival of Judah. When the Jews became weak because of their sin, and the Gentile nations became a threat to Judah, her kings frequently resorted to compromise to gain the favour of the political opposition. Further, the religions of Assyria, Babylon, Medes and Persians appeared impressive in the contest of these great world powers. The kings of Judah were thus tempted to compromise their religious heritage in order to gain favour with their national rivals.

The end result of syncretism in the Old Testament was divine judgement. Any compromise leading to infidelity brings down God's wrath upon His people. Man cannot serve God and mammon. Either man clings to his Lord and Master or he betrays that covenant relationship and allies himself with the enemy. God's Word determines for us what is permitted or forbidden. Man must choose. But syncretism is the way of disaster.

Syncretism in the Early Christian Church

The New Testament canon was written within a short period of 50 years shortly after the resurrection of Christ. Hence, under the glow of Pentecost and with the leadership of the Lord's apostles, there was little opportunity for syncretism to take hold.

However, there is evidence in the New Testament of temptations toward syncretism. It is revealing how emphatic the apostles responded to those dangers. We shall examine one such danger of syncretism in the New Testament.

When the Gospel was preached to Ephesus there were all kinds of pressures to engage in syncretism. The history of the city made syncretism a great temptation. But in contrast we find an uncompromising attitude of the Apostle Paul, resisting syncretism at every level.

Background of the Incident in Acts 19: Ephesus was a mixture of influences. Before there was a city of Ephesus, the ancient peoples living in the area erected a temple for the fertility goddess, known as "The Great Goddess, The Mother." She was the protector, teacher and mistress of the people. In this old form she was represented as a queen-bee which guided her swarming people to a new place of abode. Like other nature goddesses of the Near East, she represented "the abundance and fertility of the life force." All the people in the little villages nearby looked to the Mother Goddess and her priests for direction and protection.

When the Greeks colonized the area around 1,000 B.C., they found this fertility goddess. The Great Goddess was given a Greek varnish and bestowed the Greek name, Artemis. A Greek image was made of her, replacing the former one. But she retained her original identity, a nature goddess.

She is the expression of a religious belief, which regarded the life of God as embodying and representing the life of nature, and proceeding according to the analogy of the natural world, so that in the drama of Divine life, there is a God-Father, a Goddess-Mother, and a Son or a Daughter...born again and again in the annual cycle...of existence (Ramsay 1963:221).

A temple was built in her honour by the Greeks. When in great fear during one siege, the Ephesians dedicated the city to Artemis. Even Croesus, the conqueror, contributed the oxen of gold to the temple. The Ephesian Goddess from this time onward became "the national deity of the city."

In the second century before Christ, another change occurred. Ephesus was captured and made part of the Roman Province of Asia. As a province within Roman influence, the Imperial Cult was established with the worship of the Emperor of Rome. The reigning Emperor was considered the incarnate God in human form on earth. The people loyally accepted this as a necessary sign of loyalty.

But the peoples craved a "native Asian deity." Nothing imported would satisfy their desires. Because Ephesus was the leading city with powerful trading and financial relations with the other cities, the divinity of Ephesus became the leading goddess of the entire Province. The Romans gave her a new Roman appearance with the name, Diana. But basically, she was the old deity of fertility. She was grotesquely represented with many breasts and served by a host of priestess servants.

Within the city of Ephesus lived a large colony of Jews. Some may have been true followers of the Law. But numbered among them were some apostate Jews who used occult powers for personal gain (Acts 19:13). The city was apparently filled with much superstition in the form of magic (Acts 19:19). The Ephesian belief in the magical arts is demonstrated by the fact that the magic formula was known all over the Near East as *Ephesia Grammata*. Ephesus was also the site of the miracle worker, Apollonius of Tyana. His philosophy of syncretism taught that all gods are expressions of the one supreme sun god.

Thus, syncretism, which combined together incompatible foreign elements, was present in pagan Ephesus.

The Powerful Forces Opposing the Gospel: When Paul preached the Gospel to the Ephesians, he faced enormous pressures opposing the Gospel. What was Paul's approach when he preached the Gospel in Ephesus? Did he engage in any syncretism? There were several influences with which Paul had to contend. These may be enumerated as: social, religious, economic and political.

Socially, the city of Ephesus retained influence because of her religious heritage. Because the sea was receding progressively and the harbour difficult to use, Ephesus was a dying city. Her prestige among the peoples of the Province of Asia lay in her religion.

Religiously, the Ephesians had strong convictions about the pre-eminence of the Mother Goddess. An ancient tradition told of the statue of Artemas (or possibly a sacred stone) having fallen from heaven. The peoples, therefore, accepted this cult as authentic and regarded themselves as the protectors of this goddess.

Economically, the livelihood of an important segment of the populace was at stake (Acts 19:24). The Graeco-Roman society was divided into many guilds or unions for bankers, doctors, architects, dyers, workers in metal, stone or clay, builders and carpenters. These clubs united peoples together with similar interests. Demetrius aroused the guild of silversmiths against Paul because their business was in jeopardy.

Politically, the future influence of Ephesus seemed to lie in her recognized leadership in the prestigious cult of the Mother Goddess. As a dying city, her only claim to being the most important city in the province was in this area of religion.

The Gospel Confronts Paganism: Did Paul compromise under these tremendous pressures of tradition, culture and religion? Definitely not! When the Ephesians responded to the Gospel and became Christians, they made a total break with magic. The new converts volunteered the burning of their magical books and objects, to the sum of 50,000 days of work, a large sum by any standard (Acts 19:19).

Though Paul may not have articulated denunciation of the cult of Artemis (19:37), the implications were clear enough. He taught "that the gods made with hands are no gods at all" (Acts 19:26). The loss of trade by the silversmiths aroused their ire and led to the two hours of tumultuous chanting, "Great is Artemis of the Ephesians." (19:34).

Even among professing Christians Paul took an uncompromising stand. When believers were found who had been baptized into John's baptism, he proceeded to instruct them in the existence of the Holy Spirit and then rebaptized the believers (19:1-7).

Sceva, a Jewish exorcist, decided to add the name of Jesus Christ to his magical collection of powers. But such syncretism could not be tolerated and Sceva himself became overpowered by the very spirits he tried to exorcise.

The lesson from this incident is that the Gospel cannot be accommodated to man's weakness for syncretism. Even under tremendous tensions and pressures, the Gospel must remain pure and unadulterated.

On several other occasions, syncretism is confronted and dealt with, such as when Simon the Magician sought to exploit the gift of God for personal profit (Acts 8:4-24) and when incipient gnosticism in the form of "philosophy and empty deception" threatened the Gospel in Colossae.

The real tidal wave of syncretism, however, came later in the church. Prior to the toleration of the Christians under Constantine, the church was a persecuted minority. But this "little flock" of believers multiplied and spread abroad rapidly. And most important, they maintained integrity and purity because the cost of becoming a Christian was great.

But when Constantine openly tolerated Christianity and his three sons officially established Christianity as the religion of the Empire, the church was flooded with masses of people. Christianity was favoured by the prestige of governmental recognition. By A.D. 500 the large majority of the population of the Roman Empire was professing Christian. The northern peoples like the Goths, Visigoths, Ostrogoths, Vandals and Franks (frequently called barbarian because they did not speak Latin nor embrace the Graeco-Roman culture) gradually accepted more and more of the civilization of the Romans. Since this included Christianity, they increasingly adopted it.

Syncretism was the tragic result of the influx of large numbers of nominal Christians and a host of untaught first-generation Christians. The old pagan beliefs and practices were combined with the teachings of the Bible. The result was a kind of Christo-paganism.

"The pagan custom of raising men to the rank of gods or demigods against which the Christian apologists so vigorously protested crept into the Church in the honours paid to the apostles, martyrs and angels." (Latourette 1937:I,319). Some Christian leaders actually rejoiced in the fact that martyrs were substituted for the pagan gods and given their glory. Pagan divinities continued in the Christian church with a thin veneer of a Christian name.

When churches were built on the site of a pagan temple, the old associations continued. "The cult of the Virgin Diana may have contributed to the worship of the Virgin Mary and more than a coincidence may possibly be seen in the fact that one of the earliest churches in honour of Mary rose at Ephesus on the site of the famous Temple of Diana, and that in the same city in 431, a synod was held which first officially designated Mary the Mother of God." (Latourette 1937:I,320)

The ancient Larest in Italy were replaced by the Virgin, or the saints or figures of the child Jesus. In Sicily, the Virgin took possession of the sanctuaries of Ceres and Venus and the pagan rites associated with them were perpetuated in honour of Mary. One pagan temple of Quirinus became the Church of St. Quirino. Thus a pagan god became canonized.

Remnants of magical beliefs were carried into the church. The Gaul Christians used the sign of the cross to protect their cattle against the plague. In Egypt "a succinct recension of the essential elements of the ancient Book of the Dead was attributed to Christ and the Virgin Mary and employed by Abyssinian Christians to render men holy on earth, to preserve their bodies after death and to ensure their souls life beyond the grave and entrance into heaven." (Latourette 1937:I,323) Pagan charms in Egypt were given a Christian blessing and used to heal the sick. The name of the Trinity was pronounced over a magic drink. In some places, water was sprinkled on race horses from the horn of St. Hilarion. Pagan use of amulets was substituted by the use of relics, portions of the Gospel, crosses, medals and the like.

One could continue almost indefinitely with examples of syncretism not only in practice but in belief. See Latourette's chapter entitled, "The Effect of the Environment" (Latourette 1937:I,298-362). The result of such syncretism was a deadness and superstition which swept over the Christian church in Europe, necessitating the reformation and renewal of the church through the Protestant Reformers. The Gospel had been lost in the midst of traditions of pagan syncretism.

Syncretism in Contemporary Days

The very same problem that faced the early church in Europe faces the church in Africa today. For one reason or another, vast multitudes are accepting the Christian faith. Without adequate teaching and proper shepherding, the new converts are spontaneously bringing with them remnants of their past tradition-al religion which directly conflict with the heart of the Gospel. African Christian theologians, wishing to jettison remnants of ecclesiastical colonialism and develop an African Christianity, are consciously leading the churches into theological syncretism that does not bode well for the Gospel in Africa.

But syncretism in Africa must be understood within the larger context of Christianity worldwide. The contemporary wave of syncretism is found both in the older churches in the West and among the younger churches in the two- thirds world. This contemporary threat of syncretism has many causes which coalesce together to form a powerful surge throughout the world. The reasons are these:

Rationalism and Unbelief: Comparative Religions began in the middle of the 19th century. Those western scholars who investigated the world religions and made comparative studies became impressed with the many noble qualities of these religions and the apparent similarities between them. These western scholars of comparative religions lacked any firm Christian faith. Because of the apparent similarities and alleged virtues in all religions, they rejected any unique or absolute claim of Christianity.

Liberal Christianity has become entrenched in most old-line Protestant denominations. Having lost confidence in the absolute authority of Scripture, they have questioned such fundamental doctrines as the deity of Christ and the nature of the Gospel. The uniqueness of the Christian faith and the exclusive claims of Christ are an offense. Out of this arises a questioning and outright rejec-tion of historic Christian missions which calls people to repentance from sin and faith in Christ.

Thus an emphasis on relativity of all religions and a denial of the unique revelation in Jesus Christ has become prominent these days, even within the Christian church. Universalism thrives in this atmosphere.

Ecumenism: While there are some fine evangelicals within the member chur-ches of the ecumenical movement today, the leadership and control of the World Council of Churches is firmly in the hands of liberals who have seriously com-promised the Gospel to become another gospel. In a world that is becoming one politically, technically and economically, there is a felt need to be drawn together in a universal brotherhood of religious tolerance. At least everyone should ac-knowledge the relative worth of the other religious faiths and not be so arrogant as to claim exclusive truth. The exclusive claims of Christ are a stumbling block to many. The Old Testament is an embarrassment. In one way or another we are being challenged to unite with others and appreciate the relative value of each other's personal religious faith.

Nationalism: As the colonial era fades and the newly independent nations assert their autonomy, the old religions of Asia and Africa are being revived. Islam and Hinduism are becoming militant. As the West and the North decline and the East and the South ascend in influence, the Christian faith is confronted with renewed and invigorated non-Christian religions. This is a generally healthy climate in which syncretism can thrive.

Christianity has been associated with the strong and powerful nations of the

West. As colonialism is attacked and the influence of the West is resented, Christianity is brought into disrepute.

Resentment Over Foreign Domination: Many reversions to traditional religion have taken place over this very issue. When resentment and resistance build up over the colonial mentality of some missionaries, the Christian national rebels by forming an African Independent Church and by reclaiming some of the traditional beliefs and practices which had been rejected by the missionaries. By no means are all African Independent Churches syncretistic. And some times traditional practices ought to be reclaimed to form an authentically African Christian heritage. But when traditional beliefs and practices, incompatible with the Gospel, are incorporated into Christianity, as has been done many times by African Independent Churches, the end result is syncretistic Christianity.

Popularizing and Propagating of Rationalism: The popular beliefs taught in American and European universities, promulgated in mass media, and enshrined in contemporary philosophies are increasingly hostile to historic Christianity. Both the revolt against biblical truth and a nostalgia for other religions produces a climate favorable to syncretism.

What is true in the West is equally true in Africa. Increasingly, the intelligensia (highly educated) are not merely non-Christian but anti- Christian, hostile to evangelical Christianity. They seek to undo what has been established in the past. Newspapers and magazines, radio and television propagate liberal viewpoints. Professors in universities are seldom committed to an evangelical perspective. Through every channel imaginable rationalism is being popularized and propagated.

Political: Independent nations desire unity at any cost. Fragmented Christianity is called upon to unite. Even Christians, Muslims and those of ATR are exhorted to find the common denominator among them. Even as political pragmatism was a root cause for syncretism in Israel and Judah in the Old Testament and the motive of Roman Emperors, so we find political pressure upon the Christian churches to compromise her faith.

A Deficient Gospel: The Christian church in Africa has not always met the felt needs of the converts. In some ways, the church may not meet the people where they are nor help them with their problems. In a form of reversion, they establish independent churches which incorporate some traditional practices and beliefs. Whenever Christians leave one denomination to attend another, there must be some perceived deficiency in the one and an attraction in the other. The African Christian Church must incarnate the Gospel in such a way that these deficiencies will be minimized and the appeal of syncretistic churches is lessened.

Inadequate Biblical Teaching: Whenever the Church grows so rapidly that the converts are not properly taught the Scripture, there is bound to be a relapse into syncretism. A poorly taught, ignorant convert is subject to every kind of influence. Because churches are growing so rapidly that there are inadequate numbers of adequately trained pastors, the door is being opened for spontaneous syncretism.

This is perhaps the greatest contributing reason to the development of syncretism at the grass roots level. People are converted but not discipled. Alan Tippett comments, "Without adequate instruction after incorporation into the group, the faith which brought the convert in can be founded on error, without participation it becomes merely formal, without fellowship it becomes introvert, and without application it becomes irrelevant." (Tippett 1967:282)

Vital and relevant biblical instruction is essential to help the spiritual infant grow, develop and mature in accordance with God's Word.

Second-generation Christians Not Converted: The sons and daughters of the first generation Christians borrow the Christian ways of their fathers but fail to make a personal commitment to Jesus Christ. When boredom and dissatisfaction set in, the natural tendency is to revert to the traditional beliefs and practices. When facing a crisis of life and death, having found no security in Christ, they seek refuge in traditional religion.

Liberal Theology in the Guise of African Christian Theology: Syncretism may come forth from the church leadership. When Christian scholars loose their confidence in the absolute divine authority of the Bible, they readily mix and combine elements together which are contradictory in nature. Compromise is made in order to accommodate the contemporary cultural traditions. This has been done in the western theology in the guise of modernity and relevance. It is now sometimes done today in Africa under the guise of African Christian Theology. (read *Doing African Christian Theology: An Evangelical Perspective* by Gehman 1987).

CONCLUSION

Syncretism has been an ever present danger for God's people from the beginning of time. Nevertheless, we may say that there have been waves of syncretism throughout history with some periods more open to the danger of syncretism than others. Today we live in one of those syncretistic waves.

"To be forewarned is to be forearmed." If we are aware of the syncretistic tendencies around us, we will be able to defend the faith more adequately.

However, the defense of the faith is neither through a reactionary attitude nor a rigid defense of the status quo. A knowledge of the Bible is the *sine qua non* for maintaining the true faith handed down from the fathers. What is the Gospel? Do we know well the biblical ingredients of the Gospel?

When the Galatian Judaizers sought to add to the Gospel that which was contradictory to it, Paul vigorously rejected the false prophets, saying, "Let him be accursed." (Gal. 1:8) We can all too easily become guilty of syncretism through accretions, adding non-biblical practices and beliefs to the Christian message so as to confuse and colour the core of the Gospel. Cultural norms, local standards of behaviour, and ecclesiastical traditions may become part of the fundamentals of the faith. These may then be accepted as inseparable from basic Christianity.

The remedy for syncretism is clear. A strong, spirit-filled, biblically trained national leadership which can provide the constant discipling of all believers in the things of Christ. Evangelicals have been notorious for emphasizing evangelism but extra ordinarily weak in discipling. We plant churches and then run off to another country, trusting that the Holy Spirit will somehow and in some way nurture and teach those young believers.

Syncretism thrives on biblical illiteracy. A Spirit filled church, however, is rooted in the Scriptures. "A word to the wise is sufficient."

REVIEW QUESTIONS FOR CHAPTER 19

1. What is meant by the word, "syncretism."
2. Describe the characteristics of syncretism.
3. Syncretism has been a problem among God's people throughout history, including our times. Why is syncretism popular today?
4. Discuss how biblical revelation was compromised with pagan beliefs in church history.
5. What is the attitude in the Old Testament towards syncretism? The attitude of the New Testament?

Suggested Reading and Thought Questions for Advanced Study:

Kato, Byang. *Biblical Christianity in Africa*. 1985, pp.23-31.
Latourette, Kenneth Scott. *The History of the Expansion of Christianity*. 1970. Vol.I,pp.298-362; Vol.II,pp.409-446.
Lindsell, Harold. *The Church's Worldwide Mission*, 1966. "Syncretism," pp.85-110.
Oosthuizen, G.C. *Theological Battleground in Asia and Africa*, 1972. "The Church Among Traditional African Forces," pp.308-323.
Sundkler, B.G.M. *Bantu Prophets in South Africa*, 1961. "New Wine in Old Wineskins", pp.238-294.
Visser't Hooft, W.A. *No Other Name*, 1963.
Yamamori, Tetsunao and Charles R. Taber eds. *Christopaganism or Indigenous Christianity?* 1975, pp.13-34; pp.119-142.

1. What kind of temptations to syncretism faced the Christian church in its first millennium? How did this compromise the Gospel and weaken the Christian witness? (see above, Latourette 1970)
2. Discuss the pitfalls of syncretism which face the church of Jesus Christ today among your peoples. What lessons can we learn from Scriptural teaching and in history to guard our churches against the dangers of syncretism? (see Sundkler 1961; Kato 1985; Oosthuizen 1972)
3. Read *The Emergent Gospel* edited by Sergio Torres and Virginia Fabella (Maryknoll, NY: Orbis Books, 1978), pp.1-95. Summarize the main emphases of these papers and evaluate the underlying presuppositions which help to shape their conclusions. Do you find any tendencies toward syncretism? What evidence can you give to support your answer? What do you believe is the underlying

reason for this tendency toward or against syncretism?

4. Read *Salvation in African Tradition* by Tokunboh Adeyemo, 1979, pp.11-96). Summarize the main thoughts and evaluate the underlying presuppositions which help to shape the author's conclusions. Do you find any tendencies toward syncretism? What evidence can you give to support your answer? What do you believe is the underlying reason for this tendency toward or against syncretism?

Chapter 20

CONCLUSION

A CHRISTIAN ATTITUDE TOWARD TRADITIONAL AFRICANS

ATR is not some mere abstract belief. ATR is always practiced by people. Therefore, we as evangelicals are most concerned about the *PEOPLE* who follow ATR. What should our attitude be toward them?

A Spirit of Humility

The relativists, those who reject the uniqueness of the Christian Gospel and the exclusive claims of Christ, often accuse evangelicals of pride, arrogance and conceit. They think the evangelical must look down upon non-Christians with condescension and pride. Only those who teach that there is a little truth in all religions, so they seem to say, can approach ATR with humility.

The very opposite is true. *ONLY A BIBLICAL CHRISTIAN* can possess a true spirit of humility before non-Christians. The emphasis here is "biblical Christian." That many Christians are not biblical in their attitude is plain to all. But we must maintain the distinction between popular Christianity and biblical Christianity. The Bible judges all historical manifestations of the Christian faith. From the biblical perspective, a Christian ought to manifest a genuine spirit of humility for several reasons.

1. **A Christian stands on the same level as a non-Christian.** All men are sinners in rebellion against God apart from the grace of God.

The fundamental point of contact with any non-Christian is this mutual condition of spiritual need.

> As soon as you, as a man, encounter a person as a man, whether he be a pagan or a Mohammedan, you possess with him a common starting point, and this is first of all, the sin you both have committed, and secondly, the grace which saves you and which alone can save him when the light from Christ penetrates into the darkness, and the sinner is gripped by the mercy of God. Thus, there arises on the one hand a feeling of a common tie with the pagan, a common heart, and in that heart, there is the same 'sensus divinitatis'; that heart is disturbed by the same sin; you are by nature as heathen as he, the sole difference is the grace which has given to you, and that he too can share in (Bavinck 1960:229).

Therefore, the essential nature of a non-Christian's heart is the same as the Christian's, apart from grace. We share the same disposition, derive from the same earthly father, and have the same desperate needs of the heart. There can be no room for superiority.

Kraemer says, "The more you learn to know heathendom in its deepest motives...the more you recognize yourself therein."

2. The Christian possesses nothing of worth except what has been given him by grace.

"The feeling of superiority is essentially a cultural, and not at all a religious, product; and decidedly not a Christian one." (Kraemer 1960:109) Superiority rests on achievement. But in biblical Christianity, there is no human achievement. Salvation is all of grace.

Paul states this explicitly. "For who regards you as superior? And what do you have that you did not receive? But if you did receive it, why do you boast as if you had not received it?" (I Cor. 4:7) For a Christian to feel proud of his faith and superior to others outside the faith is to manifest utter ignorance of the nature of his salvation. A person who believes that the Christian Gospel lends itself to feelings of pride and arrogance, simply does not understand the Gospel.

One veteran missionary a generation ago put it in these words.

> We do not come to men of other creeds, Hindus, Muslims, Buddhists, seeking to impose upon them a 'Western religion,' but in the spirit of the apostle, 'I have delivered unto you that which I also received how that Christ died for our sins, that he was buried, and that he rose again the third day, according to the Scriptures.' God sent us this gospel by missionaries from Asia. We have received Christ as our Savior. And now God has sent us back to Asia, with the same gospel, not on some airplane of fancied [imagined] superiority, boasting our civilization, inventions, or national bigness, but as humble pilgrims vending [selling] priceless pearls from celestial seas (Irvin 1953:219).

3. The Christian believes in God Who is "not one to show partiality." Acts 10:34 (See Deut. 10:17; II Chron. 19:7; Rom. 2:11; Gal. 2:6; Eph. 6:9; Col. 3:25; I Pet. 1:17).

For many people, God's election of Abraham and his descendants to be God's own people to the exclusion of others seems like an act of discrimination and partiality. But that misunderstanding fails to interpret the world from God's point of view. During the early patriarchal period, men deteriorated rapidly. Once God had to destroy the world's population, saving Noah and his family alone, because "the wickedness of man was great on the earth, and that every intent of the thoughts of his heart was only evil continually." (Gen. 6:5) Once He had to disperse the people abroad because they congregated together in an act of defiance and idolatry (Gen. 11).

The very purpose of choosing Abraham was to preserve a people for Himself. To them God gave the law and through them He sent the Saviour. Though the Jews often behaved arrogantly towards the other nations, this was contrary to God's purpose. From the very beginning, God chose Abraham, not only to bless him, but that Abraham might "be a blessing," that in him "all the families of the earth" might be blessed (Gen. 12:2,3). The conversion of the Gentiles through the Jews was God's desire, though the Jews seldom understood this.

We conclude this by a quotation by Dr. Donald G. Miller, former president of the Pittsburgh Theological Seminary.

> Only the Christian faith stresses God's actions in history and claims that God finds men instead of their finding him...It is this rootage in unique historic events which makes the Christian claim of finality for Jesus Christ intelligible and frees it from religious snobbery. In making this claim for Jesus Christ, the Christian is claiming nothing for himself. The true Christian is not a proud religious man, who feels that his views are superior to those of the adherents of other religions. He is a humble, self-effacing man who knows that his views are no better than those of anyone else, who knows that he has nothing of himself, that he is merely a man in need of help. He is duty bound to tell others where help can be found (Wysham 1967:18).

An Attitude of Love

The biblical teaching of love has some direct applications to this question of a Christian's attitude toward the non-Christian. Several characteristics of New Testament love (*agape* love) are these:

Love Values and Respects. The word, *agape*, when used by the ancient Greek classics, found its distinctive meaning in this: *agape* is drawn to the one loved because of a sense of value in the object which causes one to prize him. This sense of worth, value and esteem separated *agape* from all other words for love. *Storge*, a word for natural affection, is the love of parents for children. *Eros*, a word for passion, became degenerate and referred mainly to inordinate lust and promiscuous desires. *Philia*, the word for friendship, is the affection for or liking of friends. But *agape* had a loftier sense of admiration and esteem because of the value within the person loved.

The New Testament usage of this word never quite lost that original meaning, though it is not the prominent emphasis (see I Thess. 5:13; Philemon 9)

That which a Christian treasures in a non-Christian is surely not his sin, nor his erroneous religious beliefs. But the Christian sees in the sinner a human being whom God has created in His own image, a man for whom Christ died, a man with potential for the glory of God. The Christian should, therefore, respect and value him.

Love is Self-Giving. *Agape* love is not only patient but kind; not only passive in accepting wrong doing without murmuring, but active in doing good for others; not only negative in refusing to keep hurt feelings or in refusing to retaliate, but is positive in showing deeds of kindness (I Cor. 13:4).

Agape love is active in serving others (Gal. 5:13). Christian love is patterned after Christ Who gave Himself sacrificially to the utmost (Eph. 5:2, 25). At the very heart of love is a selflessness that refuses to think of self but only of the other (Phil. 2:1-4).

Genuine love makes the difference between the man who seeks to force the Gospel down the throat of an unwilling soul and the man who gives himself for the sake of another's good, including his salvation. Acts of kindness can disarm the resistance of unbelievers.

Love Extends Universally. *Agape* love is not merely concerned about one's own group, but is concerned about everyone in need (Lk. 10:25-37; I Thess. 3:12).

The notion of being exclusive in concern, restricted in whom you love, does not derive from biblical Christianity. This is more characteristic of ethnic religions which think of God's love as limited to a particular people.

The Christian who loves with *agape* love will meet with non-Christians in an open and frank spirit, without any attempt to compel or coerce. There will be a spirit of hospitality and warm heartedness. An atmosphere of freedom and liberty will prevail.

But the love of Christ will compel him to be earnest and forthright in his witness. He will be tolerant when facing different viewpoints, patient when confronted with opposition, humble when abused and mistreated, yet persistent with compassion for the conversion of the lost.

A Paradoxical Approach

Based on what we have said concerning the nature of ATR and its relationship to biblical Christianity, we find that a Christian must maintain a paradoxical attitude.

1. He accepts truth and goodness wherever it is found as evidence of God's work of grace.

We have seen many examples of noble ideals, respectable character and great achievements that can be found among traditional Africans. Such examples include a great sense of courtesy, remarkable hospitality, love for and care of children, the aged and the unfortunate, respect for elders, a sense of community and brotherhood among the peoples, and a common sense of decency.

Within ATR we have discovered elements of truth made possible by God's common grace in General Revelation. These include: a belief in God, a knowledge of the moral law, especially the second table of the Ten Commandments, recognition of personal spiritual need, a sense of need for atonement, including animal sacrifices, belief in immortality, acceptance of the supernatural and the spirit world, and a host of other truths.

By common grace the Gospel has found a language and culture that can be transformed for Christian use. The Gospel can be communicated through the traditional African culture. The culture can be cleansed and renewed. Surely, the image of God has been stamped upon the hearts of the peoples in Africa. The religious nature of man and the element of truth found among men are due to the "seed of religion" God has planted within man.

An evangelical missionary for many years among the prisoners condemned to death in Pretoria has these remarkable words to say:

> No matter how strange this may sound, I have frequently found God in the soul of the African Bantu. Certainly, it is not the full revelation of the Father. But nevertheless, God Himself is the One Who lies hidden behind a curtain, as a shadowy figure, but the main outline is visible. A surprising and glorious experience! And when I experienced the moment that a soul surrenders, I understand the Master had been there earlier (Bavinck 1948:227).

2. But the evangelical Christian also recognizes the radical rebellion of men against God, men who are dead in trespasses and sins.

Since man's chief sin is pride and self-determination in rebellion against the sovereign rule of God, man's religion is also basically self- deification. As we have seen previously, man's religion is idolatrous, an attempt to supplant God and elevate the creature.

We must be careful when speaking of "truth" in non-Christian religions. While we find aspects of truth, fragments of truth or particles of truth, the fact is that these ideas often have different meanings from biblical truth. Moreover the "truth" is part of a larger whole and you cannot snatch the "truth" from its total contextual meaning and use without tearing the whole garment. A superficial examination highlights the similarities, but a deeper examination often discloses the discrepancies between biblical revelation and other religions. Many times "the moment of truth" is not merely deficient or inadequate, but actually a perversion or distortion of truth.

Nevertheless, we recognize that here and there, God's general revelation has been received with less distortion and serves as genuine pointers to the Gospel which centres on Christ as the embodiment of Truth. Analogies in ATR are powerful communication devices which form bridges to a knowledge of Christ.

Thus the evangelical seeks to recognize both the positive and the negative elements in ATR, both the common grace among the peoples and their rebellion. In effect, the evangelical holds to a paradoxical view of the relationship between ATR and Christianity and his attitude reflects this.

From the biblical perspective, the traditional African is not a curious museum piece or some strange curio of outdated superstition. Nor is ATR mere darkness contrasting with the sparkling light of western culture. The traditional African is a fellow creature stamped with God's image and marked by God's special love. His traditional religion is a reflection of man's peculiar nature, in active rebellion against God, yet marked by God's prevenient grace. Furthermore, every culture is marked by the fallen, corrupt Adamic nature which we have all inherited, mixed with traces of God's image.

As we approach the traditional African with the Gospel of hope and the claims of Christ, we do so with humility and *agape* love. But for the grace of God, we would be dead in trespasses and sins as he is. And by the grace of God he can be raised to new life in Christ even as we have been.

REVIEW QUESTIONS FOR CHAPTER 20

1. How can an evangelical, who believes in the uniqueness of the Gospel of Jesus Christ, approach a traditional African with humility? Do not the exclusive claims of Jesus Christ cause the Christian witness to assume an arrogant, condescending attitude toward one of another religion? Discuss.

2. Explain the kind of love which the Christian should show toward the unbeliever.

3. Define what is meant by "a paradoxical approach."

4. Discuss the "paradoxical" attitude which Christians have toward the tradi-

tional African.

Suggested Reading and Thought Questions for Advanced Study:

Kraemer, H. *The Christian Message in a Non-Christian World*, 1963. "The Missionary Approach," pp.284-335; "The Attitude Towards the Non-Christian Religions," pp.101-141.

Verkuyl, J. *Contemporary Missiology*, 1978. "Motives for Fulfilling the Missionary Task," pp.163-175.

1. What motivates the evangelical Christian to share the Gospel with a person of another religion?

2. How does the evangelical's view of ATR and biblical salvation enable him to call for repentance from dead works and yet at the same time treat the traditional African as his equal?

3. Study Paul's messages on his missionary journeys in the book of Acts (chapters 13-20), especially those sermons addressed to European pagans (14:1- 23; 17:16-34). Discuss Paul's approach to these Gentiles and his attitude toward them and their religious beliefs.

Survey of Literature on ATR

Ethnographic Studies of African Peoples. A selected list of classical studies of African peoples include:

1909	Hollis, A.C. The Nandi
1910	Routledge, W. and Katherine Routledge. With a Prehistoric People: the Akikuyu of British East Africa.
1910	Hobley, C.W. Ethnology of Akamba and Other East African Tribes
1911	Beech, Mervyn W.H. The Suk.
1912	Westermann, D. The Shilluk People
1920	Lindblom, G. The Akamba
1920	Smith, E.W. The Ila-speaking Peoples of Northern Rhodesia
1923	Roscoe, John The Banyankole and The Bakitara or Banyoro
1924	Dundas, C. Kilimanjaro and its People
1926	Talbot, P.A. The Peoples of Southern Nigeria
1928	Willoughby, W.C. The Soul of the Bantu
1930	Shapera, E. The Khoisan Peoples of South Africa
1937	Shaperia, I. ed. The Bantu-speaking Tribes of South Africa
1938	Herskovits, M.J. Dahomey
n.d.	Kenyatta, Jomo. Facing Mt. Kenya

African Traditional Religion of Particular African Peoples. Some significant books on the religious beliefs and practices of African peoples include the following:

1937	Field, M.J. Religion and Medicine of the Ga People
1937	Evans-Pritchard, E.E. Witchcraft, Oracles and Magic Among the Azande
1944	Danquah, J.B. Akan Doctrine of God
1954	Nadel, S.F. Nupe Religion
1956	Evans-Pritchard, E.E. Nuer Religion
1960	Middleton, J. Lugbara Religion
1961	Idowu, E.B. Olodumare, God in Yoruba Belief
1961	Lienhardt, G. Divinity and Experience: The Religion of the Dinka
1963	Middleton, J. and E.H. Winters eds. Witchcraft and Sorcery in East Africa
1966	Smith, E.W. ed. African Ideas of God
1969	Harjula, Raimo God and the Sun in Meru Thought
1969	Beattie, John ed. Spirit Mediumship and Society in Africa
1970	Harwood, Alan. Witchcraft, Sorcery, and Social Categories Among the Safwa
1971	P'Bitek, Okot. Religion of the Central Luo
1971	Downes, R.M. Tiv Religion
1974	Hauge, Hans-Egil. Luo Religion and Folklore
1976	Setiloane, Gabriel. The Image of God Among the Sotho-Tswana

Testimonies of Those Who Became Medicine Men or Medicine Women

A vivid account of the process of becoming a medicine man through birth is given by one Mukamba. This account demonstrates the role of the ancestors in calling, equipping and empowering of the medicine man for his profession.

My mystical power is not from anywhere but from God. It is not surprising that when I was born, my parents and the midwife witnessed that I had a beard, two bright teeth and my hands were holding two round balls, as hard as stone. These small hard balls (mbuu) had white hair covering each one. Mbuu with stiff white hair are traditionally a sign that I am a special person, dedicated to serve my Akamba society as a medicine man. The two balls indicated that my mystical powers will be for the betterment of my fellow Akamba to help them from the disturbance of witches in banning the influence of witchcraft who affect men through their powers of kyeni and kita (the powers of an evil tongue and the powers of reversing the effect of an evil tongue). The spirits of my great grandfather claimed me from the family for this duty. They taught me concerning the ways of healing men and women who have been affected by kita or kyeni. My medicine is really brought during the night through visions and direction of the ancestral spirits. I am told to go to such and such a place and I will be shown something to collect or do there. I go to such places at any time I am told by the ancestors. When I need a new revelation concerning a new sickness or event which would happen among my people, it is a requirement to drum and perform a rite so that the mystical beings may come, dine and advise me concerning the future and teach me how to play my mystical tool to help the people affected. Even the ancestors bring new power. They can direct me concerning the steps to take which will prevent any evil from happening.

When asked about the *mbuu*, he said,

They are for assurance and confirmation that my duty is prescribed. Don't fear to hear that these mbuu were originally as small as a written letter, "o". My parents took them and kept them for me. The more I grew the more the mbuu became larger and larger. When the hair fell off, my parents were informed by the ancestors to call a particular medicine man to come and perform a rite for my dedication. The night before the medicine man came, the iimu named "Kathambi" appeared before me and told me when her servant, the medicine man, would come. She gave me several revelations, tools, and taught me how to use them and commanded me to build a round house, using mud and thatch it with grass. Kathambi showed me the place to construct it and how to arrange my tools. I was directed to a certain tailor to acquire two flags, one white and the other black. These were to be erected around or beside my workshop, one to be on the left, another on the right. The place of my workshop is twenty feet from the other buildings and I have a command not to build any other building near this one, but to keep the distance given. Kathambi told me that this house is a place of work and it is where she will be meeting me.

When medicine man came, my parents were requested to give a bull for the rite. The medicine man killed the bull and the ceremony started. This was held together with a traditional dance (kilume) which started at 8:00 P.M. and extended to 4:00 A.M. After dancing for a short time, the medicine man called me to go somewhere in the bush. Reaching the place, the very spirit appeared before us and guided us where to go. At the proposed place, the medicine man changed drastically and after dancing a little with Kathambi, he was told what to do with me. He removed his clothes and ordered me to lay down. As I was doing so, I fell into surprise, confusion and dreaming. He took his official tools, then holding them, he ran around me. After this he jumped over me several times, speaking and smearing my whole body over with black powder mixed with blood of the sacrificed bull. He then tied a small bundle of mystical powders around my neck and girded me with another. He then ordered me not to take them off any time even when taking a bath. He gave me a ring to wear when I am in office. He finally rubbed me with a magic rod, saying, "Power! Power is given you"! Power to ban or overcome witchcraft (kuusya uoi). Power to divine (kuausya) and power to ban or overcome a spell (power over kita, kyeni, or kithetha)." After this I was given two very hard balls (mbuu) and he taught me how to use them when I am in my office. After this dedication, I was filled with a spirit who led me to the traditional drum dancing up to 4:00 A.M. when the medicine man ordered the dance to stop. This type of dance (kilumi) is only for the purpose of arousing the person concerned with the dedication to be filled with mystical power, to open the gate to that ministry and even make a firm connection with the ancestors who visit mightily, giving me the needed ability. Surely, since that time I was given the mystical powers which I employ in my ministry. The above mentioned powers are with me and people have appreciated and recognize me as a medicine man. And through thick or thin I am to work for the betterment of people of any color, whenever they come to me with any problem.

Esther, formerly a female medicine woman before becoming a Christian, gave a vivid account of her experience of becoming a medicine woman through inheritance from her mother and her reasons for leaving that vocation.

The devil and the forces of darkness are terribly bad. Their badness made me to reject their ministry and become a Christian. I inherited my mother's mystical power at the age of twenty, that is, two years after my marriage, though I associated with my mother in her work since I first began to understand. Through my whole life my mother taught me everything concerning witchcraft...

At first I had no desire or interest, but as time went on, I became influenced and all my interest centred on this work. At the age of 20, I was called home by my mother. When I arrived home, I found that they had killed a cow. My mother called me into a drum dancing (mbalya) in which I danced with the rest of the women and men. After a short time, I was possessed by Kathambi. Then, in that mood of helplessness, my mother took hold of my hand and led me into her workshop. There she removed her clothes and after sucking some milk from her breasts, she then mixed it with a brown smelling powder taken from her black traditional basket. She commanded me to take off my clothes, after which she told me to lie down on my back. Immediately, she began to dance while speaking some mystical words which I did not understand at that time. When she was dancing a very surprising figure joined her and danced together with her. I tried to catch one of its marvelously long tail hairs but I found that they were intangible. They were visible but not material. After two or three hours, the figure left my mother. This spirit vanished. Then my mother kissed my breasts and passed a red gourd over me. After this I was unconscious and I did not know what was going on. When I came to, I found myself dancing with the same surprising figure. This spirit had one leg, two bright eyes in front and one eye at the back. It had a neck one foot long, two sharp breasts with a very smooth body. After an hour of dancing with this strange looking woman, she ordered me to sit down and watch her while listening to whatever she would teach me. At that time my mother came in carrying with her a lot of mystical tools which the strange person had sent her to collect. My mother sat down and watched while this strange looking figure explained, advised and taught me how to use the tools. Mind you, there was no lamp in that workshop, but the young woman brightened the whole house with her three eyes. I was dedicated and commissioned to continue with this duty as a medicine woman. A place was chosen for me to go and make a house. This was to be a round house with a long post at the center. At the top, above the roof, I was told to tie a flag which my mother granted me at that time. This flag had two colors, white and black, to show that there is peace and proper relationships with the ancestors when I obey all the instructions and advice given to me. But terrible suffering will come if I forsake them.

The milk sucked from my mother's breasts and the brown smelling mystical powder were smeared around my body when I was unconscious in order to make me ready for the young woman who would later give me the power and taught me all the techniques about witchcraft. The young woman then left my mother who then shared her last word about my new profession. She then gave me a small bundle and a small gourd filled with magical medicines and ordered me to go home with her. We left the people still dancing. When we reached the place proposed for the construction of my workshop we took off our clothes. Using a mystical sword my mother dug a hole and put in it the small gourd willed with magical medicines. When we were still doing this the young woman came and witnessed this. The young woman who had re-appeared in the mean time then took us back to my mother's house and vanished. When the workshop was constructed and completed, that very night I spent in orientation under the leadership of this very strange looking young woman. This then became the meeting place with her and even the place where I performed my new profession.

When my daughters became grown up, the young woman came, demanding one to be the future heir of my mystical power. But because they had joined the Christian Church, I tried to convince her against her request. But she completely refused to listen to my advice. Then this woman appeared before me and advised me to kill the daughter who refused. She gave me the medicine to use, but I refused to do so. When the proposed night came, the strange looking woman appeared before me very angry. She ordered me to use that medicine at once to kill the girl. My love for her forbade me to do this. But immediately, sticks came from nowhere and I was beaten terribly. I cried bitterly, though the woman insisted on commanding me to kill my daughter. Within no time I ran to the pastor's house and asked for help. My husband together with my children followed me. The pastor gave me a warm welcome and good food. He read the Bible and told us about salvation. He then prayed for us. Then I received Christ as my Saviour and swore not to return to my former profession of being a medicine woman. My husband believed in Christ together with my sons and daughters. I then requested the pastor to call the elders to come with him to my house to burn my workshop and tools. The pastor and the church elders helped in burning my tools and my workshop. They sat down, prayed for my family and the Gospel was proclaimed to the people who came to witness this great event. Since that time I never met that strange looking figure or experienced her terrible presence again.

Therefore [she continued] my mystical power was hereditary. I used the power to heal people from their sicknesses, to ban any spell uttered by the witch (including kita, kyeni, and uoi). My tools were very powerful and my medicine was very effective. I was not interested with this profession. But I was forced to accept the heritage. I wanted my children to remain as Christians, though the ancestors forced me to appoint my dear daughter to be my heir. She died as a result of refusing. But her death together with the severe beatings given me, led me to hate the unmerciful ancestors and the forces of darkness. I came to seek for salvation and security. Now I don't fear to confess that in Christ there is salvation, peace, hope and security.

A medicine woman explained how she had obtained her powers to be a medicine woman through purchase.

After having this desire within me, I was taken by a very famous medicine man to Thaisu. Here we visited a certain medicine man with whom I shared my desire. I was told to give fourteen cows and two bulls. The next time I brought them to him. The cows were the fees for the services of the medicine man and the two bulls were for the sacrifice to the spirits who would associate with me in my new profession as friends and servants. After the rite was over, we had a drum dancing (kilumi) whereby old men and women, young men and women all danced together. They were given roast meat to eat for their offering in dancing, as a symbol to calm the spirits and to make them friendly to myself.

After the dancing, I was taken to a dark room in the workshop where the medicine man with the help of two spirits (majini) who accompanied us, selected tools for me to use in my new profession. I was then taught how to use each tool and how to communicate with my servants, the two majini, who the medicine man introduced to me. I was given some rules to obey in my new profession. A flag was given to me for a sign outside my workshop. The total arrangement of my workshop was designed by the medicine man who was helped by the two spirits. Then I was told to return home.

At home I directed the people in making my workshop. After it was completed, I entered. The two majini appeared before me, carrying all the tools which the medicine man gave me. We had a short talk after which the majini demanded a she goat to be killed for them. I ordered it to be killed. I then gave it for them and they drank the blood and ate some inner parts. The skin was then used by the two majini in making the mystical drum which I was ordered to be using when dancing and in need of power and revelation. From that night I gained my mystical power which I now use in helping my society in their problems.

(These vivid accounts were gathered from interviews by pastor Samuel Musyoki. See Acknowledgements.)

Further Examples of Mystical Powers Among the Akamba

There are various kinds of mystical powers among traditional Akamba which we do not place under either of the categories of *uoi* or *uwe*. For the world view of the traditional Akamba is saturated with mystical powers which can be used for good or ill.

The Curse. The traditional blessing and cursing of the Akamba parents on their children is a case in point. The power of words is found primarily in those words spoken by a senior person to a junior. An older person, holding a more powerful office or higher social status, can powerfully influence the life of a younger person simply through the spoken word (compare Lindblom 1920:182-185; Hobley 1967:145-153).

A curse begins when a parent or any older relative shakes his head because of being wronged by a son or daughter. By shaking the head the elder says that the same thing will be done to the younger person which was done to him. This cursing (known in Kikamba as *kiumo*) has lasting effects, generation after generation after generation unless it is reversed. The real essence of the curse is not the shaking of the head, but the bitter feelings in the heart toward the person.

The curse destroys whatever the person already has. The cursed person can make no progress. His character becomes rotten and he may even die for no known reason. His own sons become disobedient to him and will curse him. Some Akamba say that the curse will last forever, while others limit it to the third generation. Some believe the curse can never be reversed, while others say it can be reversed only when the proper procedure is followed early enough.

To remove the curse the victim must bring a goat early in the morning to the one who pronounced the curse. After the parents eat the goat, the one who pronounced the curse cleanses his mouth with water. Some milk and sorghum are placed in the mouth. Spittle is spat on the hands and chest of the cursed one in order to relieve him of the curse and impart a blessing. Words of good prosperity are pronounced.

If the parent who pronounced the curse has died, the cursed one approaches the uncle who will represent the father. A specialist is called, known as *mundu wa ng'ondu*.

The cursed one confesses his wrong doing, and brings a goat for sacrifice. The specialist sprinkles purifying medicines (*ng'ondu*) on the cursed one and his family to symbolize cleansing. The specialist speaks words while sprinkling the purifying medicine. The *ng'ondu* is made of water, mixed with leaves, herbs and roots. By sprinkling the cursed family with *ng'ondu* with a branch and leaves, the cursed family symbolically receives back their life and blessing.

The family eats together, feasting on the slain goat. This communal meal represents the reconciliation which has been once again attained.

The blessing of the dying father is potent and sought after by the children. Blessings are given for obedience to one's parents. A blessed person will prosper in all that he does. His children, cattle and garden will grow healthy and multiply. This blessing on the family will continue forever, unless someone is disobedient in the family and is consequently cursed.

The Oath. Another example of mystical power is the Kikamba oath known as *kithitu*. (compare Lindblom 1920:165-173; Hobley 1967:239-243; Ndeti 1972:124-128) No one knows the source of this power nor can they explain its potency. The Akamba only know that it is real and effective.

A *kithitu* is an object, usually an animal horn filled with "medicine," upon which an oath is sworn. *Kithitu* refers to the highest judicial authority to which a Mukamba could traditionally appeal for justice. Should someone swear falsely by the *kithitu*, his life or that of a nearby relative will be taken by inexplicable powers within a prescribed number of days. *Kithitu* is an evil power which harms people who are troubling the community.

The oath can be used in land disputes, theft and murder. We may illustrate this by the theft of a cow. If a cow can nowhere be found, and if the owner suspects a particular person, he may call a specialist dealing with the *kithitu* to oversee the formal ceremony in which the *kithitu* is struck. After the payment of a fee, the specialist announces the day when this will take place. He will approach the suspect, his family and clan members in order to explain the problem. If the suspect does not confess to the theft, he will be asked to strike the *kithitu* in public for all to see. The suspect strips naked and is asked to repeat words after the specialist. "If I am the one who did this," he will say, "then let me die, together with my family and clan." He then strikes the *kithitu*. After this he is given seven days. If the suspect will admit to his crime within that period, he may approach the specialist, pay the full compensation in return for the removal of the curse.

Should the victim have no suspect who might have stolen the cow, the specialist may still be called who will call the community together to explain the problem. He will ask whether anyone is guilty of stealing the cow. If no one admits this, the specialist will strike the *kithitu* saying, "Whoever has stolen Mutua's cow, let him and his family start dying after seven days." The same effect will be witnessed on the one guilty of theft.

This is the final court of appeal among the Akamba. Today in modern Kenya the government recognizes this traditional method of obtaining justice. Since Independence Kenya has been overseeing the adjudicating of land, surveying the property of people and writing official deeds of ownership. Many land disputes arise when neighbors contest ownership. As the ultimate court of appeal, the Akamba may approach the Chief of the Location who will then approve the public performance of *kithitu*. If the curse should be done privately and someone dies, then guilt will rest upon the one who initiated the use of *kithitu*. But if done publicly and officially, through the approval of the Chief, then the government recognizes this as a legitimate way of settling land disputes.

Evil Tongue: *Kyeni*. While most of the activities of the witch can be described as sorcery, the work of the person with an evil tongue is more aptly called witchcraft according to the definition given by the anthropologist. *Kyeni* is a concept that refers to an evil tongue. This type of evil mystical power can be detected when the tongue has distinguishing black marks on the tip.

Such powers are inherited, being passed down through certain families or clans. The Euani clan from Kitui are experts in ruining people, cattle and property by merely complimenting others or saying positive comments about others. A man from this clan cannot do anything about this in-born power, except to spit whenever expressing admiration for anything. When one woman went to the river to wash, another woman commented, "Your legs are really clean." Immediately, her legs became cracked and she found it difficult to walk. One Mukamba had bought a large male goat in order to improve the breed of his goat herd. The person with an evil tongue looked at the goat and remarked, "What a good looking goat!" That evening a hyena attacked the goat and killed it. People must be constantly on the alert for incidences when people speak positively about other people or property. If a man comments, "That young man can really run fast," he will be suspected of being a person with an evil tongue. When a person observes a neighbor having a healthy cow and producing a lot of milk, he may comment, "This cow has a very good udder." Soon thereafter the cow will become sick and eventually die. Therefore, complimenting others is traditionally not acceptable.

The story is told of Syontheke who once looked after some goats. When she ran off to play, the goats wandered into a neighbor's garden and began eating peas. When the owner saw this, she became angry and said to Syontheke, "Because you have allowed the goats to stray into my garden, let your eyes be full of worms." Immediately, her eyes became full of worms and she had difficulty seeing. Only a visit to the medicine man brought relief.

To reverse the intentional or unintentional effect, the person with an evil tongue must spit on the one affected. In fact, the person suspected of having an evil tongue is virtually compelled to reverse the powers emitted through positive comments. The spitting must be accompanied by words, such as, "I have no evil tongue nor do my kinsmen." Such a statement does not mean that he ceased to have the powers of an evil tongue, but only that he has effectively neutralized the effects of the evil tongue.

On the other hand, the person with an evil tongue does not always bring harm. He can make a positive statement, such as, "You will find good luck in this or that," and the person finds the prediction to come true. Through the powers of *kyeni* a person may predict misfortune and this actually occurs. The real cause is the *INTENT* of the one speaking. *Kyeni* can therefore be used for good or ill, depending on the intent of the person with this power. However, the most notorious effect of *kyeni* is negative and destructive and therefore greatly feared.

Kyeni is the destructive powers of the evil tongue, while *kita* is the solution which counteracts the *kyeni*. There are some people who have both the powers of *kyeni* and the powers of *kita* by which they can reverse the evil effects. But some people have only *kita* and not *kyeni* and vice versa.

In Kitui there are two famous men, a father and his son, who possess the powers of *kyeni* and *kita*. They competed with each other to see who was the strongest. The son went to the father's garden and saw the field ready for harvest. The son declared, "Why don't porcupines come and taste them?" All of a sudden a large number came from the bush and devoured the maize. When the father came and saw the porcupines devouring the food, he commented, "What are they doing? Why don't they stop and run back?" The porcupines all left. Then the father went to see the goats of his son, grazing and eating the leaves from the bottom of the trees as goats normally do. "Why don't they reach to the top of the trees and eat like monkeys?" said the father. The son became surprised when he saw the goats eating like monkeys. So the son replied, "Why don't they come down and eat like goats?" and they did. So the father and son shook hands and agreed that they both had great powers of *kita* and *kyena*. Their fame reaches Nairobi. But the grandfather is reputed to have had even greater powers. Somebody owed him a cow, but the man refused to pay it when he went to the house of the man owing it. So the grandfather replied, "I will never come back here again. You see that rock on the hill? That rock will come down and ask for the cow to be returned to me." In another day that huge bolder rolled down the hill and killed that man's cattle in the field. It remains there until this day. They immediately rushed a man to take a cow to the grandfather in order to stop the trouble.

In addition to the "evil tongue," some Akamba have an "evil eye." This type of mystical power can be detected when the eyes are usually red, sometimes with white secretion flowing from the eyes. The man with an "evil eye" does not need to say anything. A mere stare can unintentionally cause sickness or death. For this reason the mother will shield the smaller children from the glare of people suspected of having an "evil eye." When taking infants on a journey, the mothers would cover the child with fat from an animal which allegedly neutralizes the powers of an "evil eye" in order to protect the children from the unintentional evil affects of a glare.

The exact nature of the "evil eye" or the "evil tongue" is not known but it is experienced. For this reason the Akamba do not like people to count or to point their fingers at others when speaking, for fear that this would bring harm. Instead of pointing with the index finger, a person should point with the fingers bent downward or with the fist clenched shut. For a person with an evil tongue cannot control his powers.

Today there is a tendency for some people, especially the Christian Akamba, to believe that the power of the evil tongue comes from the ancestral spirits (*aimu*). Traditionally, this power has been unexplained and only experienced. But through Christian influence there is a tendency to perceive the power as originating from the spirit world. Such powers as the "evil tongue" and the "evil eye" are evil powers. Therefore, they cannot originate with God but must come from Satan. Christians believe that a witch, who has purchased her witchcraft, when she becomes a Christian, and when she has burned all his paraphernalia associated with witchcraft, she ceases to be a witch. But some Christians believe that if a person with an evil tongue becomes a Christian, this conversion only diminishes the power of *kyeni*. Christianity does not eliminate it completely, they say. But if *kyeni* is from Satan, then such evil power cannot remain with a Christian under the lordship of Christ. On this question Christian Akamba have different perspectives.

Therefore, we can see that there are two kinds of evil mystical powers, witchcraft (*uoi*) and an evil tongue or an evil eye (*kyeni*). The former is more closely identified with the use of materials (such as *muthea* and *kithangona*). While the latter is intrinsically bound up with the person himself, having inherited it from his parents, and needing no rites or materials to effect the evil results.

PERMISSIONS AND ACKNOWLEDGEMENTS

The author expresses his gratitude to those individuals and publishers listed below who have kindly granted permission to reproduce or utilize their materials, knowledge and research in this book. Those shorter quotations which do not require formal permission are duly acknowledged within the text.

Adeyemo, Tokunboh. Salvation in African Tradition. Nairobi: Evangel Publishing House, 1979.

Anderson, J.N.D. Christianity and Comparative Religion. London: Tyndale Press, 1955.

Arms, Jack and Lolly. Personal Interview, 1982. Permission requested.

Bavinck, J.H. The Impact of Christianity on the Non-Christian World. Grand Rapids: Wm. B. Eerdmans Pub. Co., 1948.

Beattie, John ed. Spirit Mediumship and Society in Africa. London: Routledge & Kegan Paul, 1969.

Budge, E.A. Wallis. The Book of the Dead. NY: University Books, 1960. Permission requested.

Daidanso ma Djongwe. Personal Interview, 1988.

Davis, Linnell. The Use of the Bible in the Kamba Tribal Setting. M.A. Thesis, School of World Mission, Fuller Theological Seminary, 1968. Delitzsch, Franz. Biblical Commentary on the Prophecies of Isaiah. Grand Rapids: Wm. B. Eerdmans Pub. Co., 1960.

Dickson, Kwesi and Paul Ellingworth eds. Biblical Revelation and African Beliefs. London: Lutherworth Press, 1969. Permission requested.

Dundas, Charles. Kilimanjaro and its Peoples. London: H.F. & G., 1924.

Evans-Pritchard, E.E. Witchcraft, Oracles and Magic Among the Azande. London: Oxford University Press, 1937.

Hick, John and Brian Hebbeltheaite. Christianity and Other Religions. Great Britain: Collins, Fount Paperbacks, 1980. Permission requested.

Howells, William. The Heathens. NY: Doubleday & Co., 1948.

Hughes, Langston. An African Treasury. London: Victor Gollancz, 1961. Permission requested.

Idowu, Bolaji. African Traditional Religion: Definition. London: SCM Press LTD., 1973.

Idowu, Bolaji. Olodumare: God in Yoruba Belief. London: Longmans, 1962.

Irvine, Wm. C. Heresies Exposed. NY: Loizeaux Brothers, 1953.

Jacobs, Donald R. The Cultural Themes and Puberty Rites of the Akamba. Ann Arbor: University Microfilms, 1961. Permission requested.

Kato, Byang. Theological Pitfalls in Africa. Nairobi: Evangel Pub. House, 1975.

Keightley, David. "The Religious Commitment: Shang Theology and the Genesis of Chinese Political Culture," History of Religion, 17 (Feb.- May):211-225, 1978.

Kenyatta, Jomo. Facing Mount Kenya. NY: Vintage Books Random House, n.d.).

Kittel, Gerhard ed. Theological Dictionary of the New Testament. Grand Rapids: Wm. B. Eerdmans Pub. Co., 1964.

Koch, Kurt. Occult Bondage and Deliverance. Grand Rapids: Kregel Pub., 1970) Permission requested.

Kraemer, Hendrik. The Christian Message in a Non-Christian World. Grand Rapids: Kregel Pub., 1963.

Langley, Myrtle. The Nandi of Kenya (Life Crisis Ritual in a Period of Change). London: C. Hurst & Co., Publishers, 1979) Permission applied for.

Latourette, Kenneth Scott. A History of the Expansion of Christianity. NY: Harper & Brothers, 1937.

Lindblom, Gerhard. The Akamba. Westport, Conn.:Negro University Press Greenwood, 1920.

Mbiti, John. Concepts of God in Africa. London:SPCK, 1970.

Mbiti, John. African Religions and Philosophy. London: SPCK, 1969. Permission requested.

Mbiti, John. New Testament Eschatology in an African Background. London: Oxford University Press, 1971.

Middleton, John and E.H. Winter eds. Witchcraft and Sorcery in East Africa. London: Routledge & Kegan Paul, 1963.

Musango, Jonathan. Research Paper at Scott Theological College, Kenya. Permission requested.

Musyoki, Samuel. Research Paper at Scott Theological College, Kenya.

Ndeti, Kivuto. Elements of Akamba Life. Nairobi: East African Publishing House, 1972. Permission requested.

Noss, John. Man's Religions. NY: MacMillan Co., 1963. Permission requested.

Parrinder, Geoffrey. African Traditional Religion. London: SPCK, 1962. Parrinder, Geoffrey. Witchcraft: European and African. London: Faber & Faber, 1958.

P'Bitek, Okot. African Religions in Western Scholarship. Nairobi: East African Literature Bureau, 1970.

Salalah, Charles. The Place of Ancestral Spirits in African Theology. M.A. Thesis, Columbia Graduate School of Bible and Missions, 1981.

Smith, Edwin. African Ideas of God. London: Edinburgh House Press, 1966. Permission requested.

Smith, Wilfred Cantwell. Towards a World Theology. Philadelphia: The Westminster Press, 1981. Permission requested.

Taylor, John. The Primal Vision. London: SCM Ltd., 1963. @L8H = Unger, Merrill. Biblical Demonology. Wheaton: Scripture Press, 1952. Permission requested.

Warfield, Benjamin B. Biblical and Theological Studies. Philadelphia: The Presbyterian & Reformed Pub. Co., 1952. Permission requested.

Westermann, Diedrich. Africa and Christianity. London: Oxford University Press, 1937.

Williamson, Sidney G. Akan Religion and Christian Faith. Accra: Ghana Universities Press, 1965. Permission requested.

Willoughby, W.C. The Soul of the Bantu. NY: Doubleday, Doren & Co., 1928. Permission requested.

Wysham, William N. Christians, Claim Your Heritage. NY: World Horizons Inc., 1967. Permission requested.

PERMISSIONS

Bibliography: References Cited in Text

Adeyemo, Tokumboh
  1979   Salvation In African Tradition. Nairobi: Evangel Publishing House.
Anderson, J.N.D. ed.
  1960   The World's Religions. Grand Rapids: Wm. B. Eerdmans Pub. Co.
Arensen, Jon
  1988   Anthropology Coordinator for SIL Africa. Personal Interview.
Arms, Jack and Lolly
  1982   Former missionaries with the World Presbyterian Mission, Mwingi, Kitui. Personal
          Interview.
Barrett, David B.
  1968   Schism and Renewal in Africa. London: Oxford University Press.
  1973   Kenya Churches Handbook. Kisumu, Kenya: Evangel Publishing House.
Barth, Karl
  1980   "The Revelation of God as the Abolition of Religion," Christianity and Other
          Religions. John Hick and Brian Hebbelthwaite eds., pp.32-51. Great Britain: Collins,
          Fount Paperbacks.
Bavinck, Herman
  1915   "Death.." The International Standard Bible Encyclopaedia. James Or ed., II,pp.812-813.
          Chicago: The Howard-Severance Co.
Bavinck, J.H.
  1948   The Impact of Christianity on the Non-Christian World. Grand Rapids:Wm. B.
          Eerdmans Pub. Co.
  1960   An Introduction to the Science of Missions. Philadelphia: The Presbyterian & Reformed
          Pub. Co.
Baxter, H.C.
  1943   "Religious Practices of the Pagan Wazigua: The Story of a Dying Creed." Tanganyika
          Notes and Records. 15 (June 1943), pp.49-57.
Beattie, John ed.
  1969   Spirit Mediumship and Society in Africa. London: Routledge & Kegan Paul, 1969.
Beresford-Stooke, G.
  1928a   "An Akamba Ceremony Used in Times of Drought." Man. 28 (Aug.8):139-40.
  1928b   "Akamba Ceremonies Connected with Dreams." Man. 28 (Oct.10):176,177.
  1928c   "An Akamba Fortune-Telling Ceremony." Man. 28 (Nov.):189.
Brown, Francis, S.R. Driver, Charles A. Briggs
  1983   The New Brown-Driver-Briggs-Gesenius Hebrew and English Lexicon. (Based on the
          lexicon of William Gesenius, as translated by Edward Robinson) Christian
          Copyrights. Bruce, Alexander B.
Budge, E.A. Wallis ed.
  1960   The Book of the Dead. N.Y.: University Books.
Buttrick, George Arthur ed.
  1962   The Interpreter's Dictionary of the Bible. N.Y.: Abingdon Press.
Beyerhaus, Peter
  1975   "Possessio and Syncretism in Biblical Perspective," Christopaganism or Indigenous
          Christianity? T. Yamamori and C. R. Taber eds., pp. 119-141. Pasadena: William
          Carey Library.
Carter, Jesse Bennedict
  1909   "Ancestor-Worship and Cult of the Dead (Roman)", Encyclopaedia of Religion and
          Ethics. James Hastings ed. I:461-466. Edinburgh: T & T Clark.
Cassuto, U.
  1967   A Commentary on the Book of Exodus. Jerusalem: The Magnes Press, The Hebrew
          University.
Cheng Tek'un
  1975   "New Light on Shang China. Antiquity. IL (Mar.):25-32.
Clark, Adam
  n.d.   The Holy Bible: A Commentary and Critical Notes 6 vols. N.Y.: Carlton & Porter.
Cole, R. Alan
  1974   Exodus. London: InterVarsity Press.
Cory, Hans

1960   "Religious Beliefs and Practices of the Sukuma/Nyamwezi Tribal Group." <u>Tanganyika Notes and Records.</u> 54 (March):14-26.

Culwick, A.T. and G.M.
1935   <u>Ubena of the Rivers.</u> London: George Allen & Unwin Ltd.

Daidanso ma Djongwe
1988   Associate General Secretary of the Association of Evangelicals of Africa and Madagascar. Personal Interview.

Davis, Linnell E.
1968   <u>The Use of the Bible in the Kamba Tribal Setting.</u> Unpublished Master's thesis presented to the Faculty of the School of Mission and Institute of Church Growth, Fuller Theological Seminary.

Delitzsch, Franz
n.d.   <u>Biblical Commentary on the Prophecies of Isaiah.</u> James Martin transl. 2 vols. Grand Rapids: Wm. B. Eerdmans Pub. Co. (reprint of 1877 ed.).

Dickson, Kwesi and Paul Ellingworth eds.
1969   <u>Biblical Revelation and African Beliefs.</u> London: Lutterworth Press.

Douglas, J.D. ed.
1962   <u>The New Bible Dictionary.</u> London: The Inter-Varsity Fellowship.

Dundas, Charles
1924   <u>Kilimanjaro and its Peoples.</u> London: H.F. & G. Witherby.

Ecumenical Conference on Foreign Missions
1900   <u>Ecumenical Missionary Conference.</u> Vol.I. NY: American Tract Society.

Elwell, Walter A. ed.
1984   <u>Evangelical Dictionary of Theology.</u> Grand Rapids: Baker Book House.

Evans-Pritchard, E.E.
1937   <u>Witchcraft, Oracles and Magic Among the Azande.</u> London: Oxford University Press.
1965   <u>Theories of Primitive Religion.</u> London: Oxford University Press.

Flannery, Austin ed.
1975   <u>Vatican Council II.</u> N.Y.: Costello Publishing Co.

Forde, Daryl
1954   <u>African Worlds.</u> London: Oxford University Press.

Gehman, J. Richard
1987   <u>Doing African Christian Theology: An Evangelical Perspective.</u> Nairobi: Evangel Press.

Gesenius, William
1868   <u>A Hebrew and English Lexicon of the Old Testament.</u> Boston: Crocker & Brewster.

Groot, J.J.M. de
1909   "Confucian Religion." <u>Encyclopaedia of Religion and Ethics.</u> James Hastings ed., pp.728-732. Edinburgh: T & T Clark.

Gulliver, P.H.
1951   <u>A Preliminary Survey of the Turkana.</u> A Report Compiled for the Government of Kenya. Communications from the School of African Studies (New Series No. 26, July 1951). University of Cape Town. Mimeographed.

Hadas, Moses ed.
1966   <u>Imperial Rome.</u> Time-Life International (Nederland) N.V.

Hagar, S.
1909   "Ancestor Worship and Cult of the Dead (American)." <u>Encyclopaedia of Religion and Ethics.</u> James Hastings ed., Vol.I,pp.433-437. Edinburgh: T & T Clark.

Harrison, Everett ed.
1960   <u>Baker's Dictionary of Theology.</u> Grand Rapids: Baker Book House.

Hastings, James ed.
1909   <u>Encyclopaedia of Religion and Ethics.</u> Edinburgh: T & T Clark.

Hauge, Hans-Egil
1974   <u>Luo Religion and Folklore.</u> Oslo: Scandinavian University Books.

Hays, H.R.
1958   <u>From Ape to Angel.</u> N.Y.: Alfred Knopf.

Herskovits, Melville J.
1938   <u>Dahomey: An Ancient West African Kingdom.</u> N.Y.: J.J. Augustin.

Hillman, Eugene
1968   <u>The Wider Ecumenism.</u> London: Burns & Oates.

Hobley, C.W.
    1910   Ethnology of Akamba and Other East African Tribes. Cambridge.
    1967   Bantu Beliefs and Magic With Particular Reference to the Kikuyu and Kamba Tribes.
            N.Y.: Barnes & Noble, Inc. (first edition, 1922).
Howells, William
    1948   The Heathens. N.Y.: Doubleday and Co. Inc.
Hughes, Langston
    1961   An African Treasury. London: Victor Gollancz.
Hukema, Lemart
    1988   A Biblical Solution to Kongo Witchcraft. Unpublished Th.M. Dissertation. Nairobi:
            Nairobi Evangelical Graduate School of Theology.
Idowu, E. Bolaji
    1962   Olodumare: God in Yoruba Belief. London: Longmans.
    1973   African Traditional Religion: A Definition. Maryknoll, N.Y.: Orbis Books.
International Missionary Council
    1928   The Jerusalem Meeting of the International Missionary Council, March 24-April 8,
            1928. Vol. I: The Christian Life and Message in Relation to Non-Christian Systems
            of Thought and Life. London:International Missionary Council.
    1939   The World Mission of the Church. Findings and Recommendations of the International
            Missionary Council, Tambaram, Madras, India, December 12th to 29th, 1938.
            Boston: American Board of Commissioners for Foreign Missions.
Irvine, William C.
    1953   Heresies Exposed. N.Y.: Loizeaux Bros.
Jacobs, Donald R.
    1961   The Culture Themes and Puberty Rites of the Akamba. Unpublished Ph.D.
            Dissertation. Ann Arbor: University Microfilms.
Johnston, James ed.
    1888   Report of the Centenary Conference on the Protestant Missions of the World Held in
            Exeter Hall, London, 1888. Vol.II. NY: Fleming H. Revell.
Kato, Byang H.
    1975   Theological Pitfalls in Africa. Kisumu, Kenya: Evangel Publishing House.
Keil, C.F. & F. Delitzsch
    n.d.   Biblical Commentary on the Old Testament. The Pentateuch. Vol.II. James Martin
            transl. Grand Rapids: Wm. B. Eerdmans Co.
Keightley, David N.
    1978   "The Religious Commitment: Shang Theology and the Genesis of Chinese Political
            Culture." History of Religion. 17 (Feb.-May):211-225.
Kenyatta, Jomo
    nd   Facing Mount Kenya. N.Y.: Vintage Books.
Kittel, Gerhard ed.
    1964   Theological Dictionary of the New Testament. 10 vols. Geoffrey W. Bromiley transl. &
            ed. Grand Rapids: Wm. B. Eerdmans Pub. Co.
Koch, Kurt
    1970   Occult Bondage and Deliverance. Grand Rapids: Kregel Publications.
    1981   Between Christ and Satan. Grand Rapids: Kregal Publishers.
Kraemer, Hendrik
    1963   The Christian Message in a Non-Christian World. Grand Rapids: Kregel Pub.
Kraft, Charles
    1979   Christianity in Culture. Maryknoll, N.Y.: Orbis Books.
Langley, Myrtle Sarah
    1979   The Nandi of Kenya (Life Crisis Rituals in a Period of Change). N.Y.: St. Martin's Press.
Langton, Edward
    1942   Essentials of Demonology. London: The Epworth Press.
Latourette, Kenneth Scott
    1937   A History of the Expansion of Christianity. N.Y.: Harper & Bros.
Lehmann, Edward
    1909   "Ancestor Worship and Cult of the Dead (Iranian)." Encyclopaedia of Religion and
            Ethics. James Hastings ed., I:454-455.
Leverrier, Roger
    1972   "Buddhism and Ancestral Religious Beliefs in Korea." Korea Journal. XII (May), 37-42.

Lindblom, Gerhard
    1920   The Akamba. Uppsala: Appelbergs Boktrycheri Aktiebolag.
Luzbetak, Louis
    1970   The Church and Cultures. Pasadena: William Carey Library.
Marwick, Brian Allan
    1966   The Swazi. London: Frank Case & Co., Ltd. (first edition in 1940).
Mbiti, John S.
    1966   Akamba Stories. London.
    1969   African Religions and Philosophy. London: SPCK.
    1970   Concepts of God in Africa. London: SPCK.
    1971   New Testament Eschatology in an African Background. London: Oxford University Press.
    1972   "Christianity and Traditional Religion in Africa." Crucial Issues in Missions Tomorrow. Donald McGavran ed. Chicago: Moody Press.
    1986   Bible and Theology in African Christianity. Nairobi: Oxford University Press.
Mercier, P.
    1954   "The Fon of Dahomey." African Worlds, Daryll Forde ed., pp. 210-234. N.Y.: Oxford University Press.
Middleton, John
    1953   The Kikuyu and Kamba of Kenya. London: International African Institute.
Middleton, J. and E.H. Winter eds.
    1963   Witchcraft and Sorcery in East Africa. London.
Millikin, A.S.
    1906   "Burial Customs of the Wa-Kavirondo in the Kisumu Province." Man. VI:54,55.
Montgomery, J.W. ed.
    1976   Demon Possession. Minneapolis, Minn.: Bethany Fellowship,
Montgomery, J.W.
    1981   Principalities and Powers: The World of the Occult. Minneapolis, Minn.: Bethany Fellowship.
Munro, J. Forbes
    1975   Colonial Rule and the Kambaa. Social Change in the Kenya Highlands 1889-1939. London: Oxford University Press.
Murray, Margaret
    1962   The Witch-Cult in Western Europe. London: Oxford University Press (first edition 1921).
Musango, Jonathan
    1983   Research Paper on Spirit Possession. Scott Theological College.
Musyoki, Samuel
    1983   Research Paper on Medicine Men. Scott Theological College.
Muthiani, Joseph
    1973   Akamba From Within. N.Y.: Exposition Press.
McCasland, S. Vernon
    1951   By the Finger of God. N.Y.: The Macmillan Co.
McGavran, Donald ed.
    1972   Crucial Issues in Missions Tomorrow. Chicago: Moody Press.
McVeigh, Malcolm J.
    1974   God in Africa. Hartford, Vermont: Claude Stark.
Ndeti, Kivuto
    1972   Elements of Akamba Life. Nairobi: East African Publishing House.
Newall, Venetia
    1974   The Encyclopedia of Witchcraft and Magic. London: Hamlyn.
Noss, John B.
    1963   Man's Religions. N.Y.: The MacMillan Co.
Nottingham, J.C.
    1959   "Sorcery Among the Akamba in Kenya." Journal of African Administration. (London) XI (I):2-14.
Orr, James ed.
    1952   International Standard Bible Encyclopedia. Grand Rapids: Wm. B. Eerdmans Pub. Co.
Parrinder, E. Geoffrey
    1958   Witchcraft: European and African. London: Faber & Faber.

          BIBLIOGRAPHY

1961   West African Religion. London: The Epworth Press.
1962   African Traditional Religion. London: Sheldon Press.
P'Bitek, Okot
1970   African Religions in Western Scholarship. Nairobi: East African Literature Bureau.
1971   Religion of the Central Luo. Nairobi.
Rahner, Karl.
1980   "Christianity and Non-Christian Religions," Christianity and Other Religions, John Hick
        and Brian Hebbelthwaite eds., pp.52-79. Great Britain: Collins, Fount Paperbacks.
Ramsay, W.M.
1963   The Letters to the Seven Churches of Asia. Grand Rapids: Baker Book House.
Rose, H.J.
1909   "Divination." Encyclopaedia of Religion and Ethics, James Hastings ed. Edinburgh: T &
        T Clark.
Routledge, W. and Katherine Routledge
1910   With a Prehistoric People: The Akikuyu of British East Africa. London: Edward Arnold.
Salalah, Charles S.
1981   The Place of Ancestral Spirits in African Theology: Evaluated in the Biblical Teaching.
        M.A. Thesis, Columbia Graduate School of Bible and Missions.
Sangree, Walter H.
1966   Age, Prayer and Politics in Tiriki, Kenya. London: Oxford University Press.
Schlette, Heinz Robert
1966   Towards a Theology of Religions. N.Y.: Herder & Herder.
Shorter, Aylward
1975   African Christian Theology - Adaptation or Incarnation. London: Geoffrey Chapman
        Press.
Smith, Edwin W.
1966   African Ideas of God. London: Edinburgh House Press.
Smith, George Adam
1927   The Book of Isaiah. N.Y.: Doubleday, Doran & Co., Inc.
Smith, Wilfred Cantwell
1981   Towards a World Theology. Philadelphia: The Westminster Press.
Stam, N.
1910   "The Religious Conceptions of the Kavirondo." Anthropos. V (2,3):359-362.
Summers, Montague
1973   The History of Witchcraft and Demonology. (first published in 1926)
Sundkler, Bengt G.M.
1961   Bantu Prophets in South Africa. London: Oxford University Press.
Taylor, John
1963   The Primal Vision. London: SCM Ltd.
Toynbee, Arnold
1957   Christianity Among the Religions of the World. N.Y.: Charles Scribner's Sons.
Troeltsch, Ernst
1980   "The Place of Christianity Among the World Religions." Christianity and Other
        Religions, John Hick and Brian Hebbeltwaite eds., pp.11-31. Great Britain: Collins,
        Fount Paperbacks.
Unger, Merrill F.
1952   Biblical Demonology. Wheaton: Scripture Press.
1960   Unger's Bible Dictionary. Chicago: Moody Press.
1971   The Haunting of Bishop Pike: A Christian View of the Other Side. Wheaton: Tyndale
        House Pub.
1972   Demons in the World Today. Wheaton: Tyndale House Pub.
Wagner, S.
1974   "Darash; midhrash." Theological Dictionary of Old Testament. Botterweck ed.,
        III:293-307. Grand Rapids: Wm. B. Eerdmans Pub. Co. 1974.
Warfield, Benjamin B.
1952   Biblical and Theological Studies. Philadelphia: The Prebyterian and Reformed Pub. Co.
Westermann, Diedrich
1937   Africa and Christianity. London: Oxford University Press.
Wille, W.
1970   "Some Reflections on African Traditional Religions in the Light of Historical-Critical

BIBLIOGRAPHY   307

Exegesis of the New Testament." Student Essays and Religious Papers, Limuru.

Williamson, Sidney George
1965   Akan Religion and the Christian Faith. Accra: Ghana Universities Press.

Willoughby, W.C.
1928   The Soul of the Bantu. N.Y.: Doubleday, Doren and Co.

Wolford
1981   Developing a Ministry to the Sorcery-Bound People in Shaba Province, Southern Zaire. Unpublished Doctoral Thesis. Deerfield, ILL: Trinity Evangelical Divinity School.

World Missionary Conference, 1910
1910   Report of Commission IV: The Missionary Message in Relation to Non-Christian Religions. NY: Fleming H. Revell Co.

Wright, G. Ernest
1953a   The Old Testament Against Its Enviornment. London: SCM Press.
1953b   "The Book of Deuteronomy." The Interpreter's Bible. George Arthur Buttrick ed., II:311-537. N.Y.: Abingdon-Cokesbury Press.

Wysham, William Norris
1967   Christians, Claim Your Heritage. N.Y.: World Horizons Inc.

Yamaori, Tsunao
1975   Christopaganism or Indigenous Christianity? Pasadena: Wm. Carey Library.

Young, Edward J.
1978   The Book of Isaiah. 2 vols. Grand Rapids: Wm. B. Eerdmans Pub. Co.

Zwemer, Samuel M.
1920   The Influence of Animism on Islam. N.Y.: The Macmillan Co.

BIBLIOGRAPHY

INDEX OF AUTHORS AND SUBJECTS

Adeyemo, Tokunboh	41, 42, 133, 253
ancestral spirits	139-169, 177-185
Barth, Karl	251
birth	52, 58
Beattie, John	174
charms	71, 83
circumcision	53, 59-61
Communism	37-38
contextualization	21
creation	40, 55, 217
curse	297
Daidanso ma Djongwe	78, 136, 258
death	54, 62-63
demons	47, 107-111, 171-173
Devil	28
divination	85-96, 100-102, 110-111, 143
diviner	77, 89-92
divinities	124-134
Durkheim, Emile	36
dreams	142, 156
Evans-Pritchard, E.E.	32, 71-72, 74
elders	205
evil eye	298-300
Ezeanya, Stephen	132-133
fetishism	32-33
Frazer, James	34, 67, 70
Freud, Sigmund	34-35
herbalists	77-78, 92-94
Hegal, G.W. Friedrich	246
idolatry	44-45, 231-241
Idowu, E. Bolaji	19, 24, 27, 41, 50, 68, 125, 130-133, 138, 236, 242, 249-250
Jacobs, Donald	61, 151
Kato, Byang	201
Kenyatta, Jomo	52, 68, 74, 209, 227
Koch, Kurt	107, 109-110, 174-175
Kraemer, Hendrik	252, 253, 255
Lang, Andrew	33, 34
Levy-Bruhl	36, 37
life cycle	52-54, 58-63, 143-144
living-dead	56, 139-147, 149-163
Lindblom, Gerhard	75, 86, 87, 90, 92, 145, 160, 163, 177, 195, 196, 203
Mbiti, John	10, 29, 50, 52, 56, 67, 75, 137, 139, 191, 192, 196, 199, 200, 203, 208, 216, 220, 229, 249
man: his nature	40, 46, 51-52, 56, 217, 218
Marett, R.R.	34
Marx, Karl	37
marriage	53, 61-62
medicine man	75-77, 86-94, 111-112, 159-162, 293-296
Middleton, John	67, 71, 74
Mueller, Max	36
Muthiani, Joseph	195
McVeigh, Malcolm	119
Ndeti, Kivuto	56, 57, 58, 86, 88, 154, 198, 236
necromancy	178-182
oath	298
Parrinder, E. Geoffrey	72, 76, 77, 106, 113, 119, 124-125, 126, 127, 128, 235
polygamy	54

prayer   208, 182-183
P'Bitek, Okot   22, 25-26, 72, 73
polytheism   129-130
presuppositions   24, 27
priests   77
prophets   77, 88-89, 143
puberty   52-53
Rahner, Karl   248
rainmakers   77
revelation: Christian   28, 40, 41, 42
sacrifices   207-208
Salalah, Charles   240
Sawyerr, Harry   229-230
Scripture   27, 185
Smith, Wilfred Cantwell   247
sorcery   71-74, 11-112
spirit possession   143, 158-163, 173-177
spirits   136-139, 165-169, 171-173
Supreme Being   189-202, 211-242
syncretism   270-283
Taylor, John   146, 178, 228
Toynbee, Arnold   247
Troeltsch, Ernst   246
Tylor, John   33, 67
Unger, Merrill   172, 174
Westermann, Diedrich   226
Willoughby, W.C.   140
Winter, E.H.   72
witch   73, 81, 84-85, 113
witchcraft   71-74, 80-85, 102-104, 111
worship   192-193, 202-208, 221-223

THE AUTHOR

Rev. Dr. Richard J. Gehman was born in Norristown, Pennyslvania, U.S.A., December 24, 1935. He earned a B.A. in Anthropology in 1960 from Wheaton College, Wheaton, Illinois; an M.A. in New Testament from Wheaton College Graduate School; an M.Div. in 1963 from Gordon Divinity School, Wenham, Massachusetts; and a Doctor of Missiology in 1985 from the School of World Mission, Pasadena, California.

Born in a Christian home, the son of a pastor, he was taught from earliest years of the need for conversion and a personal faith in Jesus Christ. At the age of five he was born again through repentance and faith in Christ Jesus. Later he was baptized and became a member of the Mennonite Brethren in Christ Church.

From 1963 to 1966 he taught in Berean Bible School in Allentown, Pennsylvania, from which he had graduated earlier in 1957 with a Diploma in Theology. In 1971 he was ordained to the Christian ministry by the Bible Fellowship Church in which denomination he served as pastor for one year.

Since 1966 he together with his wife, Florence, have been serving with the African Inland Mission International in Kenya, East Africa, at Scott Theological College. For eight years he served as Principal of the College, during which time the College was fully accredited by the Accrediting Council for Theological Education in Africa (ACTEA) and the Bachelor of Theology Degree programme was launched. In 1983 he handed the leadership of the college over to a Kenyan.

From 1985 to 1987 he assisted in the pastoral ministry of the Africa Inland Church in Nairobi. Since 1986 he has been co-ordinating the Theological Advisory Group of the Africa Inland Church, Kenya, which seeks the development of theological reflection in the Kenyan A.I.C. context. He has also served as a member of the Board of Governors for the Evangelical Graduate School of Theology (NEGST) in Nairobi from its very inception.

He is married to Florence A. Hilbert. They have two children, Nathan Scott and Joy Elizabeth.